The Authentic

BOOK OF

CHRISTIAN

QUOTATIONS

The Authentic

BOOK OF CHRISTIAN QUOTATIONS

Over 1000 Quotations and Illustrations from Augustine to Zinzendorf

Edited by
Robert McAnally Adams

Authentic

World Vision

Published in partnership with World Vision Press

Authentic
We welcome your comments and questions.
129 Mobilization Drive, Waynesboro, GA 30830 USA authenticusa@stl.org
and 9 Holdom Avenue, Bletchley, Milton Keynes, Bucks, MK1 1QR, UK
www.authenticbooks.com

If you would like a copy of our current catalog, contact us at:
1-8MORE-BOOKS
ordersusa@stl.org

The Authentic Book of Christian Quotations
ISBN: 1-932805-38-9

10 09 08 07 06 / 6 5 4 3 2 1

Published in 2006 by Authentic Media

Published in partnership with World Vision
34834 Weyerhaeuser Way South, P.O. Box 9716, Federal Way, WA 98063 USA
www.worldvision.org

Cover design: Paul Lewis
Interior design: Angela Duerksen
Editorial team: Betsy Weinrich

Printed in the United States of America

Dear Reader,

World Vision invites you to share your response to the message of this book by writing to World Vision Press at
worldvisionpress@worldvision.org
or by calling 800-777-7752.

For information about other World Vision Press publications, visit us at www.worldvision.org/worldvisionpress.

CONTENTS

To the memory of my father

FOREWORD

I first met Robert MacColl Adams, the editor's father, in 1965, when I spent a happy six months at the University of Texas, Austin, as a Visiting Professor. Robert Adams was then a professor of mathematics who, with his wife and family, was a wonderful Christian witness on the campus. Hospitable, open-hearted, a wise counselor to many students, Bob was a Renaissance-like figure, who read and retained omnivorously a vast amount of literature. His mind was not narrowed by his discipline, but engaged with all the world, and knowledgeable in many unexpected areas. He exemplified the notion that a mathematical scientist could be also a richly cultured humanist.

Moreover, he was an exemplary father, otherwise his own son would never have gone to this prodigious effort to sort out and edit thousands of quotations that his dad wrote out daily and accumulated over a life-time, as his way of life. My own family has warned me already, "Whatever papers are populating your study, after you're gone will go straight to the garbage heap!" We can all be so grateful to Bob that he honored his dad and indeed we as readers will also benefit from this remarkably rich thesaurus of quotations.

But why "read"? Were we not warned that the TV would reduce the reading public dramatically? Instead of which, publishing has expanded more than ever. Reading is a record of so many activities, facets of human life, directions for the perplexed, aspirations of the human heart, and for the widening of horizons. There can be no short answer other than to say, "We read because we are human." At times reading could be dangerous, as during the Inquisition, while today reading can be distracting instead because of cyberspace. Reading today can be disappointing because so much of it is filth, and certainly not a wholesome diet. So the character of the reader is readily assessed by what is read. It is said on the saintly Ambrose, that eager enquirers like Augustine could not easily approach him, for when he was not eating frugally or entertaining a guest in consultation, he was reading silently in his cell. Since Latin remained the universal language of the educated, it remained a restricted world, until the use of the vernacular and the printing-press went hand in hand. Then the florelegia of medieval devotional quotations gave place to more popularized "handbooks of devotion" for a wider public to be nurtured spiritually. So Dent's *Plain Man's Pathway to Heaven* [1601] has been replaced by *My Utmost for His Highest* [1935]. But the intent is the same, for reading makes us fuller, deeper, richer, in being both human beings and Christians too. The blend of Scripture and literature helps the believer to be bi-focal, living in the light of eternity, but having also broad lenses to see the human condition in all its scope.

But why have an anthology of quotations? Because we don't all appreciate the same literature, nor even have the taste nor time to read comprehensively. Aphorisms then are like spices, they flavor our discourse, or even act as navigation lights, to direct our way. Old Testament proverbs were not all necessarily originally divinely inspired; they may also have been collected eclectically from all the rich lore of Egypt and Mesopotamia. Literary experience is communal, it can be shared for it is meant to build up community, and when it is cogent it is there for dialogue and debate. When the collection is eclectic, as this anthology is, then it helps us sharpen focus, exercise awareness of underlying presuppositions, remind us of changes of cultural consciousness, and so educate us more fully to know what to accept and what to reject.

This collection is a treasure trove for all these possibilities. Learning to memorize many of these quotations will be to "give a word in season." They can be "sky-hooks" that lift our email electronic communications to a more imaginative level. The very names of these past voices may arouse our curiosity to read more biography, and to extend the number of our acquaintances, if not yet our friendships. It is said of a Christian lady Melania the Younger in the early fifth century, that such was her love of books, that "she would go through the lives of the Fathers as if she were eating dessert!" So when do we finish taking notes of worthy quotations, as Robert Adams has given us such a bounty? Only when we stop living. So I encourage you, fill your life with a bountiful supply.

— *James M. Houston, Emeritus Professor of Spiritual Theology and founding Principal of Regent College, Vancouver, Canada*

INTRODUCTION

T*he Authentic Book of Christian Quotations* features "the best of the best" from Christian Quotation of the Day (CQOD), which publishes a quotation from one of the thinkers and writers of Christianity each day at www.gospelcom.net/cqod.

The CQOD collection was derived primarily from my father's monumental collection of quotations, gleaned from his voracious reading over a period of more than thirty years. The success and popularity of CQOD is primarily due to his selectivity and the vast net he cast across Christian literature. According to Yahoo!, CQOD has been consistently the 1st, 2nd, or 3rd most popular source for inspirational quotes on the Internet. The value of the quotations lies not only in their compactness, but in their capacity to be absorbed and retained.

What are the quotations? They are, for the most part, expressions of truth, as their authors have come to see that truth, in compact and vivid language. They can be read as literature, but like all great literature, they require that the reader go further and consider the truth presented in the larger context of our faith and knowledge of God, Scripture, and our experience of the world.

A few warnings: Many of the quotations are dense and require some meditation. It is my hope that the recommended Scriptures will aid the reader. Go slowly. In this volume there is many a time bomb—quotations that produce a delayed reaction.

Another caveat: As I have come to know the authors in this collection, I have begun to understand the limits of their respective visions. Their work is not Scripture and should not be treated as such. Still, all the quotations have met a high standard of orthodoxy. The enforcement of this standard has not extended to the whole body of a given author's works simply because I was not able to assess that. God scatters His light around as He pleases.

Theologically, the quotation collection is overwhelmingly Evangelical. But not all of the authors wrote from the Evangelical perspective. Many times I have wanted to change something that an author wrote so it more closely agrees with my own views. I have resisted that temptation, preferring to allow the reader to receive the author's thoughts unfiltered. Still, it is amazing how far and wide the Evangelical fervor and commitment can be seen, even in writers whose ideas and lives lacked most or all other connections to the Evangelical theological framework.

As you read this volume, remember what A. W. Tozer wrote in his book, *The Divine Conquest*: "The work of a good book is to incite the reader to moral action, to turn his eyes toward God and urge him forward. Beyond that it cannot go." So, never stop prayerfully searching the Scriptures: "Pray and read. Read and pray" (John Bunyan, *Christ a Complete Saviour*).

It is difficult to express my debt of gratitude to Gospelcom.net and the vision of the Gospelcom.net team. Thanks to J. R. Whitby, Duane Smith, Robby Richardson, Warren Kramer, Dr. Quentin Schultz, and all the Gospelcom.net staff, especially Nathan Ho.

I also want to acknowledge the encouragement and criticism of my dear friends Elliott Bourne, John R. Cogdell, Tom McCasland, Frank Seay, Michael Summer, Steve Van Rooy, and Todd Wetzel. In addition, my sincere thanks to Bill Blake of Asheville, North Carolina, for the many quotations he contributed, and to David Sanford, my literary agent.

Finally, I must acknowledge the patience and forbearance of my dear wife, Ellen, who has tolerated the wreck of my office for months. She has kept me at the task and given encouragement when it was most needed. The work would not have been completed without her.

To the reader of this volume, may God's richest blessings come now and in the future.

You are invited to log onto www.gospelcom.net/cqod, where you can sign up for CQOD's daily e-mailings. While there, you also can download Believer's Desktop Companion, which presents thousands of quotations, the Scriptures, and many classic Christian writings in a searchable format.

The Authentic

BOOK OF

CHRISTIAN

QUOTATIONS

Anonymous, *Mirror of the Blessed Life of Jesus Christ, The* [1490]

1 The joy of Ascension Day

This Ascension Day is properly the most solemn feast of our Lord Jesus; for this day first in His manhood He began to sit on the Father's right hand in bliss and took full rest of all His [pilgrimage] before. Also this is properly the feast of all the blessed spirits in heaven: for this day they had a new joy of their Lord whom they saw never before there in His manhood.

The Mirror of the Blessed Life of Jesus Christ [1490]
Luke 24:50,51; Acts 1:9

Anonymous, *Theologia Germanica*, ascribed to Johannes de Francfordia, [c.1380-1440], published in 1518 anonymously by Martin Luther

2 Sin

Sin is nothing else than that the creature willeth otherwise than God willeth, and contrary to Him.

Theologia Germanica [1518]
Jas. 4:4,5

3 Preparation

Now men say, "I am in no wise prepared for this work, and therefore it cannot be wrought in me," and thus they have an excuse, so that they neither are ready nor in the way to be so. And truly there is no one to blame for this but themselves. For if a man were looking and striving after nothing but to find a preparation in all things, and diligently gave his whole mind to see how he might become prepared; verily God would well prepare him, for God giveth as much care and earnestness and love to the preparing of a man, as to the pouring in of His Spirit when the man is prepared.

Theologia Germanica [1518]
Heb. 11:13-16

4 Life of Christ

Since the life of Christ is every way most bitter to nature and the Self and the Me (for in the true life of Christ, the Self and the Me and nature must be forsaken and lost and die altogether), therefore in each of us, nature hath a deep horror of it.

Theologia Germanica [1518]
Rom. 6:5-7; Col. 3:9,10

Adams, Robert Hammond [1883-1975]

5 Inscription for a pulpit

"The hungry sheep look up, and are not fed."
The hungry sheep, that crave the living Bread.
Grow few, and lean, and feeble as can be,
When fed not Gospel, but philosophy;
Not Love's eternal story, no, not this,
But apt allusion, keen analysis.
Discourse well framed—forgot as soon as heard—
Man's thin dilution of the living Word.

O Preacher, leave the rhetorician's arts;
Preach Christ, the Food of hungry human hearts;
Hold fast to science, history, or creed,
But preach the Answer to our human need,
That in this place, at least, it may be said
No hungry sheep looks up and is not fed.

Robert Hammond Adams (my grandfather)
John 21:15-17; Acts 20:28

Adams, Robert MacColl [1913-1985]

6 Who is my true brother?

Who belongs to the Church? Who is my true brother? We cannot always tell whether or not a man believes in Christ; but we can always ask—Christianity is not a secret society. And if a man says he loves the Lord, why should I not treat him as my brother? If I should happen to welcome one who is only a professing Christian, who has not given his heart to Christ, what harm has it done? I will have offered the love of God to one who rejects it, and I will have given a few hours of my life to an enemy—but our Father holds out His hands all day long to a rebellious people, and our Savior gave His life for me when I was His enemy.

Robert MacColl Adams, "Receiving One Another"
Rom. 5:8; Eph. 5:18-20; 1 John 3:14

7 Eternal Lord, how faint and small

Eternal Lord, how faint and small
Our greatest, strongest thoughts must seem
To Thee, who overseest all,
And leads us through Life's shallow stream.

How tangled are our straightest ways;
How dimly flares our brightest star;
How earthbound is our highest praise
To Thee, who sees us as we are.

Our feet are slow where Thine are fast;
Thy kiss of grace meets lips of stone;
And we admit Thy love at last
To hearts that have none of their own.

Robert MacColl Adams
Ps. 139:1-4; Eph. 2:1

8 One of us

So here we are again, a few billion miles farther along our mysterious path among the immensities. What a comfort it is to know the Man in charge of it all. Without Him, it would be easy to think that the whole of time and space, and life itself, are without reason, purpose, or meaning—as H. G. Wells said, that it is "a bad joke beyond our understanding, a flare of vulgarity, an empty laugh braying across the mysteries." With Jesus forever between God and us, we can understand a few things, and trust Him for the rest. After all, He is one of us: a baby once, as we all were; then, and forever after, a Man, as we all shall always be.

Robert MacColl Adams, letter [1981]
Matt. 1:23; Luke 1:26-35; 2:1-21; Heb. 1:6; 2:9,10

9 On Christmas

I have this running quandary about Christmas. I get upset about it, because I feel that we American Christians make too much of it, and too little. Too little of it, because we pile all sorts of other things onto it, including some that have only the feeblest connection with the Event it is supposed to commemorate. If God did become a man, in any real sense, it is the most important thing that ever happened. Surely we, who believe it, could well devote one day a year to uninterrupted contemplation of the fact, and let Saturnalia fall on the winter solstice, where it belongs.

On the other hand, we make so much of the actual birth, and forget the things that make it more than just the birth of a baby (though even that is, in Walt Whitman's phrase, "miracle enough to stagger sextillions of infidels'")—more, even, than the birth of the greatest man who ever lived. We forget the promise to Eve of a descendant who will solve the problem of Evil; the promise to Abraham of one by whom all mankind will be blessed; the promise to Moses of a greater prophet than he, to arise from his people; and the promise to David of a Son who would be his Master. We forget about the eternal Purpose behind it all: it's like telling a story and leaving out the point. Yes, it is true that God gave us His Son, and so maybe we ought also to give gifts—but what, and to whom? It is also true that God gave us Himself, and the only sensible response to that is to give ourselves to Him. There is nothing else that He wants from us, or, if there is something, He can take it. Only I, my ego, my heart, is truly mine to give or to withhold—and is therefore the appropriate gift to Him.

([1] Walt Whitman, "Song of Myself," in *Leaves of Grass)*

Robert MacColl Adams, letter [1982]
Gen. 3:15; 12:2,3; Deut. 18:15; 2 Sam. 7:12-15;
John 3:16,17; Acts 3:20-26

Adler, Mortimer J. (Jerome) [1902-2001]

10 Affirming vs. believing

After a trip to Mexico [in 1984] . . . I fell ill. . . . The illness was protracted. . . . I suffered a mild depression. . . . When [an episcopal priest] prayed for my recovery, I choked up and wept. The only prayer I knew word for word was the Pater Noster. On that day and in the days after it, I found myself repeating the Lord's Prayer, again and again, and meaning every word of it. Quite suddenly, when I was awake one night, a light dawned on me, and I realized what had happened. . . . After many years of affirming God's existence and trying to give adequate reasons for that affirmation, I found myself believing in God.

Mortimer Adler, quoted in *Philosophers Who Believe,*
Kelly James Clark, ed. [1993]
John 4:41

Albright, William Foxwell [1891-1971]

11 Liberation in law

One of the most remarkable features of Mosaic legislation . . . is its humanity to man. It is the most humanitarian of all known bodies of laws before recent times. The laws about slavery, which envisage the liberation of Hebrew slaves after seven years, are a good example. But there are also laws protecting the poor: interest (always high in the ancient East) was prohibited, and again there was a moratorium after a term of years. . . . Even strangers, who normally had very little protection in antiquity, except when they were citizens of a strong neighboring state which might step in and protect them by force of arms, are exceptionally well cared for by Mosaic law.

William Foxwell Albright, *Yahweh and the Gods of Canaan*
[1968]
Ex. 21:2; 22:25; 23:9; Lev. 25:10; Deut. 10:19

Alcuin [c.735-804]

12 O Lord our God

O Lord our God,
    Who has called us to serve You,
In the midst of the world's affairs,   ·
    When we stumble, hold us;
When we fall, lift us up;
    When we are hard pressed with evil, deliver us;
When we turn from what is good, turn us back;
    And bring us at last to Your glory.

St. Alcuin
Isa. 8:14; Mark 12:10; 1 Cor. 8:13

Allen, Roland [1869-1947]

13 Communion is a spiritual fact

The whole point of the story of Cornelius and of the admission of the Gentiles lies in the fact that these people had not accepted what up to that moment had been considered a necessary part of the Christian teaching. The question was whether they could be admitted without accepting the teaching and undergoing the rite. It was that question which was settled by the acknowledgement that they had received the Holy Spirit. . . . The difficulty today is that Christians acknowledge that others have the Spirit, and yet do not recognize that they ought to be, and must be—because spiritually they are—in communion with one another. Men who hold a theory of the Church which excludes from communion those whom they admit to have the Spirit of Christ simply proclaim that their theory is in flat contradiction to the spiritual fact.

Roland Allen, *Pentecost and the World* [1917]
Matt. 12:18-21; Acts 11:15-18

14 Guided by the Holy Spirit

In arriving at a decision in a question of doubt, the apostles in the Acts were guided solely by their sense of the Spirit behind the action, not by any speculations as to consequences which might ensue. And so they found the truth. Gradually the results of the action manifested themselves, and, seeing them, they perceived what they had really done, and learnt the meaning of the truth revealed in the action. But if, from fear of the consequences, they had checked or forbidden the action, they would have lost this revelation. They would have missed the way to truth.

Roland Allen, *Pentecost and the World* [1917]
Acts 2:17,18; 8:29; 13:2-4; 15:28

15 Knowledge of Christ a rich treasure

Missionary zeal does not grow out of intellectual beliefs, nor out of theological arguments, but out of love. If I do not love a person I am not moved to help him by proofs that he is in need; if I do love him, I wait for no proof of a special need to urge me to help him. Knowledge of Christ is so rich a treasure that the spirit of love must necessarily desire to impart it. The mere assurance that others have it not is sufficient proof of their need. This spirit of love throws aside intellectual arguments that they can do very well without it. But if this spirit is not present, a man is easily persuaded that to impart a knowledge of Christianity (for it is noteworthy that such men always speak of Christianity rather than of Christ) is not necessary—nay, is superfluous expense of energy which might be better used in other ways.

Roland Allen, *Pentecost and the World* [1917]
Ps. 18:49; Isa. 43:5-11; Matt. 13:44; John 3:16,17

16 The Spirit of redeeming love

The Spirit is Love expressed towards man as redeeming love, and the Spirit is truth, and the Spirit is the Holy Spirit. Redemption is inconceivable without truth and holiness. But the mere fact that the Holy Spirit's first recorded action in the gospels is an expression of redeeming love should cause us to suspect a teaching which represents His work as primarily, if not solely, the sanctification of our own souls to the practical exclusion of His activity in us towards others. It is important to teach of Him as the Spirit of holiness; it is also important to teach of Him as the Spirit which in us labors for the salvation of men everywhere.

Roland Allen, *Pentecost and the World* [1917]
Acts 2:4,14-21; Rom. 1:4

17 The way to salvation

If we allow the consideration of heathen morality and heathen religion to absolve us from the duty of preaching the gospel we are really deposing Christ from His throne in our own souls. If we admit that men can do very well without Christ, we accept the Savior only as a luxury for ourselves. If they can do very well without Christ, then so could we. This is to turn our backs upon the Christ of the gospels and the Christ of Acts and to turn our faces towards law, morality, philosophy, natural religion. We look at the moral teaching of some of the heathen nations and we find it higher than we had expected . . . Or we look at morality in Christian lands, and we begin to wonder whether our practice is really much higher than theirs, and we say, "They are very well as they are. Leave them alone." When we so speak and think we are treating the question of the salvation of men exactly as we should have treated it had Christ never appeared in the world at all. It is an essentially pre-Christian attitude, and implies that the Son of God has not been delivered for our salvation. It suggests that the one and only way of salvation known to me is to keep the commandments. That was indeed true before the coming of the Son of God, before the Passion, before the Resurrection, before Pentecost; but after Pentecost that is no longer true. After Pentecost, the answer to any man who inquires the way of salvation is no longer "Keep the law," but "Believe in the Lord Jesus Christ."

Roland Allen, *Pentecost and the World* [1917]
Acts 2:36,38

18 Unity in the Holy Spirit

It will perhaps be said that in our present state of schism this assertion of spiritual principle [as in 1 Cor. 12:3] can give us no definite guidance for action, can provide us with no clear program, and must remain unfruitful. Surely that is not wholly true. It certainly must help us if we recognize that it is the presence of the Holy Spirit which creates a unity which we can never create. If men believe in the existence of this unity, they may begin to desire it, and desiring it to seek for it, and seeking it to find it. If, when they find it, they refuse to deny it, in due time, by ways now unsearchable, they will surely return to external communion.

Roland Allen, *Pentecost and the World* [1917]
1 Cor. 12:3

19 Turning to Christ

What men turn to is more important than what they turn from, even if that to which they turn is only a higher moral truth; but to turn to Christ is far more important than to turn to higher moral truth: it is to turn the face towards Him in whom is all moral truth; it is to turn to Him in whom is not only the virtue which corresponds to the known vice from which the penitent wishes to flee, but all virtue; it is to turn the face to all holiness, all purity, all grace. It was this repentance which the apostles preached after Pentecost.

Roland Allen, *Pentecost and the World* [1917]
Acts 2:38-40

20 Indifference to social evils?

We must not admit for one moment the truth of a statement often made, that the man who devotes himself to the establishment of the church, declining to be involved in all sorts of activities for the improvement of social conditions, is indifferent to, or heedless of, the sufferings and injustices under which men suffer. He is nothing of the kind: he is simply a man who is sure of his foundation, and is convinced that the only way to any true advancement is spiritual, and is Christ; and therefore he persists, in spite of all appearances, in clinging to Christ as the only foundation, and in building all his hopes for the future on the acceptance of Christ. He is not content with attacks upon symptoms of evil; they seem to him superficial: he goes to the roots. He cannot be content with teaching men Christian principles of conduct, "Christian ideals of social life"—still less with the establishment of colleges and clubs. Nothing but Christ Himself, faith in Christ, the obedience of Christ, seems to him equal to the need, and nothing else is his work but the establishment of that foundation. In doing this he is not showing indifference to social evils, he is not standing aloof from beneficent movements; he is actively engaged in laying the axe to the roots of the trees which bear the evil. That is not indifference.

Roland Allen, *Mission Activities* [1927]
Isa. 28:16; Heb. 11:10

21 Return to stern doctrines

There is in St. Paul's definite, soul-stirring assertion of the wrath of God and the reality of the judgment at hand, a truth more profound than any that underlies our somewhat enfeebled ideas of universal benevolence and the determined progress of the race. There is something more true in his denunciation of idolatry as sin than in our denial that it is possible for a man to worship an idol, or in our suggestion that all idolatry is only a road to spiritual worship of the one true God. ... One day, I think, we shall return to these stern doctrines, realizing in them a truth more profound than we now know, and then we shall preach them with conviction, and, being convinced ourselves, we shall convince others.

Roland Allen, *Missionary Methods: St. Paul's or Ours?* [1927]
1 Cor. 10:14,19-22

22 Expecting a response

To preach the Gospel requires that the preacher should believe that he is sent to those whom he is addressing at the moment, because

God has among them those whom He is at the moment calling; it requires that the speaker should expect a response.

Roland Allen, *Missionary Methods: St. Paul's or Ours?* [1927]
Matt. 4:19; 20:16

23 The Gospel according to St. Paul

The first Epistle (to the Thessalonians) was written about a year after St. Paul's preaching in the city where, according to Prof. [William] Ramsay's calculation, he had labored for only five months. Thus his stay had not been long enough for him to do more than teach the fundamental truths which seemed to him of the first importance: all the circumstances of his visit were still fresh in his memory and he was recalling to the minds of his readers what he had taught them by word of mouth. Now in that Epistle we get an extraordinarily clear and coherent account of simple mission-preaching not only implied but definitely expressed.

Briefly, that teaching contains the following elements: (1) There is one living and true God (I Thess. 1:9); (2) Idolatry is sinful and must be forsaken (I Thess. 1:9); (3) The wrath of God is ready to be revealed against the heathen for their impurity (I Thess. 4:6), and against the Jews for their rejection of Christ and their opposition to the Gospel (I Thess. 2:15,16); (4) The judgment will come suddenly and unexpectedly (I Thess. 5:2,3); (5) Jesus, the Son of God (I Thess. 1:10), given over to death (I Thess. 5:10), and raised from the dead (I Thess. 4:14), is the Savior from the wrath of God (I Thess. 1:10); (6) The Kingdom of Jesus is now set up and all men are invited to enter it (I Thess. 2:12); (7) Those who believe and turn to God are now expecting the coming of the Savior who will return from Heaven to receive them (I Thess. 1:10; 4:15-17); (8) Meanwhile, their life must be pure (I Thess. 4:1-8), useful (I Thess. 4:11-12), and watchful (I Thess. 5:14-8); (9) To that end, God has given them His Holy Spirit (I Thess. 4:8; 5:19).

This Gospel accords perfectly with the account which St. Paul gives of his preaching in the last address to the Ephesian elders, and it contains all the elements which are to be found in all the sermons and in all the notices of St. Paul's preaching in the Acts, except only the answers to the objections against the Gospel, and the proofs of its truth, which would be manifestly out of place in writing to Christians.

Roland Allen, *Missionary Methods: St. Paul's or Ours?* [1927]

24 The successful missionary

The missionary work of the non-professional missionary is essentially to live his daily life in Christ, and therefore with a difference, and to be able to explain, or at least to state, the reason and cause of the difference to men who see it. . . . His preaching is essentially private conversation, and has at the back of it facts, facts of a life which explain and illustrate and enforce his words. . . . It is such missionary work, done consciously and deliberately as missionary, that the world needs today. Everybody, Christian and pagan alike, respects such work; and, when it is so done, men wonder, and inquire into the secret of a life which they instinctively admire and covet for themselves. . . . The spirit which inspires love of others and efforts after their well-being, both in body and soul, they cannot but admire and covet—unless, indeed, seeing that it would reform their own lives, they dread and hate it, because they do not desire to be reformed. In either case, it works.

Roland Allen, *Non-Professional Missionaries* [1929]
1 Cor. 9:12; 2 Thess. 3:7-9

25 Sharing the experience

Among our own people also the church sorely needs clergy in close touch with the ordinary life of the laity, living the life of ordinary men, sharing their difficulties and understanding their trials by close personal experience. Stipendiary clergy cut off by training and life from that common experience are constantly struggling to get close to the laity by wearing lay clothing, sharing in lay amusements, and organizing lay clubs; but they never quite succeed. To get close to men, it is necessary really to share their experience, and to share their experience is to share it by being in it, not merely to come as near to it as possible without being in it.

Roland Allen, *The Case for Voluntary Clergy* [1930]
Acts 18:3

26 Examination by life experience

We demand, as [St. Paul] did, that the candidate must be of good moral character—at least, so far as that he can produce testimonials to his good conduct. We demand, as the apostle demanded, that he must hold fast the faithful word—at least, so far as that he shall not write deliberate heresy in his examination papers, and shall profess belief in the Creed. We demand, as he demanded, that the candidate must be apt to teach—at least, so far as an examination of his verbal memory can prove that he knows what he ought to teach. But there is some difference between the "without reproach" of the apostle and our testimonials; and there is a difference between the holding fast of the faith by a man tried in the furnace of life, and the soundness in the faith of a youth fresh from a theological school; and the aptness to teach of a man of experience and social authority is not quite the same thing as the aptness to teach of a young man who has just passed an examination in the subject-matter.

Roland Allen, *The Case for Voluntary Clergy* [1930]
Acts 20:17,28; 1 Tim. 3:1-13; 6:11-14; Tit. 1:5-7; 1 Pet. 5:1-4

Allison, C. (Christopher) FitzSimons [b.1927]

27 Our vulnerability to heresy

We are susceptible to heretical teachings because, in one form or another, they nurture and reflect the way that we would have it be, rather than the way God has provided, which is infinitely better for us. As they lead us into the blind alleys of self-indulgence and escape from life, heresies pander to the most unworthy tendencies of the human heart.

C. FitzSimons Allison, *The Cruelty of Heresy* [1994]
Hos.14:6; 2 Cor. 4:3,4

Allshorn, Florence [1887-1950]

28 Holiness is an effect, not a cause

Our calling is not primarily to be holy women, but to work for God and for others with Him. Our holiness is an effect, not a cause; as long as our eyes are on our own personal whiteness as an end in itself, the thing breaks down. God can do nothing while my interest is in my personal character—He will take care of this if I obey His call. In learning to love God and people as He commanded us to do, obviously your sanctification cannot but come, but not as an end in itself.

Florence Allshorn, *Notebooks* [1957]
Acts 26:14-18

29 The Christlike character

We know so well what the unique quality was that held this great and beautiful pride and exquisite humility together. It lay in the relationship he held with God. We know the familiar idea of Jesus' oneness with God: only we deal with it too much as a doctrine of the Church, not as an element in Jesus' own experience. If we never find it in reality, in life, we cannot reveal the true Christ-like character at all—we will always be trying earnestly to be something, but on too superficial and obvious a plane.

Florence Allshorn, *Notebooks* [1957]
Luke 22:26,27

30 The object of prayer

The primary object of prayer is to know God better; we and our needs should come second.

Florence Allshorn, *Notebooks* [1957]
Prov. 1:7; Hos. 6:6; Jude 1:20,21

31 The mystery

Never was a book so full of incredible sayings—everywhere the sense of mystery dominates; unless you feel that mystery, all becomes prosaic—nothing about God is prosaic.

Florence Allshorn, Notebooks [1957]
Matt. 13:35; Eph. 3:8-11

32 Forgiveness

To realize that you are safe and happy standing at God's side, with His love encompassing you because you are forgiven; too happy to take offense any more; too much in love with life to want to be made miserable with an unforgiving heart, and knowing that now every conflict is a chance to learn more of the exceeding beauty of Love: that is worth living for, and surely worth dying to this misery-making self for.

And let us be grateful beyond words for this: that God will not let us alone until we have learnt it and stand by His side. He troubles us, He brings His disturbing light back and back to us, showing us how coarse and heavy the dying self, seeking her own, is; how horrible it is that any feeling of unforgiveness, accepted and held on to, towards our brother, drives God from our side; how quickly we must do all we can to heal the separation, because we are out in the cold and the dark indeed, if divorced from that Love.

Florence Allshorn, Notebooks [1957]
Gen. 50:20; Matt. 18:21,22; Acts 13:37-39

Ambrose, Bp. [339-397]

33 Jesus, the way

Jesus is our mouth, through which we speak to the Father; He is our eye, through which we see the Father; He is our right hand through which we offer ourselves to the Father. Unless He intercedes, there is no intercourse with God.

St. Ambrose
John 17:20-24; Heb. 2:17,18; 4:15; 9:24

34 Faith, not words

It was not by dialectic that it pleased God to save His people; "for the kingdom of God consisteth in simplicity of faith, not in wordy contention."

St. Ambrose, *Exposition of the Christian Faith*, book 1, ch. 5
1 Cor. 2:4,5; 4:19,20; 2 Cor. 1:12

Anderson, J. N. D. (James Norman Dalrymple), Sir [b.1908]

35 The seal of authenticity

He frequently made claims which would have sounded outrageous and blasphemous to Jewish ears even from the lips of the greatest of prophets. He said that he was in existence before Abraham and that he was "lord" of the sabbath; he claimed to forgive sins; he continually identified himself, in his work, his person and his glory, with the one he termed his heavenly Father; he accepted men's worship; and he said that he was to be the judge of men at the last day, and that their eternal destiny would depend on their attitude to him. Then he died. It seems inescapable, therefore, that his resurrection must be interpreted as God's decisive vindication of these claims, while the alternative—the finality of the cross—would necessarily have implied the repudiation of his presumptuous and even blasphemous assertions.

J. N. D. Anderson, *Christianity: the Witness of History* [1969]
Isa. 53:2-11; Luke 6:5; John 8:58

36 Changing attitudes instead of circumstances

[Christ] was primarily concerned to change men as men rather than the political regime under which they lived; to transform their attitude rather than their circumstances; to treat the sickness of their hearts rather than the problems of their environment. But he laid down in a single pregnant sentence man's duty both to God and to the State when he said: "Render to Caesar the things that are Caesar's and to God the things that are God's;" and it is certainly not his fault that the Christian church has been so slow, down the centuries, in applying to one after another of the world's social evils the principle he emphasized so strong that we must love our neighbors as ourselves.

> J. N. D. Anderson, *Christianity: the Witness of History* [1969]
> *Matt. 22:16-22; Mark 12:13-17; Luke 20:20-26*

Andrewes, Lancelot [1555-1626]

37 What will move you?

What will move you? Will pity? Here is distress never the like. Will duty? Here is a person never the like. Will fear? Here is wrath never the like. Will remorse? Here are sins never the like. Will kindness? Here is love never the like. Will bounty? Here are benefits never the like. Will all these? Here they be all, all in the highest degree.

> Lancelot Andrewes, "Sermon on Good Friday"
> *Matt. 5:7; 21:12,13; Mark 6:34; Luke 6:34,35; 11:37-54*

Anselm of Canterbury [1033-1109]

38 Believe to understand

For I seek not to understand in order that I may believe; but I believe in order that I may understand, for I believe for this reason: that unless I believe, I cannot understand.

> Anselm of Canterbury
> *Prov. 28:5; John 7:16-18*

39 Jesus, as a mother you gather your people to you

Jesus, as a mother you gather your people to you:
 you are gentle with us as a mother with her children;
Often you weep over our sins and our pride:
 tenderly you draw us from hatred and judgment.
You comfort us in sorrow and bind up our wounds:
 in sickness you nurse us,
 and with pure milk you feed us.

Jesus, by your dying we are born to new life:
    by your anguish and labor we come forth in joy.
Despair turns to hope through your sweet goodness:
    through your gentleness we find comfort in fear.
Your warmth gives life to the dead:
    your touch makes sinners righteous.
Lord Jesus, in your mercy heal us:
    in your love and tenderness remake us.
In your compassion bring grace and forgiveness:
    for the beauty of heaven may your love prepare us.

Anselm of Canterbury
Luke 13:34; Heb. 7:19

Anstice, Joseph [1808-1836]

40 O Lord! how happy should we be

O Lord! how happy should we be,
If we could leave our cares to Thee,
    If we from self could rest;
And feel at heart that One above,
In perfect wisdom, perfect love,
    Is working for the best.
For when we kneel and cast our care
Upon our God in humble prayer,
    With strengthened souls we rise,
Sure that our Father Who is nigh,
To hear the ravens when they cry,
    Will hear His children's cries.
O may these anxious hearts of ours
The lesson learn from birds and flowers,
    And learn from self to cease,
Leave all things to our Father's will,
And in His mercy trusting still,
    Find in each trial peace!

Joseph Anstice
Matt. 6:28; 10:29; Rom. 8:28

Aquinas, Thomas [c.1225-1274]

41 Bearing wrongs, right and wrong

To bear with patience wrongs done to oneself is a mark of perfection, but to bear with patience wrongs done to someone else is a mark of imperfection and even of actual sin.

Thomas Aquinas
Acts 7:22-24

42 Seeking the truth humbly

Some there are who presume so far on their wits that they think themselves capable of measuring the whole nature of things by their intellect, in that they esteem all things true which they see, and false which they see not. Accordingly, in order that man's mind might be freed from this presumption, and seek the truth humbly, it was necessary that certain things far surpassing his intellect should be proposed to man by God.

Thomas Aquinas, *Summa Contra Gentiles* [1264]
Ps. 92:5; Matt. 7:7,8

43 Whether the firmament was made on the second day?

In questions of this sort there are two things to be observed. First, that the truth of the Scriptures be inviolably maintained. Secondly, since Scripture doth admit of diverse interpretations, that no one cling to any particular exposition with such pertinacity that, if what he supposed to be the teaching of Scripture should afterward turn out to be clearly false, he should nevertheless still presume to put it forward, lest thereby the sacred Scriptures should be exposed to the derision of unbelievers and the way of salvation should be closed to them.

Thomas Aquinas, *Summa Theologica* [1274]
Matt. 12:7; Acts 17:18-32

Arndt, John [1555-1621]

44 Crucified with Him

If thou believest that Christ was crucified for the sins of the world, thou must with Him be crucified. . . . If thou refusest to comply with this order, thou canst not be a living member of Christ, nor be united with Him by faith.

John Arndt
Gal. 6:14

Arnold, Matthew [1822-1888]

45 Condensing Christianity

Christianity is a source; no one supply of water and refreshment that comes from it can be called the sum of Christianity. It is a mistake, and may lead to much error, to exhibit any series of maxims, even those of the Sermon on the Mount, as the ultimate sum and formula into which Christianity may be run up.

Matthew Arnold
Ps. 147:4,5; Luke 10:21; John 21:25

Athanasius [c.293-373]

46 God's solution

What was God to do in the face of the dehumanizing of mankind—this universal hiding of the knowledge of Himself? So burdened were men with their wickedness that they seemed rather to be brute beasts than reasonable men, reflecting the very likeness of the Word. What, then, was God to do? What else could He possibly do, being God, but renew His Image in mankind, so that through it men might once more come to know Him? And how could this be done save by the coming of the very Image Himself, our Savior Jesus Christ? . . . Men had turned from the contemplation of God above, and were looking for Him in two opposite directions, down among created things, and things of sense. The Savior of us all, the Word of God, in His great love took to Himself a body and moved as Man among men, meeting their senses, so to speak, half-way. He became Himself an object for the senses, so that those who were seeking God in sensible things might apprehend the Father through the works which He, the Word of God, did in the body.

Human and human-minded as men were, therefore, to whichever side they looked in the sensible world, they found themselves taught the truth. Were they awe-stricken by creation? They beheld it confessing Christ as Lord. Did their minds tend to regard men as gods? The uniqueness of the Savior's works marked Him, alone of men, as Son of God. Were they drawn to evil spirits? They saw them driven out by the Lord, and learned that the Word of God alone was God and that the evil spirits were not gods at all. Were they inclined to hero-worship and the cult of the dead? Then the fact that the Savior had risen from the dead showed them how false these other deities were, and that the Word of the Father is the one true Lord, the Lord even of death. For this reason was He both born and manifested as Man, for this He died and rose, in order that, eclipsing by His works all other human deeds, He might recall man from all the paths of error to know the Father. As He says Himself, "I came to seek and to save that which was lost."

St. Athanasius, *The Incarnation of the Word of God*
Gen. 3:17; 6:5; Matt. 4:24; Luke 19:10; Rom. 1:18-23

Atkinson, B. F. C. (Basil Ferris Campbell) [b.1895]

47 Church history

The Gospel commission is the key to all problems of church history, large or small. It is the key to the success or failure of the many organizations built up to form the channels of witness to the world. Churches, societies, individuals, . . . have concerned themselves with this or that theological problem. They have made worship central instead of the Gospel commission. They have concerned themselves with their relations with the State. They have concentrated on philanthropy and social service. Wherever they have done this and have forgotten the purpose for which the Master has placed them in the world, wherever they have lost the Master's vision of a perishing humanity, wherever they have become inattentive to the cry of spiritual anguish, the Spirit has passed them by, and when they have persisted He has extinguished the light of their witness. And the pages of church history are strewn with their wreckage. They may have shouted their loyalty to Christ, they may even have suffered for Him. But if once they have forgotten that our Lord combined in a single phrase "for My sake and the Gospel's," devotion to Himself and loyalty to His commission, they have lost their influence and sunk into spiritual death.

B. F. C. Atkinson, *Valiant in Fight* [1937]
Mark 8:35,36

Auden, W. H. (Wystan Hugh) [1907-1973]

48 The force of spiritual law

All theological language is necessarily analogical, but it was singularly unfortunate that the Church, in speaking of punishment for sin, should have chosen the analogy of criminal law, for the analogy is incompatible with the Christian belief in God as the creator of Man. Criminal laws are laws, imposed on men, who are already in existence, with or without their consent, and, with the possible exception of capital punishment for murder, there is no logical relation between the nature of a crime and the penalty inflicted for committing it. If God created man, then the laws of man's spiritual nature must, like the laws of his physical nature, be laws—laws, that is to say, which he is free to defy but no more free to break than he can break the law of gravity by jumping out of the window, or the laws of biochemistry by getting drunk—and the consequences of defying them must be as inevitable and as intrinsically related to their nature as a broken leg or a hangover. To state spiritual laws in the imperative—Thou shalt love God with all thy being, Thou shalt love thy neighbor as thyself—is simply a pedagogical technique, as when a mother says to her small son, "Stay away from the window!" because the child does not yet know what will happen if he falls out of it.

W. H. Auden, *A Certain World* [1971]
Rom. 7:14-23

49 Faith without sight vs. sight without faith

Christ did not enchant men; He demanded that they believe in Him: except on one occasion, the Transfiguration. For a brief while, Peter, James, and John were permitted to see Him in His glory. For that brief while they had no need of faith. The vision vanished, and the memory of it did not prevent them from all forsaking Him when He was arrested, or Peter from denying that he had ever known Him.

W. H. Auden, *A Certain World* [1971]
Matt.17:1-3

Augustine of Hippo, Bp. [354-430]

50 Ask for better than wealth

Picture God as saying to you, "My son, why is it that day by day you rise, and pray, and genuflect, and even strike the ground with your forehead, nay sometimes even shed tears, while you say to Me: 'My Father, give me wealth!' If I were to give it to you, you would think yourself of some importance, you would fancy that you had gained something very great. Because you asked for it, you have it. But take care to make good use of it. Before you had it, you were humble; now that you have begun to be rich you despise the poor. What kind of a good is that which only makes you worse? For worse you are, since you were bad already. And that it would make you worse you knew not; hence you asked it of Me. I gave it to you, and I proved you; you have found—and you have found out! Ask of Me better things than these, greater things than these. Ask of Me spiritual things. Ask of Me Myself!"

St. Augustine
Prov. 10:2; Matt. 7:7,8; 1 John 3:17

51 Selective belief

If you believe what you like in the gospel, and reject what you don't like, it is not the gospel you believe, but yourself.

St. Augustine
2 Pet. 1:16

52 The way He's the way

He enters by the door who enters by Christ, who imitates the suffering of Christ, who is acquainted with the humility of Christ so as to feel and know that, if God became man for us, men should not think themselves God, but men. He who, being man, wishes to appear God, does not imitate Him who, being God, became man. Thou art not bid to think less of thyself than thou art, but to know what thou art.

St. Augustine
John 10:1-5; Phil. 2:5-11

53 The Body lives by the Spirit

But when does the flesh receive the bread which He calls His flesh? The faithful know and receive the Body of Christ, if they labor to be the Body of Christ; and they become the Body of Christ if they study to live by the Spirit of Christ: for that which lives by the Spirit of Christ is the Body of Christ.

St. Augustine
Rom. 8:14,29,30; 2 Tim. 2:15

54 Letters from home

The Holy Scriptures are our letters from home.

St. Augustine
John 14:2,3; 2 Cor. 5:1,2

55 The necessity of death

It is necessary to die, but nobody wants to; you don't want to, but you are going to, willy-nilly. A hard necessity that is, not to want something which can not be avoided. If it could be managed, we would much rather not die; we would like to become like the angels by some other means than death. "We have a building from God," says St. Paul, "a home not made with hands, everlasting in heaven. For indeed we groan, longing to be clothed over with our dwelling from heaven; provided, though we be found clothed, and not naked. For indeed we who are in this dwelling place groan, being burdened; in that we do not wish to be stripped, but to be covered over, so that what is mortal may be swallowed up by life." We want to reach the kingdom of God, but we don't want to travel by way of death. And yet there stands Necessity saying: "This way, please." Do you hesitate, man, to go this way, when this is the way that God came to you?

St. Augustine
Deut. 31:14; 2 Cor. 5:1

56 Imitating Christ

He enters by the door who enters by Christ, who imitates the suffering of Christ, who is acquainted with the humility of Christ so as to feel and know that, if God became man for us, men should not think themselves God, but men. He who, being man, wishes to appear God, does not imitate Him who, being God, became man. Thou art not bid to think less of thyself than thou art, but to know what thou art.

St. Augustine
John 14:6; 17:14-23

57 Hope for good

We need not despair of any man, so long as he lives. For God deemed it better to bring good out of evil than not to permit evil at all.

St. Augustine
Matt. 7:11; 2 Cor. 4:8,9

58 Procrastination

God has promised forgiveness to your repentance, but He has not promised tomorrow to your procrastination.

St. Augustine
Luke 12:16-21

59 Pride destroys good

Other sins find their vent in the accomplishment of evil deeds, whereas pride lies in wait for good deeds, to destroy them.

St. Augustine
Matt. 23:2-12; Luke 9:46-48; 18:9-14; Gal. 6:5

60 Hidden grace

It is not that we keep His commandments first, and that then He loves; but that He loves us, and then we keep His commandments. This is that grace, which is revealed to the humble, but hidden from the proud.

St. Augustine
Matt. 11:25,26

61 The heart's rest

Thou hast made us for thyself, O Lord, and our hearts are restless until they find their rest in thee.

St. Augustine, Confessions [397]
Matt. 11:28,29

62 Who is God?

What art Thou then, my God? What, but the Lord God? For who is Lord but the Lord? or who is God save our God? Most highest, most good, most potent, most omnipotent; most merciful, yet most just; most hidden, yet most present; most beautiful, yet most strong; stable, yet incomprehensible; unchangeable, yet all changing; never new, never old; all-renewing, and bringing age upon the Proud, and they know it not; ever working, ever at rest; still gathering, yet nothing lacking; supporting, filling, and over-spreading; creating, nourishing, and maturing; seeking, yet having all things.

Thou lovest, without passion; art jealous, without anxiety; repentest, yet grievest not; art angry, yet serene; changest Thy works, Thy purpose unchanged; receivest again what Thou findest, yet didst never lose; never in need, yet rejoicing in gains; never covetous, yet exacting usury. Thou receivest over and above, that Thou mayest owe; and who hath aught that is not Thine? Thou payest debts, owing nothing; remittest debts, losing nothing. And that have I now said, my God, my life, my holy joy? or what saith any man when he speaks of Thee? Yet woe to him that speaketh not, since mute are even the most eloquent.

St. Augustine, *Confessions*, I.iv. [397]
Ex. 34:14; Isa. 55:8,9

63 Fellowship

What is Christ's joy in us, but that He deigns to rejoice on our account? And what is our Joy, which He says shall be full, but to have fellowship with Him? He had perfect joy on our account, when He rejoiced in foreknowing and predestinating us; but that joy was not in us, because we did not then exist; it began to be in us, when He called us. And this joy we rightly call our own, this joy wherewith we shall be blessed; which is begun in the faith of them who are born again, and shall be fulfilled in the reward of them who rise again.

St. Augustine, *The City of God* [426]
John 15:11; Heb. 12:1,2

64 On death

Of this I am certain, that no one has ever died who was not destined to die some time. Now the end of life puts the longest life on a par with the shortest. . . . And of what consequence is it what kind of death puts an end to life, since he who has died once is not forced to go through the same ordeal a second time? They, then, who are destined to die, need not be careful to inquire what death they are to die, but into what place death will usher them.

St. Augustine, *The City of God* [426]
Luke 16:19-31; 1 Cor. 15:51,52; Heb. 9:27

65 The evil turning

When the will abandons what is above itself and turns to what is lower, it becomes evil—not because that is evil to which it turns, but because the turning itself is wicked. Therefore it is not an inferior thing which has made the will evil, but it is itself which has become so by wickedly and inordinately desiring an inferior thing.

St. Augustine, *The City of God* [426]
Eccl. 10:3

Babcock, Maltbie D. [1858-1901]

66 The real peril

The tests of life are to make, not break us. Trouble may demolish a man's business but build up his character. The blow at the outward man may be the greatest blessing to the inner man. If God, then, puts or permits anything hard in our lives, be sure that the real peril, the real trouble, is that we shall lose if we flinch or rebel.

Maltbie D. Babcock
John 16:33; Rom. 8:18; 2 Cor. 4:17

Backhouse, William [c.1779-1844) & Janson, James

67 Why He wants prayer

Though you may think yourself ever so dull and incapable of sublime attainments, yet by prayer the possession and enjoyment of God is easily obtained; for He is more desirous to give Himself to us than we can be to receive Him.

William Backhouse and James Jansen,
A Guide to True Peace [1813]
Acts 10:9

68 Fair-weather friends

It is no hard matter to adhere to God while you are in the enjoyment of His comforts and consolations; but if you would prove your fidelity to Him, you must be willing to follow Him through the paths of dryness and desertion. The truth of a friend is not known while he is receiving favors and benefits from us; but if he remain faithful to us when we treat him with coldness and neglect, it will be a proof of the sincerity of his attachment.

William Backhouse and James Jansen,
A Guide to True Peace [1813]
Matt. 26:56

Baillie, Donald M. [1887-1954]

69 Dependence upon God

Jesus lived His life in complete dependence upon God, as we all ought to live our lives. But such dependence does not destroy human personality. Man is never so fully and so truly personal as when he is living in complete dependence upon God. This is how personality comes into its own. This is humanity at its most personal.

Donald M. Baillie
Ps. 16:9; John 12:49,50

Baillie, John [1886-1960]

70 Praying for the heart

Give me a stout heart to bear my own burdens. Give me a willing heart to bear the burdens of others. Give me a believing heart to cast all burdens upon Thee, O Lord.

John Baillie
Rom. 15:1; Gal. 6:1-5

71 Seeking God for what?

To the spiritual perplexity which exercised so many of the rarest souls of the nineteenth century, God appeared as a Being whom men desired to find but could not. But such a formula, though it truly represented one side of their situation, can never represent the whole of any human situation. For God is also a Being whom it ill suits any of us to find but from whom we cannot escape. Part of the reason why men cannot find God is that there is that in Him which they do not desire to find, so that the God whom they are seeking and cannot find is not the God who truly is. Perhaps we could not fail to find God, if it were really God whom we were seeking. And indeed the deepest reality of the situation is that contained in the discovery, which alone is likely at last to resolve our perplexity, that when we were so distressfully seeking that which was not really God, the true God had already found us, though at first we did not know that it was He by whom we had been found. There is a saying, "Be careful what you seek; you might find it." And some who have sought God only as a complacent ally of their own ambitions have found Him a consuming fire.

John Baillie, *Invitation to Pilgrimage* [1942]
John 3:18,19; Heb. 12:27-29

Banning, Charles F.

72 A Christian vocabulary

Too many of us have a Christian vocabulary rather than a Christian experience. We think we are doing our duty when we're only talking about it.

Charles F. Banning
Matt. 9:13; Luke 17:7-10

Baouardy, Mariam [1846-1878]

73 Sleepers, awake!

Let us go and wake up the universe . . . and sing His praises.

Mariam Baouardy
Rev. 4:11; 5:12-14; 14:7

Barna, George

74 The lack of zeal

It occurred to me that in our work with secular organizations, the leader shapes the heart and passion of the corporate entity. In our work with non-profit organizations, we have found the same principle to be operative. When it comes to the focus of the organization, the people who serve there tend to take on many of the core personality traits of the leader toward fulfilling the mandate of the organization. If this is true, and most churches seem to lack the fervor and focus for evangelism, is it reasonable to conclude that it may be because of the lack of zeal most pastors have for identifying, befriending, loving and evangelizing non-Christian people?

George Barna
Acts 11:22-26; Gal. 1:10; Jude 1:3

Barth, Karl [1886-1968]

75 On grace

Grace is the incomprehensible fact that God is well pleased with a man, and that a man can rejoice in God. Only when grace is recognized to be incomprehensible is it grace. Grace exists, therefore, only where the Resurrection is reflected. Grace is the gift of Christ, who exposes the gulf which separates God and man, and, by exposing it, bridges it.

Karl Barth, *The Epistle to the Romans* [1933]
Rom. 1:4; 5:1,2

76 Our belief vs. His holiness

[From our side] our relation to God is unrighteous. Secretly we are ourselves the masters in this relationship. We are not concerned with God, but with our own requirements, to which God must adjust Himself. Our arrogance demands that, in addition to everything else, some super-world should also be known and accessible to us. Our conduct calls for some deeper sanction, some approbation and remuneration from another world. Our well-regulated, pleasurable life longs for some hours of devotion, some prolongation into infinity. And so, when we set God upon the throne of the world, we mean by God ourselves. In "believing" on Him, we justify, enjoy, and adore ourselves.

Karl Barth, *The Epistle to the Romans* [1933]
Rom. 1:18

77 Repentance

There is joy in heaven over one sinner that repenteth, more than over ninety and nine just persons, which need no repentance. But what is Repentance? Not the last and noblest and most refined achievement of the righteousness of men in the service of God, but the first elemental act of the righteousness of God in the service of men; the work that God has written in their hearts and which, because it is from God and not from men, occasions joy in heaven; that looking forward to God, and to Him only, which is recognized only by God and by God Himself.

Karl Barth, *The Epistle to the Romans* [1933]
Rom. 2:15; Luke 15:10

Barth, Markus [1915-1994]

78 Some strange things

It is easy to throw angels and demons and the cosmic character and relevance of Christ's work upon the scrap heap of ancient superstition and mythology, and to consider them but a manner of speech that is utterly irrelevant for our space age. But if we should feel entitled to throw out one part of the witness of Ephesians to Christ, why not the rest of it also: for instance, Christ's Lordship over the church and in the heart? It is unfair and scarcely honest to consider the Bible or parts of it as a cake from which we can pick out merely the raisins we happen to like. Speaking the truth in love and witnessing to the biblical Christ may imply the necessity to speak also of some very strange things.

Markus Barth, *The Broken Wall* [1959]
Eph. 4:1-6; 6:11-12

Basil the Great [c.330-379]

79 Keeping all the commandments

We must always be on our guard lest, under the pretext of keeping one commandment, we be found breaking another.

St. Basil the Great
Jas. 2:10

80 Tranquility

We must try to keep the mind in tranquility. For just as the eye which constantly shifts its gaze, now turning to the right or to the left, now incessantly peering up or down, cannot see distinctly what lies before it, but the sight must be fixed firmly on the object in view if one would make his vision of it clear; so too man's mind when distracted by his countless worldly cares cannot focus itself distinctly on the truth.

St. Basil the Great
Ps. 39:6; Luke 8:14; 2 Tim. 2:4

Baxter, Richard [1615-1691]

81 Ye holy angels bright

Ye holy angels bright,
Who wait at God's right hand,
Or through the realms of light
Fly at your Lord's command,
    Assist our song;
    For else the theme
    Too high doth seem
    For mortal tongue.
Ye blessed souls at rest,
Who ran this earthly race,
And now, from sin released,
Behold the Savior's face,

God's praises sound,
As in his sight,
With sweet delight,
Ye do abound.
Ye saints, who toil below,
Adore your heavenly King.
And onward as ye go
Some joyful anthem sing;
Take what he gives
And praise him still,
Through good or ill,
Who ever lives!
My soul, bear thou thy part,
Triumph in God above:
And with a well-tuned heart
Sing thou the songs of love!
Let all thy days
Till life shall end,
Whate'er he send,
Be filled with praise.

Richard Baxter
Ps. 47; 66:1-4

Bayne, Stephen F. (Fielding), Jr., Bp., [1908-1974]

82 Sending missionaries

As long as I live, I will never appeal for money for the mission of God in this world. This is a degradation of God and of ourselves, which has pauperized us in every way over the centuries. God has no need, and if the mission is God's, then we do not ask for help to give God a boost; therefore we do not appeal for funds. We allow people to take a share in God's work, and this is a very different thing.

Stephen F. Bayne, Jr.
Acts 13:2,3

83 The Church's mission?

The Church has no mission of its own. All we can have by ourselves is a club or a debating society; and our only hope, left to ourselves, is to win as many members for our own club and away from other clubs as we can. And whatever this is, it is not Mission. Mission belongs to God. The Mission was His from the beginning; it is His; it will always be His. He has His purposes from the foundation of the world, and the means to fulfill them; and the only part the Church has in this is obedience—a share in the eternal and life-giving obedience of the Son of God . . . And the most terrible judgment on the Church comes when God leaves us to our own devices because He is tired of waiting for our obedience—leaves us to be the domestic chaplains to a comfortable secular world—and goes Himself into the wilderness of human need and injustice and pain. This judgment does come on churches and nations, when they forget that God is in command, that He does the choosing.

Stephen F. Bayne, Jr., *An Anglican Turning Point* [1964]
1 Chr. 16:23,24; Ps. 96; Isa. 43:7; Luke 24:47,48; Acts 13:2-4,47; Rev. 14:6,7

Beach, W. (William) Waldo [1916-2001]

84 The common currency

It is a rare campus indeed where the Christian universe of discourse is the shared basis of allegiance and the common currency of intellectual exchange. More likely, the Christian faith is an archaic facade, a bit of Victorian fretwork on the front of the house, of which polite note is made at Commencement, but not the common premise of teaching and research and learning.

W. Waldo Beach, "Where Do We Meet?"
2 Tim. 3:7;4:4

85 Always a cross

The symbol of the New Testament and the Christian Church is a cross, which stands for a love faithful despite physical agony and rejection by the world. No amount of air-conditioning and pew-cushioning in the suburban church can cover over the hard truth that the Christian life . . . is a narrow way of suffering; that discipleship is costly: that, for the faithful, there is always a cross to be carried. No one can understand Christianity to its depths who comes to it to enjoy it as a pleasant weekend diversion.

W. Waldo Beach, *The Christian Life*
Mark 8:34,35

Beaufort, Joseph de [c.1600-?]

86 Resting on God

When an occasion of practicing some virtue offered, he addressed himself to God, saying, "Lord, I cannot do this unless Thou enablest me;" and . . . then he received strength more than sufficient. When he had failed in his duty, he simply confessed his fault, saying to God, "I shall never do otherwise if Thou leavest me to myself; it is Thou who must hinder my falling, and mend what is amiss." After this, he gave himself no further uneasiness about it.

Joseph de Beaufort, *The Character of Brother Lawrence*
Ps. 32:1-5; 51:1-5; Jas. 5:16; 1 John 1:8-10

Beecher, Henry Ward [1813-1887]

87 The Holy Ghost

I should as soon attempt to raise flowers if there were no atmosphere, or produce fruits if there were neither light nor heat, as to regenerate men if I did not believe there was a Holy Ghost.

Henry Ward Beecher
Matt. 19:26

Bell, Bernard Iddings [1886-1958]

88 Why is there evil?

What else is the meaning of our present chaos, of humanity in sorrow, but this: that contemporary man is tried before the bar of the Eternal, and found wanting? Nor can any nation survive, or re-establish lasting peace, if it rests on those foundations on which contemporary nations have been built, our own included. What are those crumbling foundations? Conceit, self-will, denial of discipline, self-expressionism, secularism, this worldliness, greed, entrenched privilege, defiance of God's desire. On base absurdities have we built. Have we now moral courage to face our common sin, or are we content to trust in one form of armed wickedness to overcome the evils of another form of the same mad folly? Merely by smashing our enemies we shall not remake the world. By Beelzebub no devils are cast out . . .

Thank God, our Christian chance is not permanently gone from us [in world affairs]. Ecclesiastics seems for the most part to have failed, failed both man and God; but God has not failed, Jesus has not failed. The God-man still remains the only leader into cooperation whose wisdom is sufficient for a permanent, competent, and free Society. The dictators and would-be dictators will not do. They overreach themselves. Eventually they will destroy one another, and kill off most of us. But even that disaster will not eradicate the desire of men and women to lay down lives for that which is more than themselves. Men will continue to demand not the freedom from that degree of unity for which the dictatorships stand, but rather a finer, more noble, more perceptive kind of unity: a human solidarity which is not nationalistic but world-embracing, a human integration which in aim and purpose is not secularist but spiritual. What the world unwittingly is groping after is allegiance to the eternal, the compassionate, the completely integrating Christ.

Bernard Iddings Bell, *Still Shine the Stars* [1941]
Ps. 133:1; Matt. 23:8; Mark 3:22-26

89 The evil of riches

The evil of riches, then, for institutions, for nations, for individuals, is that those who possess or seek to possess almost invariably overvalue possessions and so cease to live creatively. They stop loving God with all the heart and all the soul and all the strength and all the mind. They stop loving their neighbors, too. When you find a person of means who is not either a self-centered bore or a low person, you may know that God has worked a miracle.

Bernard Iddings Bell, *God is Not Dead* [1945]
Matt. 19:24; Mark 12:30,31; Luke 12:27-34

Bennett, Dan

90 Brevity

The reason that the Ten Commandments are short and clear is that they were handed down direct, and not through several committees.

Dan Bennett
Ex. 20:1-17

Bennett, John C. [b.1902]

91 Euphemisms for "sinner"

The word "sinner" often proves a great obstacle to understanding, but let us use other words. Let us say that man is the kind of creature who naturally sees the world from a very limited perspective, that he tends to be self-centered and to prefer the interests that are closest to himself and to his own social group. Let us say that man is naturally unwilling to accept his limited or finite status, that he is always seeking to extend his control over others, that he seeks to maintain his own security by means of power over all who may threaten it, that he likes to be in a position to compare himself with others to their disadvantage, that he seeks to be self-sufficient and to deny in effect his dependence upon God and to set up his own group or system or ideal in the place of God.

John C. Bennett
Ps. 5:5; Rom. 3:10-18

Berdyaev, Nikolai Alexandrovich [1874-1948]

92 The entrance to heaven

For Christian consciousness, paradise is the Kingdom of Christ and is unthinkable apart from Christ. But this changes everything. The cross and the crucifixion enter into the bliss of paradise. The Son of God and the Son of Man descends into hell to free those who suffer there. . . . To conquer evil, the good must crucify itself.

Nikolai A. Berdyaev, *The Destiny of Man* [1937]
Luke 23:43; John 14:2,3; 1 Pet. 3:18,19

Berger, Peter L.

93 Religious affirmation of secular values

There is a continuum of values between the churches and the general community. What distinguishes the handling of these values in the churches is mainly the heavier dosage of religious vocabulary involved. . . . Another way of putting this is to say that the churches operate with secular values while the secular institutions are permeated with religious terminology. . . . An objective observer is hard put to tell the difference (at least in terms of values affirmed) between the church members and those who maintain an 'unchurched' status. Usually the most that can be said is that the church members hold the same values as everybody else, but with more emphatic solemnity. Thus, church membership in no way means adherence to a set of values at variance with those of the general society; rather, it means a stronger and more explicitly religious affirmation of the same values held by the community at large.

Peter L. Berger, *The Noise of Solemn Assemblies* [1961]
Isa. 1:13,14

Bergman, Ingmar [b.1918]

94 Art and worship

It is my opinion that art lost its basic creative drive the moment it was separated from worship. It severed an umbilical cord. . . . In former days the artist remained unknown and his work was to the glory of God. . . .

Today the individual has become the highest form and the greatest bane of artistic creation.

Ingmar Bergman, *The Seventh Seal* [1957]
Ps. 145:11; 1 Pet. 2:5

Bernard of Clairvaux [1091-1153]

95 Fasting

If the appetite alone hath sinned, let it alone fast, and it sufficeth. But if the other members also have sinned, why should they not fast, too. . . . Let the eye fast from strange sights and from every wantonness, so that that which roamed in freedom in fault-doing may, abundantly humbled, be checked by penitence. Let the ear, blamably eager to listen, fast from tales and rumors, and from whatsoever is of idle import, and tendeth least to salvation. Let the tongue fast from slanders and murmurings, and from useless, vain, and scurrilous words, and sometimes also, in the seriousness of silence, even from things which may seem of essential import. Let the hand abstain from . . . all toils which are not imperatively necessary. But also let the soul herself abstain from all evils and from acting out her own will. For without such abstinence the other things find no favor with the Lord.

St. Bernard of Clairvaux
Matt. 9:14,15; 12:36,37; John 14:15; Acts 14:3; 1 Cor. 7:5

96 A dreadful offensiveness

I do a great wrong in His sight, when I beseech Him that He will hear my prayer, which as I give utterance to it I do not hear myself. I entreat Him that He will think of me; but I regard neither myself nor Him. Nay, what is worse, turning over corrupt and evil thoughts in mine heart, I thrust a dreadful offensiveness into His presence.

St. Bernard of Clairvaux
Amos 5:21-24

97 Love

Honor and glory are indeed due to God and to Him alone, but He will accept neither of them if they be not preserved in the honey of love. Love is sufficient of itself; it pleases by itself and on its own account. Love seeks no cause beyond itself and no fruit. It is its own fruit, its own enjoyment. I love because I love; I love that I may love. Love is a great thing provided it recurs to its beginning, returns to its origin, and draws always from that Fountain which is perpetually in flood. Of all the feelings and affections of the soul, love is the only one by which the creature, though not on equal terms, is able to respond to the Creator and to repay what it has received from Him. For when God loves us He desires nothing but to be loved. He loves for no other reason, indeed, than that He may be loved, knowing that by their love itself those who love Him are blessed.

St. Bernard of Clairvaux
Mark 12:32-34; Rom. 5:5; 8:28; 1 John 5:1-3

98 New wine

Prayer is a wine which makes glad the heart of man.

St. Bernard of Clairvaux
Ps. 32

99 Jesus, thou joy of loving hearts

Jesus, thou joy of loving hearts,
Thou fount of life, thou Light of men,
From the best bliss that earth imparts
We turn unfilled to Thee again.
We taste Thee, O Thou living Bread,
And long to feast upon Thee still:
We drink of Thee, the Fountainhead,

And thirst our souls from Thee to fill.
O Jesus, ever with us stay,
Make all our moments calm and bright;
Chase the dark night of sin away,
Shed o'er the world Thy holy light.

St. Bernard of Clairvaux
Matt. 26:26-28; Mark 14:22-24; Luke 22:19,20

Betz, Otto [b.1917]

100 Faith and sight

In the era of faith there is room for repentance, since each person can decide freely for Christ; in the era of sight, when the reign of Christ is manifest, only judgment is left for the undecided.

Otto Betz, *What Do We Know About Jesus?* [1968]
1 Cor. 13:12

Blackham, H. J. (Harold John) [b.1903]

101 The end of humanism

On humanist assumptions, life leads to nothing; and every pretense that it does not is a deceit.

H. J. Blackham
2 Cor. 4:1,2; 11:13-15

Blake, William [1757-1827]

102 The mind the gift of Jesus

Remember: he who despises and mocks a mental gift in another, calling it pride and selfishness and sin, mocks Jesus, the giver of every mental gift, which always appear to the ignorance-loving hypocrite as sins: but that which is a sin in the sight of cruel men, is not so in the sight of our kind God. Let every Christian, as much as in him lies, engage himself openly and publicly, before all the world, in some mental pursuit for the building up of [the Kingdom].

William Blake
Jas. 1:17; Matt. 6:33

Blewett, George John [1873-1912]

103 The best fruit of prayer

The last and highest result of prayer is not the securing of this or that gift, the avoiding of this or that danger. The last and highest result of prayer is the knowledge of God—the knowledge which is eternal life—and by that knowledge, the transformation of human character, and of the world.

George John Blewett
Ps. 85:9-13; Hos. 6:6

Boice, James Montgomery [1938-2000]

104 The unique authority

We are to believe and follow Christ in all things, including his words about Scripture. And this means that Scripture is to be for us what it was to him: the unique, authoritative, and inerrant Word of God, and not merely a human testimony to Christ, however carefully guided and preserved by God. If the Bible is less than this to us, we are not fully Christ's disciples.

James Montgomery Boice, "The Preacher & God's Word"
Matt. 5:17; 7:12; 22:37-40; Mark 7:12,13; Luke 4:4; 16:29-31

Bojaxhiu, Agnes Gonxha (Mother Teresa of Calcutta) [1910-1997]

105 Love letters

> We are all pencils in the hand of a writing God, who is sending love letters to the world.

Mother Teresa (Agnes Gonxha Bojaxhiu)
John 3:16; 2 Cor. 3:3

Bonar, Horatius [1808-1889]

106 A Bethlehem hymn

> He has come! the Christ of God;
> Left for us His glad abode,
> Stooping from His throne of bliss,
> To this darksome wilderness.
>
> He has come! the Prince of Peace;
> Come to bid our sorrows cease;
> Come to scatter with His light
> All the darkness of our night.
>
> He, the Mighty King, has come!
> Making this poor world His home;
> Come to bear our sin's sad load,—
> Son of David, Son of God!
>
> He has come whose name of grace
> Speaks deliverance to our race;
> Left for us His glad abode,—
> Son of Mary, Son of God!
>
> Unto us a Child is born!
> Ne'er has earth beheld a morn,
> Among all the morns of time,
> Half so glorious in its prime!

Unto us a Son is given!
He has come from God's own heaven,
Bringing with Him, from above,
Holy peace and holy love.

Horatius Bonar
Isa. 9:6,7

107 His work

Faith is the acknowledgment of the entire absence of all goodness in us, and the recognition of the cross as the substitute for all the want on our part. The whole work is His, not ours, from first to last.

Horatius Bonar, "The Everlasting Righteousness"
Ps. 148:13; Rom. 3:23; 2 Cor. 4:15; 1 John 1:8

Bonhoeffer, Dietrich [1906-1945]

108 A share in His sufferings

The law of Christ, which it is our duty to fulfill, is the bearing of the cross. Thus the call to follow Christ always means a call to share the work of forgiving men their sins. Forgiveness is the Christlike suffering which it is the Christian's duty to bear.

Dietrich Bonhoeffer
Mark 11:25,26; John 20:22,23; Acts 13:38,39

109 The fellowship needs the weak

In a Christian community, everything depends upon whether each individual is an indispensable link in a chain. Only when even the smallest link is securely interlocked is the chain unbreakable. A community which allows unemployed members to exist within it will perish because of them. It will be well, therefore, if every member receives a definite task to perform for the community, that he may know in hours of doubt that he, too, is not useless and unusable. Every Christian community must realize that not only do the weak need the strong, but also that the strong cannot exist without the weak. The elimination of the weak is the death of the fellowship.

Dietrich Bonhoeffer, *Life Together* [1954]
Rom. 14:13; 1 Cor. 12:22,23; Heb. 5:12-14

110 Bearing one another's burdens

It is the fellowship of the Cross to experience the burden of the other. If one does not experience it, the fellowship he belongs to is not Christian. If any member refuses to bear that burden, he denies the law of Christ.

Dietrich Bonhoeffer, *Life Together* [1954]
Rom. 15:1; Gal. 6:2

111 Life without God's Word

The deceit, the lie of the devil consists of this, that he wishes to make man believe that he can live without God's Word. Thus he dangles before man's fantasy a kingdom of faith, of power, and of peace, into which only he can enter who consents to the temptations; and he conceals from men that he, as the devil, is the most unfortunate and unhappy of beings, since he is finally and eternally rejected by God.

Dietrich Bonhoeffer, *Temptation* [1955]
Luke 4:3,4

112 Cheap grace

After all, we are told, our salvation has already been accomplished by the grace of God. . . . It was unkind to speak to men like this, for such a cheap offer could only leave them bewildered and tempt them from the way to which they had been called by Christ. Having laid hold on cheap grace, they were barred forever from the knowledge of costly grace. Deceived and weakened, men felt that they were strong now that they were in possession of this cheap grace—whereas they had in fact lost the power to live the life of discipleship and obedience. The word of cheap grace has been the ruin of more Christians than any commandment of works.

Dietrich Bonhoeffer, *The Cost of Discipleship* [1964]
2 Thess. 3:13

Bounds, E. M. (Edward McKendree) [1835-1913]

113 Peril in orthodoxy

We love orthodoxy. It is good. It is the best. It is the clean, clear cut teaching of God's Word, the trophies won by truth in its conflict with error, the levees which faith has raised against the desolating floods of honest or reckless misbelief or unbelief; but orthodoxy, clear and hard as crystal, suspicious and militant, may be but the letter well shaped, well named, and well learned, the letter which kills. Nothing is so dead as a dead orthodoxy—too dead to speculate, too dead to think, to study, or to pray.

E. M. Bounds, *Power Through Prayer* [1991]
Matt. 12:2-6,10-13; 2 Cor. 3:6

Boyle, Robert [1627-1691]

114 The object of all studies

The gospel comprises indeed, and unfolds, the whole mystery of man's redemption, as far forth as it is necessary to be known for our salvation: and the corpuscularian or mechanical philosophy strives to deduce all the phenomena of nature from adiaphorous matter, and local motion. But neither the fundamental doctrine of Christianity nor that of the powers and effects of matter and motion seems to be more than an epicycle . . . of the great and universal system of God's contrivances, and makes but a part of the more general theory of things, knowable by the light of nature, improved by the information of the scriptures: so that both these doctrines . . . seem to be but members of the universal hypothesis, whose objects I conceive to be the natural counsels, and works of God, so far as they are discoverable by us in this life.

Robert Boyle
Ps. 19:1-6

Bradley, Samuel

115 Devotional poetry

Devotional poetry . . . has to do with devotedness, with trust merged into faith, with love's steadfastness. It finds men's worthwhileness deep laid in relationship to God's worthwhileness, and this devotion is expressed in communication. It finds this world precious insofar as it . . . symbolizes God's love and therefore it runs counter to our national sin of distrust in God. (And yet, how can we trust Him without knowing and living unto Him and loving Him?)

Samuel Bradley
Ps. 66:8,9

Brainerd, David [1718-1747]

116 How precious is time!

Oh, how precious is time, and how it pains me to see it slide away, while I do so little to any good purpose. Oh, that God would make me more fruitful and spiritual.

Journal of David Brainerd
Matt. 9:37,38

Braithwaite, Albert

117 The claim of Good News

Although we have different ways of worshipping and doing things, we have only one God. So how can we claim to have . . . "Good News" unless people can see in us that Jesus Christ is breaking down barriers and bringing us together?

Albert Braithwaite
John 13:13-15

Brandon, Owen Rupert

118 The spirit of fellowship

In several striking cases of conversion I have studied, those in need were inspired and affected, not merely by the kindness of an individual . . . but by the love and sympathy of the Church as a whole. . . . Examples could be multiplied. This type of service is a great witness to the reality of Christian life and faith; but it presupposes a spirit of fellowship within the Church, a spirit which is all too rare. It means that there is mutual respect and trust between the minister and the members of his Church; and a spirit of fellowship which is outward-looking and which issues in service.

Owen Brandon, *The Battle for the Soul* [1960]
Phil. 2:1,2

Brent, Charles Henry, Bp. [1862-1929]

119 Penitence, pardon, and peace

Peace comes when there is no cloud between us and God. Peace is the consequence of forgiveness, God's removal of that which obscures His face and so breaks union with Him. The happy sequence culminating in fellowship with God is penitence, pardon, and peace—the first we offer, the second we accept, and the third we inherit.

Charles H. Brent
Eze. 34:25; 1 John 1:3,9

120 Hardness of prayer

Pray hardest when it is hardest to pray.

Charles H. Brent
Rom. 8:26

121 Power to save

It is appalling to think of a power so strong that it can annihilate with the irresistible force of its grinding heel; but it is inspiring to consider an Almightiness that transforms the works of evil into the hand-maidens of righteousness and converts the sinner into the saint. And it is this latter power which eternal Love possesses and exhibits. He persistently dwells in the sinner until the sinner wakes up in His likeness and is satisfied with it.

> Charles H. Brent, *With God in the World* [1899]
> *1 Pet. 1:5*

122 Thoughtful praying

Pray with your intelligence. Bring things to God that you have thought out and think them out again with Him. That is the secret of good judgment. Repeatedly place your pet opinions and prejudices before God. He will surprise you by showing you that the best of them need refining and some the purification of destruction.

> Charles H. Brent, *Adventures in Prayer* [1932]
> *Amos 5:14,15; Phil. 4:8*

Briejèr, C. J. (Cornelis Jan)

123 Alive and speaking

My biological work convinced me that the One who was declared dead by Nietzsche, and silent by Sartre, actually is very much alive and speaking to us through all things.

> C. J. Briejèr, letter to Rachel Carson
> *Ps. 8:2,3; Rom. 10:16-18*

Brierley, J.

124 The Kingdom

[Jesus'] life and utterance were the proclamation of this new order of things, of this new force by which man was to be ruled. When, unarmed and defenseless, He said to the Roman power, "My Kingdom is not of this world," He spoke the word of inauguration. Over the kingdom of the elemental forces, over the kingdom of the animal, over the kingdom of the intellect, He beheld rising, with Himself as prophet and embodiment, that kingdom of the spiritual whose forces should be those of purity and sacrifice, love and trust, obedience and service. It is the last of the kingdoms because it is the highest; it will be the most enduring for there is nothing that can take its place.

J. Brierley, *The Life of the Soul* [1912]
Luke 1:30-33; John 18:36

Bright, John [b.1908]

125 To be Jeremiah

Jeremiah refutes the popular, modern notion that the end of religion is an integrated personality, freed of its fears, its doubts, and its frustrations. Certainly Jeremiah was no integrated personality. It is doubtful if . . . he ever knew the meaning of the word "peace." We have no evidence that his internal struggle was ever ended, although the passing years no doubt brought an increasing acceptance of destiny. Jeremiah, if his "confessions" are any index, needed a course in pastoral psychiatry in the very worst way. . . . The feeling cannot be escaped that if Jeremiah had been integrated, it would have been at the cost of ceasing to be Jeremiah! A man at peace simply could not be a Jeremiah. Spiritual health is good; mental assurance is good; but the summons of faith is neither to an integrated personality nor to the laying-by of all questions, but to the dedication of personality—with all its fears and questions—to its duty and destiny under God.

John Bright, *The Kingdom of God* [1955]
Jer. 9:25,26; Rom. 2:28,29

Broadbent, E. H. (Edmund Hamer) [1861-1945]

126 Sectarianism

Sectarianism is limitation. Some truth taught in Scripture, some part of the divine revelation, is apprehended, and the heart responds to it and accepts it. As it is dwelt upon, expounded, defended; its power and beauty increasingly influence those affected by it. Another side of truth, another view of revelation, also contained in Scripture, seems to weaken, even to contradict, the truth that has been found to be so effectual. and in jealous fear for the doctrine accepted and taught, the balancing truth is minimized, explained away, and even denied. So on a portion of revelation, on a part of the Word, a sect is founded, good and useful because it preaches and practices Divine truth, but limited and unbalanced because it does not see all truth, nor frankly accept the whole of Scripture. Its members are not only deprived of the full use of all Scripture, but are cut off from the fellowship of many saints, who are less limited than they, or limited in another direction.

E. H. Broadbent, *The Pilgrim Church* [1935]
2 Tim. 3:16

Brogan, Denis W. (William) [1900-1974]

127 The godless establishment

[In nineteenth-century America] religion became a matter of conduct, of good deeds, of works, with only a vague background of faith. It became highly functional, highly pragmatic; it became a guarantee of success, moral and material. "The proper study of mankind is man,"[2] was the evasion by which many American divines escaped the necessity for thought about God.

([2] Alexander Pope, *An Essay on Man*)

Denis Brogan
Ps. 1:1-3

Bronnert, David

128 The light shines in the darkness

The light shines in the darkness. Candles are always popular for giving a warm romantic glow and this time of year they are to be seen on many different occasions. Of course a candle is easy to blow out! So much so that its flickering light was chosen by Shakespeare as a picture of the transitory nature of life. Out out brief candle!

Darkness is a reminder of evil, for it is in the darkness that people get lost, stumble and fall. It is in the darkness that power is misused, corruption reigns and evil is done. It is easy to imagine that in the end evil will triumph and the light will disappear. Situations change. Familiar landmarks—like this magazine!—disappear. There is the unrelenting pressure of a vanity fair society. The candle burns down and gives a thin wisp of smoke before going out.

But there are also the special party candles that keep bursting back into life. They are a much better picture of the light of the gospel! For though they have been numerous attempts down the centuries to extinguish the light, it has kept on bursting back into flame.

The light of Christ keeps on shining. New ways of sharing the good news come along. New believers are attracted to his light. Sleepy Christians are re-awakened. Fresh discoveries give even more confidence in the truth of the Bible.

The light keeps on shining in the darkness. It is a statement and a promise at the same time. It isn't that once the light shone, but rather, that in the present it shines, and it will do so in the future as well. For the light comes from the one who is, as well as who was, and is also the one who is to come.

David Bronnert
Mal. 4:2; Luke 11:35,36; John 1:4,5,9,10

129 The Scapegoat

One of the most striking parts of the Day of Atonement is that of the scapegoat. The high priest placed both his hands on the head of a goat and confessed all the sins of the nation. Then the goat carrying the sins of the people is sent off into the wilderness. But it is not just a piece of history!

There is in the modern world a quest for scapegoats though with one enormous difference. Whenever there is an accident or a tragedy, there is a search for someone to blame. Often all the modern means of communication join in; accusations, resignations, demands for compensation and the rest. If a guilty person is found, then an orgy of condemnation and vilification. Rarely a sense of, there but for the grace of God go I. Instead of dealing gently with one another's failure because of our own vulnerability to criticism, there is the presumption that we are in a fit condition to judge and to condemn.

The enormous difference? The original scapegoat followed a confession of the sins of the people. There was no blaming of someone else, but an admission of guilt and a quest for the forgiveness of God. The goat wasn't hated, but was a dramatic picture of the carrying away sins. It was the very opposite of a self-righteous victimization of someone else.

Ever since 200 A.D., Christians have seen the scapegoat as a picture of Jesus. As it was led out to die in the wilderness bearing the sins of the people, so he was crucified outside Jerusalem for our sins. We are to be both forgiven and forgiving people.

David Bronnert
Lev. 16:8-26; Ps. 32:1,2; Rom. 2:1; Heb. 10:1-14

130 The explainable fellowship

Race highlights the fact that in our congregational life we usually do not reflect the variety of cultures. There are Asian, West Indian, and Anglo-Saxon congregations worshiping and meeting close to each other. These groups meet at work and in school, but not always in church. If the church is middle-class and intellectual in the language of the services, in the music employed, in the life-style expected of Christians, in its leadership, and in the methods of presenting the gospel, then the whole atmosphere is such as to repel those who are not middle-class and intellectual. They feel out of place and unwanted, even if they are given a friendly greeting at the door. The life of the New Testament Church was evidence of the supernatural; God was in their midst. The power of Christ was a reality. The fellowship could not be explained in simple natural terms. A church divided on social and racial lines is not evidence for the supernatural, but for the simply human and social.

David Bronnert, "The Gospel and Culture"
in *The Changing World*
Matt. 12:25-28; 1 Tim. 5:21

Brooks, Phillips, Bp. [1835-1893]

131 Becoming spiritual

We never become truly spiritual by sitting down and wishing to become so. You must undertake something so great that you cannot accomplish it unaided.

Phillips Brooks
John 14:12

132 Life without prayer is foolish

If man is man and God is God, to live without prayer is not merely an awful thing: it is an infinitely foolish thing.

Phillips Brooks
Ps. 53:4; Prov. 14:16; Luke 12:16-21

133 Laboring in prayer

Do not pray for easy lives; pray to be stronger men. Do not pray for tasks equal to your powers; pray for powers equal to your tasks. Then the doing of your work shall be no miracle, but you yourself shall be a miracle. Every day you shall wonder at yourself, at the richness of life which has come to you by the grace of God.

Phillips Brooks
2 Tim. 1:7-9; Isa. 40:31

134 Pass it on

I do not believe anyone ever yet humbly, genuinely, thoroughly gave himself to Christ without some other finding Christ through him.

Phillips Brooks
Matt. 5:16

135 Freed into service and duty

God frees our souls, not from service, not from duty, but into service and into duty; and he who mistakes the purpose of his freedom mistakes the character of his freedom. He who thinks that he is being released from the work, and not set free in order that he may accomplish that work, mistakes the condition into which his soul is invited to enter.

Phillips Brooks, *The Law of Growth* [1902]
John 8:31-36; Rom. 8:15; Gal. 5:1

136 Leaving the victory to God

To hold your truth, to believe it with all your heart, to work with all your might, first to make it real to yourself and then to show its preciousness to other men, and then—not till then, but then—to leave the questions of when and how and by whom it shall prevail to God: that is the true life of the believer. There is no feeble unconcern and indiscriminateness there, and neither is there any excited hatred of the creed, the doctrine, or the Church, which you feel wholly wrong. You have not fled out of the furnace of bigotry to freeze on the open and desolate plains of indifference. You believe and yet you have no wish to persecute.

Phillips Brooks, *The Law of Growth* [1902]
John 7:16,17

Brown, Charles Reynolds [1862-1950]

137 Pride in humility

There is a false self-distrust which denies the worth of its own talent. It is not humility—it is petty pride, withholding its simple gifts from the hands of Christ because they are not more pretentious. There are men who would endow colleges, they say, if they were millionaires. They would help in the work of Bible study if they were as gifted as Henry Drummond. They would strive to lead their associates into the Christian life if they had the gifts of Dwight L. Moody. But they are not ready to give what they have and do what they can and be as it has pleased God to make them, in His service—and that is their condemnation.

Charles Reynolds Brown
Mark 12:41-44; Luke 11:39-41; 1 Cor. 12:11

Brown, P. B.

138 Essential prayer

The religious desire and effort of the soul to relate itself and all its interest to God and his will, is prayer in the deepest sense. This is essential prayer: uttered or unexpressed, it is equally prayer. It is the soul's desire after God going forth in a manifestation, . . . the soul striving after God. This is a prayer that may exist without ceasing, consisting, as it does, not in doing or saying this or that, but in temper and attitude of the spirit.

P. B. Brown
Rom. 12:1,2; 1 Thess. 5:17

Brown, Robert R.

139 From the Godward side of life

It is the Church's mission to confront the world from the Godward side of life with the Christian principles of a free and just society. The dignity, the value, and the importance of every individual are made abundantly clear by the Son of God. He has shown us what human life is intended to be, and we must be willing to stand against whatever is amiss in the temper and disposition of the world, or of any segment of it.

Robert R. Brown
1 John 5:4; 1 Pet. 2:11,12

Browne, Sir Thomas [1605-1682]

140 Discovering the Bible

Be able to be alone. Lose not the advantage of solitude, . . . but delight to be alone and single with Omnipresency. . . . Life is pure flame, and we live by an invisible sun within us.

Sir Thomas Browne
Ps. 84:11

Browning, Elizabeth Barrett [1806-1861]

141 There is sorrow

"There is no God," the foolish saith,
But none, "There is no sorrow."
And nature oft the cry of faith
In bitter need will borrow:
Eyes which the preacher could not school,
By wayside graves are raised;

And lips say, "God be pitiful,"
Who ne'er said, "God be praised."

Elizabeth Barrett Browning
Ps. 14:1; 1 Cor. 1:23-29

Browning, Robert [1812-1889]

142 Virtue in a jug

For the preacher's merit or demerit,
It were to be wished the flaws were fewer
In the earthen vessel, holding treasure,
Which lies as safe in a golden ewer;
But the main thing is, does it hold good measure?
Heaven soon sets right all other matters.

Robert Browning
2 Tim. 2:20,21

Bruce, F. F. (Frederick Fyvie) [1910-1991]

143 Impossible accommodations

However the gospel may be defended, it cannot be defended by concessions which deprive it of its essence or which detract from our Savior's title to be called The Word of God.

Frederick F. Bruce
2 Cor. 4:13,14

144 The New Testament documents

The evidence for our New Testament writings is ever so much greater than the evidence for many writings of classical authors, the authenticity of which no-one dreams of questioning. And if the New Testament were a collection of secular writings, their authenticity would generally be regarded as beyond all doubt. It is a curious fact that historians have often been much readier to trust the New Testament than have many theologians.

F. F. Bruce, *The New Testament Documents:*
Are They Reliable? [1949]

Rom. 10:17

145 The present affliction

The glory to come far outweighs the affliction of the present. The affliction is light and temporary when compared with the all-surpassing and everlasting glory. So Paul, writing against a background of recent and (even for him) unparalleled tribulation, had assured his friends in Corinth a year or two before this that 'this slight momentary affliction is preparing for us an eternal weight of glory beyond all comparison' (2Cor. 4:17). It is not merely that the glory is a compensation for the suffering; it actually grows out of the suffering. There is an organic relation between the two for the believer as surely as there was for the Lord.

F. F. Bruce, *The Letter of Paul to the Romans,*
An Introduction and Commentary [1997]
Rom. 8:18

Bruce, Michael

146 Second things put first

In church government . . . our primary concern is to reflect the nature of God. Christ became man in order that He might redeem men from their fallen state, from their selfishness and self-isolating divisions from God and from each other; so that, gathered together in one in Him, man may offer to God that likeness to Himself in love for which he was created. Church government is primarily concerned with this: with worship, with the drawing of the whole life of the whole world into this reflection of the nature of God. It is secondly—and only secondly—concerned with the quarrels and peccadilloes of those who are not, as a matter of fact, imitating God's nature very faithfully.

Michael Bruce, "The Layman and Church Government"
1 Cor. 1:13

Brunner, Emil [1889-1966]

147 Christ Himself

For the Platonic or Aristotelian philosophy it is of no importance whether Plato or Aristotle ever lived. For the mystical practice of an Indian, Persian, Chinese, or Neo-Platonic mystic it is a matter of indifference whether Rama, Buddha, Laotse, or Porphyrius are myths or not. The mystic has no personal relation to them. It is not here a question of somebody telling me the truth which of myself I cannot find, but of my finding an access to the depths of the world in the depths of my soul. And everywhere the tendency is to eliminate personality. Even where religion does not have this mystical character, it has no relation to an historical person, who communicates himself to me. That is the characteristic essence of the Christian faith alone. Even where a prophet plays the role of a mediator of divine truth, as for example in Islam, the religious act is not directed toward him but toward his teaching or message. But the Christian does not believe in the teachings of Jesus—which would not be Christian faith, but general religion—he believes in Christ Himself as being the Word of God.

Emil Brunner, *The Word and the World* [1931]
John 20:31

148 Pass it on

One who receives this Word, and by it salvation, receives along with it the duty of passing this Word on . . . Where there is no mission, there is no Church, and where there is neither Church nor mission, there is no faith.

Emil Brunner, *The Word and the World* [1931]
2 Cor. 2:14-17

149 Not guilt

It is characteristic of the thinking of our time that the problem of guilt and forgiveness has been pushed into the background and seems to disappear more and more. Modern thought is impersonal. There are, even today, a great many people who understand that man needs salvation, but there are very few who are convinced that he needs forgiveness and redemption . . . Sin is understood as imperfection, sensuality, worldliness—but not as guilt.

Emil Brunner, *The Word and the World* [1931]
Jas. 2:10

Buchanan, C. O. (Colin Ogilvie) [b.1934]

150 The one New Testament church

The doctrine of the "body" in First Corinthians . . . is a picture of the local church, (which) is distinguished by a great variety of gifts, outlooks, and cultures. The various members belong organically to each other in Christ, and are to exhibit that harmony practically in their common life. The recognition of how they differ from each other, and are yet one, is to enrich their worship, inspire their ministry, and quicken their love. To divide the local church is . . . to witness to a divided Christ, or to a discipleship to lesser masters than Christ, such as Paul or Apollos. Both implications are equally unthinkable. There is no New Testament pattern of serving the one Christ, except in one local body, formed by the incorporation given in the one baptism, and the continued life sustained by breaking and sharing the one bread.

C. O. Buchanan, "The Unity of the Church"
Acts 2:42; 1 Cor. 10:17

Buechner, Frederick [b.1926]

151 Extinct prayers

Something terrible happens, and you might say, "God help us!" or "Jesus Christ!"—the poor, crippled prayers that are hidden in the minor blasphemies of people for whom in every sense God is dead, except that they still have to speak to him, if only through clenched teeth.

Frederick Buechner
Matt. 5:22; Gal. 5:19-21; Eph. 4:26

Bunyan, John [1628-1688]

152 Abundant grace

But upon a day the good providence of God did cast me to Bedford to work on my calling, and in one of the streets of that town I came where there were three or four poor women sitting at a door in the sun and talking about the things of God; and being now willing to hear them discourse, I drew near to hear what they said, for I was now a brisk talker also myself in the matters of religion. But now I may say I heard, but I understood not; for they were far above, out of my reach; for their talk was about a new birth—the work of God on their hearts. And methought they spake as if Joy did make them speak; they spake with such pleasantness of scripture language and with such appearance of grace in all they said, that they were to me as if they had found a new world.

John Bunyan, *Grace Abounding to the Chief of Sinners* [1666]
Jer. 33:10,11; Matt. 11:15; 1 Tim. 1:15,16

153 Valiant-for-truth

After this it was noised abroad that Mr. Valiant-for-truth was taken with a summons by the same post as the other, and had this for a token that the summons was true, "That his pitcher was broken at the fountain." Eccl. 12:6. When he understood it, he called for his friends, and told them of it. Then said he, I am going to my Father's; and though with great difficulty I have got hither, yet now I do not repent me of all the trouble I have been at to arrive where I am. My sword I give to him that shall succeed me in my pilgrimage, and my courage and skill to him that can get it. My marks and scars I carry with me, to be a witness for me that I have fought His battles who will now be my rewarder. When the day that he must go hence was come, many accompanied him to the river-side, into which as he went, he said, "Death, where is thy sting?" And as he went down deeper, he said, "Grave, where is thy victory?" 1 Cor. 15:55. So he passed over, and all the trumpets sounded for him on the other side.

John Bunyan, *The Pilgrim's Progress* [1678]
Eccl. 12:6, 1 Cor. 15:55

154 Pray and read

Read and read again, and do not despair of help to understand the will and mind of God though you think they are fast locked up from you. Neither trouble your heads though you have not commentaries and exposition. Pray and read, read and pray; for a little from God is better than a great deal from men. Also, what is from men is uncertain, and is often lost and tumbled over by men; but what is from God is fixed as a nail in a sure place. There is nothing that so abides with us as what we receive from God; and the reason why the Christians in this day are at such a loss as to some things is that they are contented with what comes from men's mouths, without searching and kneeling before God to know of Him the truth of things. Things we receive at God's hands come to us as truths from the minting house, though old in themselves, yet new to us. Old truths are always new to us if they come with the smell of Heaven upon them.

John Bunyan, *Christ a Complete Saviour* [1692]
Ps. 121:1,2; Matt. 6:25-34; 1 John 4:4-5

Calvin, John [1509-1564]

155 To His glory

Now the great thing is this: we are consecrated and dedicated to God in order that we may thereafter think, speak, meditate, and do, nothing except to his glory. For a sacred thing may not be applied to profane uses without marked injury to him.

John Calvin
Ps. 119:11; 1 Pet. 5:1

156 Free gifts

Those talents which God has bestowed upon us are not our own goods but the free gifts of God; and any persons who become proud of them show their ungratefulness.

John Calvin
Jas. 1:17

157 Firm knowledge

Now we shall possess a right definition of faith if we call it a firm and certain knowledge of God's benevolence toward us, founded upon the truth of the freely given promise in Christ, both revealed to our minds and sealed upon our hearts through the Holy Spirit.

John Calvin
Acts 16:31; Rom. 10:14-17

158 God takes care of His works

Nobody seriously believes the universe was made by God without being persuaded that He takes care of His works.

John Calvin
Jer. 10:12

159 To God be the glory

We must always speak of the efficacy of the ministry in such a manner that the entire praise of the work may be reserved for God alone.

John Calvin
Matt. 10:29-31; Eph. 4:11-13; 2 Tim. 4:16,17

160 The sufficiency of Scripture

Scripture will ultimately suffice for a saving knowledge of God only when its certainty is founded upon the inward persuasion of the Holy Spirit. Indeed, these human testimonies which exist to confirm it will not be vain if, as secondary aids to our feebleness, they follow that chief and highest testimony. But those who wish to prove to unbelievers that Scripture is the Word of God are acting foolishly, for only by faith can this be known.

John Calvin
Luke 16:31

161 A sub-christian reverence?

It would be the height of absurdity to label ignorance tempered by humility "faith;" for faith consists in the knowledge of God and Christ, not in reverence for the Church.

John Calvin
Rom. 3:22; Eph. 1:15-23; Jude 1:3

162 Persevering

It behooves us to accomplish what God requires of us, even when we are in the greatest despair respecting the results.

John Calvin
Matt. 10:22; Luke 22:31,32; Heb. 2:1; 1 Pet. 1:6,7; 2 Pet. 1: 10,11

163 Contemplate His works

The most perfect way of seeking God, and the most suitable order, is not for us to attempt with bold curiosity to penetrate to the investigation of His essence, which we ought more to adore than meticulously to search out, but for us to contemplate Him in His works, whereby He renders Himself near and familiar to us, and in some manner communicates Himself.

John Calvin
Psalms 8:3,4

164 Free will

Few have defined what free will is, although it repeatedly occurs in the writings of all. Origen seems to have put forward a definition generally agreed upon among ecclesiastical writers when he said that it is a faculty of the reason to distinguish between good and evil, a faculty of the will to choose one or the other. Augustine does not disagree with this when he teaches that it is a faculty of the reason and the will to choose good with the assistance of grace; evil, when grace is absent.

John Calvin, The Institutes of the Christian Religion, ii.2.4
[1559]
Rom. 7:14-25

165 Christian freedom

Christian freedom, in my opinion, consists of three parts. The first: that the consciences of believers, in seeking assurance of their justification before God, should rise above and advance beyond the law, forgetting all law righteousness. . . . The second part, dependent upon the first, is that consciences observe the law, not as if constrained by the necessity of the law, but that freed from the law's yoke they willingly obey God's will. . . . The third part of Christian freedom lies in this: regarding outward things that are of themselves "indifferent," we are not bound before God by any religious obligation preventing us from sometimes using them and other times not using them, indifferently. . . . Accordingly, it is perversely interpreted both by those who allege it as an excuse for their desires that they may abuse God's good gifts to their own lust and by those who think that freedom does not exist unless it is used before men, and consequently, in using it have no regard for weaker brethren. . . . Nothing is plainer than this rule: that we should use our freedom if it results in the edification of our neighbor, but if it does not help our neighbor, then we should forego it.

John Calvin, *The Institutes of the Christian Religion* [1559]
1 Cor. 8:7-13; Gal. 5:13,14

166 Imperfect offerings

But sons who are more generously and candidly treated by their fathers do not hesitate to offer them incomplete and halfdone and even defective works, trusting that their obedience and readiness of mind will be accepted by their fathers, even though they have not quite achieved what their fathers intended. Such children ought we to be, firmly trusting that our services will be approved by our most merciful Father, however small, rude, and imperfect these may be.

John Calvin, The Institutes of the Christian Religion [1559]
James 1:25

167 Naturalist atheists

At this day . . . the earth sustains on her bosom many monster minds, minds which are not afraid to employ the seed of Deity deposited in human nature as a means of suppressing the name of God. Can

The Authentic **Book of Christian Quotations**

anything be more detestable than this madness in man, who, finding God a hundred times both in his body and his soul, makes his excellence in this respect a pretext for denying that there is a God? He will not say that chance has made him different from the brutes; . . . but, substituting Nature as the architect of the universe, he suppresses the name of God.

John Calvin, *The Institutes of the Christian Religion* [1559]
Ps. 14:1; Rom. 1:20,21

168 Divine deposits for our neighbors

All the blessings we enjoy are Divine deposits, committed to our trust on this condition, that they should be dispensed for the benefit of our neighbors.

John Calvin, *The Institutes of the Christian Religion* [1559]
Gal. 2:9,10

169 Free will and the Fall

Therefore Adam could have stood if he wished, seeing that he fell solely by his own will. But it was because his will was capable of being bent to one side or the other, and was not given the constancy to persevere, that he fell so easily. Yet his choice of good and evil was free.

John Calvin, *The Institutes of the Christian Religion* [1559]
Gen. 3; Deut. 30:19,20

170 Loving an adversary

A lawsuit, however just, can never be rightly prosecuted by any man, unless he treat his adversary with the same love and good will as if the business under controversy were already amicably settled and composed. Perhaps someone will interpose here that such moderation is so uniformly absent from any lawsuit that it would be a miracle if any such were found. Indeed, I admit that, as the customs of these times go, an example of an upright litigant is rare; but the thing itself, when not corrupted by the addition of anything evil, does not cease to be good and pure.

> John Calvin, *The Institutes of the Christian Religion* [1559]
> *Matt. 5:25,26; 1 Cor. 6:1-8*

171 Key to loving our enemies

Assuredly there is but one way in which to achieve what is not merely difficult but utterly against human nature: to love those who hate us, to repay their evil deeds with benefits, to return blessings for reproaches. It is that we remember not to consider men's evil intention but to look upon the image of God in them, which cancels and effaces their transgressions, and with its beauty and dignity allures us to love and embrace them.

> John Calvin, *The Institutes of the Christian Religion* [1559]
> *Matt. 5:44; 6:14; 18:35; Luke 17:3*

172 Resistance to tyrants

However these deeds of men are judged in themselves, still the Lord accomplished his work through them alike when he broke the bloody scepters of arrogant kings and when he overturned intolerable governments. Let the princes hear and be afraid. But we must, in the meantime, be very careful not to despise or violate that authority of magistrates, full of venerable majesty, which God has established by the weightiest decrees, even though it may reside with the most unworthy men, who defile it as much as they can with their own wickedness. For, if the correction of unbridled despotism is the Lord's to avenge, let us not at once think that it is entrusted to us, to whom no command has been given except to obey and suffer.

> John Calvin, *The Institutes of the Christian Religion* [1559]
> *Ps. 2:7-12; Rom. 13:1-7; Tit. 3:1*

173 Salvation from Christ

We see that our whole salvation and all its parts are comprehended in Christ. We should therefore take care not to derive the least portion of it from anywhere else. If we seek salvation, we are taught by the very name of Jesus that it is "of him." If we seek any other gifts of the Spirit, they will be found in his anointing. If we seek strength, it lies in his dominion; if purity, in his conception; if gentleness, it appears in his birth. For by his birth he was made like us in all respects that he might learn to feel our pain. If we seek redemption, it lies in his passion; if acquittal, in his condemnation; if remission of the curse, in his cross; if satisfaction, in his sacrifice; if purification, in his blood; if reconciliation, in his descent into hell; if mortification of the flesh, in his tomb; if newness of life, in his resurrection; if immortality, in the same; if inheritance of the Heavenly Kingdom, in his entrance into heaven; if protection, if security, if abundant supply of all blessings, in his Kingdom; if untroubled expectation of judgment, in the power given to him to judge. In short, since rich store of every kind of good abounds in him, let us drink our fill from this fountain, and from no other.

> John Calvin, *The Institutes of the Christian Religion* [1559]
> *Acts 4:12; 1 Cor. 1:30;8:6; Heb. 2:17; Gal. 3:3;*
> *Heb. 2:18; 4:15,16*

174 Predestination

When they inquire into predestination, they are penetrating the sacred precincts of divine wisdom. If anyone with carefree assurance breaks into this place, he will not succeed in satisfying his curiosity and he will enter a labyrinth from which he can find no exit. For it is not right for man unrestrainedly to search out things that the Lord has willed to be hidden in Himself; nor is it right for him to investigate from eternity that sublime wisdom, which God would have us revere but not understand, in order that through this also He should fill us with wonder. He has set forth by His Word the secrets of His will that He has decided to reveal to us. These He decided to reveal in so far as He foresaw that they would concern and benefit us.

> John Calvin, *The Institutes of the Christian Religion* [1559]
> *Rom. 11:2,5,6*

175 The uses of election

Few realize how much injury the dogma that baptism is necessary for salvation, badly expounded, has entailed. As a consequence, they are less cautious. For, where the opinion has prevailed that all are lost who have not happened to be baptized with water, our condition is worse than that of God's ancient people—as if the grace of God were now more restricted than under the Law!

> John Calvin, *The Institutes of the Christian Religion* [1559]
> *Eph. 1:3-6; 1 Pet. 1:2*

Campbell, Reginald John [1867-1956]

176 Love and wrath

It is no strain of metaphor to say that the love of God and the wrath of God are the same thing, described from opposite points of view. How we shall experience it depends upon the way we shall come up against it: God does not change; it is man's moral state that changes. The wrath of God is a figure of speech to denote God's unchanging opposition to sin; it is His righteous love operating to destroy evil. It is not evil that will have the last word, but good; not sorrow, but joy; not hate, but love.

> R. J. Campbell, *The Call of Christ* [1932]
> *Num. 14:11; Ps. 7:11; 76:7; 103:8; 1 Cor. 3:11-14*

Capon, Robert Farrar [b.1925]

177 It was very good

The world exists, not for what it means but for what it is. The purpose of mushrooms is to be mushrooms, wine is in order to wine: things are precious before they are contributory. It is a false piety that walks through creation looking only for lessons which can be applied somewhere else. To be sure, God remains the greatest good; but, for all that, the world is still good in itself. Indeed, since He does not need it, its whole reason for being must lie in its own natural goodness; He has no use for it, only delight.

> Robert Farrar Capon, *The Supper of the Lamb* [1969]
> *Gen. 1:31*

Carlyle, Thomas [1795-1881]

178 The terms of the call

Supply-and-demand,—alas! For what noble work was there ever yet any audible demand in that poor sense? The man of Macedonia, speaking in vision to the Apostle Paul, "Come over and help us," did not specify what rate of wages he would give.

Thomas Carlyle
Acts 16:9; 1 Cor. 9:12

179 Holiness vs. sin

The Christian must be consumed with the infinite beauty of holiness and the infinite damnability of sin.

Thomas Carlyle
Isa. 6:3; Matt. 23:33

180 The Bible, by grace

It must have been a most blessed discovery, that of an old Latin Bible which he found in the Erfurt Library about this time. He had never seen the Book before. It taught him another lesson than that of fasts and vigils. . . . Luther learned now that a man was saved not by singing masses, but by the infinite grace of God: a more credible hypothesis. He gradually got himself founded, as on the rock. No wonder he should venerate the Bible, which had brought this blessed help to him. He prized it as the Word of the Highest must be prized by such a man. He determined to hold by that, as through life and to death he firmly did.

Thomas Carlyle, *Spiritual Portrait of Martin Luther* [1859]
Matt. 7:24-27

Carmichael, Amy [1867-1951]

181 Love and giving

One can give without loving, but one cannot love without giving.

Amy Carmichael
Matt. 6:1-4; Luke 12:33,34; 1 Cor. 13; 2 Cor. 8:7-15

182 From subtle love of softening things

From subtle love of softening things,
From easy choices, weakenings,
(Not thus are spirits fortified;
Not this way went the Crucified;)
From all that dims Thy Calvary,
O Lamb of God, deliver me.
Give me the love that leads the way,
The faith that nothing can dismay,
The hope no disappointments tire,
The passion that will burn like fire;
Let me not sink to be a clod:
Make me Thy fuel, Flame of God!

Amy Carmichael, written in India, 1912
Rom. 8:22-25

183 The trifles

If monotony tries me, and I cannot stand drudgery; if stupid people fret me and the little ruffles set me on edge; if I make much of the trifles of life, then I know nothing of Calvary love.

Amy Carmichael, *If* [1938]
Ps. 37:1-3; 103:10; Prov. 24:17-20

184 The definite utterances

Someone gave me a bit of brick and a little slab of marble from Rome. It was wonderful to touch one of them and think, Perhaps the Apostle Paul or one of the martyrs touched this as they passed. But how much more wonderful is it to think that we have, for our own use, the very same sword our Lord used when the Devil attacked Him. [Brooke Foss] Westcott says "the Word of God" in Ephesians 6:17 means "a definite utterance of God." We know these "definite utterances"—we have the same Book that He had, and we can do as He did. So let us learn the "definite utterances" that they may be ready in our minds; ready for use at the moment of need—our sword which never grows dull and rusty, but is always keen and bright. So once more I say, let us not expect defeat but victory. Let us take fast hold and keep fast hold of our sword, and we shall win in any assault of the enemy.

Amy Carmichael, *Edges of His Ways* [1955]
Num. 15:40,41; 2 Tim. 2:15; Jas. 1:21-23

Carnell, Edward John [1919-1967]

185 Evidence for belief

People make mistakes when they believe. They may even want something so badly that passion creates its own evidences. Reprehensible though these habits are, they nonetheless fall within the pale of man's general effort to conform the self to things as they are. But when a person acknowledges the deficiency of evidences and yet goes right on believing, he defends a position that is large with the elements of its own destruction. Any brand of inanity can be defended on such a principle.

Edward John Carnell, *The Case for Orthodox Theology* [1959]
Matt. 24:23,24; 26:41

186 Persuading doubters, not the defiant

The heart must be kept tender and pliable; otherwise agnosticism converts to skepticism. In such a case, the value of apologetics is voided, for apologetics is aimed at persuading doubters, not at refuting the defiant. He who demands a kind of proof that the nature of the case renders impossible, is determined that no possible evidence shall convince him.

Edward John Carnell, The Case for Orthodox Theology [1959]
Matt. 12:38-41

Cary, (Arthur) Joyce (Lunel) [1888-1957]

187 The fear of God

My father had never lost his temper with us, never beaten us, but we had for him that feeling often described as fear, which is something quite different and far deeper than alarm. It was that sense which, without irreverence, I have thought to find expressed by the great evangelists when they speak of the fear of God. One does not fear God because He is terrible, but because He is literally the soul of goodness and truth, because to do Him wrong is to do wrong to some mysterious part of oneself, and one does not know exactly what the consequences may be.

Joyce Cary, Except the Lord [1953]
Ps. 19:7-9

Casteel, John L. [b.1903]

188 Growth in grace

Above all, the group must keep remembering that true growth in grace is not to be achieved by our own efforts or contriving, but must be received as the gift of God's Spirit, working in and among us. The work of the group is to keep open the channels of receptiveness through study, discipline, prayer, and self-offering. When a group learns to live in this faith, it can keep the lines of endeavor tentative and sensitive to new headings and possibilities, on the one hand; and, on the other, move forward resolutely under such light as is now given.

John L. Casteel, *Spiritual Renewal through Personal Groups* [1957]
Rom. 8:9-10

189 The class meeting

The genius of the Methodist movement, which enabled it to conquer the raw lives of workingmen in industrial England, and the raw lives of men and women on the American frontier, was the "class meeting"—ten members and their leader, meeting regularly for mutual encouragement, rebuke, nurture, and prayer.

John L. Casteel, *Spiritual Renewal through Personal Groups* [1957]
Col. 3:16

Cate, Curtis [b.1924]

190 A future religion or now?

In the "dynamic" religion that we are being promised for tomorrow, no ascetic discipline or special humbleness will any longer be required. It will be a hot-water bottle kind of piety with none of that gritty old morality it in. It will be a brand of faith that has been synthesized, vitaminized, homogenized, and capsulized, and it will be as ready-made for effortless consumption as that magically bleached, cottony, crustless, already sliced white bread which is the symbol of the modern American's massive superiority over the pagan bushwhacker.

Curtis Cate, "God and Success"
Deut. 32:31-33; Matt. 7:15; 15:2-20; 2 John 1:7-10

Catherine of Siena [1347-1380]

191 God loved us first

He has loved us without being loved. . . . We are bound to Him, and not He to us, because before He was loved, He loved us. . . . There it is, then: we cannot . . . love Him with this first love. Yet I say that God demands of us, that as He has loved us without any second thoughts, so He should be loved by us. In what way can we do this, then? . . . I tell you, through a means which he has established, by which we can love Him freely; . . . that is, we can be useful, not to Him—which is impossible—but to our neighbor. . . . To show the love that we have for Him, we ought to serve and love every rational creature and extend our charity to good and bad—as much to one who does us ill service and criticizes us as to one who serves us. For, His charity extends over just men and sinners.

Catherine of Siena
1 John 4:12, 16-21

192 Give me Yourself

O abyss, O eternal Godhead, O sea profound, what more could you give me than yourself? You are the fire that burns without being consumed; you consume in your heat all the soul's self-love; you are the fire which takes away cold; with your light you illuminate me so that I may know all your truth. Clothe me, clothe me with yourself, eternal truth, so that I may run this mortal life with true obedience, and with the light of your most holy faith.

Catherine of Siena
Ex. 3:2; Heb. 12:27-29

193 The nails

Nails were not enough to hold God-and-man nailed and fastened on the Cross, had not love held Him there.

Catherine of Siena
Matt. 27:35-50; Heb. 12:1,2

Caussade, Jean Pierre de [1675-1751]

194 Submission

Perfection does not consist in the knowledge of God's order, but in submission to it. The order of God, the good pleasure of God, the will of God, the action of God, grace—all these are one and the same thing in this life. Perfection is nothing else than the faithful cooperation of the soul with the work of God. This ultimate purpose of our life grows and increases in our souls secretly and without our knowledge.

J. P. de Caussade, *Abandonment to Divine Providence*
Jas. 1:22

Cecil, Richard [1748-1810]

195 Ministers need a devotional habit

There is a manifest want of spiritual influence on the ministry of the present day. I feel it in my own case and I see it in that of others. I am afraid there is too much of a low, managing, contriving, maneuvering temper of mind among us. We are laying ourselves out more than is expedient to meet one man's taste and another man's prejudices. The ministry is a grand and holy affair, and it should find in us a simple habit of spirit and a holy but humble indifference to all consequences. A leading defect in Christian ministers is want of a devotional habit.

Richard Cecil
Tit. 1:7-9; 1 Pet. 4:10,11

Chadwick, George Alexander [1840-1923]

196 Wise and foolish sacrifices

There is a curious betrayal of the popular estimate of this world and the world to come, in the honor paid to those who cast away life in battle, or sap it slowly in the pursuit of wealth or honors, and the contempt expressed for those who compromise life on behalf of souls, for which Christ died. Whenever, by exertion in any unselfish cause, health is broken or fortune impaired, or influential friends estranged, the follower of Christ is called an enthusiast, a fanatic, or even more plainly a man of unsound mind. He may be comforted by remembering that Jesus was said to be beside Himself when teaching and healing left Him not leisure even to eat.

G. A. Chadwick
Mark 3:20,21; 1 Cor. 1:23-28

197 Amazed, but not convicted

It is the custom of unbelievers to speak as if the air of Palestine were then surcharged with belief in the supernatural, miracles were everywhere. Thus they would explain away the significance of the popular belief that our Lord wrought signs and wonders. But in so doing they set themselves a worse problem than they evade. If miracles were so very common, it would be as easy to believe that Jesus wrought them as that He worked at His father's bench, but also it would be as inconclusive.

And how then are we to explain the astonishment which all the evangelists so constantly record? On any conceivable theory, these writers shared the beliefs of that age, and so did the readers who accepted their assurance that all were amazed, and that His report "went out straightway everywhere into all the region of Galilee." These are emphatic words, and both the author and his readers must have considered a miracle to be more surprising than modern critics believe they did. Yet we do not read of any one was converted by this miracle. All were amazed, but wonder is not self-surrender. They were content to let their excitement die out—as every violent emotion must—without any change of life, any permanent devotion to the new Teacher and His doctrine.

G. A. Chadwick, *Gospel of St. Mark* [1887]
Mark 1:23-28

The Authentic **Book of Christian Quotations**

Chalmers, Thomas [1780-1847]

198 We are all missionaries

Every man is a missionary, now and forever, for good or for evil, whether he intends or designs it or not. He may be a blot radiating his dark influence outward to the very circumference of society, or he may be a blessing spreading benediction over the length and breadth of the world. But a blank he cannot be: there are no moral blanks; there are no neutral characters.

Thomas Chalmers
Matt. 5:16; Mark 9:39,40; Phil. 2:14,15

Chambers, Oswald [1874-1917]

199 Drastic obedience

All God's revelations are sealed to us until they are opened to us by obedience. You will never get them open by philosophy or thinking. Immediately you obey, a flash of light comes. Let God's truth work in you by soaking in it, not by worrying into it. Obey God in the thing He is at present showing you, and instantly the next thing is opened up. We read tomes on the work of the Holy Spirit when . . . five minutes of drastic obedience would make things clear as a sunbeam. We say, "I suppose I shall understand these things some day." You can understand them now: it is not study that does it, but obedience. The tiniest fragment of obedience, and heaven opens up and the profoundest truths of God are yours straight away. God will never reveal more truth about Himself till you obey what you know already. Beware of being wise and prudent.

Oswald Chambers
John 9:4

Chantal, Jeanne Françoise [1572-1641]

200 Ambition vs. prayer

I have come to see that I do not limit my mind simply enough to prayer that I always want to do something myself in it, wherein I do very wrong and wish most definitely to cut off and separate my mind from all that, and to hold it with all my strength, as much as I can, to the sole regard and simple unity. By allowing the fear of being ineffectual to enter into the state of prayer, and by wishing to accomplish something myself, I spoilt it all.

Jeanne Françoise Chantal
2 Cor. 12:9

Chapin, Edwin Hubbel [1814-1880]

201 Eternal significance

Every action of our lives touches on some chord that will vibrate in eternity.

Edwin Hubbel Chapin
1 Tim. 6:12

Chapman, J. Arundel [1885-1934]

202 No road to God

The radical failure in so-called religion is that its way is from man to God. Starting with man, it seeks to rise to God; and there is no road that way.

J. Arundel Chapman, *The Theology of Karl Barth* [1931]
Isa. 40:1-5; Eph. 2:1

Chapman, Raymond [b.1924]

203 What destroys, redeems

The antithesis between death and life is not so stark for the Christian as it is for the atheist. Life is a process of becoming, and the moment of death is the transition from one life to another. Thus it is possible for a Christian to succumb to his own kind of death-wish, to seek that extreme of other-worldliness to which the faith has always been liable, especially in periods of stress and uncertainty. There may appear a marked preoccupation with death and a rejection of all temporal things. To say that this world is in a fallen state and that not too much value must be set upon it, is very far from the Manichaean error of supposing it to be evil throughout. The Christian hope finds ambivalence in death: that which destroys, also redeems.

Raymond Chapman, *The Ruined Tower* [1961]
Jer. 29:13; John 10:28; Phil. 1:21

Cherry, Edith Gilling [1872-1897]

204 We rest on Thee

We rest on Thee, our shield and our defender!
Thine is the battle, Thine shall be the praise;
When passing through the gates of pearly splendor,
Victors, we rest with Thee, through endless days.

Edith Gilling Cherry
Ps. 33:20

Chesterton, Gilbert Keith [1874-1936]

205 Left untried

The Christian ideal has not been tried and found wanting. It has been found difficult; and left untried.

G. K. Chesterton
Matt. 7:13,14

206 The universal relevance

If Christianity should happen to be true—that is to say, if its God is the real God of the universe—then defending it may mean talking about anything and everything. Things can be irrelevant to the proposition that Christianity is false, but nothing can be irrelevant to the proposition that Christianity is true. [All] things not only may have something to do with the Christian God, but must have something to do with Him if He lives and reigns.

G. K. Chesterton
2 Pet. 1:16

207 Inner vs. outer light

That Jones shall worship the "god within him" turns out ultimately to mean that Jones shall worship Jones. Let Jones worship the sun or moon—anything rather than the Inner Light; let Jones worship cats or crocodiles, if he can find any in his street, but not the god within. Christianity came into the world firstly in order to assert with violence that a man had not only to look inwards, but to look outwards, to behold with astonishment and enthusiasm a divine company and a divine captain. The only fun of being a Christian was that a man was not left alone with the Inner Light, but definitely recognized an outer light, fair as the sun, clear as the moon, terrible as an army with banners.

G. K. Chesterton, *Orthodoxy* [1909]
Isa. 64:6; Luke 18:9-14; 2 Cor. 10:17,18; Gal. 6:3

208 One is real and the other not

Those who call these cults "religions," and "compare" them with the certitude and challenge of the Church have much less appreciation than we have of what made heathenism human, or of why classic literature is still something that hangs in the air like a song. It is no very human tenderness for the hungry to prove that hunger is the same as food. It is no very genial understanding of youth to argue that hope destroys the need for happiness. And it is utterly unreal to argue that these images in the mind, admired entirely in the abstract, were even in the same world with a living man and a living polity that were worshipped because they were concrete . . . They are . . . different because one is real and the other is not. I do not mean merely that I myself believe that one is true and the other is not. I mean that one was never meant to be true in the same sense as the other.

> G. K. Chesterton, *The Everlasting Man* [1925]
> *2 Pet. 1:16; 1 John 5:19*

Cholmondeley, Hester H.

209 Thirty pieces

Still as of old
Men by themselves are priced—
For thirty pieces Judas sold
Himself, not Christ.

> Hester H. Cholmondeley
> *Matt. 26:14-16*

Christlieb, Theodor [1833-1889]

210 The amorphous idol

You meet a thousand times in life with those who, in dealing with any religious question, make at once their appeal to reason, and insist on forthwith rejecting aught that lies beyond its sphere—without, however, being able to render any clear account of the nature and proper limits of the knowledge thus derived, or of the relation in which such knowledge stands to the religious needs of men. I would invite you, therefore, to inquire seriously whether such persons are not really bowing down before an idol of the mind, which, while itself of very questionable worth, demands as much implicit faith from its worshipers as divine revelation itself.

Theodor Christlieb
Isa. 41:28,29

Church, R. W. (Richard William) [1815-1890]

211 The House of Prayer

God has set in the midst of you, as the ever present witness and figure of heaven, His holy House of Prayer. There it stands, built for no earthly purpose, different in shape, and in all things belonging to it, from earthly habitations; speaking only of heaven, and heavenly uses, and heavenly gifts, and heavenly blessings; the gate of heaven when we are brought into it as little children to Christ; the gate of heaven, if so God grant us, when we are brought to it, and pass through it the last time on our way to our grave beside it. And here we meet our God.

R. W. Church, *Village Sermons* [1897]
Isa. 56:7

Clark, F. E. (Francis Edward) [1851-1927]

212 The school of happiness

Among Christians so much prominence has been given to the disciplinary effects of sorrow, affliction, bereavement, that they have been in danger of overlooking the other and more obvious side: that by every joy, by every favor, by every sign of prosperity—yea, and by these chiefly—God designs to educate and discipline His children. This one-sided view of the truth has made many morbid, gloomy Christians, who look for God's hand only in the lightning and never think of seeing it in the sunlight.

F. E. Clark
Ps. 107:8; 145:9; Acts 14:17

Clark, Howard Hewlett [1903-1983]

213 Our common task

Whatever task God is calling us to, if it is yours, it is mine, and if it is mine, it is yours. We must do it together—or be cast aside together, and God in his absolute freedom goes on by other means to use His Church in hastening His Kingdom.

Howard Hewlett Clark
Gal. 6:2

214 God's name in the world

We must be ready, indeed eager, to see God's Name being hallowed outside the Church as well as inside. It may be that today the philosopher is honoring the Name of God when he insists that we should know what we mean when we utter our religious language and that we should be ready to have that meaning tested. It may be that other philosophers hallow the Name when they refuse to allow us to withdraw it to some supernatural realm, but insist on wrestling with the unknown God in the agony and joy of existence, crying with Jacob, "Tell me, I pray thee, thy Name." And is not the scientist honoring the Name when he patiently and obediently follows where the evidence leads? Or the social scientist when he asks us to understand what is before we begin pronouncing what ought to be? God does not spend all His time in Church.

Howard Hewlett Clark
Gen. 32:24-29; Matt. 6:9

Clarke, O. (Oliver) Fielding

215 The empty shelf in theology

In addition to the general situations in which men find themselves today, there are those things in personal life which have always tested faith: the inexplicable tragedies and injustices; the suffering of innocent people, especially of children; the seeming uselessness of prayer, and so forth. It is surely life itself that makes against belief in most cases. It is the contradiction in real life between any image of God as good—whether God is "above," "beneath," or "within"—that makes men atheists. Yet how few books and how few sermons touch on this basic problem! Our theological libraries are crammed with books devoted to every aspect of textual and higher criticism of the Bible; but of genuine theological thinking about the things which drive religion from men's hearts, there is appallingly little to be found. The archaeology of Christian origins seems largely to have replaced genuine theology.

> O. Fielding Clarke, For Christ's Sake [1963]
> *Job 40:6-14; Amos 4:6-11; Rom. 8:31*

Clement of Alexandria [c.150-c.220]

216 The princeliest goods

The Lord ate from a common bowl, and asked the disciples to sit on the grass. He washed their feet, with a towel wrapped around His waist—He, who is the Lord of the universe! He drank water from a jug of earthenware, with the Samaritan woman. Christ made use, not extravagance, His aim . . .

> St. Clement of Alexandria
> *Matt. 14:19; John 4:6-26; 13:4,5*

Clifford, John [1836-1923]

217 The vindication of prayer

I cannot answer all the curious questions of the brain concerning prayer and law, not half of them, indeed, and I will not attempt to; but I will cast my anchor here in this revealing fact, that He, the Holiest of the Holy and the Wisest of the Wise, He prays. Therefore I am assured that this anchorage of Divine example will hold the vessel in the tossings of the wildest sea of doubt, and I shall be as safe as He was, if the vessel itself is engulfed in the waves of suffering and sorrow. His act is an argument. His prayer is an inspiration. His achievements are the everlasting and all-sufficient vindication of prayer.

John Clifford, *Social Worship* [1899]
Matt. 14:23; 26:36; Mark 6:46; 14:32; Luke 6:12; 9:28; 11:1;
John 17

Clough, Arthur Hugh [1819-1861]

218 Steadfast

It fortifies my soul to know
That though I perish, truth is so;
That, wheresoe'er I stray and range,
Whate'er I do, Thou dost not change.
I steadier step when I recall
That, if I slip, Thou dost not fall.

Arthur Hugh Clough
Ps. 23; 37:23,24

Clowney, Edmund P. (Prosper) [b.1917]

219 The life of holiness

The life of holiness is the life of faith in which the believer, with a deepening knowledge of his own sin and helplessness apart from

Christ, increasingly casts himself upon the Lord, and seeks the power of the Spirit and the wisdom and comfort of the Bible to battle against the world, the flesh, and the devil.

Edmund P. Clowney, "The Church"
I John 5:18-19; 1 Cor. 1:30,31; Eph. 1:4

Cogdell, John R.

220 Jesus, the pioneer of faith

Jesus ventured to trust God far beyond the degree that any other man had trusted God. Abraham, Moses, and David were valiant believers, but compared to Jesus they were timid souls. Consider the human disappointments Jesus endured: rejected in his home town, harassed and persecuted by the religious leaders of his nation, misunderstood by his own family, betrayed with a kiss and abandoned by all his followers. Yet through it all Jesus never complained or rebelled against God; he trusted God even on the cross. Psalm 34 sets forth Jesus' pioneering discovery of God's faithfulness and delivering power. Thus Jesus was "delivered from all his fears" (Ps. 34:4), "saved . . . out of all his troubles" (Ps. 34:6), "delivered out of all his afflictions" (Ps. 34:19).

Certainly Jesus is our primary teacher and example in trusting God. If David could teach his followers to trust in God, how much more Jesus. As we see the steadfast faith of our Lord through weariness, disappointment, rejection, and even death on a cross, we cannot but be encouraged to believe that God can deliver us through our small trials. That is why we should run the race set before us looking unto Jesus.

John R. Cogdell, "The humanity of Jesus Christ,
as revealed in certain Psalms"

221 The joy set before him

This last section of Psalm 22 [i.e., verses 27-31] reminds us of Hebrews 12:2: "Looking unto Jesus the author and finisher of our faith; who for the joy that was set before him endured the cross, despising the shame, and is seated at the right hand of the throne of God." The "joy" that was set before Jesus was, we feel, knowing of the riches which would come to his brethren out of his death. In short, we are his joy, set before him when on the cross. As we have seen, only as the circle of the love of Jesus becomes world wide and as big as history will it be complete.

John R. Cogdell, "The Humanity of Jesus Christ, as revealed in certain Psalms"

Coleridge, (David) Hartley [1796-1849]

222 Be not afraid to pray

Be not afraid to pray . . . to pray is right.
Pray if thou canst with hope; but ever pray
Though hope be weak, or sick with long delay.
Whatever is good to wish, ask that of heaven;
But if for any wish thou darest not pray,
Then pray to God to cast that wish away.

Hartley Coleridge
Rom. 12:12

Coleridge, Mary Elizabeth [1861-1907]

223 Good Friday

Good Friday in my heart! Fear and affright!
My thoughts are the disciples when they fled,
My words the words that priest and soldier said,
My deed the spear to desecrate the dead.
And day, Thy death therein, is changed to night.
Then Easter in my heart sends up the sun.
My thoughts are Mary, when she turned to see,
My words are Peter, answering, 'Lov'st thou me?'

My deeds are all Thine own drawn close to Thee.
And night and day, since thou dost rise, are one.

Mary Elizabeth Coleridge
Isa. 53:2-11; John 21:15-17

Coleridge, Samuel Taylor [1772-1834]

224 The declension of love

He that begins by loving Christianity better than truth will proceed by loving his own sect or church better than Christianity, and end in loving himself better than all.

Samuel Taylor Coleridge
Matt. 5:13; Luke 11:39-52; 2 Cor. 10:17,18

225 Ingrafting

There can be no end without means; and God furnishes no means that exempt us from the task and duty of joining our own best endeavors. The original stock, or wild olive tree, of our natural powers, was not given to us to be burnt or blighted, but to be grafted on.

Samuel T. Coleridge
Rom. 11:17-21

226 The name of God written

The Jews would not willingly tread upon the smallest piece of paper in their way, but took it up; for possibly, they say, the name of God may be on it. Though there was a little superstition in this, yet truly there is nothing but good religion in it, if we apply it to men. Trample not on any; there may be some work of grace there, that thou knowest not of. The name of God may be written upon that soul thou treadest on; it may be a soul that Christ thought so much of, as to give His precious blood for it; therefore despise it not.

S. T. Coleridge, *Aids to Reflection* [1825]
Rom. 14:4

227 Virtue vs. righteousness

I dislike the frequent use of the word virtue, instead of righteousness, in the pulpit; in prayer or preaching before a Christian community, it sounds too much like pagan philosophy.

Samuel Taylor Coleridge, *Aids to Reflection* [1825]
Col. 2:16-19

Collyer, William Bengo [1782-1854]

228 Easter

Morning breaks upon the tomb,
Jesus scatters all its gloom.
Day of triumph through the skies—
See the glorious Savior rise.
Christians! Dry your flowing tears,
Chase those unbelieving fears;
Look on his deserted grave,
Doubt no more his power to save.
Ye who are of death afraid,
Triumph in the scattered shade:
Drive your anxious cares away,
See the place where Jesus lay.

William Bengo Collyer
Matt. 28:1-8; Mark 16:1-10; Luke 24:1-12; John 20:1-17

Cotterill, Thomas [1779-1823]

229 Let songs of praise fill the sky

Let songs of praises fill the sky!
Christ, our ascended Lord,
Sends down his Spirit from on high,
According to his word.

The Spirit by his heavenly breath,
    New life creates within:
He quickens sinners from the death
    Of trespasses and sin.
The things of Christ the Spirit takes,
    And shows them unto men;
The fallen soul his temple makes,
    God's image stamps again
Come, Holy Spirit, from above,
    With thy celestial fire:
Come, and with flames of zeal and love
    Our hearts and tongues inspire.

Thomas Cotterill
Acts 1:8,9; 2:1-4

Coverdale, Miles [1488-1568]

230 The blessed son of God only

The blessed son of God only
In a crib full poor did lie;
With our poor flesh and our poor blood
Was clothed that everlasting good
The Lord Christ Jesu, God's son dear,
Was a guest and a stranger here;
Us for to bring from misery,
That we might live eternally.
All this did he for us freely,
For to declare his great mercy;
All Christendom be merry therefore,
And give him thanks for evermore.

Miles Coverdale
Ps. 85:10; Luke 2:6-14

Cowan, Godfrey

231 The Christian environment

The most difficult task facing us today is to persuade the person who is enjoying Christian culture and Christian standards that these do not survive of themselves.

Godfrey Cowan
Matt. 13:20,21

Cowper, William [1731-1800]

232 The weakest saint

Satan trembles when he sees the weakest saint upon his knees.

William Cowper
Matt. 16:15-18; 2 Cor. 12:9

233 O for a closer walk with God

O for a closer walk with God,
    A calm and heavenly frame,
A light to shine upon the road
    That leads me to the Lamb
Return, O holy Dove, return,
    Sweet messenger of rest!
I hate the sins that made Thee mourn
    And drove Thee from my breast
The dearest idol I have known,
    Whate'er that idol be,
Help me to tear it from Thy throne,
    And worship only Thee.
So shall my walk be close with God,
    Calm and serene my frame;

So purer light shall mark the road
That leads me to the Lamb.

William Cowper
Luke 24:32; Rev. 5:12

Cranfield, C. E. B. (Charles Ernest Burland) [b.1915]

234 Contending for the faith

There are still those who would add to the faith human traditions and fancies, thus cluttering it up and obscuring it; and those who would take away from it, rejecting (often with little thought) whatever may seem to them to be out of harmony with the so-called modern mind; and others who would distort it, making it one way or another a pretext for injustice and oppression. But, if we are to be effective in contending for the faith against false teachings, we must certainly contend for it by striving ourselves to understand it ever more truly and more fully.

C. E. B. Cranfield, *I & II Peter and Jude* [1960]
Jude 1:3

Crashaw, Richard [1613-1649]

235 Come Love, come Lord

Come Love, come Lord, and that long day
For which I languish, come away.
When this dry soul those eyes shall see
And drink the unseal'd source of Thee,
When glory's sun faith's shades shall chase,
Then for Thy veil give me Thy face.

Richard Crashaw
2 Cor. 3:13-16

Croucher, Rowland

236 Please Christ first

Above all, desire to please Christ; dread his disapproval above everything else.

Rowland Croucher, Sunrise Sunset [1997]
Luke 16:13

Cundy, Ian P. M.

237 Spiritual unity

[The] denominational divisions which accentuate the problem are perpetrating an image of a divided Christ to the community in which we live. Such an image is at variance with the unity of the body into which we were all baptized. The same arguments that Paul used to deal with the factions and personality cults of the Corinthian church are applicable [here and now]. We can not hide behind some concept of "spiritual unity" which has little or no embodiment in structure or institution; for, not only does it drive an unnatural and unbiblical wedge between the physical and the spiritual, it is also nonsense to the world to which we are called to be in mission, and thereby denies the very basis of the unity for which Christ prayed.

Ian P. M. Cundy, "The Church as Community"
John 17:20-23; Eph. 4:1-6

Cyprian [?-258]

238 Safety

No one is safe by his own strength, but he is safe by the grace and mercy of God.

St. Cyprian
Isa. 40:31; Gal. 6:16

Dürer, Albrecht [1471-1528]

239 Prayer to the Shepherd

O God in heaven, have mercy on us! Lord Jesus Christ, intercede for your people, deliver us at the opportune time, preserve in us the true genuine Christian faith, collect your scattered sheep with your voice, your divine Word as Holy Writ calls it. Help us to recognize your voice, help us not to be allured by the madness of the world, so that we may never fall away from you, O Lord Jesus Christ.

Albrecht Dürer
John 10:14-16

D'Arcy, Martin C. [1888-1976]

240 In a dry and thirsty land

Leave Him [God] out of our explanations, and the life of thought is decapitated. . . . Without God, everything dries up.

Martin C. D'Arcy
Ps. 42:1,2

D'Oyly, George [1778-1846] & Richard Mant [1776-1848]

241 Keeping Scripture in our hearts

It is to be acknowledged that many passages in the Bible are abstruse, and not to be easily understood. Yet we are not to omit reading the abstruser texts, which have any appearance of relating to us; but should follow the example of the Blessed Virgin, who understood not several of our Savior's sayings, but kept them all in her heart. Were we only to learn humility thus, it would be enough; but we shall by degrees come to apprehend far more than we expected, if we diligently compare spiritual things to spiritual.

George D'Oyly & Richard Mant
Luke 2:19; 1 Tim. 4:13-15; 2 Pet. 3:15,16

Dale, Robert W. (William) [1829-1895]

242 Why Christ came

Christ came, not so much to preach the Gospel, as that there might be a Gospel to preach.

R. W. Dale
John 1:17

243 Happiness from God

It was not the pleasant things in the world that came from the devil, and the dreary things from God! It was sin "brought death into the world and all our woe;"[3] as the sin vanishes the woe will vanish too. God Himself is the ever-blessed God. He dwells in the light of joy as well as of purity, and instead of becoming more like Him as we become more miserable, and as all the brightness and glory of life are extinguished, we become more like God as our blessedness becomes more complete. The great Christian graces are radiant with happiness. Faith, hope, charity, there is no sadness in them; and if penitence makes the heart sad, penitence belongs to the sinner, not to the saint.

([3] from *Paradise Lost*, book 1, line 3, by John Milton)

Robert W. Dale
Rom. 5:12

Davi, Henry

244 A jealous God

It is only by forgetting yourself that you can draw near to God.

Henry Davi
Ex. 20:5; Matt. 16:24

Davidman, Joy [1915-1960]

245 Endless youth

"Thou shalt not" is the beginning of wisdom. But the end of wisdom, the new law, is, "Thou shalt." To be Christian is to be old? Not a bit of it. To be Christian is to be reborn, and free, and unafraid, and immortally young.

Joy Davidman, *Smoke on the Mountain* [1955]
Matt. 5:11,12; Gal. 5:18,22-25

246 Atheism

The old pagans had to choose between a brilliant, jangling, irresponsible universe, alive with lawless powers, and the serene and ordered universe of God and law. We modern pagans have to choose between that divine order, and the grey, dead, irresponsible, chaotic universe of atheism. And the tragedy is that we may make that choice without knowing it—not by clear conviction but by vague drifting, by losing interest in Him. A nominal deist will say: "Yes, of course there must be some sort of Force that created the galaxy. But it's childish to imagine that It has any personal relation to me!" In that belief atheism exists as an undiagnosed disease. The man who says, "One God," and does not care, is an atheist in his heart. The man who speaks of God and will not recognize him in the burning bush—that man is an atheist, though he speak with the tongues of men or angels, and appear in his pew every Sunday, and make large contributions to the church.

Joy Davidman, *Smoke on the Mountain* [1955]
Rom. 1:19,20

247 Spiritual pride

We of the churches often gather our robes away from contamination, and thank God that we are not as other men. We don't despise God's name; in fact, we call upon it constantly to justify ourselves. . . . If we object to meat-eating, we declare that God is vegetarian; if we abhor war, we proclaim a pacifist Deity. He who turned water into wine to gladden a wedding is now accused by many of favoring that abominable fluid grape juice. There can hardly be a more evil way of taking God's name in vain than this way of presuming to speak in it. For here is spiritual pride, the ultimate sin, in action—the sin of believing in one's own righteousness. The true prophet says humbly, "To me, a sinful man, God spoke." But the scribes and Pharisees declare, "When we speak, God agrees." They feel no need of a special revelation, for they are always, in their own view, infallible. It is this self-righteousness of the pious that most breeds atheism, by inspiring all decent, ordinary men with loathing of the enormous lie.

Joy Davidman, *Smoke on the Mountain* [1955]
Matt. 7:22,23; Luke 16:14,15; John 9:39-41; 2 Cor. 10:18; Gal.
6:3; Rev. 3:17,18

DeKoster, Lester

248 Disputation

The conduct of disputation by verbal brickbat, by innuendo, and by light-fingered intellectual dexterity, is a mordant reminder of the time when controversies were settled by faggot and sword. The truth is hardly less the loser because the inquisitor has altered his methods. All of us who seek to explore the wide reaches of God's revelation, and strive to bring the thinking of others under the domination of Christ, do well to seek first to bring our own rhetorical techniques under that same dominion—under the discipline, that is, of love.

Lester DeKoster
Col. 4:6; 1 Pet. 3:15,16

Denney, James [1856-1917]

249 Accepting just consequences

Each of us individually has risen into moral life from a mode of being which was purely natural; in other words, each of us also has fallen—fallen, presumably in ways determined by his natural constitution, yet certainly, as conscience assures us, in ways for which we are morally answerable, and to which, in the moral constitution of the world, consequences attach which we must recognize as our due. They are not only results of our action, but results which that action has merited; and there is no moral hope for us unless we accept them as such.

James Denney, *The Atonement and the Modern Mind* [1903]
Gen. 3:22,23

250 The unity of sin and death

What so spoke to [Paul] from the third chapter of Genesis was not a . . . story of how death invaded Paradise, but the profound experience of the human race expressed in the story, an experience in which sin and death interpenetrate, and in a sense constitute each other. To us, they are what they are only in relation to each other, and when we deny the relation we see the reality of neither. This is the truth—as I apprehend it—of all we are taught, either in the Old Testament or the New, about the relation of sin and death. It is part of the greater truth that what we call the physical and spiritual worlds are ultimately one, being constituted with a view to each other; and most of the objections which are raised against it are special cases of the objections which are raised against the recognition of this ultimate unity.

James Denney, *The Atonement and the Modern Mind* [1903]
Gen. 3; Rom. 5:12

de Diétrich, Suzanne [1891-1981]

251 Ready to obey

The Bible tells us very clearly that to "know" God is not an affair of the mind only, but an act in which our whole being—heart, mind, and will—is vitally engaged; so that sheer intellectual speculation would enable us to form certain ideas about God but never to know Him. To be grasped, God's will must be met with a readiness to obey.

Suzanne de Diétrich, *Discovering the Bible*
Rom. 6:16,17

Dibelius, Otto [1880-1967]

252 God, our guide and companion

God does not lead His children around hardship, but leads them straight through hardship. But He leads! And amidst the hardship, He is nearer to them than ever before.

Otto Dibelius
Acts 14:21,22

Dixon, John W., Jr

253 Redemptive art

Man cannot make a redemptive art, but he can make an art that communicates what he experiences of redemption as a man and what he knows of it as an artist. God in his infinite wisdom may use an art work as an instrument of redemption, but what serves or can serve that purpose is beyond the knowledge of man.

John W. Dixon, Jr.
Col. 3:23; 1 Pet. 1:18,19

Dodd, C. H. (Charles Harold) [1884-1973]

254 The Divine Commonwealth

In this Body of Christ, Paul sees "the ecclesia of God." Ecclesia is a Greek word with a splendid history. It was used in the old free commonwealths of Greece for the general assembly of all free citizens, by which their common life was governed. When political liberty went, the name still survived in the restricted municipal self-government which the Roman State allowed. It was taken over by the brotherhoods and guilds which in some measure superseded the old political associations. Among the Jews who spoke Greek, this word seemed the appropriate one to describe the commonwealth of Israel as ruled by God—the historical Theocracy. Our translation of it is "Church." That word, however, has undergone such transformations of meaning that it is often doubtful in what sense it is being used. Perhaps for ecclesia we may use the word—simpler, more general, and certainly nearest to its original meaning—"commonwealth." We have spoken throughout of the Divine Commonwealth. That phrase represents Paul's "ecclesia of God." It is a community of loving persons, who bear one another's burdens, who seek to build up one another in love, who "have the same thoughts in relation to one another that they have in their communion with Christ." It is all this because it is the living embodiment of Christ's own Spirit. This is a high and mystical doctrine, but a doctrine which has no meaning apart from loving fellowship in real life. A company of people who celebrate a solemn sacrament of Christ's Body and Blood, and all the time are moved by selfish passions—rivalry, competition, mutual contempt—is not for Paul a Church or Divine Commonwealth at all, no matter how lofty their faith or how deep their mystical experience; for all these things may "puff up;" love alone "builds up."

In the very act, therefore, of attaining its liberty to exist, the Divine Commonwealth has transcended the great divisions of men. In principle, it has transcended them all, and by seriously living out that which its association means, it is on the way to comprehending the whole race. Short of that its development can never stop. This is the revealing of the sons of God for which the whole creation is waiting.

C. Harold Dodd, *The Meaning of Paul for Today* [1920]
1 Cor. 1:2; 10:32; 11:22; 2 Cor. 1:1; Gal. 1:13; 6:16; Phil. 2:5

255 Paul's change of heart

The God of Pharisaism was like the God of the Deists, He stood aloof from the world He had made, and let law take its course. He did not here and now deal with sinful men. Paul lets us see how new and wonderful was the experience when God "flashed on his heart" in personal dealing with him. He had not suspected that God was like that. His theological studies had told him that God was loving and merciful; but he had thought this love and mercy were expressed once and for all in the arrangements He had made for Israel's blessedness. . . . It was a new thing to be assured by an inward experience admitting of no further question that God loved him, and that the eternal mercy was a Father's free forgiveness of His erring child. This was the experience that Christ had brought him: he had seen the splendor of God's own love in the face of "the Son of God, who loved me and gave Himself for me." What knowledge of Jesus Christ and His teaching lay behind the flash of enlightenment it is now impossible for us to say: but it is clear that the God whom Paul met was the "Father" of Jesus' own Gospel parables, the Shepherd who goes after the one sheep until He finds it. It was the God, in fact, whom the whole of the life of Jesus set forth, to the astonishment of those among whom He moved. Living still, He brought God to men in the same unmistakable way. The divine love that through Jesus had found Zacchaeus the publican had now through the risen Jesus found Paul the Pharisee. Henceforward the central facts of life for Paul were that while he was yet a sinner God had found and forgiven him, and that this was the work of Jesus Christ, in whose love the love of God had become plain.

C. H. Dodd, The Meaning of Paul For Today [1920]
Rom. 5:6-8; 8:35-39; II Cor. 5:14-15, 18-19; Gal. 2:20;
Eph. 1:4-7; 2:4-10; 3:18-19; 5:1-2; Col. 1:13-15

Donne, John [1573-1631]

256 Grateful for teaching

Our critical day is not the very day of our death, but the whole course of our life; I thank him, that prays for me when my bell tolls;

but I thank him much more, that catechizes me, or preaches to me, or instructs me how to live.

John Donne
John 6:27; Rom. 12:5-8; 1 Thess. 2:3,4

257 Love and death meet in Christ.

Love is strong as death; but nothing else is as strong as either; and both, love and death, met in Christ. How strong and powerful upon you, then, should that instruction be, that comes to you from both these, the love and death of Jesus Christ!

John Donne
John 3:16,17

258 Humility

Humiliation is the beginning of sanctification; and as without this, without holiness, no man shall see God, though he pore whole nights upon his Bible; so without that, without humility, no man shall hear God speak to his soul, though he hear three two-hour sermons every day.

John Donne
Ps. 25:9; Matt. 11:15; Rom. 12:3; 1 Pet. 3:4; 5:5

259 Jesus came in the fullness of time

This was the fullness of time, when Christ Jesus did come, that the Messiah should come. It was so to the Jews, and it was so to the Gentiles too. . . . Christ hath excommunicated no nation, no shire, no house, no man; He gives none of His ministers leave to say to any man, thou art not redeemed; He gives no wounded or afflicted conscience leave to say to itself, I am not redeemed.

John Donne
Matt. 12:18-21; John 3:16,17

260 He was the Word

He was the Word that spake it;
He took the bread and brake it;

And what that Word did make it
I do believe, and take it.

John Donne
John 6:32-35

261 Death, be not proud

Death, be not proud, though some have called thee
Mighty and dreadful, for thou art not so;
For those, whom thou think'st thou dost overthrow
Die not, poor Death, nor yet canst thou kill me.
From rest and sleep, which but thy pictures be,
Much pleasure, then from thee much more, must flow,
And soonest our best men with thee do go,
Rest of their bones, and soul's delivery.
Thou art slave to fate, chance, kings, and desperate men,
And dost with poison, war, and sickness dwell,
And poppy, or charms, can make us sleep as well,
And better than thy stroke. Why swell'st thou then?
One short sleep past, we wake eternally,
And Death shall be no more: Death, thou shalt die.

John Donne, *Divine Poems: Holy Sonnets*, no. 17
Rom. 14:7,8; 1 Cor. 15:26; Phil. 1:20-24; 1 Thess. 4:16;
2 Tim. 1:10; Rev. 14:13

262 Evangelism

Christ came . . . in a purpose, . . . to manifest himself in the Christian Religion, to all the nations of the world; and therefore, says David, The Lord reigneth, let the Islands rejoice—the Islands who by reason of their situation, provision, and trading have most means of conveying Christ Jesus over the world. He hath carried us up to heaven & set us at the right hand of God, & shall not we endeavor to carry him to those nations, who have not yet heard of his name? Shall we still brag that we have brought our clothes, and our hatchets, and our knives, and bread to this and this value and estimation amongst those poor ignorant Souls, and shall we never glory that we have brought the name, and Religion of Christ Jesus in estimation amongst them? Shall we stay till other nations have planted a false Christ among them? And then either continue in our sloth, or take more pains in rooting out a false Christ than would have planted the true?

John Donne, "A Sermon preached April 2, 1621"
Ps. 96,97; Luke 24:46,47

263 No other way

To me, to whom God hath revealed his Son, in a Gospel, by a Church, there can be no way of salvation, but by applying that Son of God, by that Gospel, in that Church. Nor is there any other foundation for any, nor other name by which any can be saved, but the name of Jesus. But how this foundation is presented, and how this name of Jesus is notified unto them, amongst whom there is no Gospel preached, no Church established, I am not curious in inquiring. I know that God can be as merciful as those tender Fathers present him to be; and I would be as charitable as they are. And therefore, humbly embracing that manifestation of his Son, which he hath afforded me, I leave God, to his unsearchable ways of working upon others, without further inquisition.

John Donne, *LXXX Sermons* [1640]
Acts 4:10-12; 13:48

264 The uttermost condemnation

Think thyself at that Tribunal, that judgment, now: Where thou shalt not only hear all thy sinful works, and words, and thoughts repeated, which thou thy self hadst utterly forgot, but thou shalt hear thy good works, thine alms, thy coming to Church, thy hearing of Sermons, given in evidence against thee, because they had hypocrisy mingled in them; yea, thou shalt find even thy repentance to condemn thee, because thou madest that but a door to a relapse.

John Donne, "Sermon XXXVII" in *LXXX Sermons* [1640]
Luke 13:1-5; 18:10-14; Heb. 2:1-4

Dougall, Lily [1858-1923]

265 Remembering the future

We, and all things, exist in God's infinitude now; our individuality battens with it; our personality grows strong because of it; and we know, if we know anything, that while the more we approach the good the more we please God, at the same time the more men approach the good the more nobly distinctive, the more beautifully individual do their characters become. To imagine, then, at the end of this life we shall cease to exist as conscious beings, that our characters, our personalities, will fall back into some boundless being, instead of becoming more and more definite, more and more individual, is certainly not to exalt God; for it is founded on the belief, either that God is now belittled by our present individuality, or that our present individuality is a mere delusion. In the latter case God, whom we find in the depths of our souls, is doubtless also a delusion, for if the self is not real it is no respectable witness on whose testimony we can accept God. Our deepest mature conviction is that finite and infinity interpenetrate, as time and eternity interpenetrate, and our problems must be solved in the light of that conviction.

Lily Dougall, "The Undiscovered Country" [1917]
Matt. 22:29-32

Driver, Christopher P. (Prout) [1932-1997]

266 Faithfully preaching the Gospel

Local churches which are respected and even attended by "the public"—interpreted as people who under different circumstances would not feel obliged to attend church at all—are often found to be those where, on a Christian judgment, the gospel seems to be most faithfully preached. Such churches may invite and suffer temporary periods of unpopularity—by standing up for West Indian immigrants, say, or refusing indiscriminate baptism. But on the whole, the storms are weathered by churches, and ministers, whose interest in the community and presentation of the faith [are] alert and genuine. Even so, the Church has every excuse for getting itself disliked: none at all for escaping notice.

Christopher Driver, A Future for the Free Churches? [1962]
Acts 4:19,20

Drummond, Henry [1851-1897]

267 The easy yoke

Did you ever stop to ask what a yoke is really for? Is it to be a burden to the animal which wears it? It is just the opposite: it is to make its burden light. Attached to the oxen in any other way than by a yoke, the plow would be intolerable; worked by means of a yoke, it is light. A yoke is not an instrument of torture; it is an instrument of mercy. It is not a malicious contrivance for making work hard; it is a gentle device to make hard labor light. [Christ] knew the difference between a smooth yoke and a rough one, a bad fit and a good one . . . The rough yoke galled, and the burden was heavy; the smooth yoke caused no pain, and the load was lightly drawn. The badly fitted harness was a misery; the well fitted collar was "easy." And what was the "burden"? It was not some special burden laid upon the Christian, some unique infliction that they alone must bear. It was what all men bear: it was simply life, human life itself, the general burden of life which all must carry with them from the cradle to the grave. Christ saw that men took life painfully. To some it was a weariness, to others failure, to many a tragedy, to all a struggle and a pain. How to carry this burden of life had been the whole world's problem. And here is Christ's solution: "Carry it as I do. Take life as I take it. Look at it from my point of view. Interpret it upon my principles. Take my yoke and learn of me, and you will find it easy. For my yoke is easy, sits right upon the shoulders, and therefore my burden is light."

Henry Drummond, "Pax Vobiscum"
Matt. 11:29,30

268 The most destructive sin

The peculiarity of ill temper is that it is the vice of the virtuous. It is often the one blot on an otherwise noble character. You know men who are all but perfect, and women who would be entirely perfect, but for an easily ruffled, quick-tempered, or "touchy" disposition. This compatibility of ill temper with high moral character is one of the strangest and saddest problems of ethics . . . No form of vice—not worldliness, not greed of gold, not drunkenness itself—does more to unChristianize society than evil temper. For embittering life, for breaking up communities, for destroying the most sacred relationships, for devastating homes, for withering up men and women, for taking the bloom off of childhood—in short, for sheer, gratuitous misery-producing power—this influence stands alone.

> Henry Drummond, "The Greatest Thing in the World" [1892]
> *Eph. 4:31; Jas. 1:19,20*

Drummond, William [1585-1649]

269 Bright portals of the sky

> Bright portals of the sky,
> Emboss'd with sparkling stars,
> Doors of eternity,
> With diamantine bars,
> Your arras rich uphold,
> Loose all your bolts and springs,
> Ope wide your leaves of gold,
> That in your roofs may come the King of Kings.
> O well-spring of this All!
> Thy Father's image vive;
> Word, that from nought did call
> What is, doth reason, live;
> The soul's eternal food,
> Earth's joy, delight of heaven;
> All truth, love, beauty, good:
> To thee, to thee be praises ever given!
> O glory of the heaven!
> O sole delight of earth!
> To thee all power be given,
> God's uncreated birth!

Of mankind lover true,
Indearer of his wrong,
Who doth the world renew,
Still be thou our salvation and our song!

William Drummond
Luke 2:8-14

Drury, Samuel Smith [1878-1938]

270 Splendid churches, few leaders

We are building many splendid churches in this country, but we are not providing leaders to run them. I would rather have a wooden church with a splendid parson, than a splendid church with a wooden parson.

Samuel Smith Drury

Dryden, John [1631-1700]

271 Patience

The fortitude of a Christian consists in patience, not in enterprises which the poets call heroic, and which are commonly the effects of interest, pride, and worldly honor.

John Dryden
1 Thess. 5:14

Dunstan, G. R.

272 Reconciliation

The reconciliation of man to God begins when God accepts the child of man, exactly as he is, into a relationship with himself—"this grace wherein we stand." This He does for the sake of what man is to inherit, to become. And for the means, He gives him over to a Person, Christ, and a community, the Church; and in attachment to these, personality grows, freedom is attained, sin is forgiven, estrangement is ended, capacities for relationship extend. Reconciliation is the Spirit's liberating work of love, exercised through a Person and a community of persons.

G. R. Dunstan
Rom. 5:1,2; Col. 1:20-22; Heb. 2:16-18

Dyke, Henry Van [1852-1933]

273 Thou wayfaring Jesus

Thou wayfaring Jesus—a pilgrim and stranger,
   Exiled from heaven by love at Thy birth:
Exiled again from Thy rest in the manger,
   A fugitive child 'mid the perils of earth—
Cheer with Thy fellowship all who are weary,
   Wandering far from the land that they love:
Guide every heart that is homeless and dreary,
   Safe to its home in Thy presence above.

Henry Van Dyke
Matt. 8:28

Earle, Nick [b.1926]

274 The task of the Church

It is sometimes said that even if no rules were laid down for the conduct of its affairs, the Church, being created by Jesus to "further the work of the Kingdom of God," can be judged by the extent to which it is successful in continuing his work. This supposition rests upon a misunderstanding of what is meant by "the Kingdom of God.".. The Kingdom itself is not something to be "furthered" or "built" by men's efforts. It is something which we are invited to recognize as already present, after a manner, in the life and work of Jesus. It is something to be inherited or entered into by those who believe. The task of the Church, in other words, is not to set the stage for a better world than this one but to draw the curtain from it, to reveal something that is already there.

> Nick Earle, *What's Wrong with the Church?* [1961]
> *Matt. 18:3; Luke 17:20,21; John 18:36; Rom. 14:17*

275 The source of authenticity

It was the experience of the disciples who knew Jesus both before and after the Resurrection, and the conviction which they communicated to others, that laid the foundation of faith. This faith, once given, proved to be—like the Person who gave rise to it—essentially self-authenticating. And ever since, the Church has looked to the Cross, a symbol of weakness, as its unique source of power in preaching the Gospel, its authority both to teach and to preach has been of this kind. No amount of liaison between the Church and the source of any other authority, political or moral, must be allowed to obscure the simplicity—and the mystery—of the authority of Christ.

> Nick Earle, *What's Wrong with the Church?* [1961]
> *Acts 2:22-28; 1 Cor. 1:17,18; 15:6*

Eckhart, Meister (Johannes) [c.1260- c.1327]

276 Knowing Him everywhere

A man may go into the field and say his prayer and be aware of God, or he may be in Church and be aware of God; but if he is more aware of Him because he is in a quiet place, that is his own deficiency and not due to God, Who is alike present in all things and places, and is willing to give Himself everywhere so far as lies in Him. . . . He knows God rightly who knows Him everywhere.

> Meister Eckhart
> *Ps. 139:7,8*

277 Doing vs. being

People should think less about what they ought to do and more about what they ought to be. If only their being were good, their works would shine forth brightly. Do not imagine that you can ground your salvation upon actions; it must rest on what you are. The ground upon which good character rests is the very same ground from which man's work derives its value, namely, a mind wholly turned to God. Verily, if you were so minded, you might tread on a stone and it would be a more pious work than if you, simply for your own profit, were to receive the Body of the Lord and were wanting in spiritual detachment.

Meister Eckhart
1 Cor. 2:16; Heb. 9:14

278 Loving God "because"

Some people want to see God with their eyes as they see a cow, and to love Him as they love their cow—for the milk and cheese and profit it brings them. This is how it is with people who love God for the sake of outward wealth or inward comfort. They do not rightly love God, when they love Him for their own advantage. Indeed, I tell you the truth, any object you have in your mind, however good, will be a barrier between you and the inmost Truth.

Meister Eckhart
Luke 16:13

279 Now

The now wherein God made the first man, and the now wherein the last man disappears, and the now I am speaking in, all are the same in God, where this is but the now.

Meister Eckhart
Ex. 3:14

280 More blessed than joy

Love . . . is very noticeable as fervor and devotion and jubilation, and is yet not always the best thing; for sometimes it is not from love but is caused by nature that one has such taste and sweetness; or it may be a heavenly impression or it may be produced by the senses, and those who have most of this are not always the best. For even if it should be from God, our Lord gives this to such men in order to attract and charm them, and also to detach them from others. But if these same people later grow in love, they may not have so many feelings, and then it will become clear that they have love, if they remain wholly faithful to God without any such support.

Meister Eckhart, *Spiritual Instructions*
2 Cor. 10:17,18; Phil. 1:15-18

Edersheim, Alfred [1825-1889]

281 The purpose of trial

For God to explain a trial would be to destroy its purpose, calling forth simple faith and implicit obedience.

Alfred Edersheim
John 15:10; Eph. 6:6-8; Jas. 1:22-25

Edwards, Jonathon [1703-1758]

282 Pray for ministers

If some Christians that have been complaining of their ministers had said and acted less before men and had applied themselves with all their might to cry to God for their ministers—had, as it were, risen and stormed heaven with their humble, fervent, and incessant prayers for them—they would have been much more in the way of success.

Jonathan Edwards
1 Cor. 3:5

283 Worth seeing

He that sees the beauty of holiness, or true moral good, sees the greatest and most important thing in the world. . . . Unless this is seen, nothing is seen that is worth seeing: for there is no other true excellence or beauty.

Jonathan Edwards, *Treatise concerning Religious Affections*
[1746]
1 Pet. 1:14-16

Eliot, Thomas Stearns [1888-1965]

284 Christianity useful?

What is worst of all is to advocate Christianity, not because it is true, but because it might prove useful. . . . To justify Christianity because it provides a foundation of morality, instead of showing the necessity of Christian morality from the truth of Christianity, is a very dangerous inversion; and we may reflect that a good deal of the attention of totalitarian states has been devoted with a steadfastness of purpose not always found in democracies, to providing their national life with a foundation of morality—the wrong kind, perhaps, but a good deal more of it. It is not enthusiasm, but dogma, that differentiates a Christian from a pagan society.

T. S. Eliot, *The Idea of a Christian Society* [1939]
Matt. 26:6-13

Elliot, Jim [1927-1956]

285 To touch His garment

Oh, the fullness, pleasure, sheer excitement of knowing God on Earth! I care not if I never raise my voice again for Him, if only I may love Him, please Him. Mayhap in mercy He shall give me a host of children that I may lead them through the vast star fields to explore His delicacies whose finger ends set them to burning. But if not, if only I may see Him, touch His garments, smile into His eyes—ah then, not stars nor children shall matter, only Himself.

Jim Elliot
Ps. 19:1; Dan. 7:13,14; Matt. 9:20-22

286 To gain what he cannot lose

He is no fool who gives what he cannot keep to gain what he cannot lose.

Jim Elliot, *The Journals of Jim Elliot* [1978]
Matt. 10:39; Phil. 1:21

Ellul, Jacques [1912-1994]

287 God always present

God is always present, always available. At whatever moment in which one turns to him the prayer is received, is heard, is authenticated, for it is God who gives our prayer its value and its character, not our interior dispositions, not our fervor, not our lucidity. The prayer which is pronounced for God and accepted by him becomes, by that very fact, a true prayer.

Jacques Ellul, *Prayer and Modern Man*[1973]
Ps. 46:1; 91:1,2; Rom. 8:26,27

Emrich, Richard Stanley [b.1910]

288 Giving

Living for others, commitment to God's redeeming purposes, is a means of grace. We give because of our faith, and it deepens as we give. If we permit ourselves and our people to give casually, we are really teaching contempt.

Richard S. Emrich
Matt. 6:1-4; Acts 20:35

Engstrom, Ted W.

289 The Word in our lives

The injection of the Word into our lives provides individual or corporate direction in all we do and say.

Ted W. Engstrom, former president, World Vision US
Luke 11:28

290 Guidance

Our responsibility is to walk with courage and integrity, continually looking to our Lord for Guidance.

Ted W. Engstrom, former president, World Vision US
Jer. 7:23; Mic. 6:8; Col. 2:6

291 Listening to God's voice

Our first priority is to listen to God's voice. It is our exposure to His compassion that will cause us to reach out to the oppressed, the frustrated, the angry. And it is only by listening to His voice that we will have wisdom to know how to provide workable solutions for the different groups that demand our attention.

Ted W. Engstrom, former president, World Vision US
Ps. 85:8; Matt. 12:49,50; John 12:35,36

Erasmus, Desiderius [c.1466-1536]

292 Works do not make you pious

Paul does not forbid you to use rites and ceremonies, but it is not his wish that he who is free in Christ should be bound by them. He does not condemn the law of works if only one uses it lawfully. Without these things perhaps you will not be pious; but they do not make you pious.

Desiderius Erasmus
Rom. 14:14,15,21; 1 Cor. 8:7-13; Eph. 2:8,9

293 Charity to the undeserving

It seems to me to be the best proof of an evangelical disposition, that persons are not angry when reproached, and have a Christian charity for those that ill deserve it.

Desiderius Erasmus, The Colloquies of Erasmus
1 Tim. 6:17-19

294 Where to write the Gospel

You have . . . the Gospel written upon vellum; it deserveth to be set with diamonds, except that the heart of man were a fitter repository for it.

Desiderius Erasmus, The Colloquies of Erasmus
Jer. 31:33; Rom. 2:15

Faber, Frederick W. (William) [1814-1863]

307 Why dost Thou love me so?

Jesus! why dost Thou love me so?
What hast Thou seen in me
To make my happiness so great,
So dear a joy to Thee?

Fredrick William Faber
Heb. 12:1,2

Fénelon, François [1651-1715]

295 Doing God's will

I ought to consider the business which occurs in the daily order of Providence as the work which God appoints me; and I should apply myself to it in a manner worthy of God, namely, with exactness and with tranquility. I ought not to neglect anything or be passionately vehement about anything, for it is dangerous to do the work of the Lord negligently, on the one hand; or, on the other, to appropriate it to ourselves by self-love and false zeal. In this latter case, our actions arise from a principle of self-will: we are eager and anxious for the success, and that under the pretense of seeking the glory of God. O, God, grant me Thy grace to enable me to be faithful in action and resigned in success! My only business is to do Thy will, and to do it as Thy will, not forgetting Thee in the performance of it.

François Fénelon
Matt. 12:50; Rom. 12:10-14

296 Taking courage

Never let us be discouraged with ourselves; it is not when we are conscious of our faults that we are the most wicked: on the contrary, we are less so. We see by a brighter light. And let us remember, for our consolation, that we never perceive our sins till He begin to cure them.

François Fénelon
Heb. 12:6,7

297 Without ceasing

Accustom yourself gradually to carry Prayer into all your daily occupation—speak, act, work in peace, as if you were in prayer, as indeed you ought to be.

François Fénelon
1 Thess. 5:17

298 Listening to God

God is our true Friend, who always gives us the counsel and comfort we need. Our danger lies in resisting Him; so it is essential that we acquire the habit of hearkening to His voice, or keeping silence within, and listening so as to lose nothing of what He says to us. We know well enough how to keep outward silence, and to hush our spoken words, but we know little of interior silence. It consists in hushing our idle, restless, wandering imagination, in quieting the

promptings of our worldly minds, and in suppressing the crowd of
unprofitable thoughts which excite and disturb the soul.

François Fénelon
1 Kings 19:11-13; Ps. 85:8; Matt. 12:36,37

299 Is God boring?

If God bores you, tell Him that He bores you, that you prefer the
vilest amusements to His presence, that you only feel at your ease
when you are far from Him.

François Fénelon
Ps. 14; Amos 5:14,15

300 Fidelity in little things

It is only by fidelity in little things that the grace of true love to
God can be sustained, and distinguished from a passing fervor of
spirit. . . . No one can well believe that our piety is sincere, when our
behavior is lax and irregular in its little details. What probability is
there that we should not hesitate to make the greatest sacrifices, when
we shrink from the smallest?

François Fénelon
Luke 12:42-44

301 Resisting God

There is never any peace for those who resist God.

François Fénelon
Isa. 48:22

302 The smallest things

The smallest things become great when God requires them of us;
they are small only in themselves; they are always great when they
are done for God, and when they serve to unite us with Him eternally.

François Fénelon
John 6:9

303 On prayer

As St. Cyprian well said, we may judge how ready He is to give us those good things which He Himself solicits us to ask of Him. Let us pray then with faith, and not lose the fruits of our prayers by a wavering uncertainty which, as St. James testifies, hinders the success of them. The same apostle advises us to pray when we are in trouble because thereby we should find consolation; yet we are so wretched that this heavenly employment is often a burden instead of a comfort to us. The lukewarmness of our prayers is the source of all our other infidelities.

François Fénelon, *Meditation*
Jas. 1:5-7; Rev. 3:14-16

304 Shall He find faith?

"When the Son of Man cometh, shall He find faith on the earth?" If He should now come, would He find it in us? What fruits of faith have we to show? Do we look upon this life only as a short passage to a better? Do we believe that we must suffer with Jesus Christ before we can reign with Him? Do we consider this world as a deceitful appearance, and death as the entrance to true happiness? Do we live by faith? Does it animate us? Do we relish the eternal truths it presents us with? Are we as careful to nourish our souls with those truths as to maintain our bodies with proper diet? Do we accustom ourselves to see all things in the light of faith? Do we correct all our judgments by it?

Alas! The greater part of Christians think and act like mere heathens; if we judge (as we justly may) of their faith by their practice, we must conclude they have no faith at all.

François Fénelon, *Meditation*
Hab. 2:4; Luke 18:8; 21:7

305 A right spirit

There is a great difference between a lofty spirit and a right spirit. A lofty spirit excites admiration by its profoundness; but only a right spirit achieves salvation and happiness by its stability and integrity. Do not conform your ideas to those of the world. Scorn the "intellectual" as much as the world esteems it. What men consider intellectual is a certain facility to produce brilliant thoughts. Nothing is more vain. We make an idol of our intellect as a woman who believes herself beautiful worships her face. We take pride in our own thoughts. We must reject not only human cleverness, but also human prudence, which seems so important and so profitable. Then we may enter—like little children, with candor and innocence of worldly ways—into the simplicity of faith; and with humility and a horror of sin we may enter into the holy passion of the cross.

François Fénelon, *Meditation*
Hab. 2:4; 1 Cor. 1:20,21

306 Reservations from God

If we look carefully within ourselves, we shall find that there are certain limits beyond which we refuse to go in offering ourselves to God. We hover around these reservations, making believe not to see them, for fear of self-reproach. The more we shrink from giving up any such reserved point, the more certain it is that it needs to be given up. If we were not fast bound by it, we should not make so many efforts to persuade ourselves that we are free.

François Fénelon, *Spiritual Letters*
Ps. 51:17; Rom. 12:1

Figgis, John Neville [1866-1919]

308 Gone forever

Men have, for the most part, done with lamenting their lost faith. Sentimental tears over the happy, simple Christendom of their fathers are a thing of the past. They are proclaiming now their contempt for Christ's character, and their disgust at the very name of love. Scorn and hatred, difference and division, must be more than ever our lot, if we would be the followers of Christ in these days. Conventional religion and polite unbelief are gone forever.

John Neville Figgis
1 Pet. 2:7,8

309 The wedge

Anyone can believe that Jesus was a god: what is so hard to credit is that He who hung upon the cross was the God. That is what you are asked as Christians to believe. And it is the sword, glittering but fearful. It must cut your life away from the standards of this world, away from its thought and its measures, no less than its aims and hopes. Hard and bitter is the separation, and you will be parted from many great and noble men, some perhaps your own teachers, who can accept about Jesus everything but the one thing needful. The Christian faith, if accepted, drives a wedge between its own adherents and the disciples of every other philosophy or religion, however lofty or soaring. And they will not see this; they will tell you that really your views and theirs are the same thing, and only differ in words, which, if only you were a little more highly trained, you would understand. Even among Christ's nominal servants there are many who think a little good-will is all that is needed to bridge the gulf—a little amiability and mutual explanation, a more careful use of phrases, would soon accommodate Christianity to fashionable modes of speaking and thinking, and destroy all causes of provocation. So they would. But they would destroy also its one inalienable attraction: that of being . . . a wonder, and a beauty, and a terror—no dull and drab system of thought, no mere symbolic idealism.

John Neville Figgis, *The Gospel and Human Needs* [1909]
Matt. 10:34-36; Mark 13:12,13

Fisher, Dorothy Canfield [1879-1958]

310 Wise about life

If we would only give, just once, the same amount of reflection to what we want to get out of life, that we give to the question of what to do with two weeks' vacation, we would be startled at our false standards and the aimless procession of our busy days.

Dorothy Canfield Fisher
Luke 8:8

Fletcher, Phineas [1582-1650]

311 Drop, drop, slow tears

> Drop, drop, slow tears, and bathe those beauteous feet
> Which brought from heaven the news and prince of peace.
> Cease not, wet eyes, his mercies to entreat;
> To cry for vengeance sin doth never cease;
> In your deep floods drown all my faults and fears,
> Nor let his eye see sin but through my tears.

Phineas Fletcher
Luke 7:37,38

Forsyth, P. T. (Peter Taylor) [1848-1921]

312 The mediator

Is a mediator between the eternal spirit and the finite an unreality, an intrusion? The mystic soul may impatiently think so, but the moral soul finds such mediation the way to reality; and the mystic experience is not quite trustworthy about reality. The pagan gods had no mediators, because they were not real or good gods; but the living God has a living Revealer. To know the living God is to know Christ; to know Christ is to know the living God. We do not know God by Christ but in Him. We find God when we find Christ; and in Christ alone we know and share his final purpose. Our last knowledge is not the contact of our person with a thing or a thought; it is intercourse of person and person.

P. T. Forsyth, *This Life and the Next* [1918]
Matt. 28:18; John 14:7-9

Foster, Richard J.

313 The adversary's tools

Our Adversary majors in three things: noise, hurry and crowds. If he can keep us engaged in "muchness" and "manyness," he will rest satisfied.

Richard J. Foster
Matt. 13:22

Fox, George [1624-1691]

314 The light of Jesus

These things I did not see by the help of man, nor by the letter, though they are written in the letter; but I saw them in the light of the Lord Jesus Christ, and by his immediate Spirit and power, as did the Holy men of God, by whom the Holy Scriptures were written. Yet I had no slight esteem of the Holy Scriptures; they were very precious to me, for I was in that spirit by which they were given forth; and what the Lord opened in me, I afterwards found was agreeable to them.

George Fox's Journal
1 John 5:6,7

Francis of Assisi [1182-1226]

315 Joy

Study always to have Joy, for it befits not the servant of God to show before his brother or another sadness or a troubled face.

St. Francis of Assisi
Matt. 6:16-18

François de Sales [1567-1622]

316 The useful virtues

We do not very often come across opportunities for exercising strength, magnanimity, or magnificence; but gentleness, temperance, modesty, and humility, are graces which ought to color everything we do. There may be virtues of a more exalted mold, but . . . these are the most continually called for in daily life.

François de Sales
Rom. 12:3; 1 Pet. 5:5

317 Patience

A really patient servant of God is as ready to bear inglorious troubles as those which are honorable. A brave man can easily bear with contempt, slander, and false accusations from an evil world; but to bear such injustice at the hands of good men, of friends and relations, is a great test of patience.

François de Sales
Rom. 15:2,3; Jas. 5:10,11

318 The danger of silence

One great remedy against all manner of temptation, great or small, is to open the heart and lay bare its suggestion, likings, and dislikings before some spiritual adviser; for . . . the first condition which the Evil One makes with a soul, when he wants to entrap it, is silence.

François de Sales
Jas. 5:16; Matt.18:15

319 Thy will or my will?

Alas! day by day we ask that His Will may be done, and yet, when it comes to the doing, we find it so hard! We offer ourselves so often to God—we continually say, "Lord, I am Thine, I give Thee my heart," and when He accepts it, we are such cowards. How dare we call ourselves His, if we cannot shape our own wills to His?

François de Sales
Deut. 10:12; Matt. 6:10; Eph. 6:5-8

320 Call it as it is

While extremely sensitive as to the slightest approach to slander,
you must also guard against an extreme into which some people fall
who, in their desire to speak evil of no one, actually uphold and speak
well of vice. If you have to do with one who is unquestionably a
slanderer, do not excuse him by calling him frank and free-spoken;
do not call one who is notoriously vain, liberal and elegant; do not
call dangerous levities mere simplicity; do not screen disobedience
under the name of zeal; or arrogance, of frankness; or evil intimacy,
of friendship. No, my friends, we must never, in our wish to shun
slander, foster or flatter vice in others: but we must call evil evil, and
sin sin, and so doing we shall serve God's glory.

> François de Sales, *Introduction to the Devout Life*
> *Prov. 11:9; Jas. 1:19,26; Jude 1:4,5,14-16*

321 Confession

It is an abuse to confess any kind of sin, mortal or venial, without
a will to be delivered from it, since confession was instituted for no
other end.

> François de Sales, *Introduction to the Devout Life*
> *Ps. 41:4; Jas. 5:16; 1 John 1:8-10*

Fulbert of Chartres [11th century]

322 Sing, choirs of New Jerusalem

Sing, choirs of New Jerusalem,
Your sweetest notes employ,
The paschal victory to hymn
In songs of holy joy!

For Judah's Lion burst his chains
And crushed the serpent's head;
Christ cries aloud through death's domains
To wake the imprisoned dead.

Triumphant in his glory now,
To him all power is given;
To him in one communion bow
All saints in earth and heaven.

All glory to the Father be,
All glory to the Son,
All glory to the Spirit be
While endless ages run.

Fulbert of Chartres
Gen. 3:15; 49:9,10; Matt. 28:18

Fuller, Thomas [1608-1661]

323 The pull of sin

Lord, before I commit a sin, it seems to me so shallow that I may wade through it dry-shod from any guiltiness; but when I have committed it, it often seems so deep that I cannot escape without drowning.

Thomas Fuller
Ps. 130:1-5

324 Living according to belief

He does not believe, that does not live according to his belief.

Thomas Fuller
Mark 9:24

325 Sin once more?

Lord, often have I thought to myself, I will sin but this one sin more, and then I will repent of it, and of all the rest of my sins together. So foolish was I, and ignorant. As if I should be more able to pay my debts when I owe more: or as if I should say, I will wound my friend once again, and then I will lovingly shake hands with him—but what if my friend will not shake hands with me?

Thomas Fuller, *Good Thoughts in Bad Times* [1898]
Isa. 30:1; Jer. 9:3; 2 Tim. 3:12,13; 1 John 5:16,17

326 His absence

It is to be feared lest our long quarrels about the manner of His presence cause the matter of His absence, for our want of charity to receive Him.

Thomas Fuller, *Good Thoughts in Bad Times* [1898]
Rom. 14:19-21; 1 Cor. 13

327 Offenses

It is the best sorrow in a Christian soul when his sins are loathsome and offensive unto him—a happy token that there hath not been of late in him any insensible supply of heinous offenses, because his stale sins are still his new and daily sorrow.

Thomas Fuller, *Mixt Contemplations* [1660]
1 Cor. 15:9; 1 John 2:1,2

Gasque, W. Ward

328 The historical setting

A basic principle in the interpretation of the Bible is that one must first ask what a given Scripture was intended to mean to the people for whom it was originally written; only then is the interpreter free to ask what meaning it has for Christians today. Failure to ask this primary question and to investigate the historical setting of Scripture have prevented many Christians from coming to a correct understanding of some parts of the Bible. Nowhere is this more true than in respect to the last book in the Bible. Here, there has been a singular lack of appreciation for the historical background of the book; the book has been interpreted as if it were primarily written for the day in which the expositor lives (which is usually thought to be the end time), rather than in terms of what it meant to the first-century

Christians of the Roman province of Asia for whom it was originally written. This has resulted in all sorts of grotesque and fantastic conclusions of which the author of the Revelation and its early recipients never would have dreamed.

W. Ward Gasque, *Sir William M. Ramsay: Archaeologist and New Testament Scholar* [1966]
Rev. 1:9

Glanvill, Joseph [1636-1680]

329 The love of a sect

The union of a sect within itself is a pitiful charity; it's no concord of Christians, but a conspiracy against Christ; and they that love one another for their opinionative concurrence, love for their own sakes, not their Lord's.

Joseph Glanvill
2 Pet. 2:1

Glover, T. R. (Terrot Reaveley) [1869-1943]

330 The living testament

The real conviction of the living Christ was not carried to the world by a book nor by a story. Men might allege that they had seen the risen Lord; but that was nothing till they themselves were known. The witness of the resurrection was not the word of Paul (as we see at Athens) nor of the Eleven; it was the new power in life and death that the world saw in changed men. . . . The legend of a reputed resurrection of some unknown person in Palestine nobody needed to consider; but what were you to do with the people who died in the arena, the reborn slaves with their newness of life in your own house? And when you "looked into the story," it was no mere somebody or other of whom they told it. The conviction of the people you knew, amazing in its power of transforming character and winning first the goodwill and the trust and then the conversion of others, was supported and confirmed by the nature and personality of the Man of whom they spoke, of whom you read in their books. "Never man spake like this man," you read, nor thought like this man, nor like this man believed in God. I can not but think that the factors that make a man Christian to-day were those that won the world then, our age and that age, in culture, in hopes and fears in loss of nerve, are not unlike.

Belief in immortality for us does not depend on a story, however well attested, in an ancient book. . . . No, here was a sequence of great character and emancipated spirit, all attached to and explained by such a personality as the world never saw; and the central doctrine of the risen Christ squared with the rationality and the goodness of God. . . . The wise said that God and the godlike could have no contact with suffering, but Jesus was no phantom feigning to be crucified; he truly suffered on the cross, he truly rose. Suffering is a language all can understand, and none can quite exhaust; and the suffering Christ, victorious over pain and death, meant for all who grasped his significance a new faith in God, a new freedom of mind in God.

T. R. Glover, *The Influence of Christ in the Ancient World* [1929]
John 5:21; 7:46; 2 Tim. 1:8-10

Godsey, John D. (Drew) [b.1922]

331 Opposites united

He challenged the church to rethink its own mission in the radically secular world of the twentieth century. . . . The nonbelieving brave men he met in the anti-Nazi underground, the stark realities of prison life, and his disappointment in the professional churchmen of Germany, all may have influenced Bonhoeffer to see real Christianity as "non-religious" and "worldly.". . . The opposition between sacred and secular, supernatural and natural, seemed unreal to him—the apparent opposites are united in Jesus Christ.

John D. Godsey, *The Theology of Dietrich Bonhoeffer* [1960]
1 Cor. 7:29-31

Goodspeed, Edgar J. [1871-1962]

332 In their own language

There are more readers of the English Bible in this country than in any other, and the time seemed to me to have come for a frank and direct translation of the Greek New Testament into our modern spoken American English. We take great pains to provide Asiatica and Africana with special versions, so that they may read the Bible each in his own tongue wherein he was born; and why not do as much for our young people, and our fellow citizens generally?

Edgar J. Goodspeed, *How Came the Bible?* [1940]
Acts 2:5-8

Gore, Charles [1853-1932]

333 The Spirit of Jesus

It was something more than a glorified Jesus Christ in the heavens in which [the Apostles] believed. In the beginning, John the Baptist had taught his disciples to expect from Christ the baptism—not of water only, as in his baptism—but of the Spirit. Before His death, Jesus had sought to fill His disciples' minds with the expectation of this gift. . . . And that Spirit had come in sensible power upon them some ten days after Jesus disappeared for the last time from their eyes. . . . And this Spirit was the Spirit of God, but also, and therefore, the Spirit of Jesus. Jesus was not then merely a past example, or a remote Lord, but an inward presence and power. A mere example in past history becomes in experience a feebler and feebler power. . . . But the example of Jesus was something much more than a memory. For He who had taught them in the past how to live was alive in the heavenly places and was working within them by His Spirit.

Charles Gore
Matt. 28:19,20; Acts 2:1-4

334 Divisions in the Christian Church

Do we habitually remember how it offends our Lord to see divisions in the Christian Church, nations nominally Christian armed to the teeth against one another, class against class and individual against individual in fierce and relentless competition, jealousies among clergy and church-workers, communicants who forget that the sacrament of union with Christ is the sacrament of union with their fellow men? Christians are to be the makers of Christ's peace. Something we can all do is to reconcile individuals, families, classes, churches, nations. The question is, Are we, as churchmen and citizens, by work and by prayer, in our private conduct and our public action, doing our utmost with deliberate, unsparing effort! If so, our benediction is of the highest: it is to be, and to be acknowledged as being, sons of God.

Charles Gore, *The Sermon on the Mount* [1910]
Matt. 5:9,23-26; Rom. 8:14; 15:5-7; 1 Cor. 1:13

Gossip, A. J. (Arthur John) [1873-1954]

335 Gateways to the heart

A basic trouble is that most Churches limit themselves unnecessarily by addressing their message almost exclusively to those who are open to religious impression through the intellect, whereas . . . there are at least four other gateways—the emotions, the imagination, the aesthetic feeling, and the will—through which they can be reached.

A. J. Gossip
Ps. 40:6-8; Jer. 36:7; Luke 12:11,12; John 7:16,17

336 The language of Heaven

Thanksgiving is the language of heaven, and we had better start to learn it if we are not to be mere dumb aliens there.

A. J. Gossip
Ps. 136; 1 Thess. 5:18

337 Inoculated against the Gospel

We have all been inoculated with Christianity, and are never likely to take it seriously now! You put some of the virus of some dreadful illness into a man's arm, and there is a little itchiness, some scratchiness, a slight discomfort—disagreeable, no doubt, but not the fever of the real disease, the turning and the tossing, and the ebbing strength. And we have all been inoculated with Christianity, more or less. We are on Christ's side, we wish him well, we hope that He will win, and we are even prepared to do something for Him, provided, of course, that He is reasonable, and does not make too much of an upset among our cozy comforts and our customary ways. But there is not the passion of zeal, and the burning enthusiasm, and the eagerness of self-sacrifice, of the real faith that changes character and wins the world.

A. J. Gossip, *From the Edge of the Crowd* [1924]
Deut.30:17; 2 Tim. 3:2-5

338 Salvation

Christ did not throw about that great word Salvation. But once, in the heart of an angry crowd, their enthusiasm soured suddenly into a growling muttering. He applied it confidently to a man who, under the inspiration of His friendship, had broken with his sorry past and his old selfish, unclean ways, and was doing what he could to put things right. Now that, He said, is what I call a saved man. Very solemnly He tells us that on the Day of Judgment we shall not be asked the questions we are expecting, but others that will puzzle and startle us. Those folk on the left hand were, as far as we hear, respectable folk; their business books were straight, their home life was kindly, they themselves were clean-living men and women: nothing whatever is laid to their charge excepting this, that they lived in a world needing their help and were too absorbed in something—what it was, we are not told; it may have been their souls—to give what aid they could.

A. J. Gossip, *From the Edge of the Crowd* [1924]
Matt. 11:15; 25:31-46; Luke 19:2-10

339 The Gospel is free

No doubt the gospel is quite free, as free as the Victoria Cross, which anyone can have who is prepared to face the risks; but it means time, and pains, and concentrating all one's energies upon a mighty project. You will not stroll into Christlikeness with your hands in your pockets, shoving the door open with a careless shoulder. This is no hobby for one's leisure moments, taken up at intervals when we have nothing much to do, and put down and forgotten when our life grows full and interesting. . . . It takes all one's strength, and all one's heart, and all one's mind, and all one's soul, given freely and recklessly and without restraint. This is a business for adventurous spirits; others would shrink out of it. And so Christ had a way of pulling up would-be recruits with sobering and disconcerting questions, of meeting applicants—breathless and panting in their eagerness—by asking them if they really thought they had the grit, the stamina, the gallantry, required. For many, He explained, begin, but quickly become cowed, and slink away, leaving a thing unfinished as a pathetic monument of their own lack of courage and of staying power.

A. J. Gossip, *From the Edge of the Crowd* [1924]
Matt. 7:13,14; Luke 18:18-27

340 A gift from Christ

God, as we know Him, is a gift to us from Christ.

A. J. Gossip, *From the Edge of the Crowd* [1924]
John 14:9

341 Danger in contentment

This insensibility of ours is a bad symptom. For one thing, it implies that we have no spiritual ambition, else we should not be satisfied with such poor lives; that we cannot have thought out the fact of Jesus Christ, and how immeasurably He has raised the standard. Will you hang your wretched daubs beside the works of Titian and Michelangelo and not be shamed by the enormous contrast—stand back and say, with a satisfied smirk, "That is pretty good, you know!"? And can you live face to face with Jesus Christ, and be content with what you are?

A. J. Gossip, *From the Edge of the Crowd* [1924]
Ps. 119:75; Phil. 4:11-13; Heb. 12:3-8

342 What Christ does for a soul

What exactly has Christ done for you? What is there in your life that needs Christ to explain it, and that, apart from Him, simply could not have been there at all? If there is nothing, then your religion is a sheer futility. But then that is your fault, not Jesus Christ's. For, when we open the New Testament, it is to come upon whole companies of excited people, their faces all aglow, their hearts dazed and bewildered by the immensity of their own good fortune. Apparently they find it difficult to think of anything but this amazing happening that has befallen them; quite certainly they cannot keep from laying almost violent hands on every chance passer-by, and pouring out yet once again the whole astounding story. And always, as we listen, they keep throwing up their hands as if in sheer despair, telling us it is hopeless, that it breaks through language, that it won't describe, that until a man has known Christ for himself he can have no idea of the enormous difference He makes. It is as when a woman gives a man her heart; or when a little one is born to very you; or when, after long lean years of pain and greyness, health comes back. You cannot really describe that; you cannot put it into words, not adequately. Only, the whole world is different, and life gloriously new. Well, it is like that, they say.

> A. J. Gossip, *From the Edge of the Crowd* [1924]
> *Rom. 9:22-24; Gal. 2:30; Heb. 9:11-14; 13:20,21; 2 Pet. 1:4*

343 Christlikeness

If Christ and His work and His sacrifice do not result in Christlikeness in you and me, then for us it is quite valueless, and has entirely failed; and, insofar as you and I are concerned, Christ was thrown away in vain. How, then, is it with you and me? Be very sure that upon Calvary it was no strange, immoral favoritism that came into operation, whereby because of some beliefs that remain mere dead letters, that produce no change whatever in their characters, some people living the same kind of life as others and following the same selfish interests and ends as they, are given a destiny entirely different. That is the vainest of vain dreams. Rather is this the supreme revelation of a new way of living life; and only those who—blunderingly, it may be, yet honestly—seek to adopt and imitate it can be counted really Christian folk.

A. J. Gossip, *The Galilean Accent* [1926]
1 Cor. 5:6,7; 2 Cor. 3:6; 5:17

344 What you should be

Who is it that has helped you most? Has it not been those who believed in you? Perhaps there may be few such left. The light of expectation may have died out of the most friendly and hopeful eyes; and you yourself may have lost heart. Ah! but there is still One whose faith in you has never wavered. And how wonderful it is that that one should be Jesus Christ! . . . It was a wonderful dream God dreamed, Christ says, when He created you; it was a stately being that was in His mind when you were fashioned; and I can make you all He meant that you should be.

A. J. Gossip, *The Galilean Accent* [1926]
Matt. 5:48

345 Interfering with the world

If you wanted a label for us, would you find a better than a Sadducean Age? We also are not worrying about immortality, hardly believe in it, or at least are not sure; we, too, have limited ourselves to this dust-speck of time, leaving unclaimed the vast inheritance beyond of which Christ told us; we, too, are putting all our zeal and passion and enthusiasm into things of this earth here, quite sure that that is the only road to progress, and that this everlasting chatter about the soul is quite beside the point. And they are all so earnest and so certain, work so hard, are animated often by such lofty motives, are so sure that there is really no manner of need for Christ: that given this, and this, and this, each of them pushing forward his particular panacea—the world will manage very well; that to talk about Christ, and changing people's hearts, and making us new creatures, is merely to lose precious time and wander from the practical into vague daydreaming of which nothing comes. And year by year their voices grow a little harder, and they eye Christ more and more askance, feel sourly that He is a bit of a nuisance and a stumbling-block to progress, keeping people quiet who should not be quiet, lulling them with these dim, immaterial, fantastic, spiritual hopes of His which they think have no body, and can not have. Once more the whisper grows, "Were He not far better away?" Meantime we can ignore Him, they say; and they do.

A. J. Gossip, *The Galilean Accent* [1926]
Isa. 29:13,14; Eph. 4:14; 1 Tim. 6:3-5,20,21; 2 Pet. 2:1-3

346 Merciless sin

They say it was old sins that troubled him, the past failures of the man, that made things difficult for him now. There had been days when he had been too hectoring or domineering—so, at least, these impossible people had said, though he himself denied it still. At all events, protesting to Rome, they had won the Emperor's ear, and humbled their governor. And that must not happen again. Ah, me! Is not this life of ours a fearsome thing? Take care! take care! for if you sin that sin, be sure that somehow you will pay for it—and, it may be, at how hideous a price! So Pilate found in his day; so you, too, will find it in ours. . . . Only God knows what may come out of that, if you should give way to it. Pilate was curt and domineering to the Jews one day. And it was because of that, months later, his unwilling hands set up the cross of Christ: unwilling—but they did it. Take you care! for sin is very merciless. If you have had the sweet, [sin] will see to it that you quaff the bitter to the very dregs.

A. J. Gossip, *The Galilean Accent* [1926]
Matt. 27:24

347 The waste of misdirection

When we look at the history of the Church, at the reckless fashion in which we have squandered our strength and time in fratricidal struggles between sect and sect, in embittered bickerings over matters often of secondary moment, while the world about us lies unwon, and the Church's great commission remains plainly unfulfilled, surely we can understand that outburst of Erasmus, when he cried that he wished that we would cease from our disputings altogether, and put all that energy and zeal that we are wasting upon them into the carrying of the Gospel to the heathen! Or recall the infinite pains that have been taken, down the centuries, to preserve minute orthodoxy in all points of mental belief while ugly evils flaunt along the streets and are accepted meekly as part of the makeup of things! Or recollect how easy it is to assume that we, ourselves, are Christian people. Why? Oh, well, just the usual reasons: we say our prayers, when we are not too sleepy; and we come to church, when there is nothing much to do; and so, of course, there is no doubt of it, although our tempers may remain uncurbed, and our characters are not the least like Jesus Christ's, nor growing any nearer it! Do we not need that solemn warning that Christ gives us when He tells us bluntly that many people lose their lives and souls, because they are always laying the emphasis and stress on the wrong points?

A. J. Gossip, *The Galilean Accent* [1926]
Matt. 23:13

348 You can pray

Well, to begin with, you can pray. Pray! you say scornfully, pray! I knew it would all fizzle out, and come to nothing. I could pray!

Yes, you could pray, and, whatever you may think about it, using it as a poor makeshift of a thing much lower than a second-best, not really a best at all, on which men fall back only when they can do nothing effectively, and are too fidgety to be able to do nothing at all, Christ holds that prayer is a tremendous power which achieves what, without it, was a sheer impossibility. And this amazing thing you can set into operation. And the fact that you are not so using it, and simply don't believe in it and its efficiency and efficacy as our fathers did, and that so many nowadays agree with you, is certainly a major reason why the churches are so cold, and the promises seem so tardy of fulfillment.

A. J. Gossip, *Experience Worketh Hope* [1944]
John 16:23,24; 1 Sam. 1:15; 1 Tim. 2:8

349 Gaze at the Cross

The very Nazis look at you with wonderment and an open contempt! For even they are sure that to live for nothing higher than oneself is to lose life; that life, to be called life, can be found only in serving something bigger than one's personal interests; something that crowds these out of mind and heart, till one forgets about them and lives wholly, and without exception, for that other, worthier thing. . . . It is long since Aristotle told us that only barbarians have as their ideal the wish to live as they please, and to do what they like.

And the New Testament gravely sets us down before the Cross, and bids us gaze, and still gaze, and keep gazing, till the fact has soaked itself into our minds that that, not less than that, is now the standard set us, and that whatever in our lives clashes with that is sin.

A. J. Gossip, *Experience Worketh Hope* [1944]
John 8:28

350 Camping on the border

We come to Jesus Christ: and He does for us what He promised; and the thing works out. To our amazement, it works out. And then we settle down. We have had our own first-hand and irrefutable experience. But, instead of opening the windows to the glory of the sunshine so evidently there, instead of being incited to a hugeness of faith by what Christ has already done for us, we can't believe that there can be anything more, or that even He can work, for us, anything better. That first foretaste satisfies us. And so we camp for life out on the confines of the Kingdom, and never press on to inherit what is there and meant for us.

A. J. Gossip, *Experience Worketh Hope* [1944]
Luke 17:12-19

351 God in the Sacrament

Every single time a sacrament is celebrated, God takes action, there and then—does something, not on Calvary, but in that church. And what He does is to come to each soul partaking in the Sacrament and to assure it that He stands to the best and biggest of His promises and to the fullness of His grace in Christ . . . de-universalizes the Scriptures and individualizes them, makes them a personal promise, couched no longer in general terms but offered to very you and very me, as individually as if they covered no other but referred to you and me alone. We may be cold and dead and unresponsive. None the less, something happens in the Sacrament. For God stands to His side of the Covenant, whether we stand to ours or not.

A. J. Gossip, *Experience Worketh Hope* [1944]
1 Cor. 5:8

The Authentic **Book of Christian Quotations**

352 What is worship?

But what is worship? What ought to result from it? What is the point and peak and heart and center of it? Is it the offering we bring to God of praise and adoration, of thanksgiving and sacrifice, our praise, our sacrifice to Him? That has its place, not legitimate only, but imperative. And yet to put that in the foreground is to make the service fundamentally man-centered and subjective, which, face to face with God, is surely almost unthinkably unseemly. Or is the ideal we should hold before us that other extreme, so ardently pressed on us these days, that, face to face with the Lord God Almighty, High and Holy, it is for us to forget ourselves and, leaving behind our petty little human joys and needs and sins and risings above thanksgiving and petition and confession, to lose ourselves in an awed adoration of God's naked and essential being, blessing and praising Him, not even for what he has done for us, and been for us, but for what, in Himself, He is.

To me, that seems not an advance, but a pathetic throw-back to the primitive of Brahmanism. We shall not learn to know God better, nor how to worship Him more worthily, by careful rubbing out from memory every wonder of Christ's revelation of Him. . . . The redeemed in Heaven crying continually, "Unto Him that loved us and washed us from our sins in His own blood," give, say the scriptures, an adoration which, in depth and fullness, no angel of them all can ever equal.

Yet even then, we have not reached the center. For when we worship, we are in God's presence, and it is what He says and does to us that is the all-important thing, not what we say and do toward Him. Since He is here and speaking to us, face to face, it is for us, in a hush of spirit, to listen for, and to, His voice, reproving, counseling, encouraging, revealing His most blessed will for us; and, with diligence, to set about immediate obedience. This and this, upon which He has laid His hand, must go; and this and this to which He calls us must be at once begun. And here and now I start to it. That is the heart of worship, its very core and essence.

A. J. Gossip, *Experience Worketh Hope* [1944]
Ps. 85:8; Heb. 13:15,16; Rev. 1:5,6

353 Being honest with God

Jeremy Taylor (q.v.) gives us some fundamental rules for prayer. And the chief of them is this: "Do not lie to God." And that curt piece of advice, so bluntly thrown down for us, is indeed all-important. Do not burn false fire upon God's altar; do not pose and pretend, either to Him or to yourself, in your religious exercises; do not say more than you mean, or use exaggerated language that goes beyond the facts, when speaking to Him whose word is truth.

A. J. Gossip, *In the Secret Place of the Most High* [1947]
Mark 4:22

354 God can be trusted

After Calvary, God has the right to be trusted; to be believed that He means what He says; and that His love is dependable.

A. J. Gossip, *In the Secret Place of the Most High* [1947]
Mark 15:25-37

355 He is gracious

I like to begin a service with some divine assurance of the liberality and the eager forgiveness of the God who is now meeting with us; not by beseeching Him to be gracious, but by believing that He is; that He stands to His promises; and that, quite safely, we can deal with Him on that assumption.

A. J. Gossip, *In the Secret Place of the Most High* [1947]
Acts 17:30,31

Graham, Billy [b.1918]

356 Message delivered

God proved His love on the Cross. When Christ hung, and bled, and died, it was God saying to the world, "I love you."

Billy Graham
John 3:16,17

Grant, Frederick Clifton [1891-1974]

357 How to study the Bible

We are frequently advised to read the Bible with our own personal needs in mind, and to look for answers to our own private questions. That is good, as far as it goes. . . . But better still is the advice to study the Bible objectively, . . . without regard, first of all, to our own subjective needs. Let the great passages fix themselves in our memory. Let them stay there permanently, like bright beacons, launching their powerful shafts of light upon life's problems—our own and everyone's—as they illumine, now one, now another dark area of human life. Following such a method, we discover that the Bible does "speak to our condition" and meet our needs, not just occasionally or when some emergency arises, but continually.

Frederick C. Grant
Ps. 63:5-7

Green, Bryan S. W. [1901-1993]

358 Evangelism is an attitude

Evangelism is not an activity at all. It is rather an attitude of mind behind all Christian activity. Evangelism is not a list of certain things done, but the spirit in which they are done. That is precisely why it cannot be organized. It is perhaps best described as an attitude of mind towards God and the world—an attitude which the Church must recover if she is to be true to her Lord, and to seize hold of the present opportunity.

Bryan S. W. Green, *Evangelism:*
Some principles and Experiments
Matt. 10:7,8

Green, E. M. B. (Edward Michael Bankes) [b.1930]

359 Priesthood of all believers

We instinctively contrast the ministry with the laity, the priest-hood with the people, the professional with the amateur. But the New Testament church knew nothing of this. This is perfectly astounding when you recall that every society in the world, including Israel, had had its specialized holy seasons, holy places, and holy people. In Christianity, all three were abolished. The keeping of holy days was a matter of indifference to the early Christians. They had no holy build-ings, but met in private houses—the incarnation of God had made the secular sacred. As for holy people, why, all believers were called to be that holy people, that universal priesthood envisioned long ago in the Old Testament but never hitherto realized. The mediation of Jesus has abolished the need for an intermediary caste of priests: all can have access to God in virtue of the sacrifice of Christ; all have the priestly responsibility of interceding for man to God; all have the prophetic task of speaking God's message to men. There is no priestly body within Christianity. It is a one-class society—though you would never guess as much, so grossly has conformity to pagan and Old-Testament models distorted this unique facet of Christ's community.

> E. M. B. Green, "Mission and Ministry"
> *1 Tim. 5:21; Heb. 10:10-12; Rev. 1:6*

Gregory of Nyssa [c.331- c.396]

360 The trustworthy charts

Just as at sea those who are carried away from the direction of the harbor bring themselves back on course by a clear sign, so Scripture may guide those adrift on the sea of life back into the harbor of the divine will.

> Gregory of Nyssa
> *Matt. 8:24-27; 2 Tim. 3:16*

Gregory the Great [c.540-604]

361 Sin in the workplace

There are many trades in which a man can hardly work—or simply cannot work—without sinning.

Gregory the Great
Rom. 1:28-32; Jude 1:22,23

Griffith, A. Leonard [b.1920]

362 Commitment

In religion, we are not asked to make up our minds, we are asked to make up our lives. . . . We may refuse to make up our minds, but our lives get made up, one way or the other. . . . Whatever we believe with our minds, our lives are committed either to God's way or to the God-denying way, and what matters in religion is the act of commitment.

A. Leonard Griffith, *Barriers to Christian Belief* [1962]
Ps. 86:11

Griffith Thomas, W. H. (William Henry) [1861-1924]

363 Different, yet the same

It is essential to preserve with care both sides of this truth. Christ and the Spirit are different yet the same, the same yet different. Perhaps the best expression we can give is that while their Personalities are never identical, their presence always is.

W. H. Griffith Thomas, *The Holy Spirit of God* [1913].
Rom. 8:2,3

Griffiths, Michael [b.1928]

364 Confession

At the earlier Methodist class meetings, members were expected every week to answer some extremely personal questions, such as the following: Have you experienced any particular temptations during the past week? How did you react or respond to those temptations? Is there anything you are trying to keep secret, and, if so, what? At this point, the modern Christian swallows hard! We are often coated with a thick layer of reserve and modesty which covers "a multitude of sins"—usually our own. Significantly, James 5:16-20, the original context of that phrase, is the passage which urges, "Confess your sins to one another, and pray for one another, that you may be healed."

Michael Griffiths, *Cinderella with Amnesia* [1975]

Grigg, John [b.1924]

365 Faith

"The clergy," says Canon Rhymes,[4] "are called to give to the laity the benefit of their theological understanding and so help them to account for and understand the faith which is in them." But surely there is no point in trying to account for faith: the moment it is accounted for rationally, it is no longer faith. Those whose hearts are filled with the Christian spirit . . . are best left to proclaim the Gospel in their own words and, above all, through the example of their own lives.

([4] Canon Douglas Rhymes (*q.v.*))

John Grigg
1 Thess. 1:6-8; Phlmn. 1:6; 1 Pet. 2:11,12

Grosseteste, Robert, Bp. [c.1170-1253]

366 The pastoral charge

The pastoral charge [does not] consist merely in administering the sacraments, chanting the canonical hours, celebrating masses—

though even these are not properly done by hirelings—; it consists also in feeding the hungry, giving drink to the thirsty, covering the naked, receiving guests, visiting the sick and those in prison. By the doing of these things is the people to be instructed in the holy duties of an active life.

Robert Grosseteste, Bp., in a letter [1250]
Matt. 25:31-46; 2 Cor. 6:1; 1 Pet. 5:1-4

Grou, Jean Nicolas [1731-1803]

367 Absolute importance

Nothing is small or great in God's sight; whatever He wills becomes great to us, however trifling, and if once the voice of conscience tells us that He requires anything of us, we have no right to measure its importance.

J. N. Grou
Dan. 3

368 The peace God gives

But how shall we rest in God? By giving ourselves wholly to Him. If you give yourself by halves, you cannot find full rest—there will ever be a lurking disquiet in that half which is withheld . . . All peace and happiness in this world depend upon unreserved self-oblation to God. If this be hearty and entire, the result will be an unfailing, ever-increasing happiness, which nothing can disturb. There is no real happiness in this life save that which is the result of a peaceful heart.

Jean N. Grou, *The Hidden Life of the Soul*
Rom. 12:1

Guinness, Os (Ian Oswald) [b.1941]

369 A necessary reaction

Genuine outrage is not just a permissible reaction to the hard-pressed Christian; God himself feels it, and so should the Christian in the presence of pain, cruelty, violence, and injustice. God, who is the Father of Jesus Christ, is neither impersonal nor beyond good and evil. By the absolute immutability of His character, He is implacably opposed to evil and outraged by it.

> Os Guinness, *The Dust of Death* [1973]
> *Josh. 24:19; Ps. 119:142; Nah. 1:6; Heb. 10:30,31*

Guyon, Mme. (Jeanne Marie Bouvièr de la Motte-) [1648-1717]

370 No love to give

> I love my God, but with no love of mine
>   For I have none to give;
> I love Thee, Lord, but all that love is Thine,
>   For by Thy life I live.
> I am as nothing, and rejoice to be
> Emptied and lost and swallowed up in Thee.

> Mme. Guyon
> *Phil. 3:8,9*

Gwatkin, Henry M. [1844-1916]

371 Selfishness forgotten

In the whole range of history there is no more striking contrast than that of the Apostolic churches with the heathenism around them. They had shortcomings enough, it is true, and divisions and scandals not a few, for even apostolic times were no golden age of purity and primitive simplicity. Yet we can see that their fullness of life, and hope, and promise for the future, were a new sort of power in the world. Within their own limits they had solved almost by the way the social problem which baffled Rome, and baffles Europe still. They had lifted woman to her rightful place, restored the dignity of labor, abolished beggary, and drawn the sting of slavery. The secret of the revolution is that the selfishness of race and class were forgotten in the Supper of the Lord, and a new basis for society found in love of the visible image of God in men for whom Christ died.

Henry M. Gwatkin, *Early Church History to A.D. 312* [1909]
1 Cor. 1:28,29

Hügel, Friedrich von [1852-1925]

372 The only way to joy

The mystery revealed, in a unique degree and form, in Christ's life, is really a universal spiritual human law: the law of suffering and sacrifice, as the one way to joy and possession, which has existed, though veiled till now, since the foundation of the world.

Friedrich von Hügel
Matt. 16:24,25; 1 Pet. 2:21

Hallack, Cecily Rosemary [1898-1938]

373 Lord of all pots and pans

Lord of all pots and pans and things, since I've no time to be
A saint by doing lovely things, or watching late with Thee,
Or dreaming in the dawn-light, or storming Heaven's gates,
Make me a saint by getting meals and washing up the plates.
Although I must have Martha's hands, I have a Mary mind,
And when I black the boots and shoes, Thy sandals, Lord, I find.
I think of how they trod the earth, what time I scrub the floor:
Accept this meditation, Lord, I haven't time for more.

Warm all the kitchen with Thy love, and light it with Thy peace;
Forgive me all my worrying, and make my grumbling cease.
Thou who didst love to give men food, in room or by the sea,
Accept this service that I do—I do it unto Thee.

Cecily Rosemary Hallack
Luke 10:38-42

Hallesby, O. [1879-1961]

374 Resting in His presence

It is not necessary to maintain a conversation when we are in the presence of God. We can come into His presence and rest our weary souls in quiet contemplation of Him. Our groanings, which cannot be uttered, rise to Him and tell Him better than words how dependent we are upon Him.

O. Hallesby, Prayer [1943]
Rom. 8:26,27

Ham, William T.

375 Solitary Christian?

There are many things which a person can do alone, but being a Christian is not one of them. As the Christian life is, above all things, a state of union with Christ, and of union of his followers with one another, love of the brethren is inseparable from love of God. Resentment toward any human being cannot exist in the same heart with love to God. The personal relationship to Christ can only be realized when one has "come to himself" as a member of His Body, the Christian fellowship.

William T. Ham, "Candles of the Lord," in *Spiritual Renewal through Personal Groups* [1957]
1 Cor. 1:9,10

376 Building up the members in love

The Christian Church does not want and does not need members because of a job it has to do. The Christian Church has a secret at her heart and she wants to share it. Whenever one, by repentance and forgiveness, enters this community of grace, he discovers life's end, and he too will be constrained to let this life flow out in appropriate channels. Thrilling and costly projects will come into existence, but not as ends in themselves, and the group will not become a means to [such ends]. The group will never forget that one of its primary functions is to up build the members in love.

> William T Ham, "Candles of the Lord," in *Spiritual Renewal through Personal Groups* [1957]
> *2 Cor. 5:1*

Hammarskjöld, Dag (Hjalmar Agne Carl) [1905-1961]

377 The everyday commitment

The "great commitment" is so much easier than the ordinary, everyday one—and can all too easily shut our hearts to the latter. A willingness to make the ultimate sacrifice can be associated with, and even produce, a great hardness of heart.

> Dag Hammarskjöld, *Markings* [1964]
> *Phil. 3:17-19*

378 Forgiveness

Forgiveness breaks the chain of causality because he who forgives you—out of love—takes upon himself the consequences of what you have done. Forgiveness, therefore, always entails a sacrifice.

> Dag Hammarskjöld, *Markings* [1964]
> *Matt. 6:14,15*

Hanson, Anthony T. (Tyrrell) [1916-1991]

379 Denominational blinders

With us, our denomination is a source of pride: we feel an intimate link with our fellow church-member in Fiji, and we think how wonderful it is that we belong to a communion which spans the entire globe. We do not normally reflect that this sense of solidarity is very often gained at the expense of the unity which we ought to be experiencing with our fellow-Christian next door who belongs to a different denomination.

Anthony T. Hanson
Matt. 23:8; John 17:20,21; Phil. 1:27; 1 Pet. 3:8

380 The Servant-Church

The Servant Messiah carries out his ministry in the lives of his ministers. His life is reproduced in their lives, so they also are servants. But this ministry is exercised in and towards the Church, so as to enable the Church itself to carry out the ministry of the Servant. The Messiah came as a Servant; his ministers are servants; and the Church he created is a Servant-Church.

Anthony T. Hanson, *The Church of the Servant* [1962]
Zech. 3:8; Mark 10:42-45; Phil. 2:6-8

381 The Servant of all

How did Jesus show his authority? Not by making vast claims for himself, though such claims were implicit. His authority seemed to reside in what he was and what he did rather than in what he specifically claimed to be. Especially in Mark's Gospel there is an elusive quality about his authority, the mystery of the hidden Messiah. His authority was at the same time most deeply hidden and most clearly expressed by his servanthood . . . The more the Church in its life shows forth the character of the Servant, the more will its teaching bear the marks of the authority of the Servant.

Anthony T. Hanson, *The Church of the Servant* [1962]
Mark 9:35; 10:42-45

Haskins, Minnie L. [1875-1957]

382 Better than light

And I said to the man who stood at the gate of the year: "Give me a light. that I may tread safely into the unknown." And he replied: "Go out into the darkness and put your hand into the hand of God. That shall be to you better than light, and safer than a known way."

Minnie L. Haskins, "The Desert", Introduction
Ps. 16:11; Isa. 41:10; 59:1

Hastings, Horace L. [1852-1922]

383 Everyone ought to pray

Although prayer has been defined as communion with God, aspiration after the highest things, Stopford Brooke [Irish clergyman, 1832-1916] is right when he insists that prayer, in its plainest meaning, is a petition addressed to God. When Jesus laid the duty of petition upon his disciples, He went on to assert the reasonableness of man's asking and God's answering. Jesus argues along the line of reason that, if an earthly parent does the best in his power for his children, . . . the Almighty and All-Wise Love, of which human love is only the shadow, will do better still for His great family; and therefore our Master teaches that men ought everywhere to pray, without fear, with hope, and without doubt.

Horace L. Hastings, *The Great Christian Doctrines* [1922]
Matt. 7:7-11; Luke 11:9-13; 1 Tim. 2:8

Havergal, Frances Ridley [1836-1879]

384 Jesus came!

Jesus came!—and came for me.
    Simple words! and yet expressing

Depths of holy mystery,
    Depths of wondrous love and blessing.
Holy Spirit, make me see
    All His coming means for me;
Take the things of Christ, I pray,
    Show them to my heart today.

Frances Ridley Havergal
Matt. 9:10; Mark 2:17

Head, David M.

385 Yes

Not pleading with the Father, but expressing the Father's good pleasure is the key-note of true intercession. Forgiveness is God's idea, God's desire; and it is He who appoints both the Judge and the Counsel for the Defense. It was He who inaugurated the priestly work, that men might receive His cleansing and turn to the Lamb of God slain from the foundation of the world. God has provided for himself a Lamb. It is He who sends His Son to be our Elder Brother, and to incorporate us as adopted sons into the circle of His Fatherly love. So then it is the voice of His beloved Son which is most clearly heard by the Father in heaven. In that voice of intercession, all the voices of intercession are contained and heard. The Son is talking to the Father about us, and what He says is not "Please" but "Yes," for in Him is the "Yea" and "Amen."

David Head, *Shout for Joy* [1962]
Isa. 53:12; John 17:9

386 The beginning of eternal life here

We should not draw too sharp a distinction between this "barren land" or "wilderness" of our pilgrimage, and the sweet home that God has prepared. We all know the changes and chances of this troublous life; but we can also know in this vale of tears the healthful spirit of His grace. Health for the whole man is God's gracious purpose for us here and now, often frustrated, often prevented by unbelief. The life of the saints in light must not emphasize for us simply the contrast between their state and ours, but rather the beginning of the gift of eternal life and all its benefits of inner strength and peace amid earthly vicissitudes.

David Head, *Shout for Joy* [1962]
Deut. 32:10; Rom. 7:24; 8:2; 1 Tim. 1:16

387 The cross-eyed church

The Church on earth is a cross-eyed church, with one eye on God in His heavenly benediction, and one eye on the needy world of men.

David Head, *Shout for Joy* [1962]
Eph. 1:3

Hebert, (Arthur) Gabriel [1886-1963]

388 His words

Jesus' moral teaching does not consist of a universal scheme of ethics, a series of precepts which would be universally valid, by whomever they had been spoken. They are to be heard as His word, spoken by Him, with the impact of His person behind them.

Gabriel Hebert
Matt. 7:28,29

Henry, Matthew [1662-1714]

389 The meaning of affliction

Extraordinary afflictions are not always the punishment of extraordinary sins, but sometimes the trial of extraordinary graces. Sanctified afflictions are spiritual promotions.

Matthew Henry
Job 5:17,18; Jas. 5:10,11

390 The Lord shall have them in derision

Sinners' follies are the just sport of God's infinite wisdom and power; and those attempts of the kingdom of Satan, which in our eyes are formidable, in his are despicable.

Matthew Henry
Ps. 2:4

Herbert, George [1593-1633]

391 Forgiveness

He who cannot forgive others breaks the bridge over which he himself must pass.

George Herbert
Matt. 6:12,14,15; Luke 11:4

392 Lent

It's true we cannot reach Christ's forti'th day
Yet to go part of that religious way
    Is better than to rest:
We cannot reach our Savior's purity;
Yet we are bid, 'Be holy ev'n as He':
    In both let's do our best.
Who goeth in the way which Christ hath gone
Is much more sure to meet with Him than one
    That traveleth by-ways;
Perhaps my God, though He be far before,
May turn, and take me by the hand, and more,
    May strengthen my decays.
Yet, Lord, instruct us to improve our fast
By starving sin, and taking such repast
    As may our faults control;
That ev'ry man may revel at his door,

Not in his parlor—banqueting the poor,
  And among those, his soul.

George Herbert
Isa. 35:8; 1 Pet. 1:15,16; Heb. 9:8-14

393 Blood and wine

Love is that liquor sweet and most divine
Which my God feels as blood; but I, as wine.

George Herbert
Matt. 26:28; Mark 14:23,24; Luke 22:20;
John 6:53-56; 1 Cor. 10:16

394 The shepherds sing; and shall I silent be?

The shepherds sing; and shall I silent be?
  My God, no hymn for Thee?
My soul's a shepherd too: a flock it feeds
  Of thoughts, and words, and deeds.
The pasture is Thy Word, the streams, Thy Grace
  Enriching all the place.
Shepherd and flock shall sing, and all my powers
  Out-sing the daylight hours.
Then we will chide the sun for letting night
  Take up his place and right:
We sing one common Lord; wherefore he should
  Himself the candle hold.
I will go searching, till I find a sun
  Shall stay, till we have done;
A willing shiner, that shall shine as gladly,
  As frost-nipt suns look sadly.
Then we will sing, and shine all our own day,
  And one another pay:
His beams shall cheer my breast, and both so twine,
Till ev'n his beams sing, and my music shine.

George Herbert, from *The Temple* [1633]
Luke 2:20

Hilary, Bp. of Poitiers [c.300-c.367]

395 The death of death

He took upon Him the flesh in which we have sinned, that by wearing our flesh He might forgive sins; a flesh which He shares with us by wearing it, not by sinning in it. He blotted out through death the sentence of death, that by a new creation of our race in Himself He might sweep away the penalty appointed by the former Law. . . . For Scripture had foretold that He who is God should die; that the victory and triumph of them that trust in Him lay in the fact that He, who is immortal and cannot be overcome by death, was to die that mortals might gain eternity.

In this calm assurance of safety did my soul gladly and hopefully take its rest, and feared so little the interruption of death, that death seemed only a name for eternal life. And the life of this present body was so far from seeming a burden or affliction that it was regarded as children regard their alphabets, sick men their draughts, shipwrecked sailors their swim, young men the training for their profession, future commanders their first campaign—that is, as an endurable submission to present necessities, bearing the promise of a blissful immortality.

St. Hilary, *On the Trinity*
1 Cor. 15:26,53-55; 1 John 5:5-7

Hilton, Walter [c.1330-1396]

396 Dead to sin

Since you have forsaken the world and turned wholly to God, you are symbolically dead in the eyes of men; therefore, let your heart be dead to all earthly affections and concerns, and wholly devoted to our Lord Jesus Christ. For you must be well aware that if we make an outward show of conversion to God without giving Him our hearts, it is only a shadow and pretence of virtue, and no true conversion. Any man or woman who neglects to maintain inward vigilance, and only makes an outward show of holiness in dress, speech, and behavior, is a wretched creature. For they watch the doings of other people and criticize their faults, imagining themselves to be something when in reality they are nothing. In this way they deceive themselves. Be careful to avoid this, and devote yourself inwardly to His likeness by humility, charity, and other spiritual virtues. In this way you will be truly converted to God.

Walter Hilton, The Scale of Perfection
Rom. 6:1-6,10,11; 8:10

Holland, J. G. (Josiah Gilbert) [1819-1881]

397 Untouched

A man may carry the whole scheme of Christian truth in his mind from boyhood to old age without the slightest effect upon his character and aims. It has had less influence than the multiplication table.

J. G. Holland
Rom. 1:22-26

Hooker, Richard [c.1554-1600]

398 The real presence

The real presence of Christ's most precious Body and Blood is not to be sought for in the Sacrament, but in the worthy receiver of the Sacrament.

Richard Hooker
1 Cor. 11:27-30

Hopkin, H. A. Evan

399 Self-renunciation

He looks today, as He has ever looked, not for crowds drifting aimlessly in His track, but for individual men and women whose undying allegiance will spring from their having recognized that He wants those who are prepared to follow the path of self-renunciation which He trod before them.

H. A. Evan Hopkin
Matt. 5:40-42

Hoskyns, Sir Edwyn Clement [1884-1937]

400 The tension within us

This coherence of the Bible itself, and of the Bible and the Church, is a coherence and a unity set in opposition to the world existing beyond its borders and outside its influence, so that there comes into being a tension between the world as it actually is and the Church, in so far as the Church rests upon the Biblical revelation of God. But this tension is not something that concerns the Church and the world as though they are things which exist outside us and apart from us, which we can consider and observe and discuss and have theories about. The tension between the Church and the world exists within us and is the very fiber of our being, and neither the one nor the other is superficial or trivial. For we are, all of us, of the earth, earthy; and we are also baptized members of Christ and His Church. It is precisely because we belong to two worlds that our lives consist in insecurity—that we are, in fact, a drama, the final act of which, the judgment of reward or punishment, heaven or hell, is hidden from us.

E. C. Hoskyns, *We are the Pharisees* [1960]
John 15:19; Acts 10:39-41

Houston, James M. (Macintosh) [b.1922]

401 Focused on God

When our lives are focused on God, awe and wonder lead us to worship God, filling our inner being with a fullness we would never have thought possible. Awe prepares the way in us for the power of God to transform us and this transformation of our inner attitudes can only take place when awe leads us in turn to wonder, admiration, reverence, surrender, and obedience toward God.

James Houston, The Transforming Power of Prayer [1996]
Eph. 3:14-19

Houston, Tom

402 Setting our compass

But we need to set our compass with three markers: (1) the Word of God; (2) a true analysis of the facts of our experience; and (3) the sensing of the mind of the Spirit by . . . this council.

Tom Houston, former president, World Vision International
Luke 10:21; Acts 15:28

Hovey, E. Paul [b.1908]

403 The Comforter

The word "Comforter" as applied to the Holy Spirit needs to be translated by some vigorous term. Literally, it means "with strength." Jesus promised His followers that "The Strengthener" would be with them forever. This promise is no lullaby for the faint-hearted. It is a blood transfusion for courageous living.

E. Paul Hovey
Isa. 40:31; John 14:16,17

Howard, Thomas [b.1935]

404 The fact of the Father

The desire for certitude is natural enough and explains the human tendency to mistake faith for certainty. This is not a specially religious mistake. We think of supernaturalism when faith is mentioned, but the naturalistic description of the world also operates on assumptions that require a faith as robust as does the most soaring mysticism. The usual efforts to skirt faith beg all the questions there are. A psychiatrist, for instance, who points out to you that you believe in God the Father because you need a father, or that you became a missionary to expiate your guilt feelings, may be quite correct, but he has not touched on the prior question as to whether there is, in fact, a cosmic father figure who is the archetype of all other fathers, or whether there is an evangel worth spending your life promulgating.

Thomas Howard, *Christ the Tiger* [1967]
1 Cor. 15:9

Howells, William Dean [1837-1920]

405 If I lay waste and wither up with doubt

If I lay waste and wither up with doubt
 The blessed fields of heaven where once my
 Faith possessed itself serenely safe from death;
 If I deny things past finding out;
Or if I orphan my own soul from One
That seemed a Father, and make void the place
Within me where He dwelt in Power and Grace,
What do I gain by what I have undone?

William Dean Howells
Matt. 11:2,3; 16:26; 1 Pet. 1:6,7

Hummel, Charles E. [b.1923]

406 Doing what God wants

Jesus . . . did not finish all the urgent tasks in Palestine or all the things He would have liked to do, but He did finish the work which God gave Him to do. The only alternative to frustration is to be sure that we are doing what God wants. Nothing substitutes for knowing that this day, this hour, in this place, we are doing the will of the Father. Then and only then can we think of all the other unfinished tasks with equanimity, and leave them with God.

> Charles E. Hummel, *The Tyranny of the Urgent* [1997]
> *Matt. 7:21*

Ignatius of Loyola [1491-1556]

407 God's silences

> He who hath heard the Word of God can bear his silences.
>
> St. Ignatius of Loyola
> *Heb. 4:12*

Irenaeus [c.130-c.200]

408 Beholding God

> The glory of God is a living man; and the life of man consists in beholding God.
>
> Irenæus
> *John 1:14; 2 Cor. 4:6; Heb. 1:1-4*

Ironside, Harry A. (Allen) [1876-1951]

409 Knowledge

> Scripture nowhere condemns the acquisition of knowledge. It is the wisdom of this world, not its knowledge, that is foolishness with God. . . . The history of philosophy is a story of contradictory, discarded hypotheses. . . . Many of them have failed to avail themselves of that which would unravel every knot and solve every

problem, namely, the revelation of God in Christ as given in the Holy Scriptures.

Harry A. Ironside
Matt. 16:17; 1 Cor. 1:19-27; Rev. 1:10,11

Irvine, Graeme

410 The characteristics of the Kingdom

When Christians join together to accomplish certain things, one may expect the organizations they form to reflect the characteristics of the Kingdom, but that will only happen as a consequence of the way people live and relate to each other in Christ. It will not necessarily follow from structures, policies, or documents.

Graeme Irvine, former president, World Vision International
Matt. 12:3,4; Rom. 14:17

Irving, Edward [1792-1834]

411 The basis of assurance

God's unchangeableness is the very foundation of desire and hope and activity in things religious as in things natural. The uniformity of nature's operations in the one, and the constancy of God's promises in the other, give aim and certainty to events.

Edward Irving
Num. 23:19-20; Ps. 119:89-91; Mal. 3:6;
Heb. 6:17-20; Jas. 1:17

Jenkins, E. E. (Ebenezer Evans) [1820-1905]

412 Comprehensible perfection

In the person of Christ, the formidable law of God, which by itself appalls us by its vast comprehensiveness and truth, and makes us hide ourselves from its dread sanctity, is brought down into the life of a brother, . . . and we see it illustrated and ratified in human action, we see righteousness that makes us feel more bitterly our sin, that makes us look more disparagingly upon our own efforts, yet leaves in us a longing to be like Him, as if we ought to be as He is.

E. E. Jenkins, *Life and Christ* [1896]
Matt. 11:27; John 1:18

Joad, C. E. M. (Cyril Edwin Mitchinson) [1891-1953]

413 The truth about evil

The view of evil which regards it as the by-product of circumstances which circumstances can, therefore, alter and even eliminate—has come to seem to me intolerably shallow, and the contrary view of it as endemic in man—more particularly in its Christian form, the doctrine of original sin—to express a deep and essential insight into human nature.

C. E. M. Joad, *The Recovery of Belief* [1952]
Rom. 5:12-17; James 1:14,15

John Chrysostom [c.345-407]

414 Church attendance

We assemble not in the church to pass away the time, but to gain some great benefit for our souls. If therefore we depart without profit, our zeal in frequenting the church will prove our condemnation. That so great a judgment comes not upon you, when ye go hence ponder the things ye have heard, and exercise yourselves in confirming our instruction—friend with friend, fathers with their children, masters with their slaves—so that, when ye return hither and hear from us the same counsels, ye may not be ashamed, but rejoice and be glad in the conviction that ye have put into practice the greater part of our exhortation. Not only must we meditate upon these things here—for this short exhortation sufficeth not to eradicate the evil—but at home let the husband be reminded of them by the wife, and the wife by the husband, and let an emulation obtain in families to the fulfillment of the divine law.

John Chrysostom
Ps. 19:14; Matt. 10:32,33; 1 Cor. 14:34,35; Eph. 5:22-31

415 Engraved on our hearts

I hear no one boast, that he hath a knowledge of the Scriptures, but that he owneth a Bible written in golden characters. And tell me then, what profiteth this? The Holy Scriptures were not given to us that we should enclose them in books, but that we should engrave them upon our hearts.

John Chrysostom
Jer. 31:33; Matt. 11:15; Rom. 2:14,15

416 Good resolutions

When we once begin to form good resolutions, God gives us every opportunity of carrying them out.

John Chrysostom
Matt. 25:14-30

417 Comprehension of God

A comprehended god is no god.

John Chrysostom
Job 37:5

418 The Player and the instrument

Seeing, then, it is no longer the fisherman, the son of Zebedee, but He who knoweth "the deep things of God" (I Cor. 2:10), the Holy Spirit, I mean, that striketh this lyre, let us hearken accordingly. For he will say nothing to us as a man, but what he saith, he will say from the depths of the Spirit.

John Chrysostom

419 The mind of the Scriptures

It is not possible ever to exhaust the mind of the Scriptures. It is a well that has no bottom.

John Chrysostom
Matt. 21:42; Rom. 15:4; 2 Tim. 3:16

John of Damascus [8th century]

420 The day of resurrection!

The day of resurrection!
Earth, tell it out abroad;
The passover of gladness,
The passover of God.
From death to life eternal,
From this world to the sky,
Our Christ hath brought us over
With hymns of victory.
Our hearts be pure from evil,
That we may see aright
The Lord in rays eternal
Of resurrection light,
And, list'ning to His accents,
May hear, so calm and plain
His own "All hail!" and, hearing,
May raise the victor strain.
Now let the heav'ns be joyful,
Let earth her song begin,

Let the round world keep triumph
And all that is therein;
Invisible and visible,
Their notes let all things blend;
For Christ the Lord has risen—
Our Joy that has no end.

John of Damascus
Luke 24

John of the Cross [1542-1591]

421 Contemplation

God does not reserve such a lofty vocation [as that of contemplation] to certain souls only; on the contrary, He is willing that all should embrace it. But He finds few who permit such divine things in them. Most shrink from the labor instead of submitting, as they must, with endless patience.

John of the Cross
Ps. 1:1,2; 119:11; 139:17,18; Phil. 4:8

422 The Light

Never was fount so clear,
    undimmed and bright;
From it alone, I know proceeds all light
    although 'tis night.

John of the Cross
John 1:7-9

423 The incomparability of God

No knowledge, therefore, and no conceptions in this mortal life, can serve as proximate means of this high union of the love of God. All that the understanding can comprehend; all that the will may be satisfied with; and all that the imagination may conceive; is most unlike unto God, and most disproportionate to Him.

John of the Cross, The Ascent of Mount Carmel
Job 37:5

John, Griffith [1831-1912]

424 The source of unity

The Holy Spirit is the source of spiritual unity! He is the Fount of all true joy! We as missionaries need the fullness of this joy. Without it our work will be a burden to us, and we shall toil on with the hearts of slaves; and the hearts of slaves are never strong.

Griffith John
1 Cor. 12:7-12

Johnson, Howard A. [b.1915]

425 Light enough to walk by

[Christians], at their best, know that often they don't know. They do not have all the answers. They do not have God in their pocket. We cannot answer every question that any bright boy in the back row might ask. We have only light enough to walk by.

Howard A. Johnson
John 1:9

Johnson, Paul G. (Gordon) [b.1931]

426 No place for problems

To perpetuate the clerical role of answer man, the layman when inside the church building must act as if he has only half a brain, while outside, in the world, he is expected to be an ambassador for Christ, a lay transmitter of faith. Outside, he is to be informed and vocal; inside, he must appear ignorant and mute as a sheep. Christians have within them many questions—questions that are at once elementary and profound, questions that would ripple the water were they raised. However, because a Christian is supposed to have "answers," life's important questions are not discussed outside the church building; and, because the pastor is the educated, spiritual authority, they are not discussed inside either.

> Paul G. Johnson, *Buried Alive* [1968]
> *John 21:15; Rom. 14:5; 2 Cor. 5:20*

Johnson, Samuel (1709-1784]

427 Faith in time of need?

The man who has never had religion before, no more grows religious when he is sick, than a man who has never learned figures can count when he has need of calculation.

> Samuel Johnson
> *Luke 13:24*

428 The purpose of affliction

It is by affliction chiefly that the heart of man is purified, and that the thoughts are fixed on a better state. Prosperity has power to intoxicate the imagination, to fix the mind upon the present scene, to produce confidence and elation, and to make him who enjoys affluence and honors forget the hand by which they were bestowed. It is seldom that we are otherwise than by affliction awakened to a sense of our imbecility, or taught to know how little all our acquisitions can conduce to safety or quiet, and how justly we may inscribe to the superintendence of a higher power those blessings which in the wantonness of success we considered as the attainments of our policy and courage.

> Samuel Johnson
> *1 Cor. 1:23-29*

429 The duty of Bible circulation

I did not expect to hear that it could be, in an assembly convened for the propagation of Christian knowledge, a question whether any nation uninstructed in religion should receive instruction; or whether that, instruction should be imparted to them by a translation of the holy-books into their own language. If obedience to the will of GOD be necessary to happiness, and knowledge of his will be necessary to obedience, I know not how he that withholds this knowledge, or delays it, can be said to love his neighbor as himself. He, that voluntarily continues ignorance, is guilty of all the crimes which ignorance produces; as to him that should extinguish the tapers of a light-house, might justly be imputed the calamities of shipwrecks.

Christianity is the highest perfection of humanity; and as no man is good but as he wishes the good of others, so no man can be good in the highest degree, who wishes not to others the largest measures of the greatest good. To omit for a year, or for a day, the most efficacious method of advancing Christianity [i.e., the Bible], in compliance with any purposes that terminate this side of the grave, is a crime [the like] of which I know not that the world has yet had an example.

a letter from Samuel Johnson to
William Drummond of Edinburgh, 1766
Acts 10:35; 17:30

430 Unreformed

A student may easily exhaust his life in comparing divines and moralists without any practical regard to morals and religion; he may be learning not to live but to reason . . . while the chief use of his volumes is unthought of, his mind is unaffected, and his life is unreformed.

Samuel Johnson
Eccl. 12:12,13; Matt. 5:20

431 We try to reform

We took tea, by Boswell's desire; and I eat one bun, I think, that I might not be seen to fast ostentatiously. When I find that so much of my life has stolen unprofitably away, and that I can descry by retrospection scarcely a few single days properly and vigorously employed, why do I yet try to resolve again? I try, because reformation is necessary and despair is criminal. I try, in humble hope of the help of God.

Samuel Johnson, *Prayers and Meditations*
Ps. 121:1,2; 2 Cor. 7:10

Jones, E. (Eli) Stanley [1884-1973]

432 God's heart on the cross

God, to redeem us at the deepest portion of our nature—the urge to love and be loved—must reveal His nature in an incredible and impossible way. He must reveal it at a cross. At the cross God wrapped his heart in flesh and blood and let it be nailed to the cross for our redemption.

E. Stanley Jones
Gal. 6:14

433 The Holy Spirit's power over the subconscious

If the Holy Spirit can take over the subconscious with our consent and cooperation, then we have almighty Power working at the basis of our lives, then we can do anything we ought to do, go anywhere we ought to go, and be anything we ought to be. Life is supplied with a basic adequacy. . . . The conscious mind determines the actions, the unconscious mind determines the reactions; and the reactions are just as important as the actions. Many Christians are Christians in their actions—they don't lie, steal, commit adultery, or get drunk; but they react badly to what happens to them: they react in anger, bad temper, self-pity, jealousy, and envy. . . . When the depths are upheld by the Holy Spirit, then the reaction is Christian.

E. Stanley Jones, *Conversion* [1959]
Matt. 19:26; Rom. 8:11

434 Belonging to a Person

In conversion you are not attached primarily to an order, nor to an institution, nor a movement, nor a set of beliefs, nor a code of action—you are attached primarily to a Person, and secondarily to these other things. . . . You are not called to get to heaven, to do good, or to be good—you are called to belong to Jesus Christ. The doing good, the being good, and the getting to heaven, are the by-products of that belonging. The center of conversion is the belonging of a person to a Person.

E. Stanley Jones, *Conversion [1959]*
1 Cor. 3:23

435 The unrespectability of need

In our Ashrams of East and West, places of spiritual retreat, we begin with what we call "The Morning of the Open Heart," in which we tell our needs. . . . We give four or five hours to this catharsis. The reaction of one member, who listened to it for the first time, was: "Good gracious, have we all the disrupted people in the country here?" My reply was: "No, you have a cross section of the church life honestly revealed." In the ordinary church, it is suppressed by respectability, by a desire to appear better than we really are.

E. Stanley Jones, *Conversion* [1959]
John 15:1-8; 2 Cor. 4:1,2; 5:11,12; Tit. 1:15,16;
Jas. 1:8,22-27;4:8; 1 John 1:10

436 New birth

Here he tells us that the new birth is first of all "not of blood." You don't get it through the blood stream, through heredity. Your parents can give you much, but they cannot give you this. Being born in a Christian home does not make you a Christian.

E. Stanley Jones, *Conversion* [1959]
John 3:5,6

437 The character of the Redeemer

Some have said that the power of a Redeemer would depend upon two things: first, upon the richness of the self that was given;

and second, upon the depths of the giving. Friend and foe alike are agreed on the question of the character of Jesus Christ. . . . Whatever our creed, we stand with admiration before the sublime character of Jesus. Character is supreme in life, and hence Jesus stood supreme in the supreme thing—so supreme that, when we think of the ideal, we do not add virtue to virtue, but think of Jesus Christ, so that the standard of human life is no longer a code, but a character.

E. Stanley Jones, *Now and Then*
Isa. 52:13-53:12

Jones, Rufus Matthew [1863-1948]

438 He is here

The reason why we can hope to find God is that He is here, engaged all the time in finding us. Every pulse of love is a tendril that draws us in His direction. Every verification of truth links the finite mind up into a Foundational Mind that undergirds us. Every deed of good will points toward a consummate Goodness which fulfills all our tiny adventures in faith. We can find Him because in Him we live and move and have our being.

Rufus Jones, *Pathways to the Reality of God* [1931]
Acts 17:28; Heb. 7:25

Jud, Gerald J. [b.1919]

439 Community experienced in the heart

The church is unique in that it is so able to cut across age boundaries and social-status boundaries. When one loves the Lord Jesus Christ and sincerely seeks to follow Him, then one quite by surprise comes upon a community that he did not know existed, a community that is experienced within the heart; and when this community is found, nothing is ever quite the same again.

> Gerald J. Jud, "Ministry in Colonies & Retreats," in *Spiritual Renewal through Personal Groups* [1957]
> *Acts 10:34,35; Gal. 3:28,29*

Jukes, Andrew John [1815-1901]

440 Bondage and darkness

The fall was simply this, that some creature—that is, something which is not God—took His place with man; and man, trusting the creature more than God, walked in its light—or darkness—rather than in fellowship with God. Righteousness comes back when man by faith is brought to walk with God again, and to give Him His true place by acting or being acted upon in all things according to His will. Anything, therefore, not of faith is sin. And all such sin is bondage. Self-will is bondage, for self-will or independence of God means dependence on a creature; and we cannot be dependent on a creature, be it what it may, without (more or less) becoming subject to it. What has not been given up for money, or for some creature's love? But who has ever thus served the creature more than the Creator without waking at last to feel he is a bondman? I say nothing of the worse bondage which comes from our self-will, in the indulgence of our own thoughts, or passions, or affections. Even the very energies of faith, while, as yet unchastened, it acts from self, . . . may only bring forth more bondage. . . . Who but God can set men free? And He sets them free as they walk with Him. All independence of Him is darkness.

> Andrew Jukes
> *Gal. 4:3-9*

441 The untroubled are in danger

I can tell you for an eternal truth that troubled souls are always safe. It is the untroubled that are in danger. Trouble in itself is always a claim on love, and God is love. He must deny Himself if He does not come to help the helpless. It is the prisoners, and the blind, and the leper, and the possessed, and the hungry, and the tempest-tossed, who are His special care. Therefore if you are lost and sick and bound, you are just in the place where He can meet you. Blessed are the mourners. They shall be comforted.

Andrew Jukes
Matt. 5:4; 9:11,12

Juliana of Norwich [c.1342-1417]

442 The elements of prayer

Its ground: God, by whose goodness it springeth in us.
Its use: to turn our will to His will.
Its end: to be made one with Him and like to Him in all things.

Juliana of Norwich
Ps. 130:1-6; Rom. 8:26

443 Not overcome

He said not Thou shalt not be tempested, thou shalt not be tra-vailed, thou shalt not be distressed; but He said, Thou shalt not be overcome.

Juliana of Norwich
John 16:33; Rom. 12:21; 2 Cor. 4:8-10; Jas. 1:12; 1 John 4:4

444 Jesus, the highest and the lowest

And what might this noble Lord do of more worship and joy to me than to show me (that am so simple) this marvelous homeliness [i.e., naturalness and simplicity]? Thus it fareth with our Lord Jesus and with us. For truly it is the most joy that may be that He that is highest and mightiest, noblest and worthiest, is lowest and meekest, homeli-est and most courteous: and truly this marvelous joy shall be shown us all when we see Him.

Juliana of Norwich, *Revelations of Divine Love*
Matt. 20:25-28

The Authentic **Book of Christian Quotations**

445 From without beginning

I saw full surely in this and in all, that ere God made us he loved us; which love never slackened, nor ever shall be. And in this love he hath done all his works; and in this love he hath made all things profitable to us; and in this love our life is everlasting. In our making we had beginning; but the love wherein he made us was in him from without beginning; in which love we have our beginning. And all this shall we see in God, without end.

Juliana of Norwich, *Revelations of Divine Love*
Ps. 139:13,14

Kates, Frederick Ward [b.1920]

446 Enough knowledge

The Christian clearly understands that Jesus does not reveal all that is signified by the word "God," but only as much as could be revealed through a perfect human personality living in absolute obedience to God's will. The knowledge of God that men have by virtue of Jesus' revelation is quite enough for men to live by in this life, and to live gloriously and thankfully by, Christians maintain—the knowledge that God the Creator, the Almighty and Eternal, the Lord of history, is man's Heavenly Father, and that love might well be, and indeed is, the ultimate meaning of human existence.

Frederick Ward Kates,
A Moment Between Two Eternities [1965]
Heb. 4:15

447 The reason why

"Why was I born?" "Why am I here?" Theology answers, "You are here to grow, to grow up in every way unto the full stature of a man newborn in Christ."

Frederick Ward Kates,
A Moment Between Two Eternities [1965]
Eph. 4:11-13

Keble, John [1792-1866]

448 If on our daily course

If, on our daily course, our mind
Be set to hallow all we find,
New treasures still, of countless price,
God will provide for sacrifice.

The trivial round, the common task
Will furnish all we ought to ask;
Room to deny ourselves, a road
To bring us daily nearer God.

John Keble
2 Cor. 4:7

449 The deaf may hear the Savior's voice

The deaf may hear the Savior's voice,
The fettered tongue its chains may break;
But the deaf heart, the dumb by choice,
The laggard soul that will not wake,
The guilt that scorns to be forgiven—
These baffle e'en the spells of heaven.

John Keble, *The Christian Year* [1827]
Matt. 11:15

Kelly, Thomas R. [1893-1941]

450 The one true poverty

The deepest need of men is not food and clothing and shelter, important as they are. It is God. We have mistaken the nature of poverty, and thought it was economic poverty. No, it is poverty of soul, deprivation of God's recreating, loving peace. Peer into poverty and see if we are really getting down to the deepest needs, in our economic salvation schemes. These are important. But they lie farther along the road, secondary steps toward world reconstruction. The primary step is a holy life, transformed and radiant in the glory of God.

Thomas R. Kelly, *A Testament of Devotion* [1941]
Hag. 2:8; Matt. 6:19-21; Col. 2:1-3

Kierkegaard, Søren [1813-1855]

451 Anxiety

To live thus—to cram today with eternity and not wait the next day—the Christian has learnt and continues to learn (for the Christian is always learning) from the Pattern. How did He manage to live without anxiety for the next day—He who from the first instant of His public life, when He stepped forward as a teacher, knew how His life would end, that the next day was His crucifixion; knew this while the people exultantly hailed Him as King (ah, bitter knowledge to have at precisely that moment!); knew, when they were crying, Hosanna!, at His entry into Jerusalem, that they would cry, "Crucify Him!" and that it was to this end that He made His entry. He who bore every day the prodigious weight of this superhuman knowledge—how did He manage to live without anxiety for the next day?

Søren Kierkegaard, *Christian Discourses* [1961]
Matt. 21:9; Mark 15:13,14; Luke 12:22; 21:34; 23:21-24

452 Grateful for God

To stand on one leg and prove God's existence is a very different thing from going on one's knees and thanking Him.

Søren Kierkegaard
Ps. 35:18; Eph. 5:19-21; 2 Pet. 1:16

453 Praying in Jesus' name

I cannot pray in the name of Jesus to have my own will; the name of Jesus is not a signature of no importance, but the decisive factor. The fact that the name of Jesus comes at the beginning does not make it a prayer in the name of Jesus; but this means to pray in such a manner that I dare name Jesus in it, that is to say, dare to think of Him, think His holy will together with whatever I am praying for.

Søren Kierkegaard
1 Cor. 1:2; Eph. 5:19,20; Phil. 2:9,10; Col. 3:17

454 Above human categories

If one could talk absolutely humanly about Christ, one would have to say that the words: "my God, my God, why hast thou forsaken me?" are impatient and untrue. They can only be true if God says them, and consequently also when the God-Man says them. And indeed since it is true, it is the very limit of suffering.

Søren Kierkegaard, *Journals*
Ps. 22:1; Matt. 27:46

455 Holding on to sin

Frightful this is in a sense, but it is true, and every one who has merely some little knowledge of the human heart can verify it: there is nothing to which a man holds so desperately as to his sin.

Søren Kierkegaard, *Three Discourses at
the Communion on Fridays* [1849]
Isa. 9:18; 57:20,21; Amos 5:12; John 3:19,20

Kilmer, (Alfred) Joyce [1886-1918]

456 Voiceless

Vain is the chiming of forgotten bells
That the wind sways above a ruined shrine.
Vainer his voice in whom no longer dwells

Hunger that craves immortal Bread and Wine.
Light songs we breathe, that perish with our breath,
Out of our lips that have not kissed the rod.
They shall not live who have not tasted death.
They only sing who are struck dumb by God.

Joyce Kilmer
Ps. 2:7-12; Matt. 11:4,5; Luke 1:28,59-64,67-79

Kingsley, Charles [1819-1875]

457 More than a Sunday religion

One good man, one man who does not put on his religion once a week with his Sunday coat, but wears it for his working dress, and lets the thought of God grow into him, and through and through him, till everything he says and does becomes religious, that man is worth a thousand sermons—he is a living Gospel—he comes in the spirit and power of Elias—he is the image of God. And men see his good works, and admire them in spite of themselves, and see that they are God-like, and that God's grace is no dream, but that the Holy Spirit is still among men, and that all nobleness and manliness is His gift, His stamp, His picture: and so they get a glimpse of God again in His saints and heroes, and glorify their Father who is in heaven.

Charles Kingsley
John 14:23: Col. 3:17; Tit. 2:9-12

458 The Great Physician

From Thee all skill and science flow,
    All pity, care and love,
All calm and courage, faith and hope;
    O pour them from above.
And part them, Lord, to each and all,
    As each and all shall need,
To rise like incense, each to Thee,
    In noble thought and deed.

And hasten, Lord, that perfect day
　　When pain and death shall cease,
And Thy just rule shall fill the earth
　　With health and light and peace.

Charles Kingsley
Matt. 9:11,12; Mark 6:34; Rev. 21:4

Kirk, David [b.1935]

459 The exclusive fraternity

When Jesus calls his disciples "brothers" and "friends," he is contradicting general Jewish usage and breaking through into a new concept of brotherhood which is not tribal, but open to any person.

David Kirk, *Quotations from Chairman Jesus* [1969]
Mark 3:31-35; John 15:13-15

460 The end of religion

The Way is not a religion: Christianity is the end of religion. "Religion" means here the division between sacred and secular concerns, other-worldliness, man's reaching toward God in a way which projects his own thoughts.

David Kirk, *Quotations from Chairman Jesus* [1969]
Matt. 23:2-33; Rom. 3:12,22; 11:36; 1 Cor. 3:16,17;
1 John 4:19; Heb. 11:6

461 Street confrontation

The entrance into Jerusalem [on Palm Sunday] has all the elements of the theatre of the absurd: the poor king; truth comes riding on a donkey; symbolic actions—even parading without a permit! Also, when Jesus "set his face to go to Jerusalem," what was involved was direct action, an open confrontation and public demonstration of the incompatibility of evil with the Kingdom of God.

David Kirk, *Quotations from Chairman Jesus* [1969]
Luke 9:51

Knight, G. H. (George Halley) [1835-1917]

462 Withdrawing to pray

It was no exceptional thing for Jesus to withdraw Himself "into the wilderness to pray." He was never for one moment of any day out of touch with God. He was speaking and listening to the Father all day long; and yet He, who was in such constant touch with God, felt the need, as well as the joy, of more prolonged and more quiet communion with Him . . . Most of the reasons that drive us to pray for strength and forgiveness could never have driven Him; and yet He needed prayer.

G. H. Knight, *In the Secret of His Presence* [1934]
Matt. 6:6; Luke 5:16

Kraemer, Hendrik [1888-1965]

463 What is the Church for?

The underlying questions are always: What is the Church? What is the Church for? If that is not kept in mind, the lay ministry, about which so much is being said at present, remains on the level of a many-sided activity in which the self-assertion of the laity threatens to be more evident than a new manifestation of the Church in modern society. The responsible participation of the laity in the discharge of the Church's divine calling is not primarily a matter of idealism and enthusiasm or organizational efficiency, but a new grasp and commitment to the meaning of God's redemptive purpose with mankind and with the world in the past, the present, and the future: a purpose which has its foundation and inexhaustible content in Christ.

Hendrik Kraemer, *A Theology of the Laity* [1958]
John 6:44,45; 1 Cor. 3:11; Eph. 3:8,9

Kurosaki, Kokichi [1886-1970]

464 Communion with Christ

To have faith is to rely upon Christ, the Person, with the whole heart. It is not the understanding of the mind, not the theological opinion, not creed, not organization, not ritual. It is the koinonia of the whole personality with God and Christ. . . . This experience of communion with Christ is itself the continual attitude of dependence on the Savior which we call faith.

Kokichi Kurosaki, *One Body in Christ* [1954]
John 14:23

465 The one true center of the church

Recently, some Christians have recognized the existing state of the church as sinful, or, at least, as faulty and mistaken. They are trying to save the Christians out of this labyrinth by reuniting the divided churches, by forming an alliance of churches, or by trying to form an ecumenical church. For all that, it seems very difficult to obtain the desired result, because all the present churches are still standing on the principles of the Reformation, unable to rid themselves of the sectarian spirit inherited from Catholicism. So the number of denominations and sects shows no sign of decreasing, and all efforts to unite the churches seem likely to end only in the formation of yet other sects and denominations. Yet the center of Christianity is neither institution nor organization. Nor is it even the Bible itself, as the Reformers made it, for the Ekklesia existed before the formation of the New Testament canon. Christians were in fellowship with God and one another, centering their faith in Christ, long before there was any accepted New Testament. There is only one center of Christianity—spiritual fellowship with God through Jesus Christ.

Kokichi Kurosaki, *One Body in Christ* [1954]
Matt. 18:20; John 14:23; 17:20-23; Rom. 12:5; 15:5-7

466 Different views together under God's will

Paul, using the examples of differing opinions about food and days among the believers in Rome, teaches that Christians should not despise or judge others. He does not advise them to find a happy medium between the contending opinions or to average the two extremes in a compromise. On the contrary, he admonished them that "every one be fully convinced in his own mind" (Rom. 14:5), because God is able to make both stand, as both of them are serving the Lord in obedience to their individual convictions of His will. . . . Each of us has to find personally what is the will of God for his own life, and let all others meet their responsibility to do the same. . . . For God, by giving different commands to many, and putting them together according to His plan, shall accomplish ultimately His complete will.

Kokichi Kurosaki, *One Body in Christ* [1954]

Rom. 14

467 Committed, but to what?

The primary cause of the [denominational] divisions is the institutionalism and organizationalism of the churches, which, without vivifying the life of the believers in them, smothers or drives it out of the ekklesia, and makes [the churches] merely dead institutions. Christians who really have life in Christ cannot exist within such a corpse and will at last have to come out of it. But in almost all cases, those who have come out of dead institutions want to have in their place another institution or other rituals and ceremonies, only repeating the same error. Instead of turning to Christ Himself as their center, they again seek to find fellowship and spiritual security on the very same basis that failed, not realizing that it is the institution that is killing, instead of producing, life in Christ.

Even the Bible itself is interpreted and understood in various ways, and so always becomes the center of sectarianism. Just in the same way, dogmas and creeds cannot bring Christian unity, because human minds are not so uniformly created that they can unite in a single dogma or creed. Even our understanding of Christ Himself cannot be the basis of unity, because He is too big to be understood by any one person or group, and therefore our limited understandings do not always coincide. One emphasizes this point about Christ, another that; and this again becomes the cause of divisions. If we will only take our fellowship with Christ as the center of Christian faith, all Christians will realize their oneness. . . . All our fellowship, however varied, is with the same Lord, and the same Savior is our one Head.

Kokichi Kurosaki, *One Body in Christ* [1954]
John 17:22,23; 2 Cor. 3:5,6

Lake, Kirsopp [1872-1946]

468 Faith despite the price

Faith is not belief in spite of evidence, but life in scorn of consequences—a courageous trust in the great purpose of all things, and pressing forward to finish the work which is in sight, whatever the price may be.

> Kirsopp Lake, *Landmarks in the History
> of Early Christianity* [1920]
> *Rom. 1:16,17; 4:19,20; 8:28; 2 Tim. 1:12*

Lamb, Charles [1775-1834]

469 The many forms of grace

I am disposed to say grace upon twenty other occasions in the course of the day besides my dinner. I want a form for setting out upon a pleasant walk, for a moonlight ramble, for a friendly meeting or a solved problem. Why have we none for books, those spiritual repasts—a grace before Milton, a devotional exercise proper to be said before reading [Spenser]?

> Charles Lamb

Landon, Melville D.

470 Out of business?

I hate the devil and I would kill him, but I see there are several clergymen present, and they have their families to support.

> Melville D. Landon

Lang, G. H. (George Henry) [1874-1958]

471 What is in ruins?

What is in ruins? The invisible church, composed of all Spirit-baptized persons, is indefectible, it cannot be ruined; against it "the gates of Hades shall not prevail." The local assembly may indeed by sadly ruined; but it can be restored, as, by the grace of God, has been seen times without number—at Corinth, for example. The only other institution in question is that agglomeration of sects that is called "Christendom." But that is unrecognized by the New Testament—it is not of God at all: and that it is "in ruins" is no matter for our regret.

G. H. Lang
Matt. 16:16-18

Latimer, Hugh [c.1485-1555]

472 The purpose of suffering

It may fortune thou wilt say, "I am content to do the best for my neighbor that I can, saving myself harmless." I promise thee, Christ will not hear their excuse; for He himself suffered harm for our sakes, and for our salvation was put to extreme death. I wis, if it had pleased Him, He might have saved us and never felt pain; but in suffering pains and death He did give us example, and teach us how we should do one for another, as He did for us all; for, as He saith himself, "he that will be mine, let him deny himself, and follow me, in bearing my cross and suffering my pains." Wherefore we must needs suffer pain with Christ to do our neighbor good, as well with the body and all his members, as with heart and mind.

Hugh Latimer
Matt. 16:24; 1 Pet. 2:21

Laubach, Frank C. [1884-1970]

473 Listening to God

The trouble with nearly everybody who prays is that he says "Amen" and runs away before God has a chance to reply. Listening to God is far more important than giving Him your ideas.

Frank Laubach
Ps. 85:8

474 Compassion was born at Christmas

When compassion for the common man was born on Christmas Day, with it was born new hope among the multitudes. They feel a great, ever-rising determination to lift themselves and their children our of hunger and disease and misery, up to a higher level. Jesus started a fire upon the earth, and it is burning hot today, the fire of a new hope in the hearts of the hungry multitudes.

Frank C. Laubach, *The World is Learning Compassion* [1958]
Luke 1:46-55; Rom. 15:4

Law, William [1686-1761]

475 Zeal for souls

Let a clergyman but intend to please God in all his actions, as the happiest and best thing in the world, and then he will know that there is nothing noble in a clergyman but a burning zeal for the salvation of souls; nor anything poorer in his profession [than] idleness and a worldly spirit.

William Law
Matt. 12:35-37; Jas. 5:19,20

476 Seeking God in everything

He that seeks God in everything is sure to find God in everything. When we thus live wholly unto God, God is wholly ours and we are then happy in all the happiness of God; for by uniting with Him in heart, and will, and spirit, we are united to all that He is and has in Himself. This is the purity and perfection of life that we pray for in the Lord's Prayer, that God's kingdom may come and His will be done in us, as it is in Heaven. And this we may be sure is not only necessary, but attainable by us, or our Savior would not have made it a part of our daily prayer.

William Law
Matt. 6:10; Luke 6:21

477 Can we pray about them?

Perhaps there cannot be a better way of judging of what manner of spirit we are of, than to see whether the actions of our life are such as we may safely commend them to God in our prayers.

William Law
Job 35:12,13; Ps. 66:18; Prov. 15:8;
Zech. 7:12,13; Jas. 1:6,7; 4:3

478 The greatest secret

He who has learned to pray has learned the greatest secret of a holy and happy life.

William Law
Ps. 5:3; Mark 1:35; Phil. 4:6

479 Life devoted to God

A life devoted unto God, looking wholly unto Him in all our actions, and doing all things suitably to His glory, is so far from being dull and uncomfortable, that it creates new comforts in everything that we do.

William Law, *A Serious Call to a Devout and Holy Life* [1728]
Ps. 23:5

480 The leverage of self-denial

If you were to rise early every morning, as an instance of self-denial, as a method of renouncing indulgence, as a means of redeeming your time and of fitting your spirit for prayer, you would find mighty advantages from it. This method, though it seem such a small circumstance of life, would in all probability be a means [toward] great piety. It would keep it constantly in your head that softness and idleness were to be avoided and that self-denial was a part of Christianity. . . . It would teach you to exercise power over yourself, and make you able by degrees to renounce other pleasures and tempers that war against the soul.

William Law, *A Serious Call to a Devout and Holy Life* [1728]
Matt. 16:24; Tit. 2:11-14

481 All places are holy

As a good Christian should consider every place as holy, because God is there, so he should look upon every part of his life as a matter of holiness, because it is offered unto God. The profession of a clergyman is a holy profession, because it is a ministration in holy things, an attendance at the alter. But worldly business is to be made holy unto the Lord, by being done as a service unto Him, and in conformity to His Divine will.

William Law, *A Serious Call to a Devout and Holy Life* [1728]
Ex. 3:1,2; Phil. 2:14,15; Col. 3:3

482 Avoiding perfection

It is as reasonable to suppose it the desire of all Christians to arrive at Christian perfection as to suppose that all sick men desire to be restored to perfect health; yet experience shows us, that nothing wants more to be pressed, repeated, and forced upon our minds, than the plainest rules of Christianity.

William Law, *A Serious Call to a Devout and Holy Life* [1728]
Gen. 17:1; Matt. 5:48

483 Not wanting piety

If you here stop, and ask yourselves, why you are not as pious as the primitive Christians were, your own heart will tell you, that it is neither through ignorance nor through inability, but purely because you never thoroughly intended it.

William Law, *A Serious Call to a Devout and Holy Life* [1728]
Rom. 7:14-17

484 Those that least of all deserve it

The merit of persons is to be no rule of our charity; but we are to do acts of kindness to those that least of all deserve it.

William Law, *A Serious Call to a Devout and Holy Life* [1728]
Matt. 5:3; 1 John 3:17,18

485 Living unto God

If we are to live unto God at any time, or in any place, we are to live unto Him at all times, and in all places. If we are to use anything as the gift of God, we are to use everything as His gift.

William Law, *A Serious Call to a Devout and Holy Life* [1728]
Gal. 2:19,20

486 Admirers of piety

Persons that are well affected to religion, that receive instructions of piety with pleasure and satisfaction, often wonder how it comes to pass that they make no greater progress in that religion which they so much admire.

Now the reason of it is this: it is because religion lives only in their head, but something else has possession of their heart; and therefore they continue from year to year mere admirers and praisers of piety, without ever coming up to the reality and perfection of its precepts.

William Law, *A Serious Call to a Devout and Holy Life* [1728]
Eze. 36:26; Hos. 13:6; Acts 28:26,27; Rom. 1:21

487 Devotion

Devotion signifies a life given, or devoted, to God.

He therefore is the devout man, who lives no longer to his own will, or the way and spirit of the world, but to the sole will of God, who considers God in everything, who serves God in everything, who makes all the parts of his common life parts of piety, by doing everything in the name of God, and under such rules as are conformable to His glory.

William Law, *A Serious Call to a Devout and Holy Life* [1728]
1 Thess. 5:15-23

488 Love one another

A frequent intercession with God, earnestly beseeching Him to forgive the sins of all mankind, to bless them with His providence, enlighten them with His Spirit, and bring them to everlasting happiness, is the divinest exercise that the heart of man can be engaged in.

Be daily, therefore, on your knees, in a solemn deliberate performance of this devotion, praying for others in such forms, with such length, importunity, and earnestness, as you use for yourself; and you will find all little, ill-natured passions die away, your heart grow great and generous, delighting in the common happiness of others, as you used only to delight in your own. . . .

It was this holy intercession that raised Christians to such a state of mutual love, as far exceeded all that had been praised and admired in human friendship. And when the same spirit of intercession is again in the world, when Christianity has the same power over the hearts of people that it then had, this holy friendship will be again in fashion, and Christians will be again the wonder of the world, for that exceeding love which they bear to one another.

William Law, *A Serious Call to a Devout and Holy Life* [1728]
John 13:34,35; II Cor. 1:11; Phlmn. 1:4-6

489 Natural delight in religion

When religion is in the hands of the mere natural man, he is always the worse for it; it adds a bad heat to his own dark fire and helps to inflame his four elements of selfishness, envy, pride, and wrath.

And hence it is that worse passions, or a worse degree of them are to be found in persons of great religious zeal than in others that made no pretenses to it. History also furnishes us with instances of persons of great piety and devotion who have fallen into great delusions and deceived both themselves and others. The occasion of their fall was this: . . . They considered their whole nature as the subject of religion and divine graces; and therefore their religion was according to the workings of their whole nature, and the old man was as busy and as much delighted in it as the new.

William Law, *Christian Regeneration* [1739]
Eph. 4:17-27

490 Repentance

Repentance is but a kind of table-talk, till we see so much of the deformity of our inward nature as to be in some degree frightened and terrified at the sight of it. . . . A plausible form of an outward life, that has only learned rules and modes of religion by use and custom, often keeps the soul for some time at ease, though all its inward root and ground of sin has never been shaken or molested, though it has never tasted of the bitter waters of repentance and has only known the want of a Savior by hearsay. But things cannot pass thus: sooner or later repentance must have a broken and a contrite heart; we must with our blessed Lord go over the brook Cedron, and with Him sweat great drops of sorrow before He can say for us, as He said for Himself: "It is finished."

William Law, *Christian Regeneration* [1739]
Ps. 51:17; Luke 22:44; John 18:1; 19:30; Rev. 3:19

491 The fallen spirit within

Though the light and comfort of the outward world keeps even the worst men from any constant strong sensibility of that wrathful, fiery, dark and self-tormenting nature that is the very essence of every fallen unregenerate soul, yet every man in the world has more or less frequent and strong intimations given him that so it is with him in the inmost ground of his soul. How many inventions are some people forced to have recourse to in order to keep off a certain inward uneasiness, which they are afraid of and know not whence it comes? Alas, it is because there is a fallen spirit, a dark, aching fire, within them, which has never had its proper relief and is trying to discover itself and calling out for help at every cessation of worldly joy.

William Law, Christian Regeneration [1739]
Isa. 5:11,12; Gal. 5:19-21; 1 Tim. 5:6

492 It is finished

The progress of these terrors is plainly shown us in our Lord's agony in the garden, when the reality of this eternal death so broke in upon Him, so awakened and stirred itself in Him, as to force great drops of blood to sweat from His body. . . . His agony was His entrance into the last, eternal terrors of the lost soul, into the real horrors of that dreadful, eternal death which man unredeemed must have died into when he left this world. We are therefore not to consider our Lord's death upon the Cross as only the death of that mortal body which was nailed to it, but we are to look upon Him with wounded hearts, as being fixed and fastened in the state of that twofold death, which was due to the fallen nature, out of which He could not come till He could say, "It is finished; Father, into Thy hands I commend my spirit."

William Law, An Appeal to All that Doubt [1740]
Luke 22:41-44; John 19:30

493 The condition for freedom

This therefore is a certain truth, that hell and death, curse and misery, can never cease or be removed from the creation till the will of the creature is again as it came from God and is only a Spirit of Love that wills nothing but goodness. All the whole fallen creation, stand it never so long, must groan and travail in pain, till every contrariety to the divine will is entirely taken from every creature.

Which is only saying that all the powers and properties of nature are a misery to themselves, can only work in disquiet and wrath, till the birth of the Son of God brings them under the dominion and power of the Spirit of Love.

William Law, The Spirit of Love [1752-4]
Ps. 63:1,2; Rom. 8:22,23

494 The Spirit of Love in you

Now this is the ground and original of the Spirit of Love in the creature; it is and must be a will to all goodness; and you have not the Spirit of Love in you till you have this will to all goodness at all times and on all occasions. You may indeed do many works of love and delight in them, especially at such times as they are not inconvenient to your state or temper or occurrences in life. But the Spirit of Love is not in you till it is the spirit of your life, till you live freely, willingly, and universally according to it.

William Law, *The Spirit of Love* [1752-4]
2 Tim. 1:7

495 The second Adam

The Christ of God was not then first crucified when the Jews brought Him to the Cross; but Adam and Eve were His first real murderers; for the death which happened to them in the day when they did eat of the earthly tree was the death of the Christ of God or the divine life in their souls. For Christ had never come into the world as a second Adam to redeem it, had He not been originally the life and perfection and glory of the first Adam.

William Law, *The Spirit of Love* [1752-4]
Rom. 5:14; 1 Cor. 15:22,45

496 The relentless love of God

The pure, mere love of God is that alone from which sinners are justly to expect that no sin will pass unpunished, but that His love will visit them with every calamity and distress that can help to break and purify the bestial heart of man and awaken in him true repentance and conversion to God. It is love alone in the holy Deity that will allow no peace to the wicked, nor ever cease its judgments till every sinner is forced to confess that it is good for him that he has been in trouble, and thankfully own that not the wrath but the love of God has plucked out that right eye, cut off that right band, which he ought to have done but would not do for himself and his own salvation.

William Law, *The Spirit of Love* [1749]
Job 5:17; Matt. 5:29,30

497 The dwelling of God's Spirit

If it be the earnest desire, and longing of your heart, to be merciful as he is merciful; to be full of his unwearied patience, to dwell in his unalterable meekness; if you long to be like him in universal, impartial love; if you desire to communicate every good, to every creature that you are able; if you love and practice everything that is good, righteous, and lovely, for its own sake, because it is good, righteous, and lovely; and resist no evil, but with goodness; then you have the utmost certainty, that the Spirit of God lives, dwells, and governs in you.

William Law, *The Spirit of Prayer* [1749]
Matt. 5:7; Luke 6:36; Rom. 12:21; Eph. 4:1-3;
1 Tim. 6:11,12; Jas. 1:4

498 Creation's law and order

The one supreme, unchangeable rule of love, which is a law to all intelligent beings of all worlds, and will be a law to all eternity, is this, viz., that God alone is to be loved for himself, and all other beings only in him, and for him. Whatever intelligent creature lives not under this rule of love, is so far fallen from the order of his creation, and is, till he returns to this eternal law of love, an apostate from God, and incapable of the kingdom of heaven.

Now if God alone is to be loved for himself, then no creature is to be loved for itself; and so all self-love in every creature is absolutely condemned.

And if all created beings are only to be loved in and for God, then my neighbor is to be loved, as I love myself, and I am only to love myself, as I love my neighbor, or any other created being, that is only in and for God.

William Law, *The Spirit of Prayer* [1749]
Matt. 22:39

499 Seeking the lost

[Christ] is the breathing forth of the heart, life, and Spirit of God, into all the dead race of Adam. He is the seeker, the finder, the restorer, of all that was lost and dead to the life of God. He is the love, that, from Cain to the end of time, prays for all its murderers; the love that willingly suffers and dies among thieves, that thieves may have a life with him in paradise; the love that visits publicans, harlots, and sinners, and wants and seeks to forgive, where most is to be forgiven.

William Law, *The Spirit of Prayer* [1749]
Matt. 18:11; Luke 7:37-48

Lawrence, Brother (Nicholas Herman) [c.1605-1691]

500 Continuing with God

[He said] that it was a great delusion to think that the times of prayer ought to differ from other times; that we are as strictly obliged to adhere to God by action in the time of action as by prayer in the season of prayer. That his view of prayer was nothing else but a sense of the Presence of God, his soul being at that time insensible to everything but Divine Love; and that when the appointed times of prayer were past, he found no difference, because he still continued with God, praising and blessing Him with all his might, so that he passed his life in continual joy; yet hoped that God would give him somewhat to suffer when he should have grown stronger.

Brother Lawrence
1 Thess. 5:17

501 Good when He gives

Good when He gives, supremely good;
Nor less when He denies:
Afflictions, from His sovereign hand,
Are blessings in disguise.

Brother Lawrence, *The Practice of the Presence of God*
Heb. 12:10,11

502 He is near

Lift up your heart to Him, sometimes even at your meals, and when you are in company; the least little remembrance will always be acceptable to Him. You need not cry very loud; he is nearer to us than we are aware of.

> Brother Lawrence, *The Practice of the Presence of God*
> *Ps. 25:1,2*

503 Work for the sake of love

We ought not to be weary of doing little things for the love of God, who regards not the greatness of the work, but the love with which it is performed.

> Brother Lawrence, *The Practice of the Presence of God*
> *Eccl. 11:1; 1 Cor. 13:4-7*

Leighton, Robert, Abp. [1611-1684]

504 Love will stammer

What are our lame praises in comparison with His love? Nothing, and less than nothing; but love will stammer rather than be dumb.

> Robert Leighton
> *Isa. 32:4*

Lewis, Clive Staples [1898-1963]

505 The true language of Christian doctrine

The [Christian] "doctrines" are translations into our concepts and ideas of that which God has already expressed in language more adequate, namely the actual incarnation, crucifixion, and resurrection.

> C. S. Lewis [1931]
> *1 Cor. 15:3; 1 Tim.3:15,16*

506 The badness of sadness

My own idea, for what it is worth, is that all sadness which is not now either arising from the repentance of a concrete sin and hastening towards concrete amendment or restitution, or else arising from pity and hastening towards active assistance, is simply bad.

C. S. Lewis
Eccl. 11:10; Isa. 35:10; 2 Cor. 7:10,11

507 On George MacDonald

I will attempt no historical or theological classification of [George] MacDonald's thought, partly because I have not the learning to do so, still more because I am no great friend to such pigeon-holing. One very effective way of silencing the voice of conscience is to impound in an Ism the teacher through whom it speaks; the trumpet no longer seriously disturbs our rest when we have murmured 'Thomist,' 'Barthian,' or 'Existentialist.' And in MacDonald it is always the voice of conscience that speaks. He addresses the will: the demand for obedience, for "something to be neither more nor less nor other than done" is incessant. Yet in that very voice of conscience every other faculty somehow speaks as well—intellect and imagination and humor and fancy and all the affections; and no man in modern times was perhaps more aware of the distinction between Law and Gospel, the inevitable failure of mere morality.

C. S. Lewis, preface to George MacDonald, an Anthology
Gal. 3:11,12

508 Pride is the obstacle

Don't imagine that if you meet a really humble man he will be what most people call "humble" nowadays: he won't be a sort of greasy, smarmy person, who's always telling you that, of course, he's nobody. Probably all you'll think about him is that he seemed a cheerful, intelligent chap who took a real interest in what you said to him. If you do dislike him, it will be because you feel a bit envious of anyone who seems to enjoy life so easily. He won't be thinking about himself at all. There I must stop. If anyone would like to acquire humility, I can, I think, tell him the first step. The first step is to realize that one is proud. And a biggish step, too. At least, nothing whatever can be done before it. If you think you're not conceited, it means you are very conceited indeed.

C. S. Lewis, Christian Behavior [1943]
Prov. 13:10; Matt. 5:6; Mark 12:38-40; Luke 1:51-53

509 Pride, the anti-God state of mind

The vice I am talking about is Pride or Self-Conceit: and the virtue opposite to it, in Christian morals, is called Humility. You may remember, when I was talking about sexual morality, I warned you that the center of Christian morals did not lie there. Well, now we have come to the center. According to Christian teachers, the essential vice, the utmost evil, is Pride. Unchastity, greed, drunkenness, and all that, are mere flea-bites in comparison: it was through Pride that the devil became the devil: Pride leads to every other vice: it is the complete anti-God state of mind.

C. S. Lewis, *The Problem of Pain* [1944]
Prov. 16:18; Luke 11:39-52; 1 Cor. 3:18

510 Just the pure in heart

It is safe to tell the pure in heart that they shall see God, for only the pure in heart want to.

C. S. Lewis, *The Problem of Pain* [1944]
Matt. 5:8

511 The light of Christ

I believe in Christianity as I believe that the Sun has risen: not only because I see it, but because by it I see everything else.

C. S. Lewis, *The Weight of Glory* [1949]
John 8:12; 2 Cor. 4:6

512 The price of mercy

To excuse what can really produce good excuses is not Christian charity; it is only fairness. To be a Christian means to forgive the inexcusable, because God has forgiven the inexcusable in you. This is hard. It is perhaps not so hard to forgive a single injury. But to forgive the incessant provocations of daily life—to keep on forgiving the bossy mother-in-law, the bullying husband, the nagging wife, the selfish daughter, the deceitful son—how can we do it? Only, I think, by remembering where we stand, by meaning our words when we say in our prayers each night, "Forgive us our trespasses as we forgive those who trespass against us." We are offered forgiveness on no other terms. To refuse it means to refuse God's mercy for ourselves. There is no hint of exceptions and God means what He says.

C. S. Lewis, *The Weight of Glory* [1949]
Hos. 6:6; Matt. 6:12,14,15; 18:21-35; Mark 5:25,26; Luke 6:37;
11:4; 17:3,4

513 Shadows of glory

The faint, far-off results of those energies which God's creative rapture implanted in matter when He made the worlds are what we now call physical pleasures; and even thus filtered, they are too much for our present management. What would it be to taste at the fountain-head that stream of which even these lower reaches prove so intoxicating? Yet that, I believe, is what lies before us. As St. Augustine said, the rapture of the saved soul will "flow over" into the glorified body. In the light of our present specialized and depraved appetites, we cannot imagine this [torrent of pleasure], and I warn everyone most seriously not to try. But it must be mentioned, to drive out thoughts even more misleading—thoughts that what is saved is a mere ghost, or that the risen body lives in numb insensibility. The body is made for the Lord, and these dismal fancies are wide of the mark.

C. S. Lewis, *The Weight of Glory* [1949]
Rev. 22:1-5

514 Yearnings as evidence

A man's physical hunger does not prove that that man will get any bread; he may die of starvation on a raft in the Atlantic. But surely a man's hunger does prove that he comes of a race which repairs its body by eating, and inhabits a world where eatable substances exist. In the same way, though I do not believe (I wish I did) that my desire for Paradise proves that I shall enjoy it, I think it a pretty good indication that such a thing exists and that some men will. A man may love a women and not win her; but it would be very odd if the phenomenon called "falling in love" occurred in a sexless world.

C. S. Lewis, *The Weight of Glory* [1949]
Ps. 42:1-4; Matt. 5:6

515 A pagan heart

I have often, on my knees, been shocked to find what sort of thoughts I have, for a moment, been addressing to God; what infantile placations I was really offering, what claims I have really made, even what absurd adjustments or compromises I was, half-consciously, proposing. There is a Pagan, savage heart in me somewhere. For unfortunately the folly and idiot-cunning of Paganism seem to have far more power of surviving than its innocent or even beautiful elements. It is easy, once you have power, to silence the pipes, still the dances, disfigure the statues, and forget the stories; but not easy to kill the savage, the greedy, frightened creature now cringing, now blustering in one's soul.

C. S. Lewis, *Reflections on the Psalms* [1958]
Judg. 10:15; Isa. 6:5; Ps. 40:12; 69:5

516 Success in prayer

Even if all the things that people prayed for happened, which they do not, this would not prove what Christians mean by the efficacy of prayer. For prayer is request. The essence of request, as distinct from compulsion, is that it may or may not be granted. And if an infinitely wise Being listens to the requests of finite and foolish creatures, of course He will sometimes grant and sometimes refuse them. Invariable "success" in prayer would not prove the Christian doctrine at all. It would prove something more like magic—a power in certain human beings to control, or compel, the course of nature.

C. S. Lewis, "The Efficacy of Prayer,"
in *The World's Last Night: And Other Essays* [1960]
Lev. 19:31; 2 Cor. 12:8,9

517 Answered prayers

Meanwhile, little people like you and me, if our prayers are sometimes granted, beyond all hope and probability, had better not draw hasty conclusions to our own advantage. If we were stronger, we might be less tenderly treated. If we were braver, we might be sent, with far less help, to defend far more desperate posts in the great battle.

C. S. Lewis, "The Efficacy of Prayer,"
in *The World's Last Night: And Other Essays* [1960]
Matt. 10:16; Eph. 6:10-18

518 On religion

The word religion is extremely rare in the New Testament and the writings of mystics. The reason is simple. Those attitudes and practices to which we give the collective name of religion are themselves concerned with religion hardly at all. To be religious is to have one's attention fixed on God and on one's neighbor in relation to God. Therefore, almost by definition, a religious man, or a man when he is being religious, is not thinking about religion; he hasn't the time. Religion is what we (or he himself at a later moment) call his activity from outside.

C. S. Lewis, "Lilies that Fester,"
in *The World's Last Night: And Other Essays* [1960]
Matt. 22:36-40

Lichtenberg, G. C. [1742-1799]

519 Divine service

The words "divine service" should be reassigned and no longer used for attending church, but only for good deeds.

G. C. Lichtenberg, *Aphorisms*
Luke 22:25-27

Liguori, Alphonsus [1696-1787]

520 Thanks for what we have received

Who is there that ever receives a gift and tries to make bargains about it? Let us, then, return thanks for what He has bestowed on us.

Who can tell whether, if we had had a larger share of ability or stronger health, we should not have possessed them to our destruction.

Alphonsus Liguori
1 Thess. 5:18

Lindskoog, Kathryn Ann [b.1934]

521 The persistent vision

There is much that is bad and meaningless in the universe, and the universe contains men who know that much is bad and meaningless. The Christian answer is that this is a good world gone wrong, but with a memory of what it should have been.

Kathryn Lindskoog
Gen. 1:31; 3:17-19

Littell, Franklin H. (Hamlin) [b.1917]

522 Success and surrender

The period which marked the enormous statistical success of the revival churches was also the period which saw membership standards decline almost to the vanishing point. Today the [various denominations] don't even have enough authority to keep their members out of mob violence, let alone hold them to difficult standards of theological or ethical or moral excellence.

Franklin H. Littell
Matt. 5:19

523 The Servant People

The Church, rightly conceived, is the whole covenant people called to serve in the world. The clergy are also part of the laity, and their true function is to help equip the laity to be the Servant People.

If they turn aside to rule and to secure their own status, they have betrayed the calling of the special ministry.

Franklin H. Littell
John 13:14,15

Lloyd, Roger (Bradshaigh) [b.1901]

524 The Gospel in plain language

At no point does the Gospel encourage us to believe that every man will hearken to it, charm we never so wisely. The prophets, for all their passionate sincerity, for all their courageous simplifyings of the Gospel, will meet many deaf adders who stop their ears. We must reckon with this certain fact, and refuse to be daunted by it. But also there comes a point where accommodation can go no further. It is the Gospel we have to present, however we do it. We cannot hope to do it unless we walk humbly with the modern man, as well as with God, unless we are much more eager to learn from him and about him, than to instruct him. God help us, it is all very difficult. But was there ever a task better worth trying to do, or one in which, whether we fail or succeed, we more surely find our freedom?

Roger Lloyd, The Ferment in the Church [1964]
Matt. 11:15-17; John 6:63

Loukes, Harold [1912-1980]

525 The unlimited invitation

The Church is not a tribe for the improvement in holiness of people who think it would be pleasant to be holy, a means to the integration of character for those who cannot bear their conflicts. It is a statement of the divine intention for humanity.

Harold Loukes
1 Cor. 3:16; Eph. 2:19-22

Lubbock, Sir John [1834-1913]

526 Goodness and pleasure

Many worthy people, and many good books, with no doubt the best intentions, . . . have represented a life of sin as a life of pleasure; they have pictured virtue as self-sacrifice, austerity as religion. Even in everyday life we meet with worthy people who seem to think that whatever is pleasant must be wrong, that the true spirit of religion is crabbed, sour, and gloomy; that the bright, sunny, radiant nature which surrounds us is an evil and not a blessing,—a temptation devised by the Spirit of Evil and not one of the greatest delights showered on us in such profusion by the Author of all Good.

> Sir John Lubbock, *The Use of Life* [1894]
> *Phil. 4:4*

Luccock, Halford E. [1885-1960]

527 Criticism of the church

Expressions of sharp and even violent criticism of religion and the church have been welcomed [in this collection], for they usually imply sincerity of thought. If caustic criticism of religious institutions and practices is irreligious, then Amos, Isaiah, and Jesus were very irreligious men. In fact, that is exactly what many of their contemporaries took them to be.

> Halford E. Luccock and Frances Brentano,
> *The Questing Spirit* [1947]
> *Amos 5:21-24*

528 The Gospel vs. good advice

The Christian message is not an exhortation—"try hard to be good." Good advice, but there is no saving gospel in that.

> Halford E. Luccock, *Marching Off the Map* [1952]
> *Rom. 9:31,32; Eph. 2:8,9; 2 Tim. 1:9; Tit. 3:4-7; Jas. 2:10*

529 The order of Christmas

Christmas turns things tail-end foremost. The day and the spirit of Christmas rearrange the world parade. As the world arranges it, usually there come first in importance—leading the parade with a big blare of a band—the Big Shots. Frequently they are also the Stuffed Shirts. That's the first of the parade. Then at the tail end, as of little importance, trudge the weary, the poor, the lame, the halt, and the blind. But in the Christmas spirit, the procession is turned around. Those at the tail end are put first in the arrangement of the Child of Christmas.

Halford E. Luccock, "Whoops! It's Christmas",
Abbott Christmas Book, [1959]
Matt. 19:30; 20:16; Mark 9:35-37; 10:31; Luke 13:30

530 Wrapped up in a Person

A scientist said, making a plea for exchange scholarships between nations, "The very best way to send an idea is to wrap it up in a person." That was what happened at Christmas. The idea of divine love was wrapped up in a Person.

Halford E. Luccock, "Whoops! It's Christmas",
Abbott Christmas Book, [1959]
1 John 4:8-10

Luther, Martin [1483-1546]

531 In the midst of enemies

The Kingdom is to be in the midst of your enemies. And he who will not suffer this does not want to be of the Kingdom of Christ; he wants to be among friends, to sit among roses and lilies, not with the bad people but the devout people. O you blasphemers and betrayers of Christ! If Christ had done what you are doing, who would ever have been spared?

Martin Luther
Ps. 23:5

532 In God's hands

I have held many things in my hands, and have lost them all; but whatever I have placed in God's hands, that I still possess.

Martin Luther
1 Pet. 5:6,7

533 Faith and love

The whole being of any Christian is Faith and Love. . . . Faith brings the man to God, love brings him to men.

Martin Luther
Gal. 5:6

534 The authority of the Scriptures

The authority of Scripture is greater than the comprehension of the whole of man's reason.

Martin Luther
1 Cor. 2:12-14

535 The right shape

Rest in the Lord; wait patiently for Him. In Hebrew, "Be silent in God, and let Him mould thee." Keep still, and He will mould thee to the right shape.

Martin Luther
Ps. 37:7

536 The one point under attack

If I profess with the loudest voice and clearest exposition every portion of the truth of God except precisely that little point which the world and the devil are at that moment attacking, I am not confessing Christ, however boldly I may be professing Christ. Where the battle rages, there the loyalty of the soldier is proved; and to be steady on all the battlefield besides, is mere flight and disgrace if he flinches at that point.

Martin Luther
Matt. 10:19,20; Luke 6:22,23

537 The origins of scriptural authority

Christ is the Master; the Scriptures are only the servant. The true way to test all the Books is to see whether they work the will of Christ or not. No Book which does not preach Christ can be apostolic, though Peter or Paul were its author. And no Book which does preach Christ can fail to be apostolic, although Judas, Ananias, Pilate, or Herod were its author.

Martin Luther, *Introduction to the New Testament*
John 1:1-5; 1 Cor. 15:3; Gal. 1:8,9;
1 Thess. 2:13; 2 Tim. 3:14-17

538 The flesh in Romans

You must not understand flesh here as denoting only unchastity or spirit as denoting only the inner heart. Here St. Paul calls flesh (as does Christ in John 3) everything born of flesh, i.e. the whole human being with body and soul, reason and senses, since everything in him tends toward the flesh. That is why you should know enough to call that person "fleshly" who, without grace, fabricates, teaches and chatters about high spiritual matters. You can learn the same thing from Galatians, chapter 5, where St. Paul calls heresy and hatred works of the flesh. And in Romans, chapter 8, he says that, through the flesh, the law is weakened. He says this, not of unchastity, but of all sins, most of all of unbelief, which is the most spiritual of vices.

Martin Luther, "Preface to the Letter of St. Paul to the Romans"
Rom. 8:4-13; Gal. 5:19-21

539 The priesthood

Let every man recognize what he is, and be certain that we are all equally priests, that is, we have the same power in the word and in any sacrament whatever.

Martin Luther, *The Babylonian Captivity* [1520]
1 Pet. 2:5; Rev. 1:6

540 Learning the Scriptures from God

We cannot attain to the understanding of Scripture either by study or by the intellect. Your first duty is to begin by prayer. Entreat the

Lord to grant you, of His great mercy, the true understanding of His Word. There is no other interpreter of the Word of God than the Author of this Word, as He Himself has said, "They shall be all taught of God" (John 6:45). Hope for nothing from your own labors, from your own understanding: trust solely in God, and in the influence of His Spirit. Believe this on the word of a man who has experience.

Martin Luther, What Luther Says: An Anthology
Isa. 54:13; John 3:9,10; Heb. 4:12; 2 Pet. 1:21; Rev. 2:7; 19:10

541 The ideal preacher

A good preacher should have these qualities and virtues: first, to teach systematically; second, he should have a ready wit; third, he should be eloquent; fourth, he should have a good voice; fifth, a good memory; sixth, he should know when to make an end; seventh, he should be sure of his doctrine; eighth, he should venture and engage body and blood, wealth and honor, in the world; ninth, he should suffer himself to be mocked and jeered of everyone.

Martin Luther, *Table-Talk* [1566]
1 Cor. 4:10-13; 1 Tim. 3:1-15; Heb. 13:9

Lytle, Clyde Francis [b. 1890]

542 Expecting gratitude

There were ten lepers healed, and only one turned back to give thanks, but it is to be noticed that our Lord did not recall His gift from the other nine because of their lack of gratitude. When we begin to lessen our acts of kindness and helpfulness because we think those who receive do not properly appreciate what is done for them, it is time to question our own motives.

Clyde Francis Lytle
Matt. 6:1-4; Luke 17:12-19

M'Cheyne, Robert Murray [1813-1843]

543 Your life preaches all week

Study universal holiness of life. Your whole usefulness depends on this, for your sermons last but an hour or two: your life preaches all week. If Satan can only make a covetous minister a lover of praise, of pleasure, of good eating, he has ruined your ministry. Give yourself to prayer, and get your texts, your thoughts, your words, from God.

Robert Murray M'Cheyne
Rom. 6:19-22

544 Christ in the desert

You will never find Jesus so precious as when the world is one vast howling wilderness. Then he is like a rose blooming in the midst of the desolation, a rock rising above the storm.

Robert Murray M'Cheyne
Isa. 35

545 Answering prayer

God will either give you what you ask, or something far better.

Robert Murray M'Cheyne
1 Kings 3:7-14

M'Intyre, David M. [1859-1938]

546 On the image of God

When God finished man He breathed into the human form the divine life, "and man became a living soul." Man is created to be a witness and likeness of God. God and man are so near to one another that it was possible for the Eternal Word to become Man without ceasing to be God, to re-ascend to the Highest without dehumanizing the Manhood which He had assumed; so near that the believer may say in the fullest meaning of the words, "I live, yet not I, but Christ."

David M. M'Intyre, Faith's Title Deeds [1924]
Gen. 1:26; 2:7; John 1:1-14; Gal. 2:20

Mabie, Hamilton Wright [1846-1916]

547 Without ceasing

Our wills are not ours to be crushed and broken; they are ours to be trained and strengthened. Our affections are not ours to be blighted and crucified; they are ours to be deepened and purified. The rich opportunities of life are not held out to us only to be snatched away by an invisible hand patiently waiting for the hour when the cup is sweetest; they are given to us that we may grow, alike through their rise or their withdrawal. They are real, they are sweet, and they are worthy of our longing for them; we gain nothing by calling them dross, or the world an illusion, or ourselves the victims of deception, or by exalting renunciation as the highest virtue. When these opportunities are denied us, it is a real, not an imaginary, loss which we sustain; and our part is not that of bare renunciation, of simple surrender; our part is to recognize the loss, to bear the pain, and to find a deeper and richer life in doing the will of God.

Hamilton Wright Mabie, The Life of the Spirit [1900]
Rom. 8:22

MacDonald, George [1824-1905]

548 The last resort

How often we look upon God as our last and feeblest resource! We go to Him because we have nowhere else to go. And then we learn that the storms of life have driven us, not upon the rocks, but into the desired haven.

George MacDonald
Ps. 107:21-30; Mark 4:36-41; Rom. 8:28

549 Patience

The principal part of faith is patience.

George MacDonald
Ps. 37:7-9; 40:1,2; Luke 8:15; 21:19; Rom. 2:7; 8:25;
1 Cor. 13:4,5; Heb. 12:1; James 1:3,4

550 The burden of today

It has been well said that no man ever sank under the burden of the day. It is when tomorrow's burden is added to the burden of today that the weight is more than a man can bear. Never load yourselves so, my friends. If you find yourselves so loaded, at least remember this: it is your own doing, not God's. He begs you to leave the future to Him and mind the present.

George MacDonald
Matt. 6:26-34

551 Truth

I would not favor a fiction to keep a whole world out of hell. The hell that a lie would keep any man out of is doubtless the very best place for him to go to. It is truth . . . that saves the world.

George MacDonald
John 14:6

552 All providence

To the dim and bewildered vision of humanity, God's care is more evident in some instances than in others; and upon such instances men seize, and call them providences. It is well that they can; but it would be gloriously better if they could believe that the whole matter is one grand providence.

George MacDonald
1 Sam. 2:3-10

553 Making things bad

But first I said . . . "Some people think it is not proper for a clergyman to dance. I mean to assert my freedom from any such law. If our

Lord chose to represent, in His parable of the Prodigal Son, the joy in Heaven over a repentant sinner by the figure of 'music and dancing.' I will hearken to Him rather than to man, be they as good as they may." For I had long thought that the way to make indifferent things bad, was for good people not to do them.

George MacDonald, *Annals of a Quiet Neighborhood* [1866]
Luke 15:6,22-25

554 Complete dependence upon God

You may fancy the Lord had His own power to fall back upon. But that would have been to Him just the one dreadful thing. That His Father should forget him!—no power in Himself could make up for that. He feared nothing for Himself; and never once employed His divine power to save Himself from His human fate. Let God do that for Him if He saw fit. He did not come into the world to take care of Himself . . . His life was of no value to Him but as His Father cared for it. God would mind all that was necessary for Him, and He would mind the work His Father had given Him to do. And, my friends, this is just the one secret of a blessed life, the one thing every man comes into this world to learn.

George MacDonald, *Annals of a Quiet Neighborhood* [1866]
Matt. 27:46; John 5:19,20,30

555 Ministering to the poor

I cannot imagine a much greater misfortune for a man (not to say a clergyman) than not to know, or knowing, not to minister to, any of the poor.

George MacDonald, *Annals of a Quiet Neighborhood* [1866]
Luke 7:22; Gal. 2:10

556 Love before understanding

The Gospels contain what the Apostles preached—the Epistles, what they wrote after the preaching. And until we understand the Gospel, the good news about our brother-king—until we understand Him, until we have His Spirit, promised so freely to them that ask it—all the Epistles, the words of men who were full of Him, and wrote out of that fullness, who loved Him so utterly that by that very

The Authentic **Book of Christian Quotations**

love they were lifted into the air of pure reason and right, and would die for Him, without two thoughts about it, in the very simplicity of no choice—the Letters, I say, of such men are to us a sealed book. Until we love the Lord so as to do what He tells us, we have no right to an opinion about what one of those men meant; for all they wrote is about things beyond us. The simplest woman who tries not to judge her neighbor, or not to be anxious for the morrow, will better know what is best to know, than the best-read bishop without that one simple outgoing of his highest nature in the effort to do the will of Him who thus spoke.

George MacDonald, *Annals of a Quiet Neighborhood* [1866]
2 Chr. 7:17,18; Matt. 4:4; Heb. 6:11,12; 10:36

557 Strength

[God desires] not that He may say to them, "Look how mighty I am, and go down upon your knees and worship," for power alone was never yet worthy of prayer; but that He may say thus: "Look, my children, you will never be strong but with my strength. I have no other to give you. And that you can get only by trusting in me. I can not give it you any other way. There is no other way.

George MacDonald, *Annals of a Quiet Neighborhood* [1866]
Isa. 40:31; Eph. 6:10

558 His burden is light

Do you think that the work God gives us to do is never easy? Jesus says that His yoke is easy, His burden is light. People sometimes refuse to do God's work just because it is easy. This is sometimes because they cannot believe that easy work is His work; but there may be a very bad pride in it. . . . Some, again, accept it with half a heart and do it with half a hand. But however easy any work may be, it cannot be well done without taking thought about it. And such people, instead of taking thought about their work, generally take thought about the morrow—in which no work can be done, any more than in yesterday.

George MacDonald, *The Seaboard Parish* [1868]
Matt. 11:29,30

559 Conforming to Him

The Son of God suffered unto the death, not that men might not suffer, but that their sufferings might be like His.

George MacDonald, "The Consuming Fire,"
Unspoken Sermons, Series One [1867]
1 Pet. 4:13,14

560 The Bible leading to Christ

Sad, indeed, would the whole matter be if the Bible had told us everything God meant us to believe. But herein is the Bible greatly wronged. It nowhere lays claim to be regarded as the Word, the Way, the Truth. The Bible leads us to Jesus, the inexhaustible, the ever-unfolding Revelation of God. It is Christ "in whom are hid all the treasures of wisdom and knowledge," not the Bible, save as leading to Him.

George MacDonald, "The Higher Faith,"
Unspoken Sermons, Series One [1867]
John 20:29; Col. 2:1-3

561 The Spirit teaches

There is more hid in Christ than we shall ever learn, here or there either; but they that begin first to inquire will soonest be gladdened with revelation; and with them He will be best pleased, for the slowness of His disciples troubled Him of old. To say that we must wait for the other world, to know the mind of Him who came to this world to give Himself to us, seems to me the foolishness of a worldly and lazy spirit. The Son of God is the teacher of men, giving to them of His Spirit—that Spirit which manifests the deep things of God, being to a man the mind of Christ. The great heresy of the Church of the present day is unbelief in this Spirit.

George MacDonald, "The Higher Faith,"
Unspoken Sermons, Series One [1867]
Neh. 8:8; Luke 19:47; Heb. 3:12; John 6:45; Rev. 2:7

562 The unforgivable sin?

Some misapprehension, I say, some obliquity, or some slavish adherence to old prejudices, may thus cause us to refuse the true interpretation, but we are none the less bound to refuse and wait for more light. To acccpt that as the will of our Lord which to us is inconsistent with what we learned to worship in Him already, is to introduce discord into that harmony whose end is to unite our hearts, and make them whole. "Is it for us," says the objector who, by some sleight of will, believes in the word apart from the meaning for which it stands, "to judge the character of our Lord?" I answer, "This very thing He requires of us." He requires of us that we should do Him no injustice. He would come and dwell with us, if we would but open our chambers to receive Him. How shall we receive Him if, avoiding judgment, we hold this or that daub of authority or tradition hanging upon our walls to be the real likeness of our Lord?

George MacDonald, "It Shall Not Be Forgiven,"
Unspoken Sermons, Series One [1867]
Matt. 12:31,32; Luke 12:10

563 The inexorable expulsion of sin

If God said, "I forgive you," to a man who hated his brother, and if (as is impossible) that voice of forgiveness should reach the man, what would it mean to him? How would the man interpret it? Would it not mean to him, "You may go on hating. I do not mind it. You have had great provocation, and are justified in your hate?" No doubt God takes what wrong there is, and what provocation there is, into the account; but the more provocation, the more excuse that can be urged for the hate, the more reason, if possible, that the hater should be delivered from the hell of his hate, that God's child should be made the loving child that He meant him to be. The man would think, not that God loved the sinner, but that He forgave the sin, which God never does. Every sin meets its due fate—inexorable expulsion from the paradise of God's Humanity.

George MacDonald, "It Shall Not Be Forgiven,"
Unspoken Sermons, Series One [1867]
Matt. 6:12,14,15; Mark 11:25,26; Luke 17:3,4

564 Faith in action and waiting

Faith is that which, knowing the Lord's will, goes and does it; or, not knowing it, stands and waits, content in ignorance as in knowledge, because God wills—neither pressing into the hidden future, nor careless of the knowledge which opens the path of action.

George MacDonald, "The Temptation in the Wilderness,"
Unspoken Sermons, Series One [1867]
Matt. 4:1-11; Mark 1:11,12; Heb. 11:8

565 Forgiveness

He who forgives not is not forgiven, and the prayer of the Pharisee is as the weary beating of the surf of hell, while the cry of a soul out of its fire sets the heart-strings of Love trembling.

George MacDonald, *Sir Gibbie* [1879]
Luke 11:4

566 Do it

Instead of so knowing Christ that they have Him in them saving them, they lie wasting themselves in soul-sickening self-examination as to whether they are believers, whether they are really trusting in the Atonement, whether they are truly sorry for their sins—the way to madness of the brain and despair of the heart. . . . Instead of asking yourself whether you believe or not, ask yourself whether you have, this day, done one thing because He said, Do it! or once abstained because He said, Do not do it! It is simply absurd to say you believe, or even want to believe, in Him, if you do not do anything He tells you.

George MacDonald, "The Truth of Jesus,"
Unspoken Sermons, Second Series [1885]
Eph. 4:20-23

567 Doubts

A man may be haunted with doubts, and only grow thereby in faith. Doubts are the messengers of the Living One to the honest. They are the first knock at our door of things that are not yet, but have to be, understood. . . . Doubt must precede every deeper assurance;

for uncertainties are what we first see when we look into a region hitherto unknown, unexplored, unannexed.

George MacDonald, "The Voice of Job,"
Unspoken Sermons, Second Series [1885]
Job 4:13-15; John 20:25-29; 1 Thess. 5:21

568 The rights of man

Lest it should be possible that any unchildlike soul might, in arrogance and ignorance, think to stand upon his rights against God, and demand of Him this or that after the will of the flesh, I will lay before such a possible one some of the things to which he has a right. . . . He has a claim to be compelled to repent; to be hedged in on every side; to have one after another of the strong, sharp-toothed sheep-dogs of the Great Shepherd sent after him, to thwart him in any desire, foil him in any plan, frustrate him of any hope, until he come to see at length that nothing will ease his pain, nothing make life a thing worth having but the presence of the living God within him.

George MacDonald, "The Voice of Job,"
Unspoken Sermons, Second Series [1885]
Ps. 23; Job 19:6; 1 Pet. 2:21-25

569 God pleased vs. God satisfied

That no obedience but a perfect one will satisfy God, I hold with all my heart and strength; but that there is none else that He cares for, is one of the lies of the enemy. What father is not pleased with the first tottering attempt of his little one to walk? What father would be satisfied with anything but the manly step of the full-grown son?

George MacDonald, "The Way,"
Unspoken Sermons, Second Series [1885]
Gen. 17:1; Matt. 19:21

570 Without a flaw

A God must have a God for company.
And lo! thou hast the Son-God to thy friend.
Thou honor'st his obedience, he thy law.
Into thy secret life-will he doth see;

Thou fold'st him round in live love perfectly—
One two, without beginning, without end;
In love, life, strength, and truth, perfect without a flaw.

George MacDonald, *Diary of an Old Soul* [1880]
Gen. 1:26; John 1:1-5; Heb. 5:7-9

571 On shame

Do you so love the truth and the right that you welcome, or at least submit willingly to, the idea of an exposure of what in you is yet unknown to yourself—an exposure that may redound to the glory of the truth by making you ashamed and humbled? . . . Are you willing to be made glad that you were wrong when you thought others were wrong? . . . We may trust God with our past as heartily as with our future. It will not hurt us so long as we do not try to hide things, so long as we are ready to bow our heads in hearty shame where it is fit that we should be ashamed. For to be ashamed is a holy and blessed thing. Shame is a thing to shame only those who want to appear, not those who want to be. Shame is to shame those who want to pass their examination, not those who would get into the heart of things. . . . To be humbly ashamed is to be plunged in the cleansing bath of truth.

George MacDonald, "The Final Unmasking,"
Unspoken Sermons, Third Series [1889]
Matt. 10:26; Luke 12:2; 2 Cor. 3:8,9

572 Faith is righteousness

The faith of Abraham is reckoned to him for righteousness. To call the faith of a man his righteousness is simply to speak the truth. Was it not righteous in Abraham to obey God? The Jews placed righteousness in keeping all the particulars of the law of Moses: Paul says faith in God was counted righteousness before Moses was born. You may answer, Abraham was unjust in many things, and by no means a righteous man. True; he was not a righteous man in any complete sense; his righteousness would never have satisfied Paul; neither, you may be sure, did it satisfy Abraham; but his faith was nevertheless righteousness, and if it had not been counted to him for righteousness, there would have been falsehood somewhere, for such faith as Abraham's is righteousness. It was no mere intellectual recognition of the existence of a God, which is consistent with the deepest atheism; it was that faith which is one with action: 'He went out, not knowing whither he went.' The very act of believing in God after such fashion that, when the time of action comes, the man will obey God, is the highest act, the deepest, loftiest righteousness of which man is capable, is at the root of all other righteousness, and the spirit of it will work till the man is perfect.

George MacDonald, "Righteousness,"
Unspoken Sermons, Third Series [1889]
Gen. 12:4,5; 15:6; Rom. 4:3,18-24; Phil. 3:8,9

573 God's kind of righteousness

The righteousness which is of God by faith in the source, the prime of that righteousness, is then just the same kind of thing as God's righteousness, differing only as the created differs from the creating. The righteousness of him who does the will of his father in heaven, is the righteousness of Jesus Christ, is God's own righteousness. The righteousness which is of God by faith in God, is God's righteousness. The man who has this righteousness, thinks about things as God thinks about them, loves the things that God loves, cares for nothing that God does not care about. . . . The man with God's righteousness does not love a thing merely because it is right, but loves the very rightness in it. He not only loves a thought, but he loves the man in his thinking that thought; he loves the thought alive in the man.

George MacDonald, "Righteousness,"
Unspoken Sermons, Third Series [1889]
Rom. 3:21-28

574 The Lord's day

Where every day is not the Lord's, the Sunday is his least of all. . . . There may be a sickening unreality even where there is no conscious hypocrisy.

George MacDonald, Donal Grant [1905]
Matt. 12:1-13; Tit. 1:15,16

MacGregor, (John) Geddes [1909-1998]

575 Called by its right name

In the twentieth century, the secularists, still living off the spiritual capital of Christianity, often pretended to chide Christians for having invented the term "secularist," a term which, they said, was devoid of meaning. Their leaders knew very well, however, that secularism, like any other parasite, derives its sustenance from the object on which it feeds, and so they were rather pleased when milquetoast Christians timidly offered, as a definition of secularism, "living as though God did not exist." What Christians should have called it was, rather, "a contemptibly fraudulent way of living on the cheap, by reaping the maximum fruits of Christian effort, while contributing the minimum effort of your own." When secularists accused Christians of "living in the past," the Christians ought to have retaliated by pointing out that secularists were "living off the past." By the time they got around to doing so, however, the majority of secularists had become morally incapable of seeing the point.

Geddes MacGregor, *From a Christian Ghetto* [1954]
Ps. 14:1; Prov. 1:7

Mallone, George [b.1944]

576 God is the cure

God is often faulted for creating a world full of suffering and evil. The issue is complex, both philosophically and theologically; but surely it is inappropriate to blame God for a problem He did not initiate, and [that is] in fact, one which He has sought to alleviate, at great cost to Himself. God sent His Son to inaugurate the Kingdom and to "destroy him who has the power of death, that is, the devil" (Heb. 2:14). God is not the cause of suffering and sickness; He is its cure! Jesus' ministry and death guarantee this.

George Mallone, *Those Controversial Gifts* [1983]
Heb. 2:14,15

Maltby, William Russell [1866-1951]

577 No substitute for Conversion

If [it] yields to the drift of the age and surrenders its hold of the awful but glorious individualism of the Christian salvation, . . . the Church itself will not be much enriched by an accession of panic-stricken fugitives from a Personal God. And many unhappy young people are discovering now that Church membership is not the equivalent of being reconciled to God, and a kind of Confirmation is not a substitute for Conversion.

William Russell Maltby
Eph. 1:4-6

Manley, G. T. (George Thomas)

578 How to promote Christian unity

The fundamental doctrines of our evangelical belief are . . . the full inspiration and ruling authority of Holy Scripture, with its consequences, the Divinity of Christ, the finality of His Atonement, and salvation through faith alone. These basic truths should be studied as set forth in the New Testament, that they may be asserted or defended whenever occasion requires. If this be done in a humble and Christian spirit, we shall in the long run be promoting the cause of Christian unity, which must ultimately find its basis in the truth which God has revealed.

G. T. Manley, *Christian Unity* [1945]
Rom. 10:8-11; Jude 1:3

Manton, Thomas [1620-1677]

579 Peace

We have peace with God by the righteousness of Christ, and peace of conscience by the fruits of righteousness in ourselves.

Thomas Manton
Rom. 3:24-26; Gal. 5:22,23; Eph. 2:14-17

Marshall, Catherine [1914-1983]

580 Optimism

Without realizing what was happening, most of us gradually came to take for granted the premises underlying the philosophy of optimism. We proceeded to live these propositions, though we would not have stated them as blandly as I set them forth here:

Man is inherently good.

Individual man can carve out his own salvation with the help of education and society through progressively better government.

Reality and values worth searching for lie in the material world that science is steadily teaching us to analyze, catalogue, and measure. While we do not deny the existence of inner values, we relegate them to second place.

The purpose of life is happiness, [which] we define in terms of enjoyable activity, friends, and the accumulation of material objects.

The pain and evil of life—such as ignorance, poverty, selfishness, hatred, greed, lust for power—are caused by factors in the external world; therefore, the cure lies in the reforming of human institutions and the bettering of environmental conditions.

As science and technology remove poverty and lift from us the burden of physical existence, we shall automatically become finer persons, seeing for ourselves the value of living the Golden Rule.

In time, the rest of the world will appreciate the demonstration that the American way of life is best. They will then seek for themselves the good life of freedom and prosperity. This will be the greatest impetus toward an end of global conflict.

The way to get along with people is to beware of religious dictums and dogma. The ideal is to be a nice person and to live by the Creed of Tolerance. Thus we offend few people. We live and let live. This is the American Way.

Catherine Marshall, *Beyond Our Selves* [1961]
Rom. 3:10,23; 1 John 5:19

Martin, Hugh [1890-1964]

581 The unity that is true

The Churches belong together in the Church. What that may mean for our ecclesiastical groupings we do not know. We have not discovered the kind or outward manifestation which God wills that we shall give to that inner unity. But we must seek it.

Hugh Martin
Rom. 3:21,22

Martyn, Henry [1781-1812]

582 The forerunner

I am born for God only. Christ is nearer to me than father, or mother, or sister—a near relation, a more affectionate Friend; and I rejoice to follow Him, and to love Him. Blessed Jesus! Thou art all I want—a forerunner to me in all I ever shall go through as a Christian, a minister, or a missionary.

Henry Martyn
1 Cor. 15:29; Heb. 2:18

Mascall, E. L. (Eric Lionel) [b.1905]

583 A message to the worldly

If Dr. [John A. T.] Robinson is right in saying that "God is teaching us that we must live as men who can get on very well without him," then the Church has no need to say anything whatever to secularized man, for that is precisely what secularized man already believes.

E. L. Mascall in *The Observer*, March 24, 1963
Eph. 2:11-13

584 Figurative vs. literal

Even the most traditional theologian will be anxious to point out that the classical images which have been used, with more or less success, to depict different aspects of the Redemption—the winning of a battle, the liberation of captives, the payment of a fine or debt, the curing of a disease, and so on—are not to be interpreted literally, any more than, when we say that the eternal Word "came down from Heaven," we are describing a process of spatial translation. For here we are dealing with processes and events which, by the nature of the case, cannot be precisely described in everyday language . . .

The matter is quite different with such a statement as that Christ was born of the Virgin Mary; for, whatever aspects of the Incarnation outstrip the descriptive power of ordinary language, this at least is plainly statable in it. It means that Jesus was conceived in his mother's womb without previous sexual intercourse on her part with any male human being, and this is a straightforward statement which is either true or false. To say that the birth . . . of Jesus Christ cannot simply be thought of as a biological event, and to add that this is [not] what the Virgin Birth means, is a plain misuse of language; and no amount of talk about the appealing character of the "Christmas myth" can validly gloss this over.

> E. L. Mascall, *The Secularization of Christianity* [1965]
> *Matt. 1:18-25; Luke 2:19; John 3:13; 6:38-58*

585 Faith vs. scholarship

The critical scholar is not committed, within the area of his research, to accepting the Church's presuppositions about Jesus, but he should not be committed to accepting naturalistic presuppositions either. If he does accept the latter, then the results of his research will in all probability contradict the beliefs of the Church, but this is because he has begged the question from the start. In examining, for instance, the evidence for the virginal conception [of Jesus], if he begins with the presupposition that such an event is impossible he will end with the same conclusion; if he begins with the presupposition that it is possible he may end with the conclusion that the evidence for it is good or that it is bad or that it is inconclusive. This is as far as scholarship can take him. The Christian will accept the virginal conception as part of the Church's faith.

In the rare cases where faith appears to be contradicted by scholarship whose conclusions have not been prescribed from the start, [the critical scholar] may be cast down but will not be destroyed. For he will know how temporary and mutable the conclusions of scholarship essentially are, and he will also be conscious that he himself may not have perfectly comprehended the Church's faith.

E. L. Mascall, *The Secularization of Christianity* [1965]
Prov. 3:5; Rom. 1:25

586 The shrunken Gospel

Enough has . . . been said to show that the impoverished secularized versions of Christianity which are being urged upon us for our acceptance today rest not upon a serious application of the methods of scientific scholarship nor upon a serious intuitive appreciation of the Gospels as a whole in their natural context, but upon a radical distaste for the supernatural.

E. L. Mascall, *The Secularization of Christianity* [1965]
Mark 6:5,6

587 The nature of the resurrection

There are, of course, interesting questions that can be asked about the nature of the transformation which our Lord's body underwent in his resurrection, and if we know anything about physics and biology we are quite likely to ask them. But, since we are concerned with an occurrence which is by hypothesis unique in certain relevant aspects, we are most unlikely to be able to give confident answers to them. [Paul M.] van Buren's remarks about biology and the twentieth century are nothing more than rhetoric or, at best, are simply empirical statements about his own psychology. The first century knew as well as the twentieth that dead bodies do not naturally come to life again, and no amount of twentieth-century knowledge about natural processes can tell us what may happen by supernatural means.

E. L. Mascall, *The Secularization of Christianity* [1965]
John 6:39,40

Maurice, Frederick Denison [1805-1872]

588 The spirit of judging

Of all the spirits, I believe the spirit of judging is the worst, and it has had the rule of me, I cannot tell you how dreadfully and how long. . . . This, I find has more hindered my progress in love and gentleness than all things else. I never knew what the words, "Judge not that ye be not judged," meant before; now they seem to me some of the most awful, necessary, and beautiful in the whole Word of God.

F. D. Maurice, letter to his mother
Luke 6:37

589 Not systematic

When once a man begins to build a system, the very gifts and qualities which might serve in the investigation of truth, become the greatest hindrances to it. He must make the different parts of the scheme fit into each other; his dexterity is shown, not in detecting facts, but in cutting them square. . . . I hope you will not forget that the Bible is the history of God's acts to men, not of men's thoughts about God. It begins from Him. He is acting and speaking in it throughout.

F. D. Maurice, *Ecclesiastical History* [1854]
Heb. 4:12

590 Called to unity

Unless we look upon ourselves as called to unity, we shall never be united. If God does not will that we should be united, what can our devices for producing it avail? Whereas, if we believe that it is His will, and that we are fighting against His will by our divisions, we have a right confidently to hope that He will at last bring us to repentance, or, if we do not repent, will accomplish His purposes in spite of us.

F. D. Maurice, *Hope for Mankind*
John 17:20,21; Rom. 12:16; 15:5-7; 1 Pet. 3:8,9

Maxwell, James Clerk [1831-1879]

591 The divine equation

Almighty God, who created humanity after your image and gave them living souls that they may seek you and rule your creation, teach us so to investigate the works of your hand that we may subdue the earth to our use, and strengthen our intelligence for your service. And grant that we may so receive your Word as to believe in him whom you sent to give us the science of salvation and the forgiveness of our sins. All this we ask in the name of the same Lord Jesus Christ. Amen.

> James Clerk Maxwell
> *Prov. 8:10; Luke 24:45-47; Phil. 3:8*

McCabe, Joseph E. [b.1912]

592 Beside us

Never again are we to look at the stars, as we did when we were children, and wonder how far it is to God. A being outside our world would be a spectator, looking on but taking no part in this life, where we try to be brave despite all the bafflement. A god who created, and withdrew, could be mighty, but he could not be love. Who could love a God remote, when suffering is our lot? Our God is closer than our problems, for they are out there, to be faced; He is here, beside us, Emmanuel.

> Joseph E. McCabe, *Handel's Messiah* [1978]
> *Ps. 139:7-10*

Mead, Sidney Earl [b.1904]

593 Controversy

Insofar as theology is an attempt to define and clarify intellectual positions, it is apt to lead to discussion, to differences of opinion, even to controversy, and hence to be divisive. And this has had a strong tendency to dampen serious discussion of theological issues in most groups, and hence to strengthen the general anti-intellectual bias.

Sidney E. Mead, *Church History*
Titus 3:9

Merriam, George Spring [1843-1914]

594 The spirit of faith

Faith is the soul's consciousness of its Divine relationship and exalted destiny. It is the recognition by man's higher nature of sources of comfort and hope beyond anything that sense-knowledge discloses. It is the consciousness of a Divine Father toward Whom goes out all that is in affection and highest in moral aspiration; it is the premonition of a future life of which the best attainment here is but the twilight promise. In our day, the sudden and vast revelation of material wonders unsteadies and dims for the moment the spiritual sight; but the stars will shine clear again.

The truth-seeking spirit and the spirit of faith, instead of being opposed, are in the deepest harmony. The man whose faith is most genuine is most willing to have its assertions tested by the severest scrutiny. And the passion for truth has underlying it a profound conviction that what is real is best; that when we get to the heart of things we shall find there what we most need. Faith is false to itself when it dreads truth, and the desire for truth is prompted by an inner voice of faith.

George Springs Merriam, *A Living Faith* [1876]
Heb. 11:1

Merton, Thomas [1915-1968]

595 Chilling faith

Do not be too quick to condemn the man who no longer believes in God: for it is perhaps your own coldness and avarice and mediocrity and materialism and selfishness that have chilled his faith.

Thomas Merton
Prov. 18:19; Zech. 7:5,6; Luke 6:32-34

596 Learning prayer and love

Prayer and love are learned in the hour when prayer becomes impossible and your heart has turned to stone.

Thomas Merton
Mark 14:34-36

597 The big, warm, sweet interior glow

The most dangerous man in the world is the contemplative who is guided by nobody. He trusts his own visions. He obeys the attractions of an interior voice but will not listen to other men. He identifies the will of God with anything that makes him feel, within his own heart, a big, warm, sweet interior glow. The sweeter and the warmer the feeling is, the more he is convinced of his own infallibility.

Thomas Merton, *Seeds of Contemplation* [1949]
1 John 4:1

598 Seeing Christ everywhere

We must be willing to accept the bitter truth that, in the end, we may have to become a burden to those who love us. But it is necessary that we face this also. The full acceptance of our abjection and uselessness is the virtue that can make us and others rich in the grace of God. It takes heroic charity and humility to let others sustain us when we are absolutely incapable of sustaining ourselves. We cannot suffer well unless we see Christ everywhere, both in suffering and in the charity of those who come to the aid of our affliction.

Thomas Merton, *No Man is an Island* [1955]
Isa. 53:3,4; 1 Cor. 10:27; 1 John 3:16

Meynell, Alice (Christina Gertrude Thompson) [1847-1922]

599 Given, not lent

Given, not lent,
And not withdrawn, once sent,
This Infant of mankind, this One,
Is still the little welcome Son.
New every year,
New-born and newly dear,
He comes with tidings and a song,
The ages long, the ages long.
Even as the cold
Keen winter grows not old,
As childhood is so fresh, foreseen,
And spring in the familiar green.
Sudden as sweet
Come the expected feet.
All joy is young, and new all art,
And He, too, whom we have by heart.

Alice Meynell
Luke 2:10-14

Micklem, Nathaniel [1888-1976]

600 The goal

The idea of endless and limitless progress and development seems unsatisfying both philosophically and religiously; a process only finds its meaning in its goal. However far off be the Beatific Vision, to see the King in His glory, "to know Thee and Jesus Christ whom Thou hast sent"—this is heaven, and "it were a well-spent journey though seven deaths lay between."[5]

([5] from letters of Samuel Rutherford)

Nathaniel Micklem, *Prayer and Praises* [1954]
John 17:3; 1 John 3:2

601 Christian ethics depend on Christianity's truth

This concern for the rights and liberties and welfare of the back-ward peoples is rooted in the Christian ethic of justice and of the duty to help and protect the weak, upon the Christian valuation of man as of spiritual dignity and worth, as made for freedom, as a potential child of God. These principles have no validity unless the Christian view of man be true.

Nathaniel Micklem, The Theology of Politics [1941]
Jer. 22:1-4; Amos 5: 7,8; Mic. 6:8; John 7:24

Miller, Keith

602 Marriage

A Christian marriage is [not] one with no problems or even a mar-riage with fewer problems. (It may well mean more problems.) But it does mean a life in which two people are able to accept each other and love each other in the midst of problems and fears. It means a marriage in which selfish people can accept selfish people without constantly trying to change them—and even accept themselves, because they realize personally that they have been accepted by Christ.

Keith Miller, The Taste of New Wine [1965]
1 Cor. 7:12-17

Milton, John [1608-1674]

603 Tolerance of differences among believers

[If] there be any difference among professed believers as to the sense of Scripture, it is their duty to tolerate such difference in each other, until God shall have revealed the truth to all.

John Milton
Rom. 14:5

604 Christ used force

We read not that Christ ever exercised force but once; and that was to drive profane ones out of his Temple, not to force them in.

> John Milton, "A treatise of civil power
> in ecclesiastical causes" [1659]
> *John 2:14-17*

Moffatt, James [1870-1944]

605 The least satisfied reader

This is great literature and great religious literature, this collection of ancient writings we call the Bible, and any translator has a deep sense of responsibility as he undertakes to transmit it to modern readers. He desires his transcript to be faithful to the meaning of the original, so far as he can reach that meaning, and also to do some justice to its literary qualities. But he is well aware that his aim often exceeds his grasp. Translation may be a fascinating task, yet no discipline is more humbling. You may be translating oracles, but soon you learn the risk and folly of posing as an oracle yourself. If your readers are dissatisfied at any point, they may be sure that the translator is still more dissatisfied, if not there, then elsewhere—all the more so, because, in the nature of the case, he has always to appear dogmatic in print.

> James Moffatt
> *Heb. 4:12*

Monro, Claxton [b.1914]

606 Experience agrees with the Bible

Our Christian experience must agree with the Bible. We will be taught by the Bible and fed by the Bible. But we do not believe in

Christ because He is in the Bible: we believe in the Bible because Christ is in us.

Claxton Monro
Matt. 4:4

Moody, Dwight L. (Lyman) [1837-1899]

607 Jesus is the light

The valley of the shadow of death holds no darkness for the child of God. There must be light, else there could be no shadow. Jesus is the light. He has overcome death.

Dwight L. Moody
Ps. 23:4; John 1:9-14; 8:12; 16:33; 1 Cor. 15:26

608 A small light

Remember, a small light will do a great deal when it is in a very dark place. Put one little tallow candle in the middle of a large hall, and it will give a good deal of light.

D. L. Moody
Matt. 5:14-15

Mooneyham, Stan

609 Evangelism and social action

Evangelism and social action: one is not synonymous with the other. They are the twin mandates of the New Testament, and to neglect one is not only to cripple the Church and make its message less credible but to do violence to the New Testament teachings.

Stan Mooneyham, former president, World Vision US
Gal. 2:9,10

610 Statistics for eternity only

A gospel which does not express itself to the physical needs of man is a gospel not worthy of the name . . . Man is a whole person, with body and soul. Some evangelicals act as if people are disembodied souls, statistics for eternity only.

Stan Mooneyham, former president, World Vision US
Luke 4:18,19; 14:12-14

More, Paul Elmer [1864-1937]

611 His law is right

We are born knowing nothing and with much striving we learn but a little; yet all the while we are bound by laws that hearken to no plea of ignorance, and measure out their rewards and punishments with calm indifference. In such a state, humility is the virtue of men, and their only defense; to walk humbly with God, never doubting, whatever befall, that His will is good, and that His law is right.

Paul Elmer More, *Pages from an Oxford Diary* [1937]
Ps. 19:7

Mott, John R. (Raleigh) [1865-1955]

612 Incapable of evangelism

The invasion of the Church by the world is a menace to the extension of Christ's Kingdom. In all ages conformity to the world by Christians has resulted in lack of spiritual life and a consequent lack of spiritual vision and enterprise. A secularized or self-centered Church can never evangelize the world.

John R. Mott
Mark 16:15; Rom. 12:1,2

Moule, C. F. D. (Charles Francis Digby) [b.1908]

613 Convicted, but not committed

Rational conviction, even when it can be had, is very different from commitment. . . . Commitment to Christ is a matter for the entire person, not for his mind alone; and intellectual conviction (if, indeed, it can be had at all without the whole person being involved) is not the whole business. But the whole business, precisely because it concerns the whole person, can never be achieved in defiance of the intellect. Reason, though not the whole, is part of personal response.

C. F. D. Moule, *The Phenomenon of the New Testament* [1967]
Acts 8:13,18-21

Moule, Handley C. G., Bp. [1841-1920]

614 All things work together for good

There is no situation so chaotic that God cannot from that situation create something that is surpassingly good. He did it at the creation. He did it at the cross. He is doing it today.

Bishop Handley Moule
Gen. 1:31; Rom. 8:28; Phil. 2:5-11

615 Unity

Poor and unsatisfying are the results where "Unity," "Corporate Life," and the like are the perpetual watchwords, except where they bear a primary reference to order, function, and succession in the ministry of the Church. One can not but ask the question sometimes, when contemplating phenomena of an ardent ecclesiasticism, is this the worthy goal of ten thousand efforts, of innumerable assertions of "catholicity"—this spirit and tone, these enterprises and actions, so little akin either to the love or to the simplicity, the openness, of the heavenly Gospel? Suppose such unity to be attained to the uttermost, beyond even the dreams of Rome: would it contribute at all to making "the world believe that the Father hath sent the Son, and hath loved us even as He loved Him?"

Handley C. G. Moule, *Ephesians Studies* [1927]
Matt. 9:10-13; John 17:23

Muggeridge, Malcolm [1903-1990]

616 The ultimate disaster

The only ultimate disaster that can befall us, I have come to realize, is to feel ourselves at home here on earth.

Malcolm Muggeridge
John 14:2,3; 2 Cor. 5:1-10

617 Meaning

Where, then, does happiness lie? In forgetfulness, not indulgence, of the self. In escape from sensual appetites, not in their satisfaction. We live in a dark, self-enclosed prison, which is all we see or know if our glance is fixed ever downward. To lift it upward, becoming aware of the wide, luminous universe outside—this alone is happiness. At its highest level, such happiness is the ecstasy that mystics have inadequately described. At more humdrum levels, it is human love; the delights and beauties of our dear earth, its colors and shapes and sounds; the enchantment of understanding and laughing, and all other exercise of such faculties as we possess; the marvel of the meaning of everything, fitfully glimpsed, inadequately expounded, but ever present.

Malcolm Muggeridge, *Jesus Rediscovered* [1969]
Acts 2:46,47

Mulford, Elisha [1833-1885]

618 The transcendental communique

The Word of God is the informing power of the revelation of God in the finite world. It is not, by any figure, to be identified with a book, or a temple, or a minister, or a shrine.

Elisha Mulford, *The Republic of God* [1897]
Eph. 6:17; 2 Tim. 2:8,9

Munson, Ida Norton [b.1877]

619 Because upon the first glad Easter day

Because upon the first glad Easter day
The stone that sealed His tomb was rolled away,
So, through the deepening shadows of death's night,
Men see an open door . . . beyond it, light.

Ida Norton Munson
John 10:9; Rom. 13:12

Murray, Andrew [1828-1917]

620 Limiting God

Beware in your prayer, above everything, of limiting God, not only by unbelief, but by fancying that you know what He can do.

Andrew Murray
Matt. 8:23-27

Murray, John [1898-1975]

621 The Christian and his sins

There must be a constant and increasing appreciation that though sin still remains it does not have the mastery. There is a total difference between surviving sin and reigning sin, the regenerate in conflict with sin and the unregenerate complacent to sin. It is one thing for sin to live in us: it is another for us to live in sin. It is of paramount concern for the Christian and for the interests of his sanctification that he should know that sin does not have the dominion over him, that the forces of redeeming, regenerative, and sanctifying grace have been brought to bear upon him in that which is central in his moral and spiritual being, that he is the habitation of God through the Spirit, and that Christ has been formed in him the hope of glory.

John Murray, *Redemption—Accomplished and Applied* [1955]
Eph. 2:22; Col. 1:27

Neill, Stephen [1900-1984]

622 Leadership of the church

Is the leadership of the world-wide church in the hands of men and women who know how to lead others one by one to Jesus Christ? We are so concerned with planning and administration that there is a danger lest we allow these things to serve as an excuse for not doing the one thing on which all else depends.

Stephen Neill
Acts 8:4

623 Have we not the same promise?

It was on the last night of His life, when His enemies were all around Him, that He spoke to His disciples of the joy that no man taketh away. Read again the story of His Passion: Jesus is seen throughout as calm, quiet, and confident. His last word is, "Father, into Thy hands I commit my spirit." Someone may say, "Yes, but He knew that He was going to rise from the dead." But have we not the same promise for ourselves?

The ordinary group of worshipping Christians, as the preacher sees them from the pulpit, does not look like a collection of very joyful people, in fact, they look on the whole rather sad, tired, depressed people. It is certain that such people will never win the world for Christ. . . . It is no use trying to pretend: we may speak of joy and preach about it: but, unless we really have the joy of Christ in our hearts and manifest it, our words will carry no conviction to our hearers.

Stephen Neill, *The Christian Character* [1955]
Luke 23:46; John 16:19-22,33

Newbigin, (James Edward) Lesslie, Bp. [1909-1998]

624 The quintessence of sin

If there were a righteousness which a man could have of his own, then we should have to concern ourselves with the question of how it can be imparted to him. But there is not. The idea of a righteousness of one's own is the quintessence of sin.

Lesslie Newbigin
Prov. 14:12; Isa. 5:21; 64:6; Matt. 5:20; 23:29-31;
Luke 16:14,15; Rom. 10:3; 2 Cor. 10:17,18

625 Forget self

To make the improving of our own character our central aim is hardly the highest kind of goodness. True goodness forgets itself and goes out to do the right thing for no other reason than that it is right.

Lesslie Newbigin
Eph. 4:15,16

626 The church in His mercy

The Church exists, and does not depend for its existence upon our definition of it: it exists wherever God in His sovereign freedom calls it into being by calling his own into the fellowship of His Son. And it exists solely by His mercy. God shuts up and will shut up every way except the way of faith which simply accepts His mercy as mercy. To that end, He is free to break off unbelieving branches, to graft in wild slips, and to call "No people" His people. And if, at the end, those who have preserved through all the centuries the visible "marks" of the Church find themselves at the same board with some strange and uncouth late-comers on the ecclesiastical scene, may we not fancy that they will hear Him say—would it not be so like him to say—"It is my will to give unto these last even as unto thee?" Final judgment belongs to God, and we have to beware of judging before the time. I think that if we refuse fellowship in Christ to any body of men and women who accept Jesus as Lord and show the fruits of His Spirit in their corporate life, we do so at our peril. It behooves us, therefore, to receive one another as Christ has received us.

> Lesslie Newbigin, *The Household of God* [1953]
> *Matt. 20:1-6; Rom. 11:15-21; 15:7; 1 Pet. 2:10*

627 Conformity in essentials?

We feel that other churches must accept, as the pre-conditions of fellowship, such changes as will bring them into conformity with ourselves in matters which we regard as essential, and that a failure to insist on this will involve compromise in regard to what is essential to the Church's being. But for precisely the same reason, we cannot admit a demand from others for any changes in ourselves which would seem to imply a denial that we already possess the esse of the Church.

> Lesslie Newbigin, *The Household of God* [1953]
> *Rom. 12:5,15; Gal. 6:1,2; Col. 3:12,13*

628 Pure grace

There is a covenant, . . . and God is faithful to His covenant. But the substance of that covenant is all pure mercy and grace. If men presume to claim for themselves, upon the basis of the covenant, some relationship with God other than that of the sinner needing God's grace, the covenant has been perverted. And when that has happened, God, in the sovereign freedom of His grace, destroy these pretensions, calls "No people" to be His people, breaks off natural branches and grafts in wild slips, filling them with the life that is His own life imparted to man. There is no law in His Kingdom save the law of pure grace. That is why they come from east and west to sit down with Abraham and Isaac, while the sons of the Kingdom are cast out; for the sons of the Kingdom have no place there unless they are willing to sit down with all whom the Lord of the feast shall call, and to receive His mercy in exactly the same way as the publicans and sinners.

Lesslie Newbigin, *The Household of God* [1953]
Jer. 31:31-34; Matt. 9:11-13; Rom. 11:22-24; 1 Pet. 2:10

629 Atomization

Western European civilization has witnessed a sort of atomizing process, in which the individual is more and more set free from his natural setting in family and neighborhood, and becomes a sort of replaceable unit in the social machine, His nearest neighbors may not even know his name. He is free to move from place to place, from job to job, from acquaintance to acquaintance, and—if he has attained a high degree of emancipation—from wife to wife. He is in every context a more and more anonymous and replaceable part, the perfect incarnation of the rationalist conception of man. Wherever western civilization has spread in the past one hundred years, it has carried this atomizing process with it. Its characteristic product in Calcutta, Shanghai, or Johannesburg, is the modern city into which myriads of human beings, loosened from their old ties in village or tribe or caste, like grains of sand fretted by water from an ancient block of sandstone, are ceaselessly churned around in the whirlpool of the city—anonymous, identical, replaceable units. In such a situation, it is natural that men should long for some sort of real community, for men cannot be human without it. It is especially natural that Christians should reach out after that part of Christian doctrine which speaks of the true, God-given community, the Church of Jesus Christ. We have witnessed the appalling results of trying to go back to some sort of primitive collectivity based on the total control of the individual, down to the depths of his spirit, by an all-powerful group. Yet we know that we cannot condemn this solution to the problem of man's loneliness if we have no other to offer. It is natural that men should ask with a greater eagerness than ever before, such questions as these: "Is there in truth a family of God on earth to which I can belong, a place where all men can be truly at home? If so, where is it to be found, what are its marks, and how is it related to, and distinguished from, the known communities of family, nation, and culture? What are its boundaries, its structure, its terms of membership? And how comes it that those who claim to be the spokesmen of that one holy fellowship are themselves at war with one another as to the fundamentals of its nature, and unable to agree to live together in unity and concord?" The breakdown of Christendom has forced such questions as these to the front. I think that there is no more urgent theological task than to try to give them plain and credible answers.

> Lesslie Newbigin, *The Household of God* [1953]
> *Ps. 127:1; Rom. 14:19; Col. 4:6; Phil. 1:27*

630 Chosen to be sent

Wherever the missionary character of the doctrine of election is forgotten; wherever it is forgotten that we are chosen in order to be sent; wherever the minds of believers are concerned more to probe backwards from their election into the reasons for it in the secret counsel of God, than to press forward from their election to the purpose of it, . . . that they should be Christ's ambassadors and witnesses to the ends of the earth, wherever men think that the purpose of election is their own salvation rather than the salvation of the world: then God's people have betrayed their trust.

> Lesslie Newbigin, *The Household of God* [1953]
> *1 Pet. 2:9*

631 Knowing the Spirit

The apostle asked the converts of Apollos one question: "Did ye receive the Holy Spirit when you believed?" and got a plain answer. His modern successors are more inclined to ask either "Did you believe exactly what we teach?" or "Were the hands that were laid on you our hands?" and—if the answer is satisfactory—to assure the converts that they have received the Holy Spirit even if they don't know it.

> Lesslie Newbigin, *The Household of God* [1953]
> *Acts 19:1-7*

632 The mark of the Spirit

The counterpart of this withdrawal of Christ [the ascension] from the reach of the senses was the gift to the apostles of the Holy Spirit by whom Christ was made present to them in a new way. They now knew him no more by sight and after the flesh; they had His Spirit. And this "having" is both a real possession and a foretaste, an earnest of what is in store. . . .

The Spirit assures us that we are heirs of a kingdom yet to be revealed (Rom. 8:17). The Spirit wars in us against the flesh (Gal. 5: 17) and gives us assurance that even our mortal bodies shall be quickened (Rom. 8:11). Meanwhile the very mark of the Spirit's presence is that we groan waiting for our adoption (Rom. 8:23) and hoping for that which we do not yet see (Rom. 8:24,25).

Lesslie Newbigin, *The Household of God* [1953]

633 A visible fellowship

We can all call to mind movements which have begun as pure upsurges of fresh spiritual vitality, breaking through and revolting against the hardened structure of the older body, and claiming, in the name of the Spirit, liberty from outward forms and institutions. And we have seen how rapidly they develop their own forms, their own structures of thought, of language, and of organization. It would surely be a very unbiblical view of human nature and history to think—as we so often, in our pagan way, do—that this is just an example of the tendency of all things to slide down from a golden age to an age of iron, to identify the spiritual with the disembodied, and to regard visible structure as equivalent to sin. We must rather recognize here a testimony to the fact that Christianity is, in its very heart and essence, not a disembodied spirituality, but life in a visible fellowship, a life which makes such total claim upon us, and so engages our total powers, that nothing less than the closest and most binding association of men with one another can serve its purpose.

Lesslie Newbigin, *The Household of God* [1953]
Matt. 13:45,46; 1 Cor. 12:12,13; Heb. 10:24,25; 1 John 1:7

634 No middle ground

It is common to hear churchmen speak as though they did not really regard Christian unity as a serious question this side of the End.

This is a disastrous illusion. Christians cannot behave as though time were unreal. God gives us time, but not an infinite amount of time. It is His purpose that the Gospel should be preached to all nations, and that all men should be brought into one family in Jesus Christ. His purpose looks to a real End, and therefore requires of us real decisions. If we misconstrue His patience, and think that there is an infinity of time for debate while we perpetuate before the world the scandal of our dismemberment of the Body of Christ, we deceive ourselves. In an issue regarding the doing of the will of God there is no final neutrality.

> Lesslie Newbigin, *The Reunion of the Church* [1960]
> *Matt. 11:15; John 17:20,21*

Newman, Cardinal (John Henry) [1801-1890]

635 Difficulties

Ten thousand difficulties do not make one doubt.

> Cardinal Newman
> *Luke 8:22-25*

636 Pray for a perfect heart

Pray Him to give you what the Scriptures call "an honest and good heart," or "a perfect heart;" and, without waiting, begin at once to obey Him with the best heart you have. Any obedience is better than none. You have to seek His face; obedience is the only way of seeing Him. All your duties are obediences. To do what He bids is to obey Him, and to obey Him is to approach Him. Every act of obedience is an approach—an approach to Him who is not far off, though He seems so, but close behind this visible screen of things hiding Him from us.

> Cardinal Newman
> *Ps. 24:3,4; 101:1,2; Luke 8:15*

637 Contemplating self instead of Christ

A system of doctrine has risen up during the last three centuries, in which faith or spiritual-mindedness is contemplated and rested on as the end of religion, instead of Christ. I do not mean to say that Christ is not mentioned as the author of all good, but that stress is laid on the believing rather than on the object of belief, on the comfort and persuasiveness of the doctrine than on the doctrine itself. And in this way religion is made to consist of contemplating ourselves, instead of Christ; not simply in looking to Christ, but in seeing that we look to Christ; not in His divinity and atonement, but in our conversion and faith in Him . . .

The fashion of the day has been to attempt to convert by insisting on conversion; to exhort men to be converted; to tell them to be sure they look at Christ instead of simply holding up Christ; to tell them to have faith rather than to supply its object; to lead them to work up their minds, instead of impressing upon them the thought of Him who can savingly work in them; to bid them to be sure their faith is justifying, that it is not dead, formal, self-righteous, or merely moral, instead of delineating Him whose image, fully delineated, destroys deadness, formality, self-righteousness; to rely on words, vehemence, eloquence, and the like, rather than to aim at conveying the one great idea, whether in words or not.

Cardinal Newman
John 1:23-36; Heb. 12:1-3

638 Finding out about humility

What we need, and what is given us, is not how to educate ourselves for this life; we have abundant natural gifts for human society, and for the advantage which it secures: but our great want is how to demean ourselves . . . toward our Maker, and how to gain reliable information on this supreme necessity.

Cardinal Newman
Ps. 147:6; Isa. 57:15; 66:2; Rom. 12:3; 15:17, 18; 1Cor. 3:5-7;
2Cor. 3:5; Phil. 4:11-13; 1 Pet. 5:5

Newton, John [1725-1807]

639 Preparation for joy

God often takes a course for accomplishing His purposes directly contrary to what our narrow views would prescribe. He brings a death upon our feelings, wishes and prospects when He is about to give us the desire of our hearts.

John Newton
2 Cor. 12:8,9

640 Talk about Christ

I endeavor to keep all Shibboleths, and forms and terms of distinction out of sight, as we keep knives and razors out of the way of children; and if my hearers had not some other means of information, I think they would not know from me that there are such creatures as Arminians and Calvinists in the world. But we [would] talk a good deal about Christ.

John Newton
John 17:21-23; Rom. 16:17; 1 Cor. 1:10-13; 3:1-7; 11:16-19

641 Carrying the burden for the day

I compare the troubles which we have to undergo in the course of the year to a great bundle of fagots, far too large for us to lift. But God does not require us to carry the whole at once. He mercifully unties the bundle, and gives us first one stick, which we are to carry today, and then another, which we are to carry tomorrow, and so on. This we might easily manage, if we would only take the burden appointed for each day; but we choose to increase our troubles by carrying yesterday's stick over again today, and adding tomorrow's burden to the load, before we are required to bear it.

John Newton
Matt. 6:34

642 Not idols but incentives

When everything we receive from him is received and prized as fruit and pledge of his covenant love, then his bounties, instead of being set up as rivals and idols to draw our heart from him, awaken us to fresh exercises of gratitude and furnish us with fresh motives of cheerful obedience every hour.

John Newton
Ps. 117:1,2; Matt. 6:1-18; Col. 1:12; 3:16,17

Newton, Sir Isaac [1642-1727]

643 Biblical authenticity

I find more marks of authenticity in the Bible than in any profane history whatever.

Sir Isaac Newton
Dan. 10:21

644 Thankfulness for trials

Trials are medicines which our gracious and wise Physician prescribes because we need them; and he proportions the frequency and weight of them to what the case requires. Let us trust his skill and thank him for his prescription.

Sir Isaac Newton
Eze. 20:37; John 16:20; 1 Cor. 11:32; Heb. 12:6,7

Nicolas of Cusa [1401-1464]

645 Pity

With Thee, 'tis one to behold and to pity. Accordingly, Thy mercy followeth every man so long as he liveth, whithersoever he goeth, even as Thy glance never quitteth any.

Nicolas of Cusa
Isa. 40:11; Mark 6:34; 2 Cor. 8:9

646 What is eternal life?

[Eternal life is] naught else than that blessed regard wherewith Thou never ceasest to behold me, yea, even the secret places of my soul. With Thee, to behold is to give life: It is unceasingly to impart sweetest love of Thee; 'tis to inflame me to love of Thee by love's imparting, and to feed me by inflaming, and by feeding to kindle my yearning, and by kindling to make me drink of the dew of gladness, and by drinking to infuse in me a fountain of life, and by infusing to make it increase and endure.

Nicolas of Cusa, *The Vision of God* [1554]
Isa. 35:1,2; Rom. 6:22; Rev. 7:17

Nida, Eugene A. (Albert) [b.1914]

647 The Word in its place

(Peter) Waldo, a business-man in Lyons, France, in about A.D. 1170 became intensely curious as to the content of the Scriptures. But he could not read Latin, and so the Scriptures were a closed book to him. However, he hired two money-minded priests, who, in violation of strict regulations, translated the Bible for him into Provençal, the language of southern France. The content of the Word of God made such an impression upon this earnest man that he gave up his business, took upon himself a vow of poverty, and dedicated himself to the simple preaching of the contents of God's Word.

The Latin of the Church only mystified its hearers [but] Waldo's humble preaching edified the souls of men. His words were not spectacular but powerful, as he pleaded with them to repent. Much of his preaching and that of his followers consisted in reciting long passages of Scripture in the vernacular. Many of them could not afford an expensive handwritten copy of the Bible, and the ecclesiastical authorities could too easily rob them of such a book; but they could not erase the words which were treasured in the heart.

Eugene A. Nida, *God's Word in Man's Language* [1952]
Rom. 15:4; 2 Cor. 3:3

Norbie, Donald L.

648 The world at enmity with God

For many years the Christians met in homes and never possessed any special buildings for their gatherings. As religio illicita, no thought could be had of a permanent structure for gatherings. This would only facilitate matters for the Roman government in its merciless persecutions. The early Church was very conscious of its pilgrim character in a world which was at enmity with God.

Donald L. Norbie, *New Testament Church Organization*
Luke 9:54-58; Acts 16:14,15; Heb. 11:16

Nouwen, Henri J. M. (Josef Machiel) [1932-1996]

649 The circle of prayer

Prayer and action, therefore, can never be seen as contradictory or mutually exclusive. Prayer without action grows in powerless pietism, and action without prayer degenerates into questionable manipulation. If prayer leads us into a deeper unity with the compassionate Christ, it will always give rise to concrete acts of service. And if concrete acts of service do indeed lead us to a deeper solidarity with the poor, the hungry, the sick, the dying, and the oppressed, they will always give rise to prayer. In prayer we meet Christ, and in him all human suffering. In service we meet people, and in them the suffering Christ.

Henri J. M. Nouwen, *Compassion* [1982]
Isaiah 40:11

O'Donovan, Oliver [b.1945]

650 Shared life

Within the life of the church, the paths of the single and the married should not be allowed to diverge. The shared life of the Christian community must become a context in which the differing gifts can be used for each other. There is much still to be learned about this. Are the homes of married Christians an added support for the single? Is the availability of the single Christian put at the disposal of his married friends, for "babysitting" duties and the like? And what is true of the mutual support of married and single needs to be true in a wider way of the care exercised by the married and the single for each other, so that nobody's home life becomes completely cut off from support and help.

Oliver O'Donovan, "Marriage and the Family,"
in *The Changing World*
1 Cor. 12:24-27

Olds, Glenn

651 The bottomless purse

It is through dying to concern for self that we are born to new life with God and others; in such dying and rebirth, we find that life is lent to be spent; and in such spending of what we are lent, we find there is an infinite supply.

Glenn Olds
Matt. 10:39; Rom. 6:4-13; 7:4

Olney, Helen

652 The truth taught by Jesus

The great need today among the young is the strengthening of belief in things spiritual, for in spite of the superhuman advances in science, invention, and culture, none of this is attributed to God's gift to man; in fact, the increase of knowledge and the cult of education have but given to youth a self-reliant independence where religion has no place, and beyond admitting that Christ was "the best man that ever lived," there are few who concede any other tribute to the Creator. And yet the saving principles of the world are rooted in Christ, implanted in him; the Truth by which men live is the Truth as taught and lived by Jesus.

Helen Olney, *Thoughts*
John 14:6

Oman, John [1860-1939]

653 Men judged themselves

To judge aright we must judge as Christ judged. He judged no man; yet if He judged, His judgments were just. He proclaimed none worthless, none hopeless. Yet men were continually being judged by their relations to Him. The result was infallible, because men judged themselves. Those who loved the light came to Him, those who rejected Him showed that they desired to walk in darkness.

John Oman, *Vision and Authority* [1928]
Isa. 9:2; John 1:4,5; 3:19-21

Orchard, William Edwin [1877-1955]

654 Like summer seas

Like summer seas that lave with silent tides a lonely shore,
like whispering winds that stir the tops of forest trees,
like a still, small voice that calls us in the watches of the night,
like a child's hand that feels about a fast-closed door;
    gentle, unnoticed, and oft in vain:
    so is Thy coming unto us, O God.
Like ships storm-driven into port,
like starving souls that seek the bread they once despised,

like wanderers begging refuge from the whelming night,
like prodigals that seek the father's home when all is spent;
yet welcomed at the open door, arms outstretched and kisses
for our shame;
so is our coming unto Thee, O God.
Like flowers uplifted to the sun,
like trees that bend before the storm,
like sleeping seas that mirror cloudless skies,
like a harp to the hand, like an echo to a cry, like a song to the
heart;
for all our stubbornness, our failure, and our sin:
so would we have been to Thee, O God.

William Edwin Orchard
Ps. 4:1-4

Origen [c.185-c.254]

655 Seducers?

Seducers we, they say; but they lead men astray. Oh, what a noble seduction ours, that men should change from dissolute to sober living—or towards it; to justice from injustice—or tending that way; to wisdom from being foolish—or becoming such; and from cowardice, meanness and timidity, show courage and fortitude, not least in this struggle for the sake of our religion.

Origen
Deut. 31:6; John 12:42,43

656 Discussing prayer

The discussion of prayer is so great that it requires the Father to reveal it, His firstborn Word to teach it, and the Spirit to enable us to think and speak rightly of so great a subject.

Origen
John 14:26; Rom. 8:26,27

Osiander, Andreas [1498-1552]

657 Morality and righteousness

Most men dislike a teaching which lays upon them strict moral requirements that check their natural desires. Yet they like to be considered as Christians, and listen willingly to the hypocrites who preach that our righteousness is only that God holds us to be righteous, even if we are bad people, and that our righteousness is without us and not in us, for, according to such teaching, they can be counted as holy people. Woe to those who preach that men of sinful walk can not be considered pious; most are furious when they hear this, as we see and experience, and would like all such preachers to be driven away or even killed; but where that cannot be done, they strengthen their hypocrite preachers with praise, comfort, presents and protection, so that they may go on happily and give no place to the truth, however clear it may be.

Andreas Osiander
Matt. 7:15-21

Outerbridge, Leonard M.

658 Expendable

The witness has never failed. Repeatedly, the light has shone forth in the darkness, held aloft by hands that perished in the destruction of the institution that failed. Christians tend to defend the institution of their own creation with tenacity. It is institutional Christianity that has often shackled the Church. . . . Many of the missionary institutions of the Church are expendable. They should always be treated as expendable.

Leonard M. Outerbridge, *The Lost Churches of China* [1952]
Dan. 6:10; John 1:4,5; Acts 5:29

Owen, John [1616-1683]

659 Perfect peace

There is a state of perfect peace with God which can be attained under imperfect obedience.

John Owen
Ps. 85:8; John 14:27

660 Faith at death

Faith is the leading grace in all our spiritual warfare and conflict; but all along, while we live, it hath faithful company that adheres to it and helps it. Love works, and hope works, and all other graces—self-denial, readiness to the cross—they all work and help faith. Yet when we come to die, faith is left alone. Now, try what faith will do. Not to be surprised with any thing is the substance of human wisdom; not to be surprised with death is a great part of the substance of our spiritual wisdom.

John Owen
Isa. 25:8; 1 Cor. 15:26; 1 Tim. 6:12

661 New allegiances

The Gospel leaves men, unless upon extraordinary occasions, their names, their reputations, their wealth and honors, if lawfully obtained and possessed; but the league that is between the mind and these things in all natural men must be broken. They must be no longer looked upon as the chiefest good or in the place thereof.

John Owen
Luke 16:13

662 Living faith

Faith, if it be a living faith, will be a working faith.

John Owen
Jas. 2:14-17

663 The clouds of unbelief

It is not the distance of the earth from the sun, nor the sun's withdrawing itself, that makes a dark and gloomy day; but the interposition of clouds and vaporous exhalations. Neither is thy soul beyond the reach of the promise, nor does God withdraw Himself; but the vapors of thy carnal, unbelieving heart do cloud thee.

John Owen
John 20:27; Acts 28:23-27

664 Fail but do not abandon Christ

Consider that it is not failing in this or that attempt to come to Christ, but a giving-over of your endeavors, that will be your ruin.

John Owen
Heb. 12:1-3

665 First obedience, then peace

See in the meantime that your faith bringeth forth obedience, and God in due time will cause it to bring forth peace.

John Owen
Rom. 5:1

666 Truth and holiness

Sometimes truth is lost first in a church, and then holiness, and sometimes the decay or hatred of holiness is the cause of the loss of truth. But if either is rejected, the other will not abide.

John Owen
2 Cor. 7:1; 1 Pet. 1:15-23

667 Faith's nature

We admit no faith to be justifying, which is not itself and in its own nature a spiritually vital principle of obedience and good works.

John Owen
John 14:15; Phil. 1:11

668 Being disciples of Christ

Then are we servants of God, then are we the disciples of Christ, when we do what is commanded us and because it is commanded us.

John Owen
John 14:15

669 No Spirit, no Gospel

It is sottish ignorance and infidelity to suppose that, under the Gospel, there is no communication between God and us but what is, on His part, in laws, commands, and promises; and on ours, by obedience performed in our strength and upon our convictions unto them. To exclude hence the real internal operations of the Holy Ghost, is to destroy the Gospel.

John Owen
Acts 4:31

670 Talk less and pray more

If we would talk less and pray more about them, things would be better than they are in the world: at least, we should be better enabled to bear them.

John Owen
Ps. 17:1; 28:1,2; 70:5; Dan. 9:3; Luke 18:1-7

671 Waiting on God

Men love to trust God (as they profess) for what they have in their hands, in possession, or what lies in an easy view; place their desires afar off, carry their accomplishment behind the clouds out of their sight, interpose difficulties and perplexities—their hearts are instantly sick. They cannot wait for God; they do not trust Him, nor ever did. Would you have the presence of God with you? Learn to wait quietly for the salvation you expect from Him.

John Owen
Ps. 145:15,16; Mic. 7:7; Hab. 2:3

672 First mercy, then help

When we have, through Christ, obtained mercy for our persons, we need not fear but that we shall have suitable and seasonable help for our duties.

John Owen
Ps. 72:13,14

673 A desirable fear

That fear which keeps from sin and excites the soul to cleave more firmly to God, be the object of it what it will, is no servile fear, but a holy fear and due reverence unto God and His word.

John Owen
Prov. 16:6; Matt. 10:28; Luke 12:4,5; 2 Cor. 5:10,11

674 Wisdom and folly

That wisdom which cannot teach me that God is love, shall ever pass for folly.

John Owen
1 Cor. 1:21; 1 John 4:8

675 Spiritual abilities

I do not know a warning that I judge more necessary to be given to those who are called this day, than to charge them not to trade too much with their natural gifts, and abilities, and learning. These are talents in their kind; but it is the Spirit that must manage all that learning they have, or it will prejudice them, and you also. I have known some good men who have been so addicted to their study, that they have thought the last day of the week sufficient to prepare for their ministry, though they employ all the rest of the week in other studies. But your business is to trade with your spiritual abilities . . . A man may preach a very good sermon, who is otherwise himself; but he will never make a good minister of Jesus Christ, whose mind and heart [are] not always in the work. Spiritual gifts will require continual ruminating on the things of the Gospel in our minds.

John Owen, *An Ordination Sermon*
Ps. 19:14; 119:11; 1 Tim. 4:13-15

676 The covenant of forgiveness

God could, if I may say so, more easily have made a new world of innocent creatures, and have governed them by the old covenant, than have established this new one for the salvation of poor sinners; but then, where had been the glory of forgiveness? It could not have been known that there was forgiveness with Him. The old covenant could not have been preserved and sinners pardoned. Wherefore, God choose to leave the covenant than sinners unrelieved, than grace unexalted and pardon unexercised. . . . Will we continue on the old bottom of the first covenant? All we can do therein is to set thorns and briars in the way of God, to secure ourselves from His coming against us and upon us with His indignation and fury. Our sins are so, and our righteousness is no better. And what will be the issue? Both they and we shall be trodden down, consumed, and burnt up. What way, then, what remedy is left unto us? Only this of laying hold on the arm and strength of God in that covenant wherein forgiveness of sin is provided.

John Owen, *Sacramental Sermons*
1 John 2:1,2

677 No accommodation

The world, indeed, seems to be weary of the just, righteous, holy ways of God, and of that exactness in walking according to His institutions and commands which it will be one day known that He doth require. But the way to put a stop to this declension is not by accommodating the commands of God to the corrupt courses and ways of men. The truths of God and the holiness of His precepts must be pleaded and defended, though the world dislike them here and perish hereafter. His law must not be made to lackey after the wills of men, nor be dissolved by vain interpretations, because they complain they cannot—indeed, because they will not—comply with it. Our Lord Jesus Christ came not to destroy the law and the prophets, but to fulfill them, and to supply men with spiritual strength to fulfill them also. It is evil to break the least commandment; but there is a great aggravation of that evil in them that shall teach men so to do.

John Owen, *Sermons*
Matt. 11:21; Rom. 1:18-32

678 All enter by forgiveness

Poor souls are apt to think that all those whom they read of or hear of to be gone to heaven, went thither because they were so good and so holy. . . . Yet not one of them, not any man that is now in heaven (Jesus Christ alone excepted), did ever come thither any other way but by forgiveness of sins. And that will also bring us higher, though we come short of many of them in holiness and grace.

John Owen, *Sermons*
Ps. 130:1-4; Rom. 5:20; Rev. 1:5

679 The beginnings of apostasy

"Secret" sins, such as are not known to be sins (it may be) to ourselves, make way for those that are "presumptuous." Thus pride may seem to be nothing but a frame of mind belonging unto our wealth and dignity, or our . . . abilities; sensuality may seem to be but a lawful participation of the good things of this life; passion and peevishness, but a due sense of the want of respect that we must suppose owing unto us; covetousness, a necessary care of ourselves and of our families. If the seeds of sin are covered with such pretences, they will in time spring up and bear bitter fruit in the minds and the lives of men; and the beginning of all apostasy, both in religion and in morality, lies in just such pretences. Men plead that they can do so-and-so lawfully, until they can do things openly unlawful.

John Owen, *Sermons*
Ps. 19:12,13; Matt. 12:33-35; 2 Tim. 4:3,4

680 Tolerance or indifference?

If errors must be tolerated, say some, then men may do what they please, without control. No means, it seems, must be used to reclaim them. But is gospel conviction no means? Hath the sword of discipline no edge? Is there no means of instruction in the New Testament established, but a prison and a halter?

John Owen, *Of Toleration* [1649]
2 Thess. 3:6

681 Following Jesus

If ever we intend to take one step towards any agreement or unity, it must be by fixing this principle in the minds of all men—that it is of no advantage to any man whatever church or way in Christian religion he be of, unless he personally believe the promises, and live in obedience unto all the precepts of Christ; and that for him who doth so, it is a trampling of the whole gospel under foot to say that his salvation could be endangered by his not being of this or that church or way, especially considering how much of the world hath inmixed itself into all the known ways that are in it.

John Owen, "A Vindication of the Animadversions
on 'Fiat Lux'" [1664]
John 10:27,28

682 Little hope of unity

Some pretending highly to moderation on both sides, especially among the Protestants, hope that [peace] may be attained by mutual condescension of the parties at variance, contemperation of opinions and practices unto the present distant apprehensions and interests of the chief leaders of either side: what issue and event their desires, hopes, and attempts will have, time will show to all the world. For my part, until, by a fresh outpouring of the Spirit of God from on high, I see Christians in profession agreeing in pursuing the ends of Christianity, endeavoring to be followers of Jesus Christ in a conversation becoming the Gospel, without trusting to the parties wherein they are engaged, I shall have very little hopes to see any unity amongst us that shall be one jot better than our present differences.

The present face of Christianity makes the world a wearisome wilderness; nor should I think any thing a more necessary duty than it would be for persons of piety and ability to apologize for the religion of Jesus Christ, and to show how unconcerned it is in the ways and practices of the most that profess it, and how utterly another thing it is from what in the world it is represented to be, were it not that I suppose it more immediately incumbent on them and us all to do the same work in a real expression of its power and excellency, in such a kind of goodness, holiness, righteousness, and heavenliness of conduct, as the world is only as yet in secret acquainted withal. When this is done, the way for a further agreement will be open and facile; and until it be so, . . . we shall have no end of our quarrels.

John Owen, "A Vindication of the Animadversions
on 'Fiat Lux'" [1664]
Rom. 15:5-7; Phil. 2:2

683 Amplification

When an unskillful servant gathers many herbs, flowers, and seeds in a garden, you gather them out that are useful, and cast the rest out of sight; so Christ deals with our performances. All the ingredients of self that are in them He takes away, and adds incense to what remains, and presents it to God. This is the cause that the saints at the last day, when they meet their own duties and performances, know them not, they are so changed from what they were when they went out of their hand. "Lord, when saw we Thee naked or hungry?" So God accepts a little, and Christ makes our little a great deal.

John Owen, *An Exposition upon Psalm CXXX* [1668]
Matt. 25:37-40

684 The philosophers vs. the Gospel

Some go to the light of nature and the use of "right reason" (that is, their own) as their guides; and some add the additional documents of the philosophers. They think a saying of Epictetus, or Seneca, or Arrianus, being wittily suited to their fancies and affections, to have more life and power in it than any precept of the Gospel. The reason why these things are more pleasing unto them than the commands and instructions of Christ is because, proceeding from the spring of natural light, they are suited to the workings of natural fancy and understanding; but those of Christ, proceeding from the fountain of eternal spiritual light, are not comprehended in their beauty and excellency without a principle of the same light in us, guiding our understanding and influencing our affections. Hence, take any precept, general or particular, about moral duties, that is materially the same in the writings of philosophers and in the doctrine of the Gospel; not a few prefer it as delivered in the first way before the latter.

John Owen, *A Discourse upon the Holy Spirit* [1674]
Prov. 3:5; 14:12

685 The necessary forerunner

I have seen and read somewhat of the writings of learned men concerning the state of future glory; some of them are filled with excellent notions of truth, and elegancy of speech, whereby they cannot but much affect the minds of those who duly consider what they say. But—I know not well whence it comes to pass—the things spoken do not abide nor incorporate in our minds. They please and refresh for a little while, like a shower of rain in a dry season, that soaketh not unto the roots of things; the power of them doth not enter into us. Is it not from hence, that their notions of future things are not educed out of the experience which we have of the beginnings of them in this world? Yea, the soul is disturbed, not edified, in all contemplations of future glory, where things are proposed to it whereof in this life it hath neither foretaste, sense, experience, nor evidence. No man ought to look for anything in heaven, but what one way or other he hath some experience of in this life.

John Owen, *The Glory of Christ* [1684,]
2 Cor. 4:17

Packer, J. I. [b.1926]

686 Scripture

God the Father is the giver of Holy Scripture; God the Son is the theme of Holy Scripture; and God the Spirit is the author, authenticator, and interpreter of Holy Scripture.

J. I. Packer
Matt. 21:42; 22:43; Rom. 15:4; 2 Tim. 3:15,16; 2 Pet. 1:19,20

687 Justification by faith

Martin Luther described the doctrine of justification by faith as the article of faith that decides whether the church is standing or falling. By this he meant that when this doctrine is understood, believed, and preached, as it was in New-Testament times, the church stands in the grace of God and is alive; but where it is neglected, overlaid, or denied, . . . the church falls from grace and its life drains away, leaving it in a state of darkness and death.

J. I. Packer
Gal. 3:8

688 The intolerance of the logical

All Christians believe in divine sovereignty but some are not aware that they do, and mistakenly imagine and insist that they reject it. What causes this odd state of affairs? The root cause is the same as in most cases of error in the Church—the intruding of rationalistic speculations, the passion for systematic consistency, a reluctance to recognize the existence of mystery and to let God be wiser than men, and a consequent subjecting of Scripture to the supposed demands of human logic. People see that the Bible teaches man's responsibility for his actions; they do not see how this is consistent with the sovereign Lordship of God over those actions. They are not content to let the two truths live side by side, as they do in the Scriptures, but jump to the conclusion that, in order to uphold the biblical truth of human responsibility, they are bound to reject the equally biblical and equally true doctrine of divine sovereignty, and to explain away the great number of texts that teach it. The desire to over-simplify the Bible by cutting out the mysteries is natural to our perverse minds, and it is not surprising, that even good men should fall victims to it.

J. I. Packer, *Evangelism and the Sovereignty of God* [1961]
Rom. 9:15,16; 1 Cor. 3:13-15

Palau, Luis [b.1934]

689 On belief

Have you stopped seeing great things happen in your life? Perhaps you have stopped believing that God can work in a mighty way even in our generation.

Luis Palau
Ps. 66:7

690 Disillusioned?

God is not disillusioned with us. He never had any illusions to begin with.

Luis Palau
Ps. 44:20,21; 1 John 3:18-20

691 One encounter

One encounter with Jesus Christ is enough to change you, instantly, forever.

Luis Palau
Gal. 4:4-9

692 Failure

It's bad when you fail morally. It's worse when you don't repent.

Luis Palau
1 John 1:9,10

693 Winning people to Christ

The most thrilling thing you can ever do is win someone to Christ. And it's contagious. Once you do it, you don't want to stop.

Luis Palau
Isa. 61:6

Parkhurst, Charles Henry [1842-1933]

694 The blessings of the minute

If you will study the history of Christ's ministry from Baptism to Ascension, you will discover that it is mostly made up of little words, little deeds, little prayers, little sympathies, adding themselves together in unwearied succession. The Gospel is full of divine attempts to help and heal, in the body, mind and heart, individual men. The completed beauty of Christ's life is only the added beauty of little inconspicuous acts of beauty—talking with the woman at the well;

going far up into the North country to talk with the Syrophenician woman; showing the young ruler the stealthy ambition laid away in his heart, that kept him out of the kingdom of Heaven; shedding a tear at the grave of Lazarus; teaching a little knot of followers how to pray; preaching the Gospel one Sunday afternoon to two disciples going out to Emmaus; kindling a fire and broiling fish, that His disciples might have a breakfast waiting for them when they came ashore after a night of fishing, cold, tired, discouraged. All of these things, you see, let us in so easily into the real quality and tone of God's interests, so specific, so narrowed down, so enlisted in what is small, so engrossed in what is minute.

> Charles Henry Parkhurst
> *John 21:12,13*

Pascal, Blaise [1623-1662]

695 Knowing our sin

God is none other than the Savior of our wretchedness. So we can only know God well by knowing our iniquities. . . . Those who have known God without knowing their wretchedness have not glorified him, but have glorified themselves.

> Blaise Pascal, *Pensées* [1660]
> *John 9:39-41*

696 What a pity!

What use is it to us to hear it said of a man that he has thrown off the yoke, that he does not believe there is a God to watch over his actions, that he reckons himself the sole master of his behavior, and that he does not intend to give an account of it to anyone but himself? Does he think that in that way he will have straightway persuaded us to have complete confidence in him, to look to him for consolation, for advice, and for help, in the vicissitudes of life? Do such men think that they have delighted us by telling us that they hold our souls to be nothing but a little wind and smoke—and by saying it in conceited and complacent tones? Is that a thing to say blithely? Is it not rather a thing to say sadly—as if it were the saddest thing in the world?

Blaise Pascal, *Pensées* [1660]
Ps. 14:1; Matt. 11:15; 2 Cor. 4:3-6

697 Because He loved it

I love poverty because He loved it. I love riches because they afford me the means of helping the very poor. I keep faith with everybody; I do not render evil to those who wrong me, but I wish them a situation like mine, in which I receive neither good nor evil from men. I try to be just, true, sincere, and faithful to all men; I have a tender heart for those to whom God has more closely united me; and whether I am alone, or seen by people, I do all my actions in the sight of God, who must judge them, and to whom I have consecrated them all. These are my sentiments; and every day of my life, I bless my Redeemer, who has implanted them in me, and who, out of a man full of weakness, of miseries, of lust, of pride, and of ambition, has made a man free from all these evils by the power of His grace, to which all the glory of it is due, as of myself I have only misery and error.

Blaise Pascal, *Pensées* [1660]
Job 29:11-16; Matt. 5:3; Luke 6:30; 11:41; 14:12-14;
Gal. 6:10; Jas. 2:5

698 Humble, without despair

Jesus Christ is a God whom we approach without pride, and before whom we humble ourselves without despair.

Blaise Pascal, *Pensées* [1660]
Ps. 118:22,23; Luke 7:37-48

699 The God-shaped gap

What does this desire and this inability of ours proclaim to us but that there was once in man a genuine happiness, of which nothing now survives but the mark and the empty outline; and this he vainly tries to fill from everything that lies around him, seeking from things that are not there the help that he does not get from those that are present? Yet they are quite incapable of filling the gap, because this infinite gulf can only be filled by an infinite and immutable object—that is, God, Himself. He alone is man's veritable good, and since man has deserted Him it is a strange thing that there is nothing in nature that has not been capable of taking His place for man: stars, sky, earth, elements, plants, cabbages, leeks, animals, insects, calves, serpents, fever, plague, war, famine, vices, adultery, incest. And since he has lost the true good, everything can equally appear to him as such—even his own destruction, though that is so contrary at once to God, to reason, and to nature.

Blaise Pascal, Pensées [1660]
Ps. 42; 86:10; Amos 8:11,12

700 Great and small

Do little things as though they were great, because of the majesty of Jesus Christ who does them in us, and who lives our life: and do the greatest things as though they were little and easy, because of His omnipotence.

Blaise Pascal, Pensées [1660]
Matt. 25:31-46

701 Getting at the truth

[Unbelievers] think they have made great efforts to get at the truth when they have spent a few hours in reading some book out of Holy Scripture, and have questioned some cleric about the truths of the faith. After that, they boast that they have searched in books and among men in vain.

Blaise Pascal, Pensées [1660]
John 5:39

702 Not peace but deliverance

We implore the mercy of God, not that He may leave us at peace in our vices, but that He may deliver us from them.

Blaise Pascal, Pensées [1660]
Isa. 35:3,4; 57:20,21

703 Two kinds of men

There are only two kinds of men: the righteous, who believe themselves sinners; the rest, sinners who believe themselves righteous.

Blaise Pascal, *Pensées* [1660]
Matt. 9:11,12; Mark 2:16,17

704 The centrality of Christ

Not only do we not know God except through Jesus Christ; We do not even know ourselves except through Jesus Christ.

Blaise Pascal, *Pensées* [1660]
John 14:9

705 Beginning with God

It is impossible that God should ever be the end, if He is not the beginning. We lift our eyes on high, but lean upon the sand; and the earth will dissolve, and we shall fall while looking at the heavens.

Blaise Pascal, *Pensées* [1660]
Rev. 1:8; 21:6

Patmore, Coventry (Kersey Dighton) [1823-1896]

706 Kind souls

Kind souls, you wonder why, love you,
    When you, you wonder why, love none.
We love, Fool, for the good we do,
    Not that which unto us is done.

Coventry Patmore
Matt. 5:46

707 God's answers

God usually answers our prayers so much more according to the measure of His own magnificence, than of our asking, that we do not recognize His benefits to be those for which we sought Him.

Coventry Patmore
Rom. 10:13

708 Unencumbered

Let me love Thee so that the honor, riches, and pleasures of the world may seem unworthy even of hatred—may not even be encumbrances.

Coventry Patmore
Phil. 3:8

709 All that God can give

To love another as oneself is only the halfway house to Heaven, though it seems as far as it was prudent to bid man go. The "greater love than this" of which our Lord speaks, though He does not command it, is to give oneself for one's friends. And when one does this, or is ready to do this, prayer even for "us" seems too selfish—and it is unnecessary, for we then possess all that God Himself can give us. The easy renunciation of self for the Beloved becomes the very breath of life.

Coventry Patmore
Lev. 19:18; John 15:13

Paton, David M. (MacDonald) [b.1913]

710 The meaning of "almighty"

We ought indeed to expect to find the works of God in such things as the advance of knowledge. Knowledge of the physical universe is not to be thought of as irrelevant to Christian faith [simply] because it does not lead to saving knowledge of God. In so far as it is concerned with God's creation, physical science is a fitting study for God's children. Moreover, the advance of scientific knowledge does negatively correct and enlarge theological notions—at the least, the geologists and astrophysicists have helped us to rid ourselves of parochial notions of God, and filled in some of the meaning of such phrases as "almighty."

> David M. Paton, *Christian Missions and*
> *the Judgment of God* [1953]
> *Heb. 11:3*

Peabody, R. G.

711 The decisive factor

However important it may be to have a creed that is sound, or an emotion that is warm, the Christian life according to the Gospels is primarily determined by the direction of the will, the fixing of the desire, the habit of obedience, the faculty of decision. If you are determined in your purpose, if you have the will to do the Will, then with half a creed and less than half a pious ecstasy, you are at least in the line of the purpose of Jesus Christ; and as you will to do His will, may come some day to know the teaching.

> R. G. Peabody
> *Matt. 7:21*

Perrin, Henri [1914-1954]

712 Dear to Christ

A great many of those about me would be imprisoned under any law; in France, as here, they would be regular jail-birds. But I loved them better and better—and still I knew how little was my love for them compared to Christ's. It is easy enough for a man to be honest and a "Good Christian" and keeper of "the moral law," when he has his own little room, his purse well filled—when he is well shod and well fed. It is far less easy for a man who has to live from day to day, roaming from city to city, from factory to factory. It is far less easy for someone just out of jail, with nothing to wear but old down-at-the-heels shoes and a shirt in rags. All of a sudden, I understood our Lord's words: "I was in prison . . . and you visited me not." All these men, lazy, outside the law, starving: these failures of all kinds—they were dear to Christ—they were Christ, waiting in prison for someone to lean over Him—and if we were true Christians, we would do them every kindness.

Henri Perrin, *Priest-Workman in Germany* [1947]
Ps. 69:32,33; Matt. 25:36

Phelps, Arthur Stevens [1863-1948]

713 Prayer supplemented by action

Prayer is the preface to the book of Christian living; the test of the new life sermon; the girding on of armor for battle; the pilgrim's preparation for his journey. It must be supplemented by action or it amounts to nothing.

Arthur Stevens Phelps
Ex. 14:15; Ps. 43:3; Luke 18:10-14

Phelps, Elizabeth Stuart [1844-1911]

714 In the pure soul

In the pure soul, whether it sing or pray,
The Christ is born anew from day to day.
The life that knoweth Him shall bide apart
And keep eternal Christmas in the heart.

Elizabeth Stuart Phelps
Luke 2:1-40

Phelps, William Lyon [1865-1943]

715 Knowledge

A knowledge of the Bible without a college course is more valuable than a college course without a knowledge of the Bible.

William Lyon Phelps
1 Cor. 1:19-21

Phillips, J. B. (John Bertram) [1906-1982]

716 Communion with God

Jesus, like all other religious leaders, taught men to pray, that is, He taught them to look away from the world of ordinary sense impressions and to open the heart and spirit to God; yet He is always insistent that religion must be related to life. It is only by contact with God that a better quality of living can be achieved—and Jesus Himself, as the records show, spent many hours in communion with God—yet that new quality of life has to be both demonstrated and tested in the ordinary rough-and-tumble of plain living. It is in ordinary human relationships that the validity of a man's communion with God is to be proved.

J. B. Phillips
Matt. 6:9-13; Mark 1:35; Luke 5:16; 11:1-4

717 Wholeness from the parts

In his enthusiasm, the evangelist often finds it difficult seriously to imagine that anyone could be called not to be an evangelist. The man of vision and imagination finds it difficult to see the value of those who do no more than plod on faithfully along a well-tried road. The man whose concern is in personal dealing with people and leading them to understand God better finds it difficult to be patient with the theologian or the Christian philosopher whose work is in the quiet of a book-lined study. Yet the truth is that the wholeness which God is working to achieve is never complete in an individual, but through

individuals living together as one body, each supplying the deficien-
cies of the others.

J. B. Phillips, *Making Men Whole* [1952]
Rom. 12:4

718 Words to pass the defenses

The preacher and the writer may seem to have an . . . easy task. At
first sight, it may seem that they have only to proclaim and declare;
but in fact, if their words are to enter men's hearts and bear fruit, they
must be the right words, shaped cunningly to pass men's defenses
and explode silently and effectually within their minds. This means,
in practice, turning a face of flint toward the easy cliché, the well-
worn religious cant and phraseology—dear, no doubt, to the faithful,
but utterly meaningless to those outside the fold. It means learning
how people are thinking and how they are feeling; it means learning
with patience, imagination and ingenuity the way to pierce apathy
or blank lack of understanding. I sometimes wonder what hours of
prayer and thought lie behind the apparently simple and spontaneous
parables of the Gospel.

J. B. Phillips, *Making Men Whole* [1952]
Luke 12:11,12; Col. 3:16,17

719 Our expectations of God

From the crude cry which we have so often heard during the war
years: "If there is a God, why doesn't He stop Hitler?" to the unspoken questioning in many a Christian heart when a devoted servant of
Christ dies from accident or disease at what seems to us a most inop-
portune moment, there is this universal longing for God to intervene,
to show His hand, to vindicate His purpose. I do not pretend to understand the ways of God any more than the next man; but it is surely
more fitting as well as more sensible for us to study what God does
do and what He does not do as He works in and through the complex
fabric of this disintegrated world, than to postulate what we think
God ought to do and then feel demoralized and bitterly disappointed
because He fails to fulfill what we expect of Him.

J. B. Phillips, *Making Men Whole* [1952]
Ps. 106:13-15

720 God's slowness

Most Christians are affected far more than they know by the standards and methods of the surrounding world. In these days when power and size and speed are almost universally admired, it seems to me particularly important to study afresh the "weakness," the "smallness of entry," and the "slowness" of God as He begins His vast work of reconstructing His disordered world. We are all tempted to take short cuts, to work for quick results, and to evade painful sacrifice. It is therefore essential that we should look again at love incarnate in a human being, to see God Himself at work within the limitations of human personality, and to base our methods on what we see Him do.

J. B. Phillips, *Making Men Whole* [1952]
Phil. 3:7,8

721 Absolute sovereignty

It is necessary to point out that our responsibility is a relative one only, for as we think of the world-wide disintegration of the human family, the prospect before us could easily fill us with alarm and despondency, if we were not sure first of the absolute sovereignty of God who (I speak reverently) knows what He is doing in conducting this enormous experiment that we call life.

J. B. Phillips, *Making Men Whole* [1952]
1 Chr. 29:10-12; Ps. 24; Hag. 2:7; John 10:29; Rev. 4:11

722 God gracious to the wicked

Jesus once declared that God is "good to the ungrateful and the wicked" (St. Luke 6:35), and I remember preaching a sermon on this text to a horrified and even astonished congregation who simply refused to believe (so I gathered afterwards) in this astounding liberality of God. That God should be in a state of constant fury with the wicked seemed to them only right and proper, but that God should be kind towards those who were defying or disobeying His laws seemed to them a monstrous injustice. Yet I was but quoting the Son of God Himself, and I only comment here that the terrifying risks that God takes are part of His Nature. We do not need to explain or modify His unremitting love towards mankind.

J. B. Phillips, *Making Men Whole* [1952]

723 We are involved

We may with complete detachment study and form a judgment upon a religion, but we cannot maintain our detachment if the subject of our inquiry proves to be God Himself. This is, of course, why many otherwise honest intellectual people will construct a neat by-pass around the claim of Jesus to be God. Being people of insight and imagination, they know perfectly well that once to accept such a claim as fact would mean a readjustment of their own purposes and values and affections which they may have no wish to make. To call Jesus the greatest Figure in History or the finest Moral Teacher the world has ever seen commits no one to anything. But once to allow the startled mind to accept as fact that this man is really focused— God may commit anyone to anything! There is every excuse for blundering in the dark, but in the light there is no cover from reality. It is because we strongly sense this, and not merely because we feel that the evidence is ancient and scanty, that we shrink from committing ourselves to such a far-reaching belief as that Jesus Christ was really God.

J. B. Phillips, *Your God is Too Small* [1953]
Ps. 110:1; John 1:1-5; 10:10; Phil.2:5-11

724 Friends with God

A man can not be "friends with" God on any other terms than complete obedience to Him, and that includes being "friends with" his fellow man. Christ stated emphatically that it was quite impossible, in the nature of things, for a man to be at peace with God and at variance with his neighbor. This disquieting fact is often hushed up, but it is undeniable that Christ said it, and the truth of it is enshrined in the petition for forgiveness in the "Lord's Prayer."

J. B. Phillips, *Your God is Too Small* [1953]
Matt. 5:23,24

725 Divisions in the church

The 'outsider' who knows nothing of the mixture of tradition, conviction, honest difference, and hidden resentment, that lies behind the divisions of the Christian Church sees clearly the advantage of a united Christian front and cannot see why the Churches cannot 'get together'. The problem is doubtless complicated, for there are many honest differences held with equal sincerity, but it is only made insoluble because the different denominations are (possibly unconsciously) imagining God to be Roman or Anglican or Baptist or Methodist or Presbyterian or what have you. If they could see beyond their little inadequate god, and glimpse the reality of God, they might even laugh a little and perhaps weep a little. The result would be a unity that actually does transcend differences, instead of ignoring them with public politeness and private contempt.

J. B. Phillips, *Your God is Too Small* [1953]
Neh. 4:4; Matt. 12:25; Rom. 15:5; 1 Cor. 1:10-13

726 The reliability of the Resurrection

It is, of course, impossible to exaggerate the importance of the historicity of what is commonly known as the Resurrection. If, after all His claims and promises, Christ had died and merely lived on as a fragrant memory, He would only be revered as an extremely good but profoundly mistaken man. His claims to be God, His claims to be Himself the very principle of life, would be mere self-delusion. His authoritative pronouncements on the nature of God and Man and Life would be at once suspect. Why should He be right about the lesser things, if He was proved to be completely wrong in the greater?

J. B. Phillips, *Your God is Too Small* [1953]
1 Cor. 15:14

727 Christ and mysticism

It should be noted, at least by those who accept Christ's claim to be God, that he by no means fits into the picture of the "mystic saint." Those who are fascinated by the supposed superiority of the mystic soul might profitably compile a list of its characteristics and place them side by side with those of Christ. The results would probably expose a surprising conclusion. There is, in fact, no provision for a "privileged class" in genuine Christianity.

J. B. Phillips, *Your God is Too Small* [1953]
Rom. 2:11; Gal. 3:28,29

728 God's Living Spirit

Every time we say, 'I believe in the Holy Spirit,' we mean that we believe that there is a living God able and willing to enter human personality and change it.

J. B. Phillips, *Plain Christianity* [1954]
Acts 1:8

729 A living sacrifice

Following the way of Jesus Christ and doing all we can for His cause and for our fellow men expresses something of our worship in action. But how to give Him a present to express our love is a bit of a problem. How can you give God anything when He owns everything? But does He? How about that power to choose, that precious free will that He has given to every living personality and which He so greatly respects? That is the only present we can give—our selves, with all our powers of spirit, mind, and body, willingly, freely given because we love Him. That is the best and highest worship that you and I can offer, and I am sure that it is this above all that God most highly appreciates.

J. B. Phillips, *Plain Christianity* [1954]
Rom. 12:1,2

730 Christianity is not a religion

Suppose Christianity is not a religion but a way of life, a falling in love with God, and, through Him, a falling in love with our fellows. Of course, such a way is hard and costly, but it is also joyous and rewarding even in the here-and-now. People who follow that Way know beyond all possible argument that they are in harmony with the purpose of God, that Christ is with them and in them as they set about His work in our disordered world. If anyone thinks this is perilous and revolutionary teaching, so much the better. That is exactly what they thought of the teaching of Jesus Christ. The light He brought to bear upon human affairs is almost unbearably brilliant: but it is the light of Truth, and in that light human problems can be solved.

J. B. Phillips, *When God Was Man* [1954]
Matt. 5; 6

731 Count the cost

There is joy and strength, of course, in this holy food and drink, but it is also an inevitable joining forces with the vast Scheme of reconciliation and redemption. Now there is something in our natural selves that may well make us wary of such a contact. The man who in his heart intends to go on being selfish or proud, or who has already decided how far his Christian convictions should carry him, is probably obeying a sound instinct when he keeps away from this glorious but perilous Sacrament. For, if the truth be told, men are often willing to put their trust in a god who in the end must be triumphant, simply because they want to be on the winning side; but they are not nearly so ready to bear any part of the cost of that winning. Yet the fellowship of the broken bread and the poured-out wine can mean no less than that.

J. B. Phillips, *Appointment with God* [1956]
Luke 14:28-30

732 Finding unity in communion

It is a singularly unpleasant thought that a book about Holy Communion is more likely to produce disagreement and controversy than one written on almost any other Christian subject. It seems a truly terrible thing that this Sacred Appointment, which was surely meant to unite, in actual practice divides Christians more sharply than any other part of their worship. Christians of various denominations may, and frequently do, work together on social projects, they may study the Scripture together, and they may . . . pray together. But the moment attendance at the Lord's Table is suggested, up go the denominational barriers. . . . I would make a strong plea that we do not exclude from the Lord's Table in our Church those who are undoubtedly sincere Christians. I cannot believe that to communicate together with our Lord should be regarded as the consummation, the final pinnacle, of the whole vast work of Reunion. Suppose it is the means and not the end. We might feel far more sharply the sin of our divisions and of our exclusiveness if we came humbly together to receive the Body and Blood of our Lord, and in that reception we might find such a quickening of our common devotion to Him that the divisions between us might be found not nearly so insuperable as we supposed.

J. B. Phillips, *Appointment with God* [1956]
Matt. 26:17-30; Mark 14:22-24; Luke 13:26; 22:19,20;
John 13:1-4; Acts 2:42,46,47; 20:7; 1 Cor. 10:16,17,21,22; 11:20-34

733 A terrifying ignorance

To me there is a much more frightening ignorance in our modern world than the "ignorance of the heathen." I am referring to the almost total ignorance of the content and implication of the Christian Faith shown by many "clever" people today. Frankly, I find it horrifying to discover that men who are experts in their own line—in astronomy, genetics, or nuclear physics, for example—have no adult knowledge of what the Church of Christ stands for, and a complete blank ignorance of what the Church is achieving today. It is the more horrifying because people who rightly respect the expert for his knowledge in his own field have no idea that he has not carefully examined and reluctantly discarded Christianity; but in all probability he has never studied it at all!

J. B. Phillips, *The Church Under the Cross* [1956]
Rom. 15:21

734 Tragic idealist?

It is easy to criticize the many failings of the Church; it is all too easy to criticize the lives of those who profess and call themselves Christians; but I should say that it is almost impossible to read the Gospels thoroughly with adult, serious attention and then dismiss the central Figure as a mere human prophet or a tragic idealist. The reaction to such a study may indeed prove to be conversion or open hostility, but it would at least mean the end of childish and ill-informed attacks upon what is supposed to be the Christian religion.

J. B. Phillips, *New Testament Christianity* [1956]
Jer. 9:3

735 The morality of justification by faith

One of Paul's most important teachings . . . is the doctrine of what we call "justification by faith." It frequently appears to the non-Christian mind that this is an immoral or at least unmoral doctrine. Paul appears to be saying that a man is justified before God, not by his goodness or badness, not by his good deeds or bad deeds, but by believing in a certain doctrine of Atonement. Of course, when we come to examine the matter more closely, we can see that there is nothing unmoral in this teaching at all. For if "faith" means using a God-given faculty to apprehend the unseen divine order, and means, moreover, involving oneself in that order by personal commitment, we can at once see how different that is from merely accepting a certain view of Christian redemption. . . . That which man in every religion, every century, every country, was powerless to affect, God has achieved by the devastating humility of His action and suffering in Jesus Christ. Now, accepting such an action as a fait accompli is only possible by this perceptive faculty of "faith." It requires not merely intellectual assent but a shifting of personal trust from the achievements of the self to the completely undeserved action of God. To accept this teaching by mind and heart does, indeed, require a metanoia [Gr. "transformation"], a revolution in the outlook of both heart and mind.

J. B. Phillips, *New Testament Christianity* [1956]
Rom. 12:2

736 The whole Gospels

This astonishing sense of spiritual attack which, it seems to me, must inevitably follow the continual reading of the four Gospels, without preconception but with an alert mind, is not the sole privilege of the translator. It can happen to anyone who is prepared to abandon proof-texts and a closed attitude of mind, and allow not merely the stories but the quality of the Figure who exists behind the stories to meet him afresh. Neat snippets of a few verses are of course useful in their way, but the overall sweep and much of the significance of the Gospel narratives are lost to us unless we are prepared to read the Gospels through, not once but several times.

J. B. Phillips, *New Testament Christianity* [1956]
Matt. 10:26-28

The Authentic **Book of Christian Quotations**

737 Why they call it Good Friday

Those who think God did this almost incredible thing call it Good Friday because only an extremely good God could do a thing like that. All religions attempt to bridge the gulf between the terrific purity of God and the sinfulness of man, but Christianity believes that God built that bridge Himself. This particular Friday commemorates His deliberate action in allowing Himself to be caught up in the sin-suffering-death mechanism which haunts mankind. He didn't let it end there, for He went on, right through death. But the men who believe in Him can't forget the kind of Person such an act reveals. That's why they call it Good Friday.

J. B. Phillips, *Is God at Home?* [1957]
Isa. 53:2-11; John 19:16-30

Phillips, Wendell [1811-1884]

738 A battle

Christianity is a battle, not a dream.

Wendell Phillips
2 Cor. 10:3; 1 Tim. 6:12

Pierce, Robert [1914-1978]

739 In the midst of suffering

Jesus Christ can so interfere in a human life that it can look up and say, "Bless the Lord, O my soul, and forget not all His benefits," even in the midst of sorrow or suffering.

Robert Pierce, founder and president, World Vision
Ps. 103:2-5

740 How beautiful the feet

God is wanting you to give Him the despised, the humdrum things in your life—like feet—and let Him make them beautiful.

Robert Pierce, founder and president, World Vision
Isa. 52:7

741 What God blesses

I don't ask God to bless what I do. I pray He will help me to do what He blesses.

Robert Pierce, founder and president, World Vision
Matt. 25:37-40

742 Reckless giving

May the Spirit of God help you to give of yourself as recklessly for the cause of Christ throughout the whole world as God "recklessly" gave His Son, Jesus Christ.

Robert Pierce, founder and president, World Vision
Rom. 8:32; 12:1,2

Pike, Kenneth L. [1912-2001]

743 Camouflage

"Help!"
"Sorry! 'monmywaytochurch."
The deepest sins are camouflaged as holiness.

Kenneth L. Pike
Luke 10:30-37

744 Morally responsible for assumptions

Assumptions based on faith are apparently an ever-present component in any system of belief—whether these assumptions include the existence of a personal God, or whether they begin with non-rational directionally-emergent forces governed by statistical probabilities.

Our argument does not claim that evidences are so clear that faith is not needed. We do intend to imply, however, that the choice of a set of assumptions is a moral choice. Adherence to an epistemology is not something which merely "happens to" a person, but instead it reflects a component of his moral development. In some sense he is, in my judgment, morally responsible for adopting an epistemology even though it can be neither proved nor disproved to the satisfaction of those who oppose it.

Kenneth L. Pike, *With Heart and Mind* [1962]
1 Tim. 6:20-21

745 Pagan words for Christian thoughts

Upon a little reflection one can see that no concepts which are restricted to Christianity could possibly be found in a language spoken only by pagans. How could pagans have developed words for Christian ideas which have never occurred to them? This identical situation existed when the Holy Spirit inspired the New Testament. At that time many pagan words, with pagan-thought background, were used in Christian contexts; by the contexts the present Christian meaning eventually built up, until it was possible to express all the Christian meaning in the pagan terms.

Kenneth L. Pike, *With Heart and Mind* [1962]
Acts 2:6

746 Cause and effect

He may effect us directly by His Spirit, with the force of a thunderbolt, or He may choose to woo us gently by stirring up our conscience. But, in addition, God affects us by determining that in the universe certain causes shall bring about certain effects. Cause and effect is, therefore, the operation of God through normal channels rather than through special channels. We have our normal way of acting when we drive a car. We can more or less put it in "automatic pilot" while we carry on a conversation, but when an emergency arises, we take conscious personal control. I have a hunch that God has something for which this automatic pilot will serve as an illustration. That is, His routine way of operating is cause and effect, and He is in control of it, so that when cause and effect affects us, then God is affecting us. That is what the Apostle Paul means in Galatians when he says, "Do not kid yourself—God is not blind. What you do, you will get paid for." The causes which we have set in operation by our own personal choices will inevitably bring about certain results. But God is involved because God makes cause and effect to work.

But since cause and effect is under the personal control of God, He can introduce into the situation other causes than the ones which we ourselves can control. When in faith we come to God for cleansing from the mess we have made of things, and when we ask for power to reverse causes we have set in motion, God sends in other causes by His Holy Spirit. It may be by direct intervention, or by a combination of circumstances which He controls. We can, therefore, be delivered from the wrath to come, because God will add other causes than those that we have initiated.

Kenneth L. Pike, *With Heart and Mind* [1962]
Gal. 6:7-9

Pink, A. W. (Arthur Walkington) [1886-1952]

747 The hands of the Lord

Nothing is too great and nothing is too small to commit into the hands of the Lord.

A. W. Pink
Ps. 22:9,10

748 Done with unbelief

None but the Lord himself can afford us any help from the awful workings of unbelief, doubtings, carnal fears, murmurings. Thank God one day we will be done forever with "unbelief."

A. W. Pink
Mark 9:23,24; John 7:5; 1 Cor. 1:22,23

749 The Godhood of God

From every pulpit in the land it needs to be thundered forth that God still lives, that God still observes, . . . still reigns. Faith is now in the crucible, it is being tested by fire, and there is no fixed . . . resting place for the heart and mind but in the Throne of God. What is needed now, as never before, is a full, positive, constructive setting forth of the Godhood of God.

A. W. Pink, *The Sovereignty of God* [1918]
Ex. 20:2; Ps. 46:10

Pinnock, Clark H. [b.1937]

750 The demand for exclusion

Most Christians would agree with C. S. Lewis when he says [of the doctrine of the Final Judgment], "There is no doctrine which I would more willingly remove from Christianity than this, if it lay in my power."[6] But we cannot do so, for two reasons: first, because it enjoys the full support of Christ's own teaching; and second, because it makes a good deal of sense. If the gospel is extended to us for our acceptance, it must be possible also to reject and refuse it. The alternative would be for God to compel an affirmative response.

It would be nice to be able to say that all will be saved, but the question arises, Does everyone want to be saved? What would love for God be like if it were coerced? There is a hell because God respects our freedom and takes our decisions seriously—more seriously, perhaps, than we would sometimes wish. God wants to see hell completely empty; but if it is not, He cannot be blamed. The door is locked only on the inside. It is not Christians but the unrepentant who "want" it [to be locked].

([6] C. S. Lewis, *The Problem of Pain*)

Clark H. Pinnock, *Reason Enough* [1980]
John 5:26-30

751 Another retreat from reality

There has been a tendency of late to interpret alienation from faith in intellectual rather than experiential terms. Academically oriented Christians especially tend to think that the barriers to faith should be removed by repackaging the content of the message in a way more congenial to the modern outlook. But it is quite possible that we are dealing not so much with a failure of intellect as with an alienation from the experiential roots of Christianity itself so amply attested in the New Testament.

Clark H. Pinnock, *Reason Enough* [1980]
Matt. 24:12; 2 Tim. 3:1-4;4:3,4

Porter, Kenneth W. (Wiggins) [1905-1981]

752 Good nails

... They haled him, trembling, to the Judgment Seat.
"O Lord, behold the man who made the nails that pierced Thy feet!"
The Master laid a thin, scarred hand upon the shame-bowed head.
"They were good nails," he said ...

Kenneth W. Porter
John 20:24-29

Powell, Lyman Pierson [1866-1946]

753 The fountainhead

I read in Shakespeare of the majesty of the moral law, in Victor Hugo of the sacredness of childhood, in Tennyson the ugliness of hypocrisy, in George Eliot the supremacy of duty, in Dickens the divinity of kindness, and in Ruskin the dignity of service. Irving teaches me the lesson of cheerfulness, Hawthorne shows me the hatefulness of sin, Longfellow gives me the soft, tranquil music of hope. Lowell makes us feel that we must give ourselves to our fellow men. Whittier sings to me of divine Fatherhood and human brotherhood. These are Christian lessons: who inspired them? Who put it into the heart of Martin Luther to nail those theses on the church door of Wittenberg?

Who stirred and fired the soul of Savonarola? Who thrilled and electrified the soul of John Wesley? Jesus Christ is back of these all.

Lyman Pierson Powell
John 1:1; 1 Cor. 2:12-14

Pusey, Edward B. (Bouverie) [1800-1882]

754 In Thy hand

Into God's hands let us now—for the coming year, and for all the years of time, and for Eternity—commend our spirits. Whether for the Church or for ourselves, let us not take ourselves into our own hands, or choose our own lot. "My times are in Thy hand." He loveth the Church, which He died to purchase, His own Body, and all the members of the Body, better than we can; He loveth us better and more wisely than we ourselves; He who made us loveth us better than we who unmade ourselves; He who died for us, better than we who destroy ourselves: He who would sanctify us for a Holy Temple unto Himself, better than we who have defiled what He has hallowed. Fear we not, therefore, anything which threateneth, shrink we not back from anything which falleth on us. Rather let us, though with trembling, hold up our hearts to Him, to make them His Own, in what way He willeth.

Edward B. Pusey
Ps. 31:15,16

Quarles, Francis [1592-1644]

755 He is my Altar

He is my Altar, I His holy place;
I am His guest, and He my living food;
I'm His by penitence, He is mine by grace;
I'm His by purchase, He is mine by blood;

He's my supporting elm, and I His vine:
Thus I my Best-beloved's am; thus He is mine.

Francis Quarles
Acts 20:28; 1 Cor. 3:16,17

Raleigh, Sir Walter [c.1552-1618]

756 Denying Him by works

We profess that we know God, but by works we deny Him; for beatitude doth not consist in the knowledge of divine things, but in a divine life, for the devils know them better than man.

Sir Walter Raleigh
Jas. 2:14-17

Ramsay, Sir William Mitchell [1851-1939]

757 To hesitate is to be lost

Nothing could have saved the infant Church from melting away into one of those vague and ineffective schools of philosophic ethics except the stern and strict rule that is laid down here [Rev. 2:15, 16] by St. John. An easy-going Christianity could never have survived; only the most convinced, resolute, almost bigoted adherence to the most uncompromising interpretation of its own principles could have given the Christians the courage and self-reliance that were needed. For them to hesitate or to doubt was to be lost.

Sir William M. Ramsay, *The Letters to the Seven Churches* [1904]
Rev 2:15-16

758 The Divine Nature

The central idea of the Christian religion, the idea which cannot be doubted or minimized without sacrificing the essential truth of Christianity, is that God, who had always through His messengers and prophets communicated His word to man, at last, as the climax of His grace, sent His only Son into the world. The Divine Nature, which is omnipresent and eternal, free from the human limitations of space and time, materialized itself in human form upon the earth, voluntarily subjecting itself to those limitations and yet continuing to be Divine . . . In so far as it was human, this expression of the Divine Nature in the world must have a beginning, a history for a term of years, and an end, i.e., a birth, life, and death. Yet, on the other hand, as being Divine, it was preexistent and deathless. The Word was in the beginning, and the Word was God. Birth and death have no bearing on the eternal Divine Nature. Thus the Divine Nature makes itself in appearance to us double, and this double nature is called by the terms Father and Son, which must of course be regarded as symbolical names attempting to make the Divine mystery intelligible to the human mind with its necessarily limited powers of understanding.

It was therefore an essential part of the Divine purpose, that those who had known the Divine Word in its human expression as the man Jesus, should become aware that death had no real power over Him. This result was accomplished by various events after such fashion that a sufficient number of persons were firmly convinced of the truth, and constituted a body of witnesses whose evidence might convince the world and give effect to the Divine will.

After this conviction was produced, we come to the final stage, the apparent departure of the embodied Divine Nature, the man Jesus, from the world. The earthly period had fulfilled its purpose and reached its climax. This is the Ascension. This term, like many of the other words which must be employed by man in discussing the subject, is an attempt to express Divine truth—which as Divine is not subject to worldly conditions—in the language of human imperfection. The Divine Nature is omnipresent. It does not lie more in one direction from us than in another; it is neither above nor below: it is everywhere. To say that Jesus went up into heaven is a merely symbolic expression.; it has not a local significance; it is an emblematic statement of the truth. The truth which has to be conceived in the mind is that, at the due stage and the proper moment, Jesus ceased to be apparent to human senses in the world, and is God with God.

Sir William M. Ramsay, *Pictures of the Apostolic Church* [1910]
Luke 24:46-51; Acts 1:8; 1 Cor. 15:3-9; 1 John 4:8-10

Rashdall, James Hastings [1858-1924]

759 Following Christ

Belief in God through Christ is the most important of all aids to the following of Christ, but (let us never forget) the following is the great thing. To those who, by whatever means they are attracted to Him, really seek to do God's will as He revealed it, Christ will prove a Savior—a Savior from sin, a Savior from the power of sin here, and from the misery which sin brings with it here and hereafter.

James Hastings Rashdall, *Principles and Precepts* [1927]
Matt. 16:24

760 Coming in penitence

It does not make a very great difference what side of Christ's work attracts us and appeals to us most; doubtless Christ has many ways of drawing men to Himself. One side of Christ's work will appeal most to one mind, another to another. The mistake that is often made by those who speak most about Christian experience is that they are so apt to insist upon everyone else's experience—on penalty of its utter worthlessness—being exactly the same as their own. The great thing is that we should be attracted by Christ in some way, that we should come to God in that spirit of penitence which Christ taught was the one condition of acceptance with Him, and with that steady purpose of amendment which is, as he always taught, a part of true penitence.

James Hastings Rashdall, *Principles and Precepts* [1927]
Acts 8:22

761 Do we believe?

The great question for us now is, Do we believe in that love of God which Christ taught by His words, and of which His followers saw in His voluntary death a crowning manifestation? And remember that even belief in the love of God will do us no good unless it awakes answering love in ourselves—unless it adds to our hatred of the sin which separates us from God and increases our love of other men.

James Hastings Rashdall, *Principles and Precepts* [1927]
Rom. 7:13

Rauschenbusch, Walter [1861-1918]

762 Speculative thought

Theologians have felt no hesitation in founding a system of speculative thought on the teachings of Jesus; and yet Jesus was never an inhabitant of the realm of speculative thought.

Walter Rauschenbusch
Matt. 10:37

Reardon, Patrick Henry

763 Praying against principalities and powers

To relinquish any of the Psalms on the excuse that its sentiments are too violent for a Christian is a clear sign that a person has also given up the very battle that a Christian is summoned to fight. The Psalms are prayers for those who are engaged in an ongoing, spiritual conflict. No one else need bother even opening the book.

Patrick Henry Reardon, *Christ in the Psalms* [2000]
Ps. 5:10; 109:9-20

Redwood, Hugh [b.1883]

764 The cause of evil

[Christ] tells us plainly, and without any qualifications, that we are involved in a war in which there is no room for neutrals. Yet people attempt to evade His statement. Generally speaking, these are the very people who are the quickest in laying the blame upon God for all the sorrow and sin in the world. They argue that He could prevent it. They excuse their own do-nothing attitude by making of evil's apparent predominance a ground for doubt of His loving kindness. It never seems to occur to them to look for the cause in mankind.

Hugh Redwood, *Live Coals* [1935]
Mark 9:40-42

Rees, Thomas [1869-1926]

765 Testing the spirits

The first principle of differentiation was laid down by Paul, when dealing with the problems of the spiritual phenomena that had arisen at Corinth. . . . In the confusion of spiritual phenomena, . . . it was possible that evil spirits, as well as the Holy Spirit, inspired some of the manifestations. One in particular Paul singles out as being in obvious contradiction to the work of the Spirit of God: "No man speaking in the Spirit of God saith, Jesus is anathema (cursed)." On the other hand, "No man can say, Jesus is Lord, but in the Holy Spirit" (I Cor. 12:3). It is difficult to conceive the state of mind of a member of a Christian congregation who would curse the name of Jesus. Yet it is evident that at Corinth, people gave way to such uncontrollable frenzy that, either in folly or in momentary reversion to Judaism or heathenism, they cursed the name in whose honor they had met. . . . But the spirit that inspired disloyalty to Jesus Christ could not be the Holy Spirit, for in Paul's experience and theology, the two beings were, if not identical, at least in perfect harmony of principle and action. This, then, was Paul's first criterion for deciding which spiritual phenomena could be approved by Christians as the work of the Holy Spirit. They must be loyal to Jesus Christ as Lord of life, and as the object of faith and love for every believer.

Another criterion was loyalty to the community of Christ both as gathered congregation and as organized church. The pride of spiritual gifts had led the Corinthians to jealousy and strife. They had divided into factions owning the leadership, one of Paul, one of Apollos, another of Cephas, and another of Christ—but such factions, the apostle tells them, were not characteristics of the "spiritual," but of the carnal. To divide the Church was to destroy the temple of God, where the Holy Spirit dwelt among them (I Cor. 3:1, 3, 16). And the very gifts about which they quarreled should have been a power to unite them, for they all proceeded from one and the same Spirit, from one and the same Lord, from one and the same God, who worketh all in all. The Spirit was indeed the principle of unity in the Church, "for in one Spirit were we all baptized into one body" (I Cor. 12:13). Therefore, to divide the Church was to drive away the Spirit. . . . The tests of spiritual phenomena in the life of the community, and the proofs that they were of the Holy Spirit, were unity, order, and edification.

The supreme antidote against strife and confusion, the supreme principle of unity and service in the Church, was also the greatest gift of the Spirit and the perfect and abiding proof of its presence, namely, love. This introduces a third criterion of the Spirit, and on the wider stage of the moral life. It is loyalty to the moral ideal of Christ. "If we live by the Spirit, by the Spirit let us also walk" (Gal. 5:25). Where the Spirit dwells, it produces a new, a higher, a unique type of moral life. For Paul, the Christian life was not the normal and natural product of human activity, but a gracious divine gift, received by the descent of the Spirit into the human heart, for "the fruit of the Spirit is love, joy, peace, long-suffering, kindness, goodness, faithfulness, meekness, temperance" (Gal. 5:22-23). And there is yet one higher manifestation of the Spirit, the participation in the divine sonship of Jesus Christ. "And because ye are sons, God sent forth the Spirit of His Son into our hearts, crying, Abba, Father" (Gal. 4:6). Where sonship is, there the Spirit is. On the other hand, "as many as are led by the Spirit of God, these are the sons of God" (Rom. 8:14). Where the Spirit leads, there sonship is. . . . The possession of the Spirit and participation in Christ's sonship are but two aspects of the same experience. Here, the phenomenon, if it may be so called, bears its own credentials. Sonship is a self-evident work of the Spirit. But the evidence is available only for its owners in order that the Spirit of adoption may attest itself to others, it must issue in the life according to the Spirit, by walking in the spirit and bearing the fruit of the Spirit.

Thomas Rees, *The Holy Spirit in Thought and Experience* [1915]

766 The Holy Spirit

The experiencing of divine sonship, of adoption, is the act of the Spirit in our hearts crying Abba, Father (Gal. 4:6; Rom. 8:15,16). . . . Liberty, peace, and joy are correlative factors in the same moment of experience, and they are all attributed to the Holy Spirit (Rom. 8:2,6; 14:17; Gal. 5:22,23; 1 Thess. 1:6). In the allegory of Abraham's two sons, Paul contrasts the state of bondage under the Law with that of liberty under grace, and defines the one as being after the flesh, but the other after the Spirit (Gal. 4:21-29). . . . The first great moment of the new life, whether it be called justification by faith, the realization of sonship, or peace with God, is a work of the Holy Spirit, through the preaching of the Word. But [Paul] does not indicate . . . the exact logical or historical sequence of the various elements in the experience, and it may be doubted whether he would have entertained any idea of sequence within the complex experience of justification.

That Paul regarded the subsequent development of Christian life and character as in its totality the work of the Spirit is not questioned. All the Christian virtues are the fruit of the Spirit (Gal. 5:22,23). He is the Spirit of holiness (Rom. 1:4), of sanctification (II Thess. 2:13), and of a new life (Rom. 7:6). Love, the greatest of the Christian graces, is the pre-eminent gift of the Spirit (I Cor. 13; Col. 1:8; Rom. 15:30), not only as the grace of character, but also as a principle of unity in the Church (Eph. 4:1-6; cf. Eph. 2:18, 22). The Spirit bestows wisdom and knowledge on the individual and in the Church. Paul spoke "God's wisdom in a mystery . . . through the Spirit, for the Spirit searcheth all things, yea, the deep things of God" (I Cor. 2:7-10). "For to one is given through the Spirit the word of wisdom, and to another the word of knowledge, according to the same Spirit" (I Cor. 12:8). All Christian knowledge was derived from the Spirit, both by Paul and [the Apostle] John (Eph. 1:17, 23; 3:16-19; John 16:13; I John 2:20, 27; cf. James 1:5; 3:15, 17).

The Spirit was the power manifested in the resurrection of Christ (Rom. 1:4), in the inner life of man (Rom. 15:13; Eph. 3:16), and in the preaching of the word (I Thess. 1:5; 1Cor. 2:4). He is the Spirit of life, both now and hereafter (Gal. 6:8; I Cor. 15:45); and the Spirit of assurance, the guarantee of the new life, whereby man obtains confidence towards God and courage in the face of the world's evil (II Cor. 1:22; Rom. 5:5; 8:16, 23; Eph. 1:13; 4:30). Man, therefore, as the dwelling-place of the Spirit, is the inalienable possession of God (I Cor. 3:16, 17; 6:19)

As the Christian life in the individual is the work of the Spirit, it follows that the corporate realization of that life, in the Church built upon the foundation of apostles and prophets, is also His creation. . . . The great creative acts and significant turning-points were recognized, either by the Church or by its historian, as determined by the Spirit. The Spirit confirmed and preserved the community from the outset, by the descent at Pentecost (Acts 2:4). The extension of the Gospel beyond Judea and the first mission to the Gentiles were commanded and approved by the Spirit (Acts 8:29; 10:19, 44; 13:2, 4). Paul, on his journeys, was led by the Spirit (Acts 16:6, 7). He himself was especially conscious that his whole ministry was inspired by the

Holy Ghost (Rom. 15:18,19). All the apostles were conspicuously men of the Spirit.

The Spirit guided the Church in the creation of organization and officers (Acts 6:3; 20:28). The first three gifts of the Spirit which God had set in the Church were apostles, prophets, and teachers, in addition to which the whole Church had a gift of government (I Cor. 12:4, 28). The decisions of the first council of the Church were first of all decrees of the Spirit (Acts 15:28). Paul had preached and created churches by the power of the Spirit (I Cor. 2:4; 1Thess. 1:5,6; Gal. 3:2). In one Spirit were all believers baptized into one body (I Cor. 12:13: cf. Phil. 1:27). The Spirit therefore dwells in the Church as the principle of its entire united and common life (Eph. 2:18,22; cf. I Cor. 3:16).

Thomas Rees, *The Holy Spirit in Thought and Experience*
[1915]

Reeves, (Richard) Ambrose, Bp. [1899-1980]

767 Understanding unity

Whatever may be our differences of color, culture, and class, the unity that is ours in Christ is given visible expression at every Synod. Here we all gather around the one Altar, here we all share in shaping the policy of the Church in this diocese; here we all take part in making provision for carrying on the work of the Church during the coming year. At this time, year by year, we are specially conscious of our unity in Christ, and are made aware afresh that we are members of this new race of human beings which is made up of all those of every ethnic group who have been added to Christ. We are members of that Kingdom in which all human antagonisms are transcended. Yet we shall not interpret aright this unity which is ours in Christ Jesus unless we continually remind ourselves that it has its origin in His death and resurrection. The Church springs out of the deeds of Jesus done in the flesh, and we can only fulfill our destiny in the Church as we learn that we are utterly dependent upon the whole Body of Christ.

Ambrose Reeves [1956]
1 Pet. 2:9

768 Meeting Jesus

What makes life worth living is the mutual enrichment of people through understanding, intelligence and affection. It is just here that our awareness that Jesus is our contemporary and that Calvary is relevant to our present human situation ought to help us greatly. And that is not merely because in his relationships with others during his earthly life in Palestine Jesus exemplified all that I have tried to say about human relationships. In every genuine human encounter with another person we may become aware of Jesus, and meet with him. This may sound fanciful, but there is much in the Scriptures and in Christian experience which suggests that Jesus is frequently met in the traffic of person with person, provided that there is a genuine encounter between them. Jesus himself showed that for this to happen demands courage and a willingness to move from a life that is centered in itself. So if we are to pass out of that lonely world of isolation then we must be prepared to take the risks that are always involved when we allow persons to confront us as persons and do not regard them as things. Yet, dangerous though it may be to live in this way, it is the only way to live.

Ambrose Reeves, *Calvary Now* [1965]
Matt. 19:13-15; 25:34-40

Reich, Max I. (Isaac) [1867-1945]

769 Messianic prophecy fulfilled

[The entire Old Testament] ground-plan is the whole scheme of Messianic prophecy, from the germinal revelation in Genesis concerning the suffering, yet triumphant Seed of the Woman to the coming to His Temple of the long-absent "Angel of the Covenant" in Malachi. That hope alone explains the Book, giving meaning and consistency to its story. Was it a chimera, an hallucination? According to the prophecy of Micah, the messianic Shepherd of Israel had to be born in Bethlehem. It is unthinkable that an heir to the throne of David could be born in Bethlehem now, and be also able to prove his legitimacy by documentary evidence. The event must clearly have taken place already, or Micah is a false prophet, a raiser of false hopes, along with the other writers in the Old Testament.

Max I. Reich
Gen. 3:15; Mic. 3:1; 5:2; Rom. 1:1-4

Reid, Gavin [b.1950]

770 On outreach

This is the age of the conference and study group—people talking about what they know they should be doing. In a subtle way, talking about something becomes an excuse for not doing it. This new bolt-hole of the conference and study group is not confined to the local congregation. It is a painful fact of life in the central structures of the churches. We have a welter of reports, commissions, surveys, liaison bodies, and so on. They have the appearance of progressive thinking and readiness to face change, combined with the function of being delaying devices. They are the sacraments of current Christianity, and its dilemma. Outreach is a move from power structures to meekness structures, and, in spite of the fact that Christians believe that it is the meek who shall inherit the earth, they show (as in the ecumenical movement) a distinct reluctance to relinquish power-structure thinking.

Gavin Reid, *The Gagging of God* [1969]
Col. 2:8

771 The language of the Gospel

If those who say that we must preach the same message as Paul and the other apostles mean that we should also exhibit the same adaptability and sensitivity to the background culture, then they are right. . . . If, however, they mean that we should expect results merely by repeating the actual phrases found in the New Testament, then they are mistaken. They are making, in fact, one of the basic mistakes in verbal communication, which is to confuse words with what they describe. The gospel is something God has done, not a series of phrases describing it. Saying this does not undermine the Christian's belief in the inspiration of the Bible, for the important thing about the

Bible is what it talks about, rather than the way it does the talking. If we considered that there was the same degree of essential inspiration in the way it does the talking, then we would have to insist that every Christian learn Hebrew and Greek. The mere fact that we in the Western world read translations of the scriptures is a clear admission that times and cultures have changed.

Gavin Reid, *The Gagging of God* [1969]
Acts 17:16-23

Reindorp, G. E., Bp.

772 The unenlightened conscience

To say of an act done, "My conscience is quite clear," sounds smug and satisfactory. It does not by any means follow that the speaker's conscience ought to be clear. It may simply show that [it] is sadly unenlightened.

G. E. Reindorp
John 16:2; 1 Tim. 4:2; Tit. 1:15

Rhymes, Douglas [1914-1996]

773 Sunday piety

If our faith is not relevant to our daily life in the world and in the parish, then it is no use; and if we cannot be Christians in our work, in the neighborhood, in our political decisions, then we had better stop being Christians. A piety reserved for Sundays is no message for this age.

Douglas Rhymes
Matt. 13:54-58; 1 John 5:4

774 Service and the church

The laity . . . living in the world as an integral part of it, is the primary body through which the reality of the phrase "the Church is service" has to be manifested in all spheres of secular life: the Church has to show in her own life and attitude towards others the evidences of the redemptive order which is in Christ an operative fact: Christ the Lord is also Christ the servant: the Church which is the lord of all life is also the servant of all life, and the lordship is shown only through the service. The world wants to see redemption: it is not interested in being talked to about it. A church which is not outward looking . . . has ceased to be a church as the Body of Christ and has instead become a club for the benefit of its members.

Douglas Rhymes
2 Cor. 4:5

Richard of Chichester, Bp. [1197-1253]

775 Each day

Thanks be to thee, O Lord Jesus Christ, for all the benefits which Thou hast given us; for all the pains and insults which Thou hast borne for us. O most merciful redeemer, friend and brother, may we know thee more clearly, love Thee more dearly, and follow Thee more nearly; For Thine own sake.

St. Richard of Chichester
2 Cor. 4:15,16

Rieu, E. V. (Emil Victor) [1887-1972]

776 The Magna Carta of the human spirit

Let the Gospels speak. Of what I have learnt from these documents in the course of my long task, I will say nothing now. Only this, that they bear the seal of the Son of Man and God, they are the Magna Charta of the human spirit. Were we to devote to their comprehension a little of the selfless enthusiasm that is now expended on the riddle of our physical surroundings, we would cease to say that

Christianity is coming to an end—we might even feel that it had only just begun.

E. V. Rieu, The Four Gospels [1952]
Phil. 1:27,28

Robertson, Frederick W. [1816-1853]

777 Prayer

The Divine Wisdom has given us prayer, not as a means whereby to obtain the good things of earth, but as a means whereby we learn to do without them; not as a means whereby we escape evil, but as a means whereby we become strong to meet it.

Frederick W. Robertson
Ps. 5:7; 85:8; Rom. 8:34

Robinson, John [c.1576-1625]

778 More truth yet

If God reveal anything to you by any other instrument of His, be as ready to receive it as ever you were to receive any truth by my ministry: for I am verily persuaded, the Lord has more truth yet to break forth out of His holy Word.

John Robinson to the Mayflower emigrants
2 Pet. 3:15,16

Rolle, Richard [c.1290-1349]

779 Fastened on God

It behooves thee to love God wisely; and that may thou not do but if thou be wise. Thou art wise when thou art poor, without desire of this world, and despisest thyself for the love of Jesus Christ; and expendeth all thy wit and all thy might in His service. Whoso will love wisely, it behooves him to love lasting things lastingly, and passing things passingly; so that his heart be set and fastened on nothing but in God.

Richard Rolle
1 Tim. 6:17-19

780 Three degrees of love

That thou mayest win to the sweetness of God's love, I set here three degrees of love, in the which thou shouldst be aye waxing. The first is called insuperable, the second inseparable, the third singular. Thy love is insuperable when nothing may overcome it, that is, neither weal, nor woe, nor anguish, just of flesh nor the liking of this world. . . . Thy love is inseparable when all thy thoughts and thy wills are gathered together and fastened wholly in Jesus Christ, so that thou mayest no time forget Him, but aye thou thinkest on Him. . . . Thy love is singular when all thy delight is in Jesus Christ and in no other thing finds joy and comfort.

Richard Rolle, *The Commandments*
John 14:21; 15:9-12

781 Love of the Lord

The commandment of God is, that we love Our Lord in all our heart, in all our soul, in all our thought. In all our heart; that is, in all our understanding without erring. In all our soul; that is, in all our will without gainsaying. In all our thought; that is, that we think on Him without forgetting. In this manner is very love and true, that is work of man's will. For love is a willful stirring of our thoughts unto God, so that it receive nothing that is against the love of Jesus Christ, and therewith that it be lasting in sweetness of devotion; and that is the perfection of this life.

Richard Rolle, *The Commandments*
Matt. 22:37,38

782 Prayer to the Holy Spirit

O Holy Spirit, Who breathe where you will, come into me and snatch me up to yourself. Fortify the nature you have created, with gifts so flowing with honey that, from intense joy in your sweetness, it may despise and reject all which is in this world, that it may accept spiritual gifts, and through melodious jubilation, it may entirely melt in holy love, reaching out for uncircumscribed Light.

Richard Rolle, *Concerning the Love of God*
John 8:12; 2 Cor. 5:8; 2 Tim. 4:8

Rooy, Cammie van

783 Beauty from ashes

I know there are many who have pitied my beginnings, thinking it tragic that I had to endure such traumas both as a child and throughout my life, but I confess that I have rather pitied those who have never tasted the bitterness of a trial "too severe." For how is one to appreciate the contrast of light's dawning hope if his soul has never trembled through the dark hours of a nightmare's watch? Or how can one prove God's faithfulness if he never is granted the privilege of wandering through a barren desert, where only pools of Christ's Presence can possibly provide survival? It is a great honor to be apportioned pain. Christ Himself, though God incarnate, learned obedience through what He suffered. Dare we assume that we as His children can be taught by any wiser or kinder instructor than the severity of unwanted pain? We dare not steel ourselves against our trials, running away from the fires where our pruned branches crumble to ashes. For if we escape those flames, we will risk barrenness of soul and will miss out on the beauty that only is born through the ashes of yesterday's grief.

Cammie Van Rooy [2002]
Isa. 61:1-3

Rossetti, Christina G. (Georgina) [1830-1894]

784 Love is strong as death

> "I have not sought Thee, I have not found Thee,
>   I have not thirsted for Thee:
> And now cold billows of death surround me,
> Buffeting billows of death astound me,
>   Wilt Thou look upon, wilt Thou see
>   Thy perishing me?"
>
> "Yea, I have sought thee, yea, I have found thee,
>   Yea, I have thirsted for thee,
> Yea, long ago with love's bands I bound thee:
> Now the Everlasting Arms surround thee,
>   Through death's darkness I look and see
>   And clasp thee to Me."

Christina Rossetti

Ps. 22; 23

785 A better resurrection

> I have no wit, no words, no tears;
> My heart within me like a stone
> Is numbed too much for hopes or fears.
> Look right, look left, I dwell alone;
> I lift mine eyes, but dimmed with grief
> No everlasting hills I see;
> My life is in the falling leaf:
> O Jesus, quicken me.
> My life is like a faded leaf,
> My harvest dwindled to a husk:
> Truly my life is void and brief
> And tedious in the barren dusk;
> My life is like a frozen thing,
> No bud nor greenness can I see:
> Yet rise it shall—the sap of spring;
> O Jesus, rise in me.
> My life is like a broken bowl,

A broken bowl that cannot hold
One drop of water for my soul
Or cordial in the searching cold;
Cast in the fire the perished thing;
Melt and remold it, till it be
A royal cup for Him, my King:
O Jesus, drink of me.

Christina Rossetti
Heb. 11:35

Rufinus, T. [c.345-410]

786 By example

As, then, a consummate master teaches both by example and by precept, so Christ taught the obedience, which good men are to render even at the cost of death, by Himself first dying in rendering it.

Rufinus
Phil. 2:5-12

Rupp, (Ernest) Gordon [1910-1986]

787 The City of God

Here in Pilgrim's Progress there is the ultimate human nostalgia for the City of God, which is the restless heart's true home. And even the cynical, the unbelieving and half-believing reader who goes with Christian to the end of the road must be a little shaken, may tremble to see something like a gate and also some of the glory of the place, and, glimpsing something of the company within the golden gates, may wish himself among them.

Gordon Rupp, "John Bunyan" in
Six Makers of English Religion, 1500-1700 [1957]
Rev. 21:10-27

Ruskin, John [1819-1900]

788 To know Him

To live is nothing, unless to live be to know Him by whom we live.

John Ruskin
2 Tim. 1:12

Rust, E. C. (Eric Charles)

789 The unifying principle

We cannot find in the Old Testament the fondly drawn distinction of our latter days between the natural and the supernatural, for the whole of the natural order is so directly linked with God that its conservation must be regarded as a kind of continuous creation, quite as dependent on God's creative Word as when first the heavens and the earth were made.

E. C. Rust, *Nature and Man in Biblical Thought* [1953]
Gen. 1:29,30; Ps. 23; Luke 12:24-28

Rutherford, Samuel [1600-1664]

790 Rich in grace

Every man thinketh he is rich enough in grace, till he take out his purse, and . . . then he findeth it but poor and light in the day of a heavy trial. I found I had not enough to bear my expenses, and should have fainted, if want and penury had not chased me to the storehouse of all.

Samuel Rutherford, letter [1637]
Eph. 2:5

791 On being cut off

I get not my feasts without some mixture of gall; neither am I free of old jealousies; for he hath removed my lovers and friends far from me; he hath made my congregation desolate, and taken away my crown; and my dumb sabbaths are like a stone tied to a bird's foot, that wanteth not wings; they seem to hinder my flight, were it not that I dare not say one word, but "Well done, Lord Jesus."

Samuel Rutherford, letter while in exile [1637]
Lam. 3:19-23

792 The balance sheet

I desire now to make no more pleas with Christ; verily, he hath not put me to a loss by what I suffer; he oweth me nothing; for in my bonds, how sweet and comfortable have the thoughts of him been to me, wherein I find a sufficient recompense of reward!

Samuel Rutherford, a letter while in exile [1637]
Heb. 10:35

793 Infinite grace

Millions of hells of sinners cannot come near to exhaust infinite grace.

Samuel Rutherford, a letter [1646]
Eph. 2:5

Ruysbroeck, Jan van [1293-1381]

794 The universality of His love

Christ was common to all in love, in teaching, in tender consolation, in generous gifts, in merciful forgiveness. His soul and his body, his life and his death and his ministry were, and are, common to all. His sacraments and his gifts are common to all. Christ never took any food or drink, nor anything that his body needed, without intending by it the common good of all those who shall be saved, even unto the last day.

Jan van Ruysbroeck, *Adornment of the Spiritual Marriage* [1350]
Luke 20:38; 2 Cor. 4:13-15; 5:14,15; 1 Tim. 2:6,7

Ryle, J. C. (John Charles), Bp. [1816-1900]

795 World understands humility and love

Humility and love are precisely the graces which the men of the world can understand, if they do not comprehend doctrines. They are the graces about which there is no mystery, and they are within reach of all classes. . . . [The poorest] Christian can every day find occasion for practicing love and humility.

J. C. Ryle
Matt. 5:16; 1 Cor. 13:4-7; 1 Pet. 3:4

Ryrie, Charles C. [b.1925]

796 Faith and works

What is said in the passage [James 2:14 ff.] is like a two coupon train or bus ticket. One coupon says, "Not good if detached" and the other says, "Not good for passage." Works are not good for passage; but faith detached from works is not saving faith.

Charles C. Ryrie, from *The Ryrie Study Bible*,
note on James 2:24
Jas. 2:14-18

Sadiq, John W. [1910-1980]

797 Manifesto

When our Lord began his ministry he announced a manifesto, far more comprehensive, thoroughgoing, and revolutionary than any socialism, which spoke of the good news to the poor, release for prisoners, and recovery of sight to the blind. The Church must learn to stand solidly behind all efforts to bring fuller life to people.

John W. Sadiq
Isa. 61:1,2; Luke 4:17-21

Saphir, Adolph [1831-1891]

798 Believing the future as well as the past

What think ye, is the Word of God to be fulfilled? Do you believe the Word of God? Do you believe what is fulfilled in the Word of God because it is fulfilled? or do you believe because God has said so? If you believe the past fulfillment because it is past, then you do not believe God. If you believe God, you must believe the future as well as the past.

Adolph Saphir
Ps. 27:1-3; 37:33; John 14:1-4; 1 Cor. 1:9; Tit. 1:2

799 The lamp of consciousness

God, though present everywhere, has His special residence, as being a pure Spirit, in our minds—"In Him we live, and move, and have our being." He is somewhere in the recesses of our soul, in the springs of our existence, a light in that mysterious region of our nature where the wishes, feelings, thoughts, and emotions take their earliest rise. The mind is a sanctuary, in the center of which the Lord sits enthroned, the lamp of consciousness burning before Him.

Adolph Saphir, *The Hidden Life* [1877]
Acts 17:24-28

800 Grace in the "Old" Testament

What is meant by calling the writings of Moses and the Prophets [the] "Old Testament"? Do they not set forth the covenant of grace? The doctrine of justification by faith—does not Paul in his Epistle to the Romans prove it from Genesis and from the Psalms? Where is the doctrine of substitution and the vicarious sufferings of the messiah set forth more clearly than in Leviticus and in the 53rd of Isaiah? The term "Old Testament" leads people to fancy it is an antiquated book; whereas, in many respects, it is newer than the New Testament, referring more fully to the age of glory and blessedness on the earth which is still before us.

> Adolph Saphir, *Christ and Israel* [1911]
>
> Isa. 53

801 Creed vs. actuality

It is one thing to believe in justification by faith, it is another thing to be justified by faith.

> Adolph Saphir, *Christ and Israel* [1911]
> *Matt. 9:13; Rom. 1:16,17; 3:25, 26; 4:20, 22;*
> *Phil. 3:8-11; Gal. 2:16*

802 The humanity of Christ

Let us not forget the humanity of the Lord Jesus Christ. Let us not think of it vaguely, and fall into the heretical fancy that the Son of God became man merely to transact certain things which were necessary to secure the salvation of men, and that after this object was achieved His human nature recedes into the background and impenetrable obscurity. No, it is not so; all-important as His work on earth was—the only foundation of our hope and blessedness—let us adore the revealed mystery that God gave us His Son, never to recall Him, as it were, and take Him away from us; He spared Him not and gave Him to us, allowing Him to become man, exalting Him as the Son of Man, enthroning Him because of his obedience unto death, and giving unto Him as the Son of Man all power in heaven and earth.

> Adolph Saphir, *Christ and Israel* [1911]
> *Rom. 8:32; Phil. 2:5-11*

803 The missionary character of the church

Let us remember how very soon the missionary character of the Church was forgotten, and the Church, instead of obeying the commandment of Jesus to go and make disciples of all nations (in fact, that it was chiefly a missionary association), neglected this great and important calling. . . . It is astonishing how a commandment so simple and distinct, and how a duty which you would have imagined would be eagerly greeted by the impulse of gratitude, of affection, and of compassion, was forgotten for so long a time, in the churches of the Reformation especially. Now we are accustomed to hear of mission work among the heathen nations, and to find that a great multitude of people are interested in it, and regard it with respect; but it was only at the commencement of the last century, and with great difficulty, [that] the attention of the Church was roused to this important duty; and even in the. . . . Church of Scotland there were a number of ministers who thought that the state of heathenism was so utterly corrupt, and that there was so much to be done in our own country, that it was altogether a Utopian project to think of converting the idolaters, and that it was not our imperative duty to trouble ourselves with their wretched condition.

Adolph Saphir, *Christ and Israel* [1911]
Matt. 28:19,20

804 All Scripture is Gospel

When Paul speaks [II Cor. 3] of our being ministers of the New Testament, he does not refer to books most of which were not yet written, but to the gospel, which he found in the Scripture he possessed. The Jews could only see "Old Testament" in Moses and the prophets, because they were blind. To the spiritual all Scripture is gospel, or New Testament (the Law being the schoolmaster, bringing us to Christ), but to the natural and self righteous, as we ought to know from experience and observation, all Scripture (gospels and epistles included) is Old Testament, or Covenant of Works.

Adolph Saphir, *Christ and Israel* [1911]
Gen. 15:6; 2 Cor. 3:6; Gal.3:24,25

805 God loves

The abstract metaphysical monotheism, the constant emphasis laid on God's unity and infinite and incomprehensible essence, could not give light to the mind or peace to the heart. . . . How human is the God of the Old Testament—the God who appears, speaks, guides, who loves and is loved, even as the Man of the New Testament, Christ Jesus, is divine! This difference between the idea of an absolute and infinite God and the God of Scripture is, after all, that which separates the true believer and Christian from the natural man.

Adolph Saphir, Christ and Israel [1911]
Heb. 1:1-4; 3:1,6

806 Not the doctrine, but the Person

There was no point of controversy between Jesus and the Jews; Jesus brought no new doctrine unto them. Jesus said, What the masters in Israel teach, what the Pharisees and the Scribes teach, is perfectly correct. There was no dogma which was the cause of controversy between Jesus and the nation; there was no new custom that Jesus introduced: He went into the Temple every day, He observed the ordinances and festivals of Israel. What was the subject of dispute and controversy between Jesus and the Jews? It was no doctrine, it was no innovation, it was Jesus Himself whom they rejected. There was an antipathy in them to the person of Jesus: it was the Lord Himself whom they hated, because they hated the Father. . . . But Jesus knew . . . that it was because He was one with the Father, because He was the express image of His being, because He was the perfect manifestation of the character of God, that they hated Him; and therefore Jesus was pained, not because they hated Him, but because they hated in Him the Father.

Adolph Saphir, Christ and Israel [1911]
John 1:11; 15:23-25

Saucy, Robert L.

807 Where the church can be seen

It is true that the New Testament uses the term ekklesia for the spiritual reality of the body of Christ and also for the assembly, in which the genuineness of the spiritual reality of every individual professing member cannot be known. To this extent, the exact membership of any individual church and the universal church at large cannot be known and is thereby invisible. But even this invisible membership is very visible in the reality of life. As for membership in an invisible church without fellowship with any local assembly, this concept is never contemplated in the New Testament. The universal church was the universal fellowship of believers who met visibly in local assemblies.

> Robert L. Saucy, *The Church in God's Program* [1972]
> *2 Tim. 2:19*

Sayers, Dorothy Leigh [1893-1957]

808 Contempt of materialism

Contempt of material things as such is, in fact, no more orthodox than pantheism—it is the great dualist heresy which always lies in wait for an over-spiritualized Christianity.

> Dorothy Leigh Sayers
> *2 Pet. 2:1,2*

809 Jesus, God and man

If Jesus were God and nothing else, his immortality means nothing to us; if he were a man and no more, His death is no more important than yours or mine. But if he were really both God and man, then when the man Jesus died, God died too, and when the God Jesus rose from the dead, then man rose too, because they were one and the same person.

> Dorothy Leigh Sayers
> *1 Cor. 15:22; 2 Cor. 5:21*

810 Christian principles without Christ

That you cannot have Christian principles without Christ is becoming increasingly clear [in the world today], because their validity as principles depends on Christ's authority.

Dorothy Leigh Sayers
Mark 1:21,22

Schaeffer, Francis [1912-1984]

811 Confidence in pastor or God?

You must not lose confidence in God because you lost confidence in your pastor. If our confidence in God had to depend upon our confidence in any human person, we would be on shifting sand.

Francis Schaeffer
1 Cor. 3:4-6

812 A cold kind of burning

Men today do not, perhaps, burn the Bible, nor does the Roman Catholic Church any longer put it on the Index, as it once did. But men destroy it in the form of exegesis: they destroy it in the way they deal with it. They destroy it by not reading it as written in normal, literary form, by ignoring its historical-grammatical exegesis, by changing the Bible's own perspective of itself as propositional revelation in space and time, in history.

Francis Schaeffer, *Death in the City* [1969]
Matt. 23:29-36

813 Christian sociology

This is the real Church of the Lord Jesus Christ—not merely organization, but a group of people, individually the children of God, drawn together by the Holy Spirit for a particular task, either in a local situation or over a wider area. The Church of the Lord Jesus should be a group of those who are redeemed and bound together on the basis of true doctrine. But subsequently they should show together a substantial "sociological healing" of the breaches between men, which have come about because of . . . man's sin. The Christian sociological position is that the sociological problems which we find . . . are a result of the separation that has come between men because of sin.

Now the world should be able to see in the Church those marks [which show] that there is a substantial sociological healing possible in the present generation. It is not enough for the Church to be engaged with the State in healing social ills, though this is important at times. But when the world can turn around and see a group of God's people exhibiting substantial healing in the area of human relationships in their present life, then the world will take notice. Each group of Christians is, as it were, a pilot plant, showing that something can be done in the present situation, if only we begin in the right way.

Francis A. Schaeffer, *The God Who Is There* [1968]
Eph. 2:20-22; Col. 3:9-11

Schaff, Philip [1819-1893]

814 United in Christ

If Christians are ever to be united, they must be united in Christ, their living head and the source of their spiritual life.

Philip Schaff
Heb. 4:15

Scofield, C. I. [1843-1921]

815 The church's divergence

The church has failed to follow her appointed pathway of separation, holiness, heavenliness and testimony to an absent but coming Christ; she has turned aside from that purpose to the work of civilizing the world, building magnificent temples, and acquiring earthly power and wealth, and, in this way, has ceased to follow in the footsteps of Him who had not where to lay His head.

C. I. Scofield, *Addresses on Prophecy* [1914]
Matt. 8:20; 23:13-33; 2 Pet. 1:16

816 Lowering the purpose of the church

Instead of pursuing her appointed path of separation, persecution, world-hatred, poverty, and non-resistance, [the Church] has used . . . Scripture to justify her in lowering her purpose to the civilization of the world, the acquisition of wealth, the use of an imposing ritual, the erection of magnificent churches, the invocation of God's blessing upon the conflicts of armies, and the division of an equal brotherhood into "clergy" and "laity."

C. I. Scofield, *Rightly Dividing the Word of Truth* [1930]
Amos 5:10; Matt. 5:10-12; 10:28; Mark 13:11-13; John 7:6-8

Selden, John [1584-1654]

817 Faith and works

In my intellect, I may divide [faith and works], just as in the candle I know there is both light and heat; yet put out the candle, and both are gone.

John Selden
Jas. 2:14

Sergeant, Lewis [d.1902]

818 The principles of the Lollards

The gist of what Wycliffe[7] has to say on every point is practically this, that where the Church and the Bible do not agree, we must prefer the Bible; that where authority and conscience appear to be rival guides, we shall be much safer in following conscience; and that where the letter and the spirit seem to be in conflict, the spirit is above the letter.

(⁷ John Wycliffe, "morningstar of the Reformation" (q.v.))

Lewis Sergeant
2 Cor. 3:6; Gal. 1:8; 2 Tim. 3:16

Shedd, Charlie W. [b.1915]

819 Empty people

The problem is not that the churches are filled with empty pews, but that the pews are filled with empty people.

Charlie Shedd
Luke 1:53

Sheppard, H. R. L. (Hugh Richard Lawrie) [1880-1937]

820 The finished work

"It is finished." It is hard for us to know the intonation with which these words of the dying Christ were spoken. If they came as the sufferer's sigh of relief, they must also have been the worker's glad cry of achievement. Everything had been done that could be, man had been offered a sight of God as He really was. For those of us who believe that, in seeing Jesus, we see God, the Cross is not a coarse framework of blood-stained wood, but the most precious emblem of man's dearest hopes; it is the great pledge which we sorely need, that love is stronger than hate, grace than sin, life than death.

H. R. L. Sheppard, Two Days Before [1924]
John 19:30

Sherrill, Lewis J. (Joseph) [1892-1957]

821 Lost

It is a Gospel to men who are without God, sinful, bewildered, anxious, discouraged, self-sufficient and proud yet destroying themselves and others, caught in a desperate plight from which they cannot extricate themselves. The Bible characterizes men in such a state as "lost," and as being "without hope in the world." . . . And let no one suppose that such a term as "lost" is merely a bit of conventional theological jargon. It stands for a terrible reality, a reality which modern man in his modern predicament knows only too well from his own bitter experience. It gives rise to the voices of despair which haunt our radios, our newspapers, our fiction and poetry, our stage and screen, our doctors' offices, our hospital wards, our grisly nightmare of atomic war, and the conversation of common people who no sooner meet than they begin to bemoan the fate that has overtaken the world.

Lewis J. Sherrill, *Lift Up Your Eyes* [1949]
Isa. 8:21,22; Jer. 18:12; Rom. 15:21; Eph. 2:12

Shoemaker, Samuel M. [1893-1963]

822 The source of power

True spiritual power of the Christian order is a kind of possessedness. It arises in and flows through a life hid with Christ in God. Its source is the grace of our Lord Jesus Christ, and the potency of the Holy Spirit. True spiritual power is the child of two parents: the truth as it is revealed in Jesus and our own experience resulting upon our acceptance of Him and His truth. The objective factor is that whole set of facts and truths, of historic events, and of interpretation of them, which is held by the church and set forth in the Bible. The subjective factor is what happens in the crucible of your life and mine when we accept the set of facts and truths and interpretations, and it begins to work in us.

Samuel M. Shoemaker
Col. 3:3

823 A redemptive community

There are, I should say, four elements in a redemptive community. It is personal, with things happening between people as well as to and in them individually; it is compassionate, always eager to help, observant but non-judgmental toward others, breathing out hope and concern; it is creative, with imagination about each one in the group and its work as a whole, watching for authentic new vision coming from any of them; and it is expectant, always seeking to offer to God open and believing hearts and minds through which He can work out His will, either in the sometimes startling miracles He gives or in steady purpose through long stretches where there is no special "opening." It may fairly be said that unless one enmeshes himself in this "redemptive fellowship" of the church, he lessens his chances of steady growth and effectiveness, in his Christian life and experience.

Samuel M. Shoemaker, *The Experiment of Faith* [1957]
Eph. 4:14-16

Short, Robert L. (Lester) [b.1932]

824 Nominal Christians

The nominal Christian, then, will see Jesus as a name, a representative, a symbol, a personification, a prototype, a figure, a model, an exemplar for something else. The nominal Christian pays homage to something about Jesus, rather than worshipping the man himself. For this reason, nominal Christians will extol the moral teachings of Jesus, the faith of Jesus, the personality of Jesus, the compassion of Jesus, the world view of Jesus, the self-understanding of Jesus, etc. None of these worships Jesus as the Christ, but only something about him, something peripheral to the actual flesh-and-blood man. This is why when the almighty God came into the world in Jesus, he came as the lowest of the low, as weakness itself, as a complete and utter nothing, in order that men would be forced into the crucial decision about him alone and would not be able to worship anything about him.

Robert L. Short, *The Parables of Peanuts* [1968]
2 Cor. 13:4

825 Disillusionment in prayer

The childish idea that prayer is a handle by which we can take hold of God and obtain whatever we desire, leads to easy disillusionment with both what we had thought to be God and what we had thought to be prayer.

Robert L. Short, *The Parables of Peanuts* [1968]
1 Cor. 14:20

Simeon, Charles [1759-1836]

826 Repentance

Repentance is in every view so desirable, so necessary, so suited to honor God, that I seek that above all. The tender heart, the broken and contrite spirit, are to me far above all the joys that I could ever hope for in this vale of tears. I long to be in my proper place, my hand on my mouth, and my mouth in the dust. . . . I feel this to be safe ground. Here I cannot err. . . . I am sure that whatever God may despise. . . . He will not despise the broken and contrite heart.

Charles Simeon
Ps. 51:17; Luke 5:32

827 Thy increase, my decrease

I would have the whole of my experience one continued sense— first, of my nothingness, and dependence on God; second, of my guiltiness and desert before Him; third, of my obligations to redeeming love, as utterly overwhelming me with its incomprehensible extent and grandeur.

Charles Simeon
2 Cor. 5:14,15

828 A broken heart

By constantly meditating on the goodness of God and on our great deliverance from that punishment which our sins have deserved, we are brought to feel our vileness and utter unworthiness; and while we continue in this spirit of self-degradation, everything else will go on easily. We shall find ourselves advancing in our course; we shall feel the presence of God; we shall experience His love; we shall live in the enjoyment of His favor and in the hope of His glory. . . . You often feel that your prayers scarcely reach the ceiling; but, oh, get into this humble spirit by considering how good the Lord is, and how evil you all are, and then prayer will mount on wings of faith to heaven. The sigh, the groan of a broken heart, will soon go through the ceiling up to heaven, aye, into the very bosom of God.

Charles Simeon
Rom. 8:26,27

Singh, Sadhu Sundar [1889-1929]

829 Salt

Salt, when dissolved in water, may disappear, but it does not cease to exist. We can be sure of its presence by tasting the water. Likewise, the indwelling Christ, though unseen, will be made evident to others from the love which he imparts to us.

Sadhu Sundar Singh
Matt. 5:13

830 The limitless patience

God's patience is infinite. Men, like small kettles, boil quickly with wrath at the least wrong. Not so God. If God were as wrathful, the world would have been a heap of ruins long ago.

Sadhu Sundar Singh
Ex. 34:6,7; Ps. 86:15; 103:8-10; Luke 20:9-16

831 The Living Water

From time immemorial men have quenched their thirst with water without knowing anything about its chemical constituents. In like manner we do not need to be instructed in all the mysteries of doctrine, but we do need to receive the Living Water which Jesus Christ will give us and which alone can satisfy our souls.

Sadhu Sundar Singh
John 4:7-14

832 Bearing the cross

From my many years experience I can unhesitatingly say that the cross bears those who bear the cross.

Sadhu Sundar Singh
Matt. 10:38; 16:24,25

Smart, Christopher [1722-1771]

833 Rejoice in the Lamb

Rejoice in God, O ye tongues; give the glory to the Lord, and the Lamb.

Nations, and languages, and every creature, in which is the breath of Life.

Let man and beast appear before him, and magnify his name together.

Let Noah and his company approach the throne of Grace, and do homage to the Ark of their Salvation.

Let Abraham present a Ram, and worship the God of his Redemption.

Let Jacob with his speckled Drove adore the good Shepherd of Israel.

. . .

Let Daniel come forth with a Lion, and praise God with all his might, through faith in Christ Jesus.

. . .

Let David bless with the bear—
    The beginning of victory to the Lord—
    to the Lord the perfection of excellence—

Hallelujah from the heart of God, and from the hand
of the artist inimitable, and from the echo of the heavenly harp in
sweetness magnifical and mighty.

Christopher Smart, *Jubilate Agno* [1759]
Lev. 26:6; Ps. 9:1,2; 63:11; Rev. 5:12

834 The flowers

For the flowers are great blessings.
For the Lord made a Nosegay in the meadow with his disciples
    and preached upon the lily.
For the flowers have great virtues for all senses.
For the flower glorifies God and the root parries the adversary.
For the flowers have their angels even the words of God's
    creation.
For there is a language of flowers.
For there is a sound reasoning upon all flowers.
For flowers are peculiarly the poetry of Christ.

Christopher Smart, *Jubilate Agno* [1759]
Matt. 6:28

Smith, Carl R. & Lynn, Robert W.

835 The end or the means?

Doubt, rather than faith, is high among the causes of the religious
boom. And the church's response to this current situation will reveal,
better than anything else, our faith in God—or our faithlessness. If
we churchmen interpret such pervasive doubt as a threat, then we
will do as the church has done so often in the past: we will substitute
the church for God, and make our church-centered activities into an
ersatz kingdom of God. Our faithlessness will be evident in the easy
paraphrase of the hard truth of the gospel, and in the lapse from the
critical loyalty that God requires of us, into the vague and corrupting
sentimentalism that has so marred American Protestantism. Or the
church can interpret the present religious situation as a promise, as
God's recall of His people to a new reformation. Our faithfulness to

God-in-Christ will be manifest in the willingness to be honest with ourselves and with the gospel. Then we may view the church, not as an end in itself, but as the point of departure into the world for which the Son of God died. Which will it be?

Carl R. Smith & Robert W. Lynn, "Experiment in Suburbia," in
Spiritual Renewal through Personal Groups [1957]
Prov. 2:3-5; Rom. 14:17

Smith, Franc (S. F. X. Dean)

836 Keeping quiet

[At the Garden of Olives Monastery]
"Why are you all so quiet all the time?" I say, still whispering at him in this hoarse voice.

"We are teachers and workers," he says, "not talkers."

"Workers, O.K.," I say, "but how can a teacher be quiet all the time and teach anybody anything?"

"Christ was the best," he says, thinking of something. "He lived thirty-three years. Thirty years he kept quiet; three years he talked. Ten to one for keeping quiet."

Franc Smith, *Harry Vernon at Prep* [1959]
Matt. 13:34

Smith, Miles [d. 1624]

837 A tongue they understand

We are so far off from condemning any of their labors that travailed before us in this kind, either in this land or beyond sea, . . . that we acknowledge them to have been raised up of God, . . . and that they deserve to be had of us and of posterity in everlasting remembrance. . . . Therefore blessed be they, and most honored be their name, that break the ice and give the onset upon that which helpeth forward to the saving of souls. Now what can be more available thereto, than to deliver God's book unto the God's people in a tongue which they understand? . . . So if we, building upon their foundation that went before us, and being helped by their labors, do endeavor to make that better which they left so good; no man, we are sure, has cause to mislike us; they, we persuade ourselves, if they were alive, would thank us. For is the Kingdom of God become words or syllables? Why should we be in bondage to them if we may be free?

Miles Smith, preface to the King James Bible [1611]
Acts 2:7-12

Smith, Sydney [1771-1845]

838 The feasts and the fasts

The observances of the Church feasts and fasts are tolerably well kept, upon the whole, since the rich keep the feasts and the poor keep the fasts.

Sydney Smith

Soper, Donald O. [1903-1998]

839 God limited by His goodness

I can see no intellectual objection to the statement that God's power is not limited by anything outside His own creative purpose: in that sense He is omnipotent, but it is even impossible for Him to exercise that power in certain ways without thereby ceasing to be our Father. In that sense God is not omnipotent: He is limited by His own nature, by His perfect goodness and mercy; for the omnipotence of God means nothing apart from His Fatherly love. In particular, this limitation of the power of God is to be found in the measure of freedom which, as His children, we enjoy. God shares His power with us so that, for a time at least, if we so determine, we can break His laws and frustrate His plans, but also so that we can give to Him, if we choose, the free allegiance of our hearts and minds, and become

The Authentic **Book of Christian Quotations**

children at His Family Table, drawn together by the compulsion of His love, and not the exercise of His might.

Donald O. Soper, *Popular Fallacies* [1938]
Ps. 85:10; Nah. 1:3; Matt. 19:26

Spurgeon, Charles Haddon [1834-1892]

840 Religious luxury

Oh, Brethren, it is sickening work to think of your cushioned seats, your chants, your anthems, your choirs, your organs, your gowns, and your bands, and I know not what besides, all made to be instruments of religious luxury, if not of pious dissipation, while ye need far more to be stirred up and incited to holy ardor for the propagation of the truth as it is in Jesus.

C. H. Spurgeon
Mark 4:13-20; Jas. 5:1-5

841 The best soldiers

The Lord gets his best soldiers out of the highlands of affliction.

C. H. Spurgeon
Ps. 126:5,6; 2 Tim. 2:11-13; Heb. 12:6,7; 1 Pet. 5:10

842 Seeking the lost

If sinners be dammed, at least let them leap to Hell over our bodies. If they will perish, let them perish with our arms about their knees. Let no one go there unwarned and unprayed for.

C. H. Spurgeon
Rom. 15:21; Jude 1:22,23

843 Carrying one's cross

There are no crown wearers in heaven who were not cross bearers here below.

C. H. Spurgeon, *Gleanings among the Sheaves* [1869]
Matt. 10:38; 16:24,25

Stace, W. T. (Walter Terence) [b.1886]

844 Getting around the problem

The problem of evil assumes the existence of a world-purpose. What, we are really asking, is the purpose of suffering? It seems purposeless. Our question of the why of evil assumes the view that the world has a purpose, and what we want to know is how suffering fits into and advances this purpose. The modern view is that suffering has no purpose because nothing that happens has any purpose: the world is run by causes, not by purposes.

W. T. Stace, *Religion and the Modern Mind* [1953]
Ps. 89:30-32; 1 Pet. 2:21

Stark, Rodney & Charles Glock

845 Enemies within the citadel

While many Americans are still firmly committed to the traditional, supernatural conceptions of a personal God, a Divine Savior, and the promise of eternal life, the trend is away from these convictions. The fact is that a demythologized modernism is overwhelming the traditional Christ-centered, mystical faith. For the modern skeptics are not the apostates, village atheists, or political revolutionaries of old. The leaders of today's challenge to traditional beliefs are principally theologians—those in whose care the church entrusts its sacred teachings.

Rodney Stark & Charles Glock, *Trans-Action*
Mark 13:21,22; Luke 6:39; 21:8; 2 Tim. 4:1-4

Stearns, Richard

846 Active love

In today's world, wracked by terrorism, poverty, lawlessness, disease, and violence, the message of the gospel and the need for Christians who put their faith into action has never been more acute. We, the followers of Jesus Christ, are an integral part of God's plan for the world—the same world that God loved so much—"that he gave his one and only son, that whoever believes in him shall not perish but have everlasting life" (John 3:16). In this famous verse we see the depth of God's love for our world. It was not a passive and sentimental love but rather a dynamic, active, and sacrificial love. For God so loved the world that he acted!

> Richard Stearns, President, World Vision United States,
> Introduction to *Faith In Action Study Bible: Living God's Word*
> *in a Changing World* [2005]
> *John 3:16-17; 1 John 3:17-18*

Steen, Thomas M.

847 Lacks that one thing

The church has magnificent buildings, superb equipment, trained leadership, excellent teaching materials, organizational ability, and yet lacks that one thing that could take all these tools and make them the channel of God's will. In spite of its ever-increasing membership, the church lacks the spirit of God's growing love and understanding that can transform it from an efficient organization into a loving, dynamic fellowship where men and women become vitally alive with faith, love, and hope.

> Thomas M. Steen, "Renewal in the Church," in
> *Spiritual Renewal through Personal Groups* [1957]
> *2 Cor. 1:21,22*

Steuart, R. H. J. (Robert Henry Joseph) [1874-1948]

848 Understanding what Christ is

The truth is that the only key to the Christian life is the life of Christ; that the only solution to the many problems that thicken round our lives as we live them is to be found in the study of His life as He lived it; and that we shall never begin to understand what we ourselves are until we have begun to understand what He is.

R. H. J. Steuart
Mark 8:27-30

Stevenson, Robert Louis [1850-1894]

849 Prayer for a family

Lord, behold our family here assembled. We thank Thee for this place in which we dwell; for the love that unites us; for the peace accorded us this day; for the hope with which we expect the morrow; for the health, the work, the food, and the bright skies that make our lives delightful; for our friends in all parts of the earth, and our friendly helpers in this foreign isle [Samoa]. . . . Give us courage, gaiety, and the quiet mind. Spare to us our friends, soften to us our enemies. Bless us, if it may be, in all our innocent endeavors. If it may not be, give us the strength to encounter that which is to come, that we be brave in peril, constant in tribulation, temperate in wrath, and in all changes of fortune and down to the gates of death, loyal and loving to one another.

Robert Louis Stevenson
Ps. 9:13; Rom. 12:20; Heb. 13:6

Stott, John R. W. [b.1921]

850 A two-footed stance

The loving service which God sends His people into the world to render includes both evangelism and social action, for each is in itself an authentic expression of love, and neither needs the other to justify it.

John R. W. Stott
Rom. 12:1

851 We have the means

We have the means to evangelize our country; but they are slumbering in the pews of our churches.

John R. W. Stott
Rom. 13:11,12; Eph. 5:14

852 A persuasive demonstration

Instead of always being one of the chief bastions of the social status quo, the Church is to develop a Christian counter-culture with its own distinctive goals, values, standards, and lifestyle—a realistic alternative to the contemporary technocracy which is marked by bondage, materialism, self-centeredness, and greed. Christ's call to obedience is a call to be different, not conformist. Such a Church—joyful, obedient, loving, and free—will do more than please God: it will attract the world. It is when the Church evidently is the Church, and is living a supernatural life of love by the power of the Holy Spirit, that the world will believe.

John R. W. Stott, "Obeying Christ in a Changing World"
John 4:31-34; Eph. 2:19-22; 2 Tim. 1:7

853 The Spirit in discipleship

The essential contrast which Paul paints is between the weakness of the law and the power of the Spirit. For over against indwelling sin, which is the reason the law is unable to help us in our moral struggle (Rom. 7:17, 20), Paul now sets the indwelling Spirit, who is both our liberator now from 'the law of sin and death' (Rom. 8:2) and the guarantee of resurrection and eternal glory in the end (Rom. 8:11, 17, 23). Thus the Christian life is essentially life in the Spirit, that is to say, a life which is animated, sustained, directed and enriched by the Holy Spirit. Without the Holy Spirit true Christian discipleship would be inconceivable, indeed impossible.

John R. W. Stott, *Romans: Encountering
the Gospel's Power* [1998]
Rom. 8:3

Streeter, B. H.

854 God shares our suffering

In the Old Testament, we find the idea that God enters into the sufferings of His people. "In all their afflictions, He was afflicted." (Isa. 63:9) The relation of God to the woes of the world is not that of a mere spectator. The New Testament goes further, and says that God is love. But that is not love which, in the presence of acute suffering, can stand outside and aloof. The doctrine that Christ is the image of the unseen God means that God does not stand outside.

B. H. Streeter
1 John 4:8

Studd, C. T. [1860-1931]

855 The Great-God Party

I belong to the "Great-God Party," and will have nothing to do with the "Little-God Party." Christ does not want nibblers of the possible, but grabbers of the impossible.

C. T. Studd
Ps. 48:1

856 Prime qualifications

A lost reputation is the best degree for Christ's service.

C. T. Studd
Rom. 12:1-3

857 Enlist!

We Christians too often substitute prayer for playing the game. Prayer is good; but when used as a substitute for obedience, it is nothing but a blatant hypocrisy, a despicable Pharisaism. . . . To your knees, man! and to your Bible! Decide at once! Don't hedge! Time flies! Cease your insults to God, quit consulting flesh and blood. Stop your lame, lying, and cowardly excuses. Enlist!

C. T. Studd
Matt. 4:19; Luke 6:43-49; Rom. 2:1

858 Location, location, location

Some want to live within the sound of church or chapel bell; I want to run a rescue shop within a yard of hell.

C. T. Studd
1 Pet. 3:19; Jude 1:22,23

Studdert Kennedy, Geoffrey Anketell [1883-1929]

859 Comfort

We have taught our people to use prayer too much as a means of comfort—not in the original and heroic sense of uplifting, inspiring, strengthening, but in the more modern and baser sense of soothing sorrow, dulling pain, and drying tears—the comfort of the cushion, not the comfort of the Cross.

G. A. Studdert Kennedy
Acts 14:21-23

860 The bread of life

Variety may be the spice of life, but it is not life itself. It is that bread of life, that peace of God which is the very staff of life itself, for which men's souls are starving in these days.

G. A. Studdert Kennedy, *The Wicket Gate* [1923]
Amos 8:11,12

861 The spread of evil

We have forgotten that evil is infectious, as infectious as small-pox; and we do not perceive that if we allow whole departments of our life to become purely secular, and to create and maintain moral or immoral standards on their own, in time the whole of life is bound to become corrupt.

G. A. Studdert Kennedy, *The Wicket Gate* [1923]
Ps. 14:1-3

862 Confronting the world

The tremendous power of mass-suggestion, which we call the world, can only be confronted, and its victims cured, if they are received into a body which is filled with a vivid, vigorous, and conscious community life of the Spirit. Individuals are powerless to cope with a power so subtle and all-pervasive as this mass-suggestion is. If we are to save and rescue sinners, there must grow up in our Church a Spirit of Love and Brotherhood, a Christian community-life, transcending class and national distinctions, as pungent, as powerful, as impossible to escape as the Spirit of the world. No Apostolic Succession, no Ecclesiastical correctness, no rigidity of orthodox doctrine, can be themselves and in themselves give us this; it comes, and can only come, from a clearer vision of the Christ, a more complete surrender to His call and to the bearing of His Cross.

G. A. Studdert Kennedy, *The Wicket Gate* [1923]
1 Cor. 1:17,18

863 The only satisfaction

If I am a son of God, nothing but God will satisfy my soul; no amount of comfort, no amount of ease, no amount of pleasure, will

The Authentic **Book of Christian Quotations**

give me peace or rest. If I had the full cup of all the world's joys held up to me, and could drain it to the dregs, I should still remain thirsty if I had not God.

G. A. Studdert Kennedy, *The Wicket Gate* [1923]
Ps. 42:1,2; Matt. 5:6; Eph. 2:19; 1 John 3:1,2

Summers, W. H. (William Henry)

864 Wycliffe's dominion founded in grace

[John] Wycliffe's doctrine of "dominion founded in grace" was a peculiar feature of his system. He taught that God, as the great feudal superior of the universe, allotted to all earthly authorities their rule in fief as subject to Himself. The priesthood was not an office of dominion, but of service, and its prerogatives ceased when service was not rendered. Dominion was not granted to one person as God's Vicar on earth, but the King was as much God's Vicar as the Pope; nay, every Christian held his rights immediately of God.

W. H. Summers, *Our Lollard Ancestors* [1904]
Rom. 13:1-7

Swete, Henry Barclay [1835-1917]

865 Inarticulate longing

There are times when we cannot pray in words, or pray as we ought; but our inarticulate longings for a better life are the Spirit's intercessions on our behalf, audible to God who searches all hearts, and intelligible and acceptable to Him since they are the voice of His Spirit, and it is according to His will that the Spirit should intercede for the members of His Son.

Henry Barclay Swete,
The Holy Spirit in the New Testament [1909]
Rom. 8:26

Synge, F. C. (Francis Charles)

866 The vocation

Every Christian, by virtue of membership in the Church, has a vocation to share in the ministry of Christ to the world which has been entrusted to the Church. The vocation is answered in the home and office and factory and field. There it is that the People of God bears its witness to the vocation of the People of God, a people with a people's diversity and complex vitality, a people comprising a multiplicity of cultures and histories and colors and tongues, a people and not a collection of individuals, a people bound together in allegiance to one King and in obedience to one purpose.

F. C. Synge
2 Cor. 3:12

Tabb, John Banister [1845-1909]

867 I had no God but these

I had no god but these,
The sacerdotal trees,
And they uplifted me,
    "I hung upon a Tree."
The sun and moon I saw,
And reverential awe
Subdued me day and night,
    "I am the perfect light."
Within a lifeless stone—
All other gods unknown—
I sought Divinity,
    "The Corner-stone am I."
For sacrificial feast
I slaughtered man and beast,
Red recompense to gain.
    "So I, a Lamb, was slain."
"Yea, such My hungering Grace
That whereso'er My face

Is hidden, none may grope
Beyond eternal Hope."

John Banister Tabb
Ps. 118:22; Matt. 21:42; Mark 12:10; Luke 20:17;
1 Pet. 3:15; Rev. 5:12

Tauler, Johannes [c.1300-1361]

868 The only safety

If thou desirest to be safe, turn at once in thy emptiness to God. If thou hast been inconsistent, how canst thou better become consistent again than in God only? How canst thou better escape death than by the true, real Life—which is God Himself?

Johannes Tauler
Ps. 71:1-3

869 The price of true peace

If we ever are to attain to true Divine Peace, and be completely united to God, all that is not absolutely necessary, either bodily or spiritually, must be cast off; everything that could interpose itself to an unlawful extent between us and Him, and lead us astray: for He alone will be Lord in our hearts, and none other; for Divine Love can admit of no rival.

Johannes Tauler, *The Inner Way*
Matt. 6:24

870 A judging spirit

He who desires to become a spiritual man must not be ever taking note of others, and above all of their sins, lest he fall into wrath and bitterness, and a judging spirit towards his neighbors.

John Tauler, *Sermons*
Luke 6:37,38

Taylor, (James) Hudson [1832-1905]

871 The source of power

Since the days of Pentecost, has the whole church ever put aside every other work and waited upon Him for ten days, that the Spirit's power might be manifested? We give too much attention to method and machinery and resources, and too little to the source of power.

Hudson Taylor
Acts 4:31; 1 Thess. 1:5

Taylor, Jeremy [1613-1667]

872 Lord, come away

Lord, come away;
Why dost thou stay?
Thy road is ready and thy paths made straight
With longing expectations wait
The consecration of thy beauteous feet.
Ride on triumphantly; behold! we lay
Our lusts and proud wills in thy way.
Hosannah! welcome to our hearts: Lord, here
Thou hast a temple too, and full as dear
As that of Sion; and as full of sin—
Nothing but thieves and robbers dwell therein;
Enter and chase them forth, and cleanse the floor,
Crucify them, that they may never more
Profane that holy place
Where thou hast chose to set thy face.
And then if our still tongues shall be
Mute in the praises of thy deity,
The stones out of the temple wall
Shall cry aloud and call
Hosannah! and thy glorious footsteps greet.

Jeremy Taylor
Luke 19:37-40

873 The triumph of pride

Pride has a greater share than goodness of heart in the remonstrances we make to those who are guilty of faults; we reprove, not so much with a view to correcting them, as to persuade them that we are exempt from those faults ourselves.

Jeremy Taylor, *Holy Dying* [1651]
Matt. 7:1,2

874 Care for little things

Love is careful of little things, of circumstances and measures, and of little accidents; not allowing to itself any infirmity which it strives not to master, aiming at what it cannot yet reach, desiring to be of an angelic purity, and of a perfect innocence, and a seraphical fervor, and fears every image of offense; is as much afflicted at an idle word as some at an act of adultery, and will not allow to itself so much anger as will disturb a child, nor endure the impurity of a dream. And this is the curiosity and niceness of divine love: this is the fear of God, and is the daughter and production of love.

Jeremy Taylor, *Holy Living* [1650]
Mark 14:3-9

875 Beatitude

Love is the greatest thing that God can give us; for Himself is love: and it is the greatest thing we can give to God; for it will also give ourselves, and carry with it all that is ours. The apostle calls it the band of perfection; it is the old, and it is the new, and it is the great commandment, and it is all the commandments; for it is the fulfilling of the Law. It does the work of all the graces without any instrument but its own immediate virtue. For as the love of sin makes a man sin against all his own reason, and all the discourses of wisdom, and all the advices of his friends, and without temptation and without opportunity, so does the love of God: it makes a man chaste without the laborious arts of fasting and exterior disciplines, temperate in the midst of feasts, and is active enough to choose it without any intermedial appetites, and reaches at glory through the very heart of grace, without any other aims but those of love. It is a grace that loves God for Himself, and our neighbors for God. The consideration of God's goodness and bounty, the experience of those profitable and excellent emanations from Him, may be, and most commonly are, the first motive of our love; but when we are once entered, and have tasted the goodness of God, we love the spring for its own excellency, passing from passion to reason, from thanking to adoring, from sense to spirit, from considering ourselves to union with God: and this is the image and little representation of heaven; it is beatitude in picture, or rather the infancy and beginning of glory.

Jeremy Taylor, *Holy Living* [1650]
Ps. 34:8; 1 Pet. 2:1-3

876 Fix my thought

Fix my thoughts, my hopes, and my desires upon heaven and heavenly things; teach me to despise the world, to repent deeply for my sins; give me holy purposes of amendment and ghostly strength, and assistance to perform faithfully whatsoever I shall intend piously. Enrich my understanding with an eternal treasure of Divine Truths, that I may know thy will: and thou, who workest in us to will and to do of thy good pleasure, teach me to obey all thy commandments, to believe all thy revelations, and make me partaker of all thy gracious promises.

Jeremy Taylor, *Holy Living* [1650]
Ps. 25:1-5; 119:11,12,25-40,64-68; Matt. 13:34,35,51,52

877 Present in hearts

God is especially present in the hearts of His people, by His Holy Spirit; and indeed the hearts of holy men are temples in the truth of things, and in type and shadow they are heaven itself. For God reigns in the hearts of His servants; there is His Kingdom. The power of grace hath subdued all His enemies; there is His power. They serve Him night and day, and give Him thanks and praise; that is His glory. This is the religion and worship of God in the temple.

The temple itself is the heart of man, Christ is the high priest, who from thence sends up the incense of prayers, and joins them to His own intercession and presents all together to His Father; and the Holy Ghost by His dwelling there hath also consecrated it into a temple; and God dwells in our hearts by faith, and Christ by His Spirit, and the spirit by His purities: so that we are also cabinets of the mysterious Trinity, and what is this short of heaven itself, but as infancy is short of manhood? . . . The same state of life it is, but not the same age. It is heaven in a looking glass, dark but yet true, representing the beauties of the soul, and the grace of God, and the images of His eternal glory, by the reality of a special presence.

Jeremy Taylor, Holy Living [1650]
Ps. 91:1,2; 141:1,2; 1 Cor. 6:19,20; Heb. 7:26-28; 9:24

Temple, William, Abp. [1881-1944]

878 Worship

To worship is to quicken the conscience by the holiness of God, to purge the imagination by the beauty of God, to open the heart to the love of God, and to devote the will to the purpose of God.

William Temple
Ps. 5:7; 22:22; 26:6-8; 84:1-4; 103:1-4; 122:1; 1 Cor. 14:15

879 Faith is fellowship with God

Faith is not the holding of correct doctrines, but personal fellowship with the Living God. . . . What is offered to man's apprehension in any specific revelation is not truth concerning God but the Living God Himself.

William Temple
Heb. 11:6

880 The life of faith

The life of faith does not earn eternal life: it is eternal life. And Christ is its vehicle.

William Temple
Rom. 6:4

881 The Ascension

In the days of His earthly ministry, only those could speak to him who came where He was: if He was in Galilee, men could not find Him in Jerusalem; if He was in Jerusalem, men could not find Him in Galilee. His Ascension means that He is perfectly united with God; we are with Him wherever we are present to God; and that is everywhere and always. Because He is "in Heaven" He is everywhere on earth: because He is ascended, He is here now. Our devotion is not to hold us by the empty tomb; it must lift up our hearts to heaven so that we too "in heart and mind thither ascend and with Him continually dwell:"[8] it must also send us forth into the world to do His will; and these are not two things, but one.

([8] from the collect for Ascension, *Book of Common Prayer*, 1928)

William Temple, *Readings in St. John's Gospel* [1939]
John 20:17

ten Boom, Corrie [1892-1983]

882 All things possible

If all things are possible with God, then all things are possible to him who believes in him.

Corrie ten Boom
Gen. 18:14; Jer. 32:17; Matt. 19:26

Teresa of Avila [1515-1582]

883 The power of obedience

I know the power obedience has of making things easy which seem impossible.

Teresa of Avila
Rom. 16:19; Eph. 2:10; Phil. 2:12

884 Disturbed by trivia

Our souls may lose their peace and even disturb other people's, if we are always criticizing trivial actions—which often are not real defects at all, but we construe them wrongly through our ignorance of their motives.

Teresa of Avila
Jas. 4:11

Tertullian (Quintus S. Florens Tertullianus) [c.160-c.230]

885 Through Christ

We say, and we say openly, and while ye torture us, mangled and gory we cry out, "We worship God through Christ!" Believe Him a man: it is through Him and in Him that God willeth Himself to be known and worshipped.

Tertullian (Q. S. F. Tertullianus)
Rom. 8:35-39

Thérèse de Lisieux (Marie-Françoise-Thérèse Martin) [1873-1897]

886 The life of love

The eve His life of love drew near its end,
Thus Jesus spoke: "Whoever loveth Me,
And keeps My word as Mine own faithful friend,
My Father, then, and I his guests will be;
Within his heart will make Our dwelling above.

Our palace home, true type of heaven above.
There, filled with peace, We will that he shall rest,
With us, in love."

Thérèse de Lisieux
John 14:23-27

Thomas à Kempis [1380-1471]

887 Humility

What doth it profit thee to enter into deep discussions concerning the Holy Trinity, if thou lack humility, and be thus displeasing to the Trinity? For verily it is not deep words that make a man holy and upright; it is a good life which maketh a man dear to God. I had rather feel contrition than be skillful in the definition thereof. If thou knewest the whole Bible, and the sayings of all the philosophers, what should this profit thee without the love and grace of God?

Thomas à Kempis, *Of the Imitation of Christ* [1418]
1 Cor. 13:1,2; 1 Pet. 3:4

888 Few bearers of His cross

Jesus hath many lovers of His heavenly kingdom, but few bearers of His Cross. He hath many seekers of comfort, but few of tribulation. He findeth many companions of His table, but few of His fasting. All desire to rejoice with Him, few are willing to undergo anything for His sake. Many follow Jesus that they may eat of His loaves, but few that they may drink of the cup of His passion. Many are astonished at His miracles, few follow after the shame of His Cross. Many love Jesus so long as no adversities happen to them. Many praise Him and bless Him, so long as they receive any comforts from Him. But if Jesus hide Himself and withdraw a little while, they fall either into complaining or into too great dejection of mind.

Thomas à Kempis, *Of the Imitation of Christ* [1418]
Matt. 8:21-27; 16:24,25

889 The love of the sufferer

When Christ was in the world, He was despised by men; in the hour of need He was forsaken by acquaintances and left by friends to the depths of scorn. He was willing to suffer and to be despised; do you dare to complain of anything? He had enemies and defamers; do you want everyone to be your friend, your benefactor? How can your patience be rewarded if no adversity tests it? How can you be a friend of Christ if you are not willing to suffer any hardship? Suffer with Christ and for Christ if you wish to reign with Him.

Had you but once entered into perfect communion with Jesus or tasted a little of His ardent love, you would care nothing at all for your own comfort or discomfort but would rejoice in the reproach you suffer; for love of Him makes a man despise himself.

Thomas à Kempis, *Of the Imitation of Christ* [1418]
Mark 13:13; Acts 9:16; Rom. 15:3

890 The need to begin

If we would put some slight stress on ourselves at the beginning, then afterwards we should be able to do all things with ease and joy. It is a hard thing to break through a habit, and a yet harder thing to go contrary to our own will. Yet, if thou overcome not slight and easy obstacles, how wilt thou overcome greater ones? Withstand thy will at the beginning, and unlearn an evil habit, lest it lead thee little by little into worse difficulties. Oh, if thou knewest what peace to thyself thy holy life should bring, . . . and what joy to others, methinketh thou wouldst be more zealous for spiritual profit.

Thomas à Kempis, *Of the Imitation of Christ* [1418]
John 8:31,32; 1 Thess. 3:12,13

891 Knowledge is not enough

Every man naturally desires knowledge; but what good is knowledge without fear of God? Indeed a humble rustic who serves God is better than a proud intellectual who neglects his soul to study the course of the stars.

Thomas à Kempis, *Of the Imitation of Christ* [1418]
Ps. 25:14

892 The profitability of suffering

If indeed there had been anything better and more profitable to the health of men than to suffer, Christ would surely have shown it by word and example.

Thomas à Kempis, *Of the Imitation of Christ* [1418]
1 Pet. 4:13,14; 5:10

893 Suffering the Cross

Sometimes thou shalt be forsaken of God, sometimes thou shalt be troubled by thy neighbors; and what is more, oftentimes thou shalt be wearisome even to thyself. Neither canst thou be delivered or eased by any remedy or comfort; but so long as it pleaseth God, thou oughtest to bear it. For God will have thee learn to suffer tribulation without comfort, and that thou subject thyself wholly to Him, and by tribulation become more humble. No man hath so cordial a feeling of the Passion of Christ, as he that hath suffered the like himself.

The Cross therefore is always ready, and everywhere waits for thee. Thou canst not escape it, whithersoever thou runnest; for wheresoever thou goest, thou carriest thyself with thee, and shalt ever find thyself. Both above and below, without and within, which way so ever thou dost turn thee, everywhere thou shalt find the Cross; and everywhere of necessity thou must hold fast patience, if thou wilt have inward peace, and enjoy an everlasting crown.

Thomas à Kempis, *Of the Imitation of Christ* [1418]
Ps. 22:1; Luke 9:23; 2 Tim. 3:11,12

894 Temporal vs. eternal

For a small reward, a man will hurry away on a long journey; while for eternal life, many will hardly take a single step.

Thomas à Kempis, *Of the Imitation of Christ*
Matt. 6:5,6; 19:16-26

895 Loving the unlovely

It is no great matter to associate with the good and gentle; for this is a naturally pleasing to all, and everyone willingly enjoyeth peace, and loveth those best that agree with him. But to be able to live peaceably with hard and perverse persons, or with the disorderly, or with such as go contrary to us, is a great grace, and a most commendable thing.

Thomas à Kempis, Of the Imitation of Christ [1418]
Matt. 5:43-48

896 The requirement of faith

Faith is required of thee, and a sincere life, not loftiness of intellect, nor deepness in the mysteries of God. If thou understandest not . . . the things which are beneath thee, how shalt thou comprehend those which are above thee? Submit thyself unto God, and humble thy sense to faith, and the light of knowledge shall be given thee, as shall be profitable and necessary unto thee.

Thomas à Kempis, Of the Imitation of Christ [1418]
Heb. 5:8,9; Luke 8:10; 1 Cor. 2:7-10

897 Fellowship

Why do we talk and gossip so continually, seeing that we so rarely resume our silence without some hurt done to our conscience? . . . Devout conversation on spiritual things helpeth not a little to spiritual progress, most of all where those of kindred mind and spirit find their ground of fellowship in God.

Thomas à Kempis, Of the Imitation of Christ [1418]
Rom. 12:9

898 Excusing others

Thou knowest well how to excuse and color thine own deeds; but thou art not willing to receive the excuses of others. It were more just that thou shouldest accuse thyself, and excuse thy brother.

Thomas à Kempis, Of the Imitation of Christ [1418]
Matt. 18:23-35; Jas. 2:13

899 Adversity

If thou art willing to suffer no adversity, how wilt thou be the friend of Christ?

Thomas à Kempis, *Of the Imitation of Christ* [1418]
Matt. 24:9

900 When things go ill

Count not thyself to have found true peace, if thou hast felt no grief; nor that then all is well if thou hast no adversary; nor that this is perfect, if all things fall out according to thy desire.

Thomas à Kempis, *Of the Imitation of Christ* [1418]
Ps. 119:75; Jon. 1:14-2:4; Acts 16:23-25

901 The fear of death

He who loveth God with all his heart feareth not death, nor punishment, nor judgment, nor hell, because perfect love giveth sure access to God. But he who still delighteth in sin, no marvel if he is afraid of death and judgment.

Thomas à Kempis, *Of the Imitation of Christ* [1418]
Matt. 10:28; Rom. 8:5,6; Rev. 2:11

Tillotson, John, Abp. [1630-1694]

902 Wealth an opportunity for doing good

Wealth and riches, that is, an estate above what sufficeth our real occasions and necessities, is in no other sense a 'blessing' than as it is an opportunity put into our hands, by the providence of God, of doing more good.

John Tillotson
Luke 12:15; Jas. 2:6,7; 1 John 3:17

903 Count the cost

Men expect that religion should cost them no pains, that happiness should drop into their laps without any design and endeavor on their part, and that, after they have done what they please while they live, God should snatch them up to heaven when they die. But though "the commandments of God be not grievous," yet it is fit to let men know that they are not thus easy.

John Tillotson
Luke 14:26-30; 1 John 5:1-4

904 Trusting God for the outcome

We distrust the providence of God when, after we have used all our best endeavors and begged His blessing upon them, we torment ourselves about the wise issue and event of them.

John Tillotson
Luke 12:6,7; Heb. 3:14

905 Ashamed of the Gospel

We have no cause to be ashamed of the Gospel of Christ; but the Gospel of Christ may justly be ashamed of us.

John Tillotson
Rom. 1:16,17

906 Assurance vs. speculation

Every man hath greater assurance that God is good and just than he can have of any subtle speculations about predestination and the decrees of God.

John Tillotson
Matt. 7:11; 1 John 4:8

907 Resolutions

Resolution is no strange and extraordinary thing; it is one of the most common acts that belong to us as we are men. But we do not ordinarily apply it to the best purposes. It is not so ordinary for men to resolve to be good as to resolve to be rich and great, not so common for men to resolve against sin as to resolve against poverty and suffering. It is not so usual for men to resolve to keep a good conscience as to keep a good place.

John Tillotson
2 Tim. 2:3; 4:5; Heb. 12:3

908 Disinclined

The true ground of most men's prejudice against the Christian doctrine is because they have no mind to obey it.

John Tillotson
1 John 4:3

909 Ghostly consolation

The common custom is, when the physician has given over his patient, then and not till then to send for the minister, not so much to inquire into the man's condition and to give him suitable advice as to minister comfort and to speak peace to him at a venture. But let me tell you that herein you put an extremely difficult task upon us, in expecting that we should pour wine and oil into the wound before it be searched, and speak smooth and comfortable things to a man that is but just brought to a sense of the long course of a lewd and wicked life impenitently continued in. Alas! what comfort can we give to men in such a case? We are loath to drive them to despair; and yet we must not destroy them by presumption; pity and good nature do strongly tempt us to make the best of their case and to give them all the little hopes which with any kind of reason we can—and God knows it is but very little that we can give to such persons upon good ground, for it all depends upon the degree and sincerity of their repentance, which God only knows, and we can but guess at.

John Tillotson, *Sermons*
Heb. 12:16,17; Jas. 4:8-10; Rev. 2:5

910 A new commandment

Are we not all members of the same Body and partakers of the same Spirit and heirs of the same blessed hope of eternal life? . . . Why do we not, as becomes brethren, dwell together in unity, but are so apt to quarrel and break out into heats, to crumble into sects and parties, to divide and separate from one another upon every trifling occasion? Give me leave . . . in the name of our dear Lord . . . to recommend to you this new commandment of his, that ye love one another. Which is almost a new commandment still, and hardly the worse for wearing, so seldom is it put on, and so little hath it been practiced among Christians.

John Tillotson, *Sermons*
John 13:34; Rom. 6:8,9; 15:5-7

911 Repentance

Let no man deceive you with vain words or vain hopes or false notions of a slight and sudden repentance. As if heaven were a hospital founded on purpose to receive all sick and maimed persons that, when they can live no longer to the lusts of the flesh and the sinful pleasures of this world, can but put up a cold and formal petition to be admitted there. No, no, as sure as God is true, they shall never see the Kingdom of God who, instead of seeking it in the first place, make it their last refuge and retreat.

John Tillotson, *Sermons*
Matt. 6:33; Luke 8:14; 1 Tim. 5:5,6

912 Life without leaving the world

It is further objected that he hath left to us no example of that which by many is esteemed the only religious state of life, viz. perfect retirement from the world, for the more devout serving of God and freeing us from the temptations of the world—such as is that of monks and hermits. This perhaps may seem to some a great oversight and omission. But our Lord in great wisdom thought fit to give us a pattern of a quite different sort of life, which was, not to fly the conversation of men and to live in a monastery or a wilderness, but to do good among men, to live in the world with great freedom and with great innocence. He did indeed sometimes retire himself for the more free and private exercise of devotion, as we ought to do; but he passed his life chiefly in the conversation of men, that they might have all the benefit that was possible of his instruction and example. We read that "he was carried into the wilderness to be tempted," but not that he lived there to avoid temptation. He hath given us an example of denying the world without leaving it.

John Tillotson, *Sermons*
Matt. 4:1,12-17; Luke 4:1,14,15

913 True enemy vs. false friend

A mere form of religion does upon some accounts bring a man under a heavier sentence than if he were openly profane and irreligious. He that makes a show of religion flatters God, but all the while he acts and designs against him; whereas the profane man deals plainly, and tho' he be a monstrous and unnatural rebel, yet he is a fair and open enemy. And the kisses of a false friend are more hateful than the wounds of an open enemy.

John Tillotson, *Sermons*
Matt. 23:13,15

Tippett, Alan Richard

914 The purpose of the privilege

The concept of Israel as the chosen people does not imply a certain divine favoritism, as some seem to think, but an opportunity of grace, a calling that involved the assumption of the servant role among the nations. It was the fact that they had interpreted themselves as special objects of God's favor, and rejected the servant role, that led to their own rejection.

A. R. Tippett, *Church Growth and the Word of God* [1970]
Isa. 42:6,7; 53; Rom. 3:1-4

Tolstoy, Lyof N. (Nikolayevich) [1828-1910]

915 Freedom

A Christian cannot help being free, because in the pursuit and attainment of his object, no one can either hinder or retard him.

Lyof N. Tolstoy
Gal. 5:1

Torrey, R. A. (Reuben Archer) [1856-1928]

916 None too small

We sometimes fear to bring our troubles to God, because they must seem small to Him who sitteth on the circle of the earth. But if they are large enough to vex and endanger our welfare, they are large enough to touch His heart of love. For love does not measure by a merchant's scales, not with a surveyor's chain. It hath a delicacy . . . unknown in any handling of material substance.

R. A. Torrey
Matt. 10:29-31; John 3:16,17; 1 Cor. 6:19,20

Tourville, Abbe de [1842-1903]

917 Hard to please?

I implore you in God's name, not to think of Him as hard to please, but rather as generous beyond all that you can ask or think.

Abbe de Tourville
John 10:10; 2 Cor. 4:15

Towne, Charles Hanson [1877-1949]

918 Lord, I am glad

Lord, I am glad for the great gift of living,
Glad for Thy days of sun and of rain;
Grateful for joy, with an endless thanksgiving,
Grateful for laughter—and grateful for pain.
Lord, I am glad for the young April's wonder,
Glad for the fullness of long summer days;
And now when the spring and my heart are asunder,
Lord, I give thanks for the dark autumn ways.
Sun, bloom, and blossom, O Lord, I remember,

The dream of the spring and its joy I recall;
But now in the silence and pain of November,
Lord, I give thanks to Thee, Giver of all!

Charles Hanson Towne
Ps. 19:1; Eph. 5:19,20

Tozer, A. W. (Aiden Wilson) [1897-1963]

919 Surrendering to society

Religion today is not transforming people; rather it is being transformed by the people. It is not raising the moral level of society; it is descending to society's own level, and congratulating itself that it has scored a victory because society is smilingly accepting its surrender.

A. W. Tozer
2 Tim. 4:3,4

920 The means and the end

The sacred page is not meant to be the end, but only the means toward the end, which is knowing God himself.

A. W. Tozer
Prov. 2:3-5; Rom. 11:33

921 The one fixed point

When God would make His name known to mankind, He could find no better word than "I AM." "I am that I am," says God, "I change not." Everyone and everything else measures from that fixed point.

A. W. Tozer, *The Pursuit of God* [1948]
Ex. 3:14

922 Priorities

Let the seeking man reach a place where life and lips join to say continually, "Be thou exalted," and a thousand minor problems will be solved at once. His Christian life ceases to be the complicated thing it had been before and becomes the very essence of simplicity.

A. W. Tozer, *The Pursuit of God* [1948]
Ps. 108:5

923 Prayer life

A satisfying prayer life elevates and purifies every act of body and mind and integrates the entire personality into a single spiritual unit. In the long pull we pray only as well as we live.

A. W. Tozer, *The Pursuit of God* [1948]
John 15:16

924 Instantly free

Let a man set his heart only on doing the will of God and he is instantly free. If we understand our first and sole duty to consist of loving God supremely and loving everyone, even our enemies, for God's dear sake, then we can enjoy spiritual tranquility under every circumstance.

A. W. Tozer, *The Pursuit of God* [1948]
Matt. 22:36-40

925 The winsome God

The blessed and inviting truth is that God is the most winsome of all beings and in our worship of Him we should find unspeakable pleasure.

A. W. Tozer, *The Pursuit of God* [1948]
Ezra 6:15,16; Ps. 5:11,12; 27:6; Rom. 15:13

926 The vastness within

The widest thing in the universe is not space, it is the potential capacity of the human heart. Being made in the image of God, it is capable of almost unlimited extension in all directions. Christians

should seek for inner enlargement till their outward dimension gives
no hint of the vastness within.

A. W. Tozer, *The Pursuit of God* [1948]
Prov. 28:14

927 God's words

God did not write a book and send it by messenger to be read at a
distance by unaided minds. He spoke a Book and lives in His spoken
words, constantly speaking His words and causing the power of them
to persist across the years.

A. W. Tozer, *The Pursuit of God* [1948]
2 Tim. 3:14,15

928 Out of the world's parade

The moment we make up our minds that we are going on with this
determination to exalt God overall, we step out of the world's parade.
. . . We acquire a new viewpoint; a new and different psychology
will be formed within us; a new power will begin to surprise us by its
upsurgings and its outgoings.

A. W. Tozer, *The Pursuit of God* [1948]
Matt. 6:24; 1 Pet. 4:4

929 Gazing upon God

Constantly practice the habit of inwardly gazing upon God. You
know that something inside your heart sees God. Even when you
are compelled to withdraw your conscious attention in order to
engage in earthly affairs, there is within you a secret communion
always going on.

A. W. Tozer, *The Pursuit of God* [1948]
Isa. 6:1-8; John 14:23

930 The wonders of His Word

The doctrine of justification by faith (a Biblical truth, and a
blessed relief from sterile legalism and unavailing self-effort) has in
our times fallen into evil company and has been interpreted by many

in such a manner as actually to bar men from the knowledge of God. The whole transaction of religious conversion has been made mechanical and spiritless. Faith may now be exercised without a jar to the moral life and without embarrassment to the Adamic ego. Christ may be "received" without creating any special love for Him in the soul of the receiver. The man is "saved," but he is not hungry or thirsty after God. In fact, he is specifically taught to be satisfied and encouraged to be content with little. The modern scientist has lost God amid the wonders of His world; we Christians are in real danger of losing God amid the wonders of His Word.

A. W. Tozer, *The Pursuit of God* [1948]
Matt. 5:6; 7:9,10; Rom. 3:20

931 Heaven on earth

When the eyes of the soul looking out meet the eyes of God looking in, heaven has begun right here on this earth.

A. W. Tozer, *The Pursuit of God* [1948]
Rev. 3:20

932 Eyes on God

We get our moral bearings by looking at God. We must begin with God. We are right when, and only when, we stand in a right position relative to God, and we are wrong so far and so long as we stand in any other position.

A. W. Tozer, *The Pursuit of God* [1948]
Matt. 6:24; 12:50; Rev. 22:14

933 Focusing on God, rather than unity

One hundred worshipers meeting together, each one looking away to Christ, are in heart nearer to each other than they could possibly be were they to become "unity" conscious and turn their eyes away from God to strive for closer fellowship.

A. W. Tozer, *The Pursuit of God* [1948]
Rom. 14:5-8

934 Counterfeits for the Spirit

A generation of Christians reared among push buttons and automatic machines is impatient of slower and less direct methods of reaching their goals. We have been trying to apply machine-age methods to our relations with God. We read our chapter, have our short devotions, and rush away, hoping to make up for our deep inward bankruptcy by attending another gospel meeting or listening to another thrilling story told by a religious adventurer lately returned from afar. The tragic results of this spirit are all about us. Shallow lives, hollow religious philosophies, the preponderance of the element of fun in gospel meetings, the glorification of men, trust in religious externalities, quasi-religious fellowships, salesmanship methods, the mistaking of dynamic personality for the power of the Spirit; these and such as these are the symptoms of an evil disease, a deep and serious malady of the soul.

A. W. Tozer, *The Pursuit of God* [1948]
Matt. 10:19,20; 1 Cor. 1:17-22; 2:4,5; Col. 2:18,19

935 God as He is

Much of our difficulty as seeking Christians stems from our unwillingness to take God as He is and adjust our lives accordingly. We insist upon trying to modify Him and bring Him nearer to our own image.

A. W. Tozer, *The Pursuit of God* [1948]
Jas. 4:7,8

936 On being

The Lord of all being is far more than the Lord of all beings. He is the Lord of all actual existence. He is the Lord of all kinds of beings—spiritual being, natural being, physical being. Therefore, when we rightly worship Him we encompass all being.

A. W. Tozer, *The Pursuit of God* [1948]
John 4:23,24

937 The Person behind the Bible

A loving Personality dominates the Bible, walking among the trees of the garden and breathing fragrance over every scene. Always a living Person is present, speaking, pleading, loving, working, and manifesting himself whenever and wherever his people have the receptivity necessary to receive the manifestation.

A. W. Tozer, *The Pursuit of God* [1948]
Luke 5:1-3

938 Continuous love

God desires and is pleased to communicate with us through the avenues of our minds, our wills, and our emotions. The continuous and unembarrassed interchange of love and thought between God and the souls of the redeemed men and women is the throbbing heart of the New Testament.

A. W. Tozer, *The Pursuit of God* [1948]
1 Thess. 5:17

939 Journey into the Presence

The interior journey of the soul from the wilds of sin into the enjoyed presence of God is beautiful. Ransomed men need no longer pause in fear to the Holy of Holies. God wills that we should push on into His presence and live our whole life there.

A. W. Tozer, *The Pursuit of God* [1948]
Matt. 27:51; Mark 15:38; Luke 23:45

940 The gaze of faith

If faith is the gaze of the heart at God, and if this gaze is but the raising of the inward eyes to meet the all-seeing eyes of God, then it follows that it is one of the easiest things possible to do.

A. W. Tozer, *The Pursuit of God* [1948]
John 8:28

941 Solitude

Modern civilization is so complex as to make the devotional life all but impossible. It wears us out by multiplying distractions and beats us down destroying our solitude, where otherwise we might drink and renew our strength, before going out to face the world again. "The thoughtful soul to solitude retires," said the poet[9] of other and quieter times; but where is the solitude to which we can retire today? "Commune with your own heart upon your bed and be still," is a wise and healing counsel; but how can it be followed in this day of the newspaper, the telephone, the radio and television? These modern playthings, like pet tiger cubs, have grown so large and dangerous that they threaten to devour us all. What was intended to be a blessing has become a positive curse. No spot is now safe from the world's intrusion. The need for solitude and quietness was never greater than it is today. What the world will do about it is their problem. Apparently the masses want it the way it is, and the majority of Christians are so completely conformed to this present age that they, too, want things the way they are. They may be annoyed a bit by the clamor and by the goldfish-bowl existence they live, but apparently they are not annoyed enough to do anything about it.

([9] from *Rubáiyát* of Omar Khayyám, stanza IV)

A. W. Tozer, *Of God and Men* [1960]
Ps. 4:4

942 Sin as a misdirection

Unbelief is actually perverted faith, for it puts its trust, not in the living God but in dying men. The unbeliever denies the self-sufficiency of God and usurps attributes that are not his. This dual sin dishonors God and ultimately destroys the soul of man.

A. W. Tozer, *The Knowledge of the Holy* [1961]
Lam. 3:17,18; Heb. 3:12

943 A disturbing adoration

The love of Christ both wounds and heals, it fascinates and frightens, it kills and makes alive, it draws and repulses. There can be nothing more terrible or wonderful than to be stricken with love for Christ so deeply that the whole being goes out in a pained adoration of His person, an adoration that disturbs and disconcerts while it purges and satisfies and relaxes the deep inner heart.

A. W. Tozer, *That Incredible Christian* [1964]
Acts 9:16

944 The supernatural Book

The Bible is a supernatural book and can be understood only by supernatural aid.

A. W. Tozer, *Man: The Dwelling Place of God* [1966]
1 Cor. 2:9-16

Traherne, Thomas [c.1637-1674]

945 The context of all meaning

He knoweth nothing as he ought to know it, who thinketh he knoweth anything without seeing its place and the manner how it relateth to God, angels, and men, and to all the creatures in earth, heaven and hell, time and eternity.

Thomas Traherne
2 Tim. 3:2-7

Troeltsch, Ernst [1865-1923]

946 The Kingdom within us

Faith is the source of energy in the struggle of life, but life still remains a battle which is continually renewed upon ever-new fronts. For every threatening abyss that is closed, another yawning gulf appears. The truth is—and this is the conclusion of the whole matter—the Kingdom of God is within us. But we must let our light shine before men in confident and untiring labor that they may see our good works and praise our Father in Heaven. The final ends of all humanity are hidden within His hands.

Ernst Troeltsch, The Social Teaching of the
Christian Churches [1981]
Matt. 5:16; Luke 17:21

Troutman, Charles H. (Henry, Jr.) [1914-1990]

947 Why we can pray

The criterion for our intercessory prayer is not our earnestness, nor our faithfulness, nor even our faith in God, but simply God Himself. He has taken the initiative from the beginning, and has built our prayers into the structure of the universe. He then asks us to present these requests to Him that He may show His gracious hand.

Charles H. Troutman
Matt. 6:8; Eph. 3:14-19

Trueblood, (David) Elton [1900-1994]

948 Difficulties

If we are honest, we freely admit that the Christian system involves difficulties; but so does every other system. No thoughtful person gives up a position merely because he finds difficulties in it; he does not abandon it until he is able to find other and alternative systems with fewer difficulties. . . . I learned from my professors of philosophy . . . that, while philosophy might not provide me with a watertight intellectual defense of the Christian faith, it would, if used aright, help me to reveal the weakness of its enemies. By careful analysis it is possible to see that there are glaring weaknesses and non-sequiturs in atheism, naturalism, positivism, scientism, and psychologism. The Christian must be a fighter, for he is always under attack. The Church will not be as strong as it ought to be until each local pastor uses his precious freedom from outside employment in order to become a scholarly participant in the intellectual struggle of our day and generation.

Elton Trueblood, The Incendiary Fellowship [1967]
Eph. 4:14,15

Tyndale, William [c.1492-1536]

949 On Romans

Now go to, reader, and according to the order of Paul's writing [in Romans], even so do thou. First behold thyself diligently in the law of God, and see there thy just damnation. Secondarily, turn thine eyes to Christ, and see there the exceeding mercy of thy most kind and loving Father. Thirdly, remember that Christ made not this atonement that thou shouldest anger God again; neither cleansed he thee, that thou shouldest return (as a swine) unto thine old puddle again: but that thou shouldest be a new creature and live a new life after the will of God and not of the flesh. And be diligent lest through thine own negligence and unthankfulness thou lose this favor and mercy again.

William Tyndale, Prologue to Romans [1531]
Rom. 3:23-26; 6:1,2

Underhill, Evelyn [1875-1941]

950 The spiritual life

The spiritual life is a stern choice. It is not a consoling retreat from the difficulties of existence, but an invitation to enter fully into that difficult existence, and there apply the Charity of God, and bear the cost.

Evelyn Underhill
John 14:21; Rom. 5:8; 1 John 3:1;4:8-10

951 The interior life

By the quality of our inner lives I do not mean something charac-terized by ferocious intensity and strain. I mean rather such a humble and genial devotedness as we find in the most loving of the saints. I mean the quality which makes contagious Christians, makes people catch the love of God from you.

Evelyn Underhill, *Concerning the Inner Life* [1926]
1 John 4:12; Jude 1:21

952 On conflicts

Most of our conflicts and difficulties come from trying to deal with the spiritual and practical aspects of our life separately instead of realizing them as parts of one whole. If our practical life is cen-tered on our own interests, cluttered up by possessions, distracted by ambitions, passions, wants and worries, beset by a sense of our own rights and importance, or anxieties for our own future, or longings for our own success, we need not expect that our spiritual life will be a contrast to all this. The soul's house is not built on such a convenient plan; there are few soundproof partitions in it. Only when the convic-tion—not merely the idea—that the demand of the Spirit, however inconvenient, rules the whole of it, will those objectionable noises die down which have a way of penetrating into the nicely furnished little oratory and drowning all the quieter voices by their din.

Evelyn Underhill, *The Spiritual Life* [1937]
1 John 2:16

953 Words a medium for God

Words are merely carriers of the secret, supernatural communica-tions, the light and call of God. That is why spiritual books bear such different meanings for different types and qualities of soul, why each time we read them they give us something fresh, as we can bear it.

Evelyn Underhill, *Light of Christ* [1944]
Luke 4:22; 1 Cor. 14:9

Vaughan, Henry [1622-1695]

954 When night comes, list thy deeds

When night comes, list thy deeds; make plain the way
'Twixt heaven and thee; block it not with delays;
    But perfect all before thou sleep'st: then say:
    There's one sun more strung on my Bead of days.
What's good, score up for joy; the bad, well scanned.
    Wash off with tears, and get thy Master's hand.

Henry Vaughan
Ps. 4

955 I greet Thy sepulcher

I greet Thy sepulcher, salute Thy grave,
That blest enclosure, where the angels gave
The first glad tidings of Thy early light,
And resurrection from the earth and night.
I see that morning in Thy convert's tears,
Fresh as the dew, which but this downing wears.
I smell her spices; and her ointment yields
As rich a scent as the now primrosed fields:
The Day-star smiles, and light, with Thee deceased,
Now shines in all the chambers of the East.

Henry Vaughan
John 20:11-18

Vauvenargues, Marquis de. (Luc de Clapier) [1715-1747]

956 I shall see God

Newton, Pascal, Bossuet, Racine, Fénelon—that is to say, some
of the most enlightened men on earth, in the most philosophical of
all ages—have been believers in Jesus Christ; and the great Condé,

when dying, repeated these noble words, "Yes, I shall see God as He is, face to face!"

Vauvenargues
1 Cor. 13:12

Vidler, Alec R. [b.1899]

957 The unconditioned spirit

The Spirit of Christ can set men free, and can enable them to become their true selves, without requiring their dependence on any particular religious organization.

Alec Vidler
2 Cor. 4:13,14

Wallis, Arthur

958 Apostolic preaching

Apostolic preaching is not marked by its beautiful diction, or literary polish, or Cleverness of expression, but operates in demonstration of the Spirit and of power.

Arthur Wallis
Matt. 10:19

Wand, J. W. C. (John William Charles) [1885-1977]

959 From authority to persuasion

Almost everywhere political secularization was accompanied at length by a general decrease in religious observance. Theological matters ceased to be, if they had ever genuinely been, the main interest of the people. This does not mean that religion died out: far from it. But it became the interest, not of the whole, but of a section of the people. The Church, instead of being a recognized ruling authority, became what its Founder said it was, a little yeast in a large lump of dough. In some countries it barely maintained the right to exist; in others it had to adapt its methods to new conditions. But wherever possible it has continued openly to pursue the same ends, and has not ceased to declare what it believes to be the will of God even in the political sphere. Indeed, we may recognize a gain in the new situation. What it could once do by authority, it now seeks to do by persuasion.

J. W. C. Wand, *The Church Today* [1960]
Matt. 13:33

Warfield, Benjamin B. [1851-1921]

960 Inspiration

If criticism has made such discoveries as to necessitate the abandonment of the doctrine of plenary inspiration, it is not enough to say that we are compelled to abandon only a "particular theory of inspiration." . . . We must go on to say that that "particular theory of inspiration" is the theory of the apostles and of the Lord, and that in abandoning it we are abandoning them.

B. B. Warfield, *The Inspiration and Authority of the Bible* [1948]
2 Tim. 3:16,17

Watson, David

961 The beam in our own eye

If we see a speck in a brother's eye, we must first see if there is a log in our own eye; perhaps that speck in our brother's eye is only a reflection of the beam in our own.

David Watson
Matt. 7:3-5

Watts, Isaac [1674-1748]

962 The King of Glory sends his Son

> The King of glory sends his Son,
> To make his entrance on this earth;
> Behold the midnight bright as noon,
> And heav'nly hosts declare his birth!
> About the young Redeemer's head,
> What wonders, and what glories meet!
> An unknown star arose, and led
> The eastern sages to his feet.
> Simeon and Anna both conspire
> The infant Savior to proclaim;
> Inward they felt the sacred fire,
> And bless'd the babe, and own'd his name.
> Let pagan hordes blaspheme aloud,
> And treat the holy child with scorn;
> Our souls adore th' eternal God
> Who condescended to be born.

> Isaac Watts, *Hymns and Spiritual Songs* [1707]
> *Matt. 2:1-11; Luke 2:1-20, 25-38*

963 The Witnessing and Sealing Spirit

> Why should the children of a king
>   Go mourning all their days?
> Great Comforter, descend and bring
>   Some tokens of thy grace.
>
> Dost though not dwell in all thy saints,
>   And seal the heirs of heaven?
> When wilt thou banish my complaints,
>   And show my sins forgiven?

Assure my conscience of her part
    In the Redeemer's blood;
And bear thy witness with my heart,
    That I am born of God.

Thou are the earnest of his love,
    The pledge of joys to come;
And thy soft wings, celestial Dove,
    Will safe convey me home.

> Isaac Watts, *Hymns and Spiritual Songs* [1707]
> *Rom. 8:14,16. Eph. 1:13,14*

964 Jesus invites His saints

Jesus invites His saints
    To meet around His board;
Here pardon'd rebels sit and hold
    Communion with their Lord.

For food He give His flesh,
    He bids us drink His blood;
Amazing favor! matchless grace
    Of our descending God!

This holy bread and wine
    Maintains our fainting breath,
By union with our living Lord
    And interest in His death.

Let all our powers be join'd
    His glorious name to raise;
Pleasure and love fill every mind,
    And every voice be praise.

> Isaac Watts, *Hymns and Spiritual Songs* [1707]
> *1 Cor. 10:16,17*

965 Hosanna to the royal Son

Hosanna to the royal Son
    Of David's ancient line!
His natures two, his person one,
    Mysterious and divine.

The root of David here, we find,
    And Offspring are the same;
Eternity and time are join'd
    In our Immanuel's name.

Bless'd he that comes to wretched men
    With peaceful news from heaven;
Hosannas of the highest strain
    To Christ the Lord be given!

Let mortals ne'er refuse to take
    The hosanna on their tongues,
Lest rocks and stones should rise, and break
    Their silence into songs.

> Isaac Watts, *Hymns and Spiritual Songs* [1707]
> *Matt. 21:9; Luke 19:38,40*

966 There is a stream

There is a stream, whose gentle flow
Supplies the city of our God;
Life, love, and joy still gliding through,
And watering our divine abode:
That sacred stream, thine holy word,
That all our raging fear controls;
Sweet peace thy promises afford,
And give new strength to fainting souls.

> Isaac Watts, *Psalms of David Imitated* [1719]

> The Lord can clear the darkest skies
>> Can give us day for night.
> Make drops of sacred sorrow rise
>> To rivers of delight.

Isaac Watts, Psalms, Hymns, and Spiritual Songs

Webster, Douglas [b.1920]

968 The missionary motive

The missionary goes out to men of other faiths and of no faith, not to argue, not to make comparisons, never to claim a superior knowledge or revelation, but to tell of a glorious deed, of the New Creation that has occurred and of the New Being that has appeared and into which men may enter. This is testimony, the apostolic testimony, and this, with the energy of love, is the missionary motive. The insistent task of missionary education and responsibility is to engender this motive throughout the Church, a task that can only be accomplished as men are confronted anew with the message of the Bible and with its supreme and central story, the story of the cross.

Douglas Webster, Local Church and World Mission [1964]
Acts 3:14,15; 2 Cor. 4:13,14; 2 Thess. 1:10

Wedel, Theodore O. [1892-1970]

969 Prodigals no more!

Prodigal sons, forgiven and reconciled with their heavenly Father, could they do other than forgive one another? A fellowship of prodigal sons came into being—the church of Christ. Love begets love. A new power . . . was let loose upon our suffering world, the power to love those who have not deserved love, the unworthy, the unlovely and unlovable, a man's enemies, and even his torturers. Christians, in imitation of the Savior, became, as it were, Christs to one another and to the world.

Theodore O. Wedel
John 13:34; Rom. 12:21; 14:13

Weil, Simone [1909-1943]

970 To be always relevant

To be always relevant, you have to say things which are eternal.

Simone Weil
Ps. 30:12; Matt. 24:34,35

Wesley, Charles [1707-1788]

971 But lo' the snare is broke

But lo' the snare is broke, the captive's freed,
By faith on all the hostile powers we tread,
And crush through Jesus' strength the Serpent's head.
Jesus hath cast the cursed Accuser down,
Hath rooted up the tares by Satan sown:
All nature bows to His benign command,
And two are one in His almighty hand.
One in His hand, O may we still remain,
Fast bound with love's indissoluble chain;
(That adamant which time and death defies,
That golden chain which draws us to the skies!)
His love the tie that binds us to His throne,
His love the bond that perfects us in one,
His only love constrains our hearts t' agree,
And gives the rivet of Eternity.

Charles Wesley
Gen. 3:15; Luke 4:18; Eph. 4:1-4

972 The infinite God

Jesus, the infinite I AM,
With God essentially the same,
With him enthroned above all height,
As God of God, and Light of Light,
Thou art by thy great Father known,
From all eternity his Son.

Thou only dost the Father know,
And wilt to all thy followers show,
Who cannot doubt thy gracious will
His glorious Godhead to reveal;
Reveal him now, if thou art he,
And live, eternal Life, in me.

Charles Wesley
Matt. 11:27

973 Come, Holy Ghost

Come, Holy Ghost, for moved by thee
The prophets wrote and spoke;
Unlock the truth, thyself the key,
Unseal the sacred book.

Charles Wesley
Acts 1:8

Wesley, John [1703-1791]

974 Suffering

Suffer all, and conquer all.

John Wesley
Rom. 8:36,37

975 Virtue leads to pride

Wherever riches have increased, the essence of religion has decreased in the same proportion. Therefore I do not see how it is possible in the nature of things for any revival of religion to continue long. For religion must necessarily produce both industry and frugality, and these cannot but produce riches. But as riches increase, so will pride, anger, and love of the world in all its branches. How then is it possible that Methodism, that is a religion of the heart, though it flourishes now as the green bay tree, should continue in this state? For the Methodists in every place grow diligent and frugal; consequently, they increase in goods. Hence, they proportionately increase in pride, in anger, in the desire of the flesh, the desire of the eyes, and the pride of life. So, although the form of religion remains, the spirit is swiftly vanishing away. Is there no way to prevent . . . this continual decay of pure religion?

John Wesley
Mark 10:25

976 Why the gifts were withdrawn

The grand reason why the miraculous gifts were so soon withdrawn was not only that faith and holiness were well-nigh lost, but that dry, formal, orthodox men began then to ridicule whatever gifts they had not themselves and to cry them all [down] as evil madness or imposture.

John Wesley
2 Cor. 3:6

977 Preaching in the field

I could scarcely reconcile myself at first to this strange way of preaching in the fields, of which Whitfield set me an example on Sunday; having been all my life (till very lately) so tenacious of every point relating to decency and order, that I should have thought the saving of souls almost a sin, if it had not been done in a church.

John Wesley's Journal
1 Cor. 9:22

Westcott, Brooke Foss [1825-1901]

978 The danger of understanding

The idea of "conviction" is complex. It involves the concepts of authoritative examination, of unquestionable proof, of decisive judgment, of punitive power. Whatever the final issue may be, he who "convicts" another places the truth of the case in dispute in a clear light before him, so that it must be seen and acknowledged as truth. He who then rejects the conclusion which the exposition involves, rejects it with his eyes open and at his peril. Truth seen as truth carries with it condemnation to all who refuse to welcome it.

Brooke Foss Westcott, *The Gospel According to St. John* [1882]
John 6:44,45; 2 Thess. 2:10

Wetzel, Todd H. [b.1946]

979 Be ready for suffering

Like many of the leaders and teacher [in the church], perhaps I failed to prepare people for the way of suffering. I had not suffered much myself and did not help people to be ready for it. But the fact is: when you follow Jesus, what happened to Him happens to you.

Todd H. Wetzel, *Steadfast Faith* [1997]
1 Pet. 4:13,14

Whale, John Seldon [1896-1997]

980 The Man in the midst

It is God Himself, personally present and redeemingly active, who comes to meet men in this Man of Nazareth. Jesus is more than a religious genius, such as George Fox, and more than a holy man, such as the lovable Lana in Kipling's Kim. He himself knows that he is more. The Gospel story is a tree rooted in the familiar soil of time and sense; but its roots go down into the Abyss and its branches fill the

Heavens; given to us in terms of a country in the Eastern Mediterranean no bigger than Wales, during the Roman Principate of Tiberius Caesar in the first century of our era, its range is universal; it is on the scale of eternity. God's presence and his very Self were made manifest in the words and works of this Man. In short, the Man Christ Jesus has the decisive place in man's ageless relationship with God. He is what God means by 'Man'. He is what man means by 'God'.

J. S. Whale, *Christian Doctrine* [1966]
Matt. 3:13-17

981 Explanations?

The Gospels cannot explain the Resurrection; it is the Resurrection which alone explains the Gospels.

John S. Whale, *Christian Doctrine* [1966]
John 5:25

Whately, Richard [1787-1863]

982 Accustomed to blessings

It is generally true that all that is required to make men unmindful of what they owe God for any blessing is that they should receive that blessing often and regularly.

Richard Whately
Deut. 6:10-16; 8:11-17

Whitefield, George [1714-1770]

983 Tearing down the old house

The renewal of our natures is a work of great importance. It is not to be done in a day. We have not only a new house to build up, but an old one to pull down.

George Whitefield
1 Cor. 3:9-17

984 Such feeble return

Gladly shall I come whenever bodily strength will allow to join my testimony with yours in Olney pulpit, that God is love. As yet I have not recovered from the fatigues of my American expedition. My shattered bark is scarce worth docking any more. But I would fain wear, not rust, out. Oh! my dear Mr. Newton, indeed and indeed I am ashamed that I have done and suffered so little for Him that hath done and suffered so much for ill and hell-deserving me.

George Whitefield, letter to John Newton
Phil. 3:7,8

985 Preaching more than a half hour

To preach more than half an hour, a man should be an angel himself, or have angels for hearers.

George Whitefield

Whitehead, Alfred North [1861-1947]

986 Apart from God

Apart from God every activity is merely a passing whiff of insignificance.

Alfred North Whitehead
Eccl. 3:14,15

Whitemell, C. T., Mrs.

987 The light of Christ

In darkness there is no choice. It is light that enables us to see the differences between things; and it is Christ who gives us light.

Mrs. C. T. Whitemell, *Christ in Flanders*
Mal. 4:2; Luke 2:29-32; John 1:4-9

Whittier, John Greenleaf [1807-1892]

988 One fixed trust

> I see the wrong that round me lies,
>   I feel the guilt within;
> I hear, with groan and travail-cries,
>   The world confess its sin.
> Yet, in the maddening maze of things,
>   And tossed by storm and flood,
> To one fixed trust my spirit clings
>   I know that God is good!

> John Greenleaf Whittier
> *Ps. 34:8*

Wilberforce, William [1759-1833]

989 On Sunday

All these several artifices, whatever they may be, to unhallow the Sunday, and to change its character (it might be almost said, to mitigate its horrors,) prove but too plainly, however we may be glad to take refuge in religion, when driven to it by the loss of every other comfort, and to retain, as it were, a reversionary interest in an asylum, which may receive us when we are forced from the transitory enjoyments of our present state; that in itself wears to us a gloomy and forbidding aspect, and not a face of consolation and joy; that the worship of God is with us a constrained, not a willing, service, which we are glad therefore to abridge, though we dare not omit it.

> William Wilberforce, *A Practical View* [1958]
> *Ps. 5:7; 122:1*

990 Ignoring the eternal things

The generality of nominal Christians . . . are almost entirely taken up with the concerns of the present world. They know indeed that they are mortal, but they do not feel it. The truth rests in their understandings, and cannot gain admission into their hearts. This speculative persuasion is altogether different from that strong practical impression of the infinite importance of eternal things, which, attended with a proportionate sense of the shortness and uncertainty of all below, while it prompts to activity from a conviction that the night cometh when no man can work, produces a certain firmness of texture, which hardens us against the buffetings of fortune, and prevents our being very deeply penetrated by the cares and interests, the good or evil, of this transitory state.

William Wilberforce, *A Practical View* [1958]
2 Tim. 2:3,4

Wilde, Oscar (Fingal O'Flahertie Wills) [1854-1900]

991 The broken gates

> And thus we rust Life's iron chain
>   Degraded and alone:
> And some men curse, and some men weep,
>   And some men make no moan:
> But God's eternal Laws are kind
>   And break the heart of stone.
> And every human heart that breaks,
>   In prison-cell or yard,
> Is as that broken box that gave
>   Its treasure to the Lord,
> And filled the unclean leper's house
>   With the scent of costliest nard.
> Ah! happy they whose hearts can break
>   And peace of pardon win!
> How else may man make straight his plan
>   And cleanse his soul from sin?
> How else but through a broken heart
>   May Lord Christ enter in?

Oscar Wilde, *The Ballad of Reading Gaol* [1898]
Ps. 51:17; Isa. 57:15; Matt. 5:8; Rev. 3:20

Willard, Dallas [b.1935]

992 A conversational relationship with God

Our union with God—his presence with us, in which our alone-ness is banished and the meaning and full purpose of human exis-tence is realized—consists chiefly in a conversational relationship with God while we are each consistently and deeply engaged as his friend and colaborer in the affairs of the kingdom of the heavens.

Dallas Willard, *Hearing God* [1999]
Matt. 9:37,38; 1 John 4:13

Williams, Charles [1886-1945]

993 Contrition

Every contrition for sin is apt to encourage a not quite charitable wish that other people should exhibit a similar contrition.

Charles Williams
Rom. 2:3

Williams, Daniel Day [1910-1973]

994 One true God

The first article of Christian faith is that man has one and only one true object of worship. There is one Holy God, creator of heaven and earth. He is Lord of all life. To Him we are beholden for our life in all its meaning and its hope. Monotheism for the Christian means that anything else which is put in the place of our loyalty to God is an idol. The worship of national power, or racial prestige, or financial success, or cultural tradition, is a violation of the one truth about life, that all created things come from God. To commit life to the one true God is to refuse to have any other gods at all. Values there are in abundance, interests, plans, programs, loyalties to family and nation. But these are not gods; they do not save us; they are not holy in themselves.

Daniel Day Williams, *Interpreting Theology* [1953]
1 Kings 18:21-40; Ex. 20:3; Matt. 4:10; Col. 3:5

Williams, Roger [c.1603-1683]

995 Unity

We find not in the Gospel, that Christ hath anywhere provided for the uniformity of churches, but only for their unity.

Roger Williams
1 Cor. 12:12-18

996 12 needful things

(1) God's children ought to walk in constant amazement of spirit as to God, His nature, and works. (2) The glorifying of God is the great work of God's children. (3) Delightful privacy with God argues strong affection. (4) Frequent prayer an argument of much of God's Spirit; true prayer is the pouring out of the heart to God; God's children are most in private with God; the prayers of God's people most respect spiritual mercies; God's people wait for and rest in God's answer. (5) God's people are sensible of their unworthiness. (6) God Himself is regarded as the portion of His people. (7) Ready obedience to God. (8) The patience of God's children under God's hand. (9) The mournful confession of God's people. (10) God's people long after God in an open profession of His ordinances. (11) Their hearts are ready and prepared. (12) God's people's sense of their own insufficiencies.

Roger Williams, *Experiments of Spiritual Life and Health* [1652]
1 Cor. 6:20; 10:31

Wilson, Thomas, Bp. [1698-1755]

997 If we loved God

The world would use us just as it did the martyrs, if we loved God as they did.

Bp. Thomas Wilson
Ps. 2:1-3; John 12:25; Acts 7:55-60; Rom. 8:36

Winter, Gibson [b.1916]

998 Structure in the Church

The introverted church is one which puts its own survival before its mission, its own identity above its task, its internal concerns before its apostolate, its rituals before its ministry. Undue emphasis on the static structure of the Church has led to the disappearance of a significant lay ministry in denominational Protestantism.

Gibson Winter, *The Suburban Captivity of the Churches* [1961]
Rev. 2:4,5

Woods, C. Stacey

999 In alien society

The Church is an organism that grows best in an alien society.

C. Stacey Woods
Ps. 39:12; Acts 8:1

1000 Prayer makes fellow laborers

The history of our student movement [Inter-Varsity] has demonstrated that a prayer-less chapter is a fruitless chapter. Prayer spells all the difference between working for God in our own strength and wisdom or being fellow laborers together with Him in the work that He is seeking to do in the University.

C. Stacey Woods
1 Cor. 3:8-11

Wycliffe, John [c.1320-1384]

1001 Understanding of Scripture

Christian men and women, old and young, should study well in the New Testament, for it is of full authority, and open to understanding by simple men, as to the points that are most needful to salvation. Each part of Scripture, both open and dark, teaches meekness and charity; and therefore he that keeps meekness and charity has the true understanding and perfection of all Scripture. Therefore, no simple man of wit should be afraid to study in the text of Scripture. And no cleric should be proud of the true understanding of Scripture, because understanding of Scripture without charity that keeps God's commandments, makes a man deeper damned . . . and pride and covetousness of clerics is the cause of [the Church's] blindness and heresy, and deprives them of the true understanding of Scripture.

John Wycliffe, *The Wicket*
Matt. 5:5; 1 Cor 13:13

Zinzendorf, Count Nicolaus Ludwig von [1700-1760]

1002 One passion

I have but one passion—it is He, it is He alone. The world is the field and the field is the world; and henceforth that country shall be my home where I can be most used in winning souls for Christ.

Count Nicolaus Ludwig von Zinzendorf
Luke 24:46-48; Acts 4:18-20; 13:47; 1 Cor. 9:22; 12:3; 16:9

Of Rice and Men
Published under the title "Rice Christians"

by Robert MacColl Adams

Everybody knows what "rice Christians" are, I suppose. People here in the United States have tended to look down upon the beggarly Chinese (or Indian, or what-not) who would crawl to the mission compound and pretend to be a convert to Christianity just for a bowlful of boiled rice a day. But it is a strangely hard heart that will scorn a man for choosing to be a "rice Christian" instead of a no-rice Buddhist, for example . . . a strangely hard heart, I say, and doubly strange in a Christian, who might be expected to be glad if a man has forsaken the worship of Buddha for that of Christ, no matter what the inducement was.

But it is no use, you may say (as I did), to give up worshipping Buddha unless you become a real Christian, and these rice Christians cared only for the rice: they had not given their hearts to Christ. Perhaps not. But if not, who is to blame?

The rice Christian should have realized what is involved in being a real Christian; but it would be easier to condemn his ignorance if he had ever seen real Christians. The rice Christian might be illiterate, but he knew something of the world. He might even know, in a dim way, that for every rice-doling missionary in China, there were hundreds and thousands of Christians back in America whose missionary zeal and Christian love supported the missionary and provided the meager rations of rice he doled out. Can you blame the poor man with the bowl of rice if he got the impression that being a Christian doesn't make any very heavy demands on a person?

Of course, the poor fellow may not have known—and the missionary may have omitted to tell him—that, for most American Christians, being a Christian is almost entirely external, a matter of conformity to a certain socially approved pattern of behavior at certain limited times, and that—far from demanding a man's heart—American Christianity has a hard time prying him loose from his pocket change. However, a lot of the beggars did know this: even among the illiterate, the word gets around. And so the rice Christian may well have thought himself as much a Christian as anyone else.

But surely, you will say, the hypothetical well-informed rice Christian had seen one real Christian, by anyone's definition: what about the missionary? All right, what about him? The beggar may simply have thought of him as an exception. If he really understood the price the missionary was paying for his Christianity, he also knew about the many "Christians" who declined to pay any such price . . . indeed, any price at all. And it is hard to blame the beggar for concluding that devotion is, to say the least, optional for Christians. More likely, though, he didn't know about the price. You and I know how badly the missionary was supported, and how much he gave up. But the beggar saw him as one of the kings of the earth, wealthy beyond the dreams of avarice (didn't he have food to give away?), protected by unseen Powers, the darling of Fortune. Can any of us appreciate, I wonder, how the average American looks to a man who has never had a full meal in his life?

All four Evangelists record that, when Jesus had fed the five thousand, they were all filled. You and I might not think much of the chance of stuffing ourselves on dry rye bread and sun-cured herring; but to the people actually involved, it was an unparalleled miracle—they walked halfway around the Sea of Galilee in the broiling sun the next day just on the chance of finding this Jesus again. And some of them did find Him. He knew that they had not followed Him for His teaching, but because of that startling, that mind-shattering miracle of the full bellies. But He did not scorn them: He only went on to teach them the difference between a rice Christian and a real one.

Those rice Christians who used to come to our mission stations in China—they may have come only because of the rice, but they came to the right place, didn't they? They came to Christ as He was held out to them, and they were taught there about being real Christians. We don't have any rice-bearing missionaries in China any more, but there are still Christians there. Not many, you say. Who knows? And who knows how many Christians there would be in our own fair land ten years after the rice was cut off?

For we all began as rice Christians, you know. All of us came first because we were hungry—no higher reason. Even the mushiest rice gruel is better than hunger pangs. Did you come to Him through fear of Hell? There's a low motive for you: "Let Jesus Christ save you; following Him is better than an eternity of torment." But many a Christian came to Christ first for just that reason. There is energy in even plain boiled rice. Did you come to Him because you couldn't carry your load of guilt any more? There's another low-level appeal, isn't it? "Let Jesus Christ bear your burden; following Him is better than total collapse." Yet this low-level appeal brought many a Christian to Christ, and still does.

There are vitamins in unpolished rice, unattractive though it is. Did you come to Him because of deficiency diseases in your soul— no hope, no direction, no purpose in living? What a pitifully low appeal: "Let Jesus Christ give you a reason for living; following Him is better than suicide." A low appeal indeed—so low, in fact, that it reached down to me when (it seemed) nothing else could; and so I, for one, can't look down on it.

Well, there are crunchier, flakier, yummier forms of rice. American technology enables rice to be presented in a variety of forms, not all easily recognized as rice. There's the golden rice flake of Christian respectability: here we are in our proper place of service and testimony to the community; how good it is to know that we are on God's side! There's the dainty rice puff of Christian intellectuality: we love those "studies" which require of us only that slight degree of intellectual effort which is a pleasure; how good it is to be learning to understand God! And there's the fragile rice crispy of Christian fellowship: in this finest of all forms of togetherness there is only the slightest touch of snobbery, sometimes; and the glow we get from being with God's family may last for hours.

Now there is some real nourishment in these things, even if they have a way of starting you to wondering about lunch at about 10: 30 A.M. But all rice, all grain, all food, is like that. They are only the "meat which perisheth", after all—good enough to bring us to Jesus Christ, but not good enough to sustain us long without Him. And the yummiest, crunchiest, nuttiest form of rice now being offered to people is, I think, the notion that Christianity is fun: "Become a Christian and all your troubles are over", is the general idea. The Christian life is presented as one long, sweet song, a triumphal procession of jolly associations, marvelous sessions of prayer and study, happy-happy worship services, the grandest conquest over sin and weakness and error, a successful avoidance of all the snares of the world without missing any of its joys. Everything is great, everything is going to be great from here on in.

Well, we all began as rice Christians, and not many of us can be sure, even yet, that the rice means absolutely nothing to us. It is not for one rice Christian to say that another cannot be sincere, or that the Lord Jesus may not draw a man to Himself by any means that will serve His purpose. And there is joy in belonging to Him: it is a real joy, a happiness beyond anything the world can give. Looking back, I can see that I was never really happy before I met Him; looking for-

The Authentic **Book of Christian Quotations**

ward, I know that there can be no happiness without Him again, ever again. And I wouldn't want any prospective Christian not to know this, or not to realize that our final destiny is complete happiness.

But being a Christian here and now is not all cokes and bowling. In coming to know Jesus, you have come to know yourself, too: naturally, this is more pleasant for some than for others, but to see yourself as you really are can never be entirely pleasant. And when a Christian fails at something he ought to have done, it isn't just the failure that hurts—there is also the knowledge that he has let Jesus down. And those little shortcomings of ours, that used to matter so little, compared with the glaring faults of others: we know now that our temper, or our gloom, or our selfishness, reflects on Jesus; and knowing that people are judging your Lord by you is not always a joyous thought to live with. Even the growing up to His measure is hard on a man: we have so little aptitude for such a transformation that it always means conflict, and often rebellion. And temptations hurt as they never did before: not just in the conscience, but in the heart. The assaults of temptation are not on our prudence now, or even on our morals, but on the love for Jesus. His love for us has made Him quite defenseless against our hurting Him, and so temptation is no longer an urge to do a bad thing but an urge to hurt a loving Person.

No, being a real Christian isn't all fun, and don't tell anyone it is. You come for the rice, and it's good . . . as far as it goes. But it doesn't last forever. No matter what kind of rice brought you to Jesus, it won't last. If you have really come to Him, that doesn't matter. But if you haven't, you will saunter up to the mission station one day, and the door will be shut. And there you will be with your empty bowl, seeing—just your helpless self staring at the empty place in you where Jesus wasn't allowed to come.

Yes, we all started as rice Christians. But if all you have found is advantage, whether it is fun or profit or security, then you haven't started following Him yet. His way is the way of the Cross. The world can be very hard on those it hates. If it is not hard on you, perhaps it sees nothing in you to hate. But then it doesn't see Jesus in you, for it hates Jesus with an undying hatred. While your way is still all fun, all easy, all jolly, it is only your way: when you turn from it to follow His way, it will cost. It may cost you everything you have. That is what it cost Him.

2 February, 1962

AUTHOR INDEX*

* refers to the quotation number, not to the page number

Augustine of Hippo, Bp. (354-430) — 50, 51, 52, 53, 54, 55, 56, 57, 58, 59, 60
——, *City of God, The* [426], — 63, 64, 65
——, *Confessions* [397], — 61, 62
Babcock, Maltbie D. (1858-1901) — 66
Backhouse, William (1779/80-1844), *Guide to True Peace, A*, with James Janson [1813]
        — 67, 68
Baillie, Donald M. (1887-1954) — 69
Baillie, John (1886-1960) — 70
——, *Invitation to Pilgrimage*, Scribner, New York: 1942 — 71
Banning, Charles F. — 72
Baouardy, Mariam (1846-1878) — 73
Barna, George — 74
Barth, Karl (1886-1968), *Epistle to the Romans, The*, tr. Edwyn C. Hoskyns, Oxford
        University Press, London: 1933 — 75, 76, 77
Barth, Markus (1915-1994), *Broken Wall, The*, Judson Press, Chicago: 1959 — 78
Basil the Great (330?-379) — 79, 80
Baxter, Richard (1615-1691) — 81
Bayne, Stephen F. (Fielding), Jr., Bp., (1908-1974) — 82
——, *Anglican Turning Point, An*, Church Historical Society, Austin: 1964 — 83
Beach, W. (William) Waldo (1916-2001), *Christian Life, The*, CLC Press, Richmond,
        Va.:1966 — 85
——, "Where Do We Meet?" — 84
Beaufort, Joseph de (17th C), *Character of Brother Lawrence, The* — 86
Beecher, Henry Ward (1813-1887) — 87
Bell, Bernard Iddings (1886-1958), *God is Not Dead*, Harper & Brothers, NY: 1945
        — 89
——, *Still Shine the Stars*, Harper & brothers, New York, London: 1941 — 88
Bennett, Dan — 90
Bennett, John C. (b.1902) — 91
Berdyaev, Nikolai Alexandrovich (1874-1948), *Destiny of Man, The*, Geoffrey Bles,
        London: 1937 — 92
Bergman, Ingmar (b.1918) — 94
Berger, Peter L. *Noise of Solemn Assemblies, The*, Doubleday, Garden City: 1961 — 93
Bernard of Clairvaux (1091-1153) — 95, 96, 97, 98, 99
Betz, Otto (b.1917), *What Do We Know About Jesus?*, Westminster Press, Philadelphia:
        1968 — 100
Blackham, H. J. (Harold John) (b.1903) — 101
Blake, William (1757-1827) — 102
Blewett, George John (1873-1912) — 103
Boice, James Montgomery (1938-2000), "Preacher and God's Word, The" — 104
Bojaxhiu, Agnes Gonxha (Mother Teresa of Calcutta) (1910-1997) — 105
Bonar, Horatius (1808-1889) — 106
——, "Everlasting Righteousness, The" [1874] — 107
Bonhoeffer, Dietrich (1906-1945) — 108
——, *Cost of Discipleship, The*, SCM Press, London: 1964 — 112
——, *Life Together*, Harper, New York: 1954 — 109, 110
——, *Temptation*, SCM Press, London: 1955 — 111
Bounds, E. M. (Edward McKendree) (1835-1913), *Power Through Prayer*, n.d. — 113
Boyle, Robert (1627-1691) — 114

Bradley, Samuel — 115
Brainerd, David (1718-1747), *Journal* [1749] — 116
Braithwaite, Albert — 117
Brandon, Owen Rupert, *Battle for the Soul, The*, Hodder & Stoughton, London: 1960 — 118
Brent, Charles Henry, Bp. (1862-1929) — 119, 120
——, *Adventures in Prayer*, Harper, NY: 1932 — 122
——, *With God in the World* [1899] — 121
Briejèr, C. J. (Cornelis Jan) — 123
Brierley, J., *Life of the Soul, The*, James Clarke & Company, London: 1912 — 124
Bright, John (b.1908), *Kingdom of God, The*, Lutterworth Press, London: 1955 — 125
Broadbent, E. H. (Edmund Hamer) (1861-1945) — 126
Brogan, Denis W. (William) (1900-1974) — 127
Bronnert, David, "Gospel and Culture, The" in *The Changing World*, v.3 of *Obeying Christ in a Changing World*, Glasgow : William Collins & Co. Ltd, [c1977] — 130
——, "The Light Shines in the Darkness" — 128
——, "The Scapegoat" — 129
Brooks, Phillips, Bp. (1835-1893) — 131, 132, 133, 134
——, *Law of Growth, The*, E. P. Dutton, New York: 1902 — 135, 136
Brown, Charles Reynolds (1862-1950) — 137
Brown, P. B. — 138
Brown, Robert R. — 139
Browne, Sir Thomas (1605-1682) — 140
Browning, Elizabeth Barrett (1806-1861) — 141
Browning, Robert (1812-1889) — 142
Bruce, F. F. (Frederick Fyvie) (1910-1991) — 143
——, *Letter of Paul to the Romans, An Introduction and Commentary, The*, 2nd edition, Eerdmans, Grand Rapids, Mich.: 1997 — 145
——, *New Testament Documents: Are They Reliable? The*, InterVarsity Press, Downers Grove, Illinois: 1949. By permission. — 144
Bruce, Michael, "Layman and Church Government, The" — 146
Brunner, Emil (1889-1966), *Word and the World, The*, Student Christian Movement Press, London: 1931 — 147, 148, 149
Buchanan, C. O. (Colin Ogilvie) (b.1934), "Unity of the Church, The" — 150
Buechner, Frederick (b.1926) — 151
Bunyan, John (1628-1688), *Christ a Complete Saviour* [1692] — 154
——, *Grace Abounding to the Chief of Sinners* [1666] — 152
——, *Pilgrim's Progress, The* [1678] — 153
Calvin, John (1509-1564) — 155, 156, 157, 158, 159, 160, 161, 162, 163
——, *Institutes of the Christian Religion, The* [1559], — 164, 165, 166, 167, 168, 169, 170, 171, 172, 173, 174, 175
Campbell, Reginald John (1867-1956), *Call of Christ, The*, (publisher unk.) Lond. [1932] — 176
Capon, Robert Farrar (b.1925), *Supper of the Lamb, The*, Doubleday, New York: 1969 — 177
Carlyle, Thomas (1795-1881) — 178, 179
——, *Spiritual Portrait of Martin Luther* [1859] — 180
Carmichael, Amy (1867-1951) — 181

——, *Journals of Jim Elliot, The*, Old Tappan, N.J. : F. H. Revell Co., c1978. — 286

Ellul, Jacques (1912-1994), *Prayer and Modern Man*, The Seabury Press, New York: 1973 — 287

Emrich, Richard Stanley (b.1910) — 288

Engstrom, Ted W., former president, World Vision US, by permission. — 289, 290, 291

Erasmus, Desiderius (1466?-1536) — 292

——, *Colloquies* — 293, 294

Faber, Frederick W. (William) (1814-1863) — 307

Fénelon, François (1651-1715) — 295, 296, 297, 298, 299, 300, 301, 302

——, *Meditations* — 303, 304, 305

——, *Spiritual Letters* — 306

Figgis, John Neville (1866-1919) — 308

——, *Gospel and Human Needs, The*, Longman's, Green & Co., London: 1909 — 309

Fisher, Dorothy Canfield (1879-1958) — 310

Fletcher, Phineas (1582-1650) — 311

Forsyth, P. T. (Peter Taylor) (1848-1921), *This Life and the Next*, MacMillan, NY: 1918 — 312

Foster, Richard J. — 313

Fox, George (1624-1691), *Journal* — 314

Francis of Assisi (1182-1226) — 315

François de Sales (1567-1622) — 316, 317, 318, 319

——, *Introduction to the Devout Life* — 320, 321

Fulbert of Chartres (11th century) — 322

Fuller, Thomas (1608-1661) — 323, 324

——, *Good Thoughts in Bad Times*, United Society of Christian Endeavor, Boston, Chicago: 1898 — 325, 326

——, *Mixt Contemplations* [1660] — 327

Gasque, W. Ward, *Sir William M. Ramsay: Archaeologist and New Testament Scholar*, Baker Book House, Grand Rapids: 1966 — 328

Glanvill, Joseph (1636-1680) — 329

Glover, T. R. (Terrot Reaveley) (1869-1943), *Influence of Christ in the Ancient World, The*, Yale University Press, New Haven: 1929 — 330

Godsey, John D. (Drew) (b.1922), *Theology of Dietrich Bonhoeffer, The*, Westminster Press: 1960 — 331

Goodspeed, Edgar J. (1871-1962), *How Came the Bible?*, Abingdon, New York: 1940 — 332

Gore, Charles (1853-1932) — 333

——, *Sermon on the Mount, The* [1910] — 334

Gossip, A. J. (Arthur John) (1873-1954) — 335, 336

——, *Experience Worketh Hope*, T. & T. Clark, Edinburgh: 1944 — 348, 349, 350, 351, 352

——, *From the Edge of the Crowd*, T. & T. Clark, Edinburgh: 1924 — 337, 338, 339, 340, 341, 342

——, *Galilean Accent, The*, T. & T. Clark, Edinburgh: 1926 — 343, 344, 345, 346, 347

——, *In the Secret Place of the Most High*, Charles Scribner's Sons, New York: 1947 — 353, 354, 355

Graham, Billy (b.1918) — 356

Grant, Frederick Clifton (1891-1974) — 357

Green, Bryan S. W. (1901-1993), *Evangelism: Some principles and Experiments* — 358

Green, E. M. B. (Edward Michael Bankes) (b.1930), "Mission and Ministry" — 359

Gregory the Great (540?-604) — 361

Gregory of Nyssa (331?-396?) — 360

Griffith, A. Leonard (b.1920), *Barriers to Christian Belief*, Hodder and Stoughton, London: 1962 — 362

Griffith Thomas, W. H. (William Henry) (1861-1924), *Holy Spirit of God, The*, Longmans, Green, London: 1913 — 363

Griffiths, Michael (b.1928), *Cinderella with Amnesia*, InterVarsity Press, Downers Grove, IL: 1975 — 364

Grigg, John (b.1924) — 365

Grosseteste, Robert, Bp. (c.1170-1253) — 366

Grou, Jean Nicolas (1731-1803) — 367

——, *Hidden Life of the Soul, The* — 368

Guinness, Os (Ian Oswald) (b.1941), *Dust of Death, The*, Inter-Varsity Press, Leicester: 1973 — 369

Guyon, Mme. (Jeanne Marie Bouvièr de la Motte-) (1648-1717) — 370

Gwatkin, Henry M. (1844-1916), *Early Church History to A.D. 312*, Macmillan, London: 1909 — 371

Hallack, Cecily Rosemary (1898-1938) (in *Treasury of Religious Verse*, no copyright, no date) — 373

Hallesby, O. (1879-1961), *Prayer*, Inter-Varsity Fellowship, London: 1943 — 374

Ham, William T., "Candles of the Lord," in *Spiritual Renewal through Personal Groups*, Association Press, NY: 1957 — 375, 376

Hammarskjöld, Dag (Hjalmar Agne Carl) (1905-1961) — 377

——, *Markings*, tr. Leif Sjöberg & W. H. Auden (*q.v.*), Alfred A. Knopf, New York: 1964 (post.) — 378

Hanson, Anthony T. (Tyrrell) (1916-1991) — 379

——, *Church of the Servant, The*, SCM Press, London: 1962 — 380, 381

Haskins, Minnie L. (1875-1957), "The Desert" (c.1908) — 382

Hastings, Horace L. (1852-1922), *Great Christian Doctrines, The* [1922] — 383

Havergal, Frances Ridley (1836-1879) — 384

Head, David M., *Shout for Joy*, London: Epworth Press, 1962 — 385, 386, 387

Hebert, (Arthur) Gabriel (1886-1963) — 388

Henry, Matthew (1662-1714) — 389, 390

Herbert, George (1593-1633) — 391, 392, 393, 394

Hilary, Bp. of Poitiers (ca. 300-367?), *On the Trinity* — 395

Hilton, Walter (1330?-1396), *Scale of Perfection, The* [early 15th century] — 396

Holland, J. G. (Josiah Gilbert) (1819-1881) — 397

Hooker, Richard (1554?-1600) — 398

Hopkin, H. A. Evan — 399

Hoskyns, Sir Edwyn Clement (1884-1937), *We are the Pharisees*, SPCK, London: 1960 — 400

Houston, James M. (Macintosh) (b.1922), *Transforming Power of Prayer, The*, NavPress, Colorado Springs, Colo.: 1996 — 401

Houston, Tom, former president, World Vision International, by permission. — 402

Hovey, E. Paul (b.1908) — 403

Howard, Thomas (b.1935), *Christ the Tiger*, Lippincott, Philadelphia: 1967 — 404

Howells, William Dean (1837-1920) — 405

Hügel, Friedrich von (1852-1925) — 372

Hummel, Charles E. (b.1923), *[Freedom from] Tyranny of the Urgent, The*, InterVarsity
    Press, Downers Grove, Ill.: 1997 — 406
Ignatius of Loyola (1491-1556) — 407
Irenaeus (c.130-c.200) — 408
Ironside, Harry A. (Allen) (1876-1951) — 409
Irvine, Graeme, former president, World Vision International, by permission. — 410
Irving, Edward (1792-1834) — 411
Jenkins, E. E. (Ebenezer Evans) (1820-1905), *Life and Christ* [1896] — 412
Joad, C. E. M. (Cyril Edwin Mitchinson) (1891-1953), *Recovery of Belief, The*, Faber and
    Faber, London: 1952 — 413
John Chrysostom (345?-407) — 414, 415, 416, 417, 418, 419
John of Damascus (8th century) — 420
John of the Cross (1542-1591) — 421, 422
——, *Ascent of Mount Carmel, The* — 423
John, Griffith (1831-1912) — 424
Johnson, Howard A. (b.1915) — 425
Johnson, Paul G. (Gordon) (b.1931), *Buried Alive*, John Knox Press, Richmond: 1968
    — 426
Johnson, Samuel (1709-1784) — 427, 428, 429, 430
——, *Prayers and Meditations* — 431
Jones, E. (Eli) Stanley (1884-1973) — 432
——, *Conversion*, Abingdon Press, New York: 1959 — 433, 434, 435, 436
——, *Now and Then* — 437
Jones, Rufus Matthew (1863-1948), *Pathways to the Reality of God*, MacMillan, New
    York: 1931 — 438
Jud, Gerald J. (b.1919), "Ministry in Colonies & Retreats," in *Spiritual Renewal through
    Personal Groups*, Association Press, NY: 1957 — 439
Jukes, Andrew John (1815-1901) — 440, 441
Juliana of Norwich (1342?-1417) — 442, 443
——, *Revelations of Divine Love* — 444, 445
Kates, Frederick Ward (b.1920), *Moment Between Two Eternities, A*, Harper & Row,
    New York: 1965 — 446, 447
Keble, John (1792-1866) — 448
——, *Christian Year, The* [1827] — 449
Kelly, Thomas R. (1893-1941), *Testament of Devotion, A*, Quaker Home Service,
    London: 1941 — 450
Kierkegaard, Søren (1813-1855) — 451, 452, 453
——, *Christian Discourses*, translated, with an introduction by Walter Lowrie, Oxford
    University Press, New York: 1961 — 454, 455
Kilmer, (Alfred) Joyce (1886-1918) — 456
Kingsley, Charles (1819-1875) — 457, 458
Kirk, David (b.1935), *Quotations from Chairman Jesus*, Templegate Publishers,
    Springfield, Ill.: 1969 — 459, 460, 461
Knight, G. H. (George Halley) (1835-1917), *In the Secret of His Presence*, Augustana
    Book Concern, Rock Island, Ill.: 1934 — 462
Kraemer, Hendrik (1888-1965), *Theology of the Laity, A*, Lutterworth Press, London:
    1958 — 463
Kurosaki, Kokichi (1886-1970), *One Body in Christ*, Eternal Life Press, Kobe, Japan:
    1954 — 464, 465, 466, 467

McCabe, Joseph E. (b.1912), *Handel's Messiah*, Westminster Press, Philadelphia: 1978 — 592

M'Cheyne, Robert Murray (1813-1843) — 543, 544, 545

MacDonald, George (1824-1905) — 548, 549, 550, 551, 552

——, *Annals of a Quiet Neighborhood* [1866] — 553, 554, 555, 556, 557

——, "Consuming Fire, The," *Unspoken Sermons*, Series One [1867] — 559

——, *Diary of an Old Soul* [1880] — 570

——, *Donal Grant*, Kegan Paul, Trench, Trubner & Co., 1905 — 574

——, "Final Unmasking, The," *Unspoken Sermons*, Third Series [1889] — 571

——, "Higher Faith, The," *Unspoken Sermons*, Series One [1867] — 560, 561

——, "It Shall Not Be Forgiven," *Unspoken Sermons*, Series One [1867] — 562, 563

——, "Righteousness," *Unspoken Sermons*, Third Series [1889] — 572, 573

——, *Seaboard Parish, The* [1868] — 558

——, *Sir Gibbie* [1879] — 565

——, "Temptation in the Wilderness, The," *Unspoken Sermons*, Series One [1867] — 564

——, "Truth of Jesus, The," *Unspoken Sermons*, Second Series [1885] — 566

——, "Voice of Job, The," *Unspoken Sermons*, Second Series [1885] — 567, 568

——, "Way, The," *Unspoken Sermons*, Second Series [1885] — 569

MacGregor, (John) Geddes (1909-1998), *From a Christian Ghetto*, Longmans, Green, London: 1954 — 575

M'Intyre, David M. (1859-1938), *Faith's Title Deeds*, Morgan & Scott, London: 1924 — 546

Mallone, George (b.1944), *Those Controversial Gifts*, Hodder & Stoughton, London: 1983 — 576

Maltby, William Russell (1866-1951) — 577

Manley, G. T. (George Thomas), *Christian Unity*, Inter-Varsity Fellowship, London: 1945 — 578

Manton, Thomas (1620-1677) — 579

Marshall, Catherine (1914-1983), *Beyond Our Selves*, McGraw-Hill, New York: 1961 — 580

Martin, Hugh (1890-1964) — 581

Martyn, Henry (1781-1812) — 582

Mascall, E. L. (Eric Lionel) (b.1905) — 583

——, *Secularization of Christianity, The*, Darton, Longman & Todd: 1965 — 584, 585, 586, 587

Maurice, Frederick Denison (1805-1872) — 588

——, *Ecclesiastical History* [1854] — 589

——, *Hope for Mankind* — 590

Maxwell, James Clerk (1831-1879) — 591

Mead, Sidney Earl (b.1904) — 593

Merriam, George Spring (1843-1914), *Living Faith, A* [1876] — 594

Merton, Thomas (1915-1968) — 595, 596

——, *No Man is an Island*, Harcourt Brace Jovanovich, New York: 1978, c1955 — 598

——, *Seeds of Contemplation*, Hollis & Carter: 1949 — 597

Meynell, Alice (Christina Gertrude Thompson) (1847-1922) — 599

Micklem, Nathaniel (1888-1976), *Prayer and Praises*, Independent Press, London: 1954 — 600

——, *Theology of Politics, The*, Oxford University Press, London: 1941 — 601

Miller, Keith, *Taste of New Wine, The*, Word Books, Waco, Texas: 1965 — 602

Milton, John (1608-1674) — 603

—— "Treatise of civil power in ecclesiastical causes, A" [1659] — 604

Moffatt, James (1870-1944) — 605

Monro, Claxton (b.1914) — 606

Moody, Dwight L. (Lyman) (1837-1899) — 607, 608

Mooneyham, Stan, former president, World Vision US, by permission. — 609, 610

More, Paul Elmer (1864-1937), *Pages from an Oxford Diary*, Princeton University Press: 1937 — 611

Mott, John R. (Raleigh) (1865-1955) — 612

Moule, C. F. D. (Charles Francis Digby) (b.1908), *Phenomenon of the New Testament, The*, SCM: 1967 — 613

Moule, Handley C. G., Bp. (1841-1920) — 614

——, *Ephesians Studies*, Chas. J. Thynne & Jarvis, Ltd, London: 1927 — 615

Muggeridge, Malcolm (1903-1990) — 616

——, *Jesus Rediscovered*, Garden City, N.Y., Doubleday: 1969 — 617

Mulford, Elisha (1833-1885), *Republic of God, The* [1897] — 618

Munson, Ida Norton (b.1877) — 619

Murray, Andrew (1828-1917) — 620

Murray, John (1898-1975), *Redemption—Accomplished and Applied*, W. B. Eerdmans Pub. Co., Grand Rapids: 1955 — 621

Neill, Stephen (1900-1984) — 622

——, *Christian Character, The*, Lutterworth Press, London: 1955 — 623

Newbigin, (James Edward) Lesslie, Bp. (1909-1998) — 624, 625

——, *Household of God, The*, SCM Press, London: 1953 — 626, 627, 628, 629, 630, 631, 632, 633

——, *Reunion of the Church, The*, SCM Press, London: 1960 — 634

Newman, John Henry Cardinal (1801-1890) — 635, 636, 637, 638

Newton, Sir Isaac (1642-1727) — 643, 644

Newton, John (1725-1807) — 639, 640, 641, 642

Nicolas of Cusa (1401-1464) — 645

——, *Vision of God, The* [1554] — 646

Nida, Eugene A. (Albert) (b.1914), *God's Word in Man's Language*, Harper: 1952 — 647

Norbie, Donald L., *New Testament Church Organization*, Interest, Chicago: n.d. (Master's thesis) (other works, 1974, 1992) — 648

Nouwen, Henri J. M. (Josef Machiel) (1932-1996), *Compassion*, Darton, Longman and Todd: 1982 — 649

O'Donovan, Oliver (b.1945), "Marriage and the Family: Personal and Ethical Implications for Christians" in *The Changing World*, v.3 of *Obeying Christ in a Changing World*, Glasgow : William Collins & Co. Ltd, [c1977] — 650

Olds, Glenn — 651

Olney, Helen, *Thoughts* — 652

Oman, John (1860-1939), *Vision and Authority*, Hodder and Stoughton, London: 1928 — 653

Orchard, William Edwin (1877-1955) — 654

Origen (185?-254?) — 655, 656

Osiander, Andreas (1498-1552) — 657

Outerbridge, Leonard M., *Lost Churches of China, The*, Westminster Press, Philadelphia: 1952 — 658

Owen, John (1616-1683) — 659, 660, 661, 662, 663, 664, 665, 666, 667, 668, 669, 670, 671, 672, 673, 674
——, *Discourse upon the Holy Spirit, A* [1674] — 684
——, *Exposition upon Psalm CXXX, An* [1668] — 683
——, *Glory of Christ, The* [1684, 1691] — 685
——, *Of Toleration* [1649] — 680
——, *Ordination Sermon, An* — 675
——, *Sacramental Sermons* — 676
——, *Sermons* — 677, 678, 679
——, "Vindication of the Animadversions on 'Fiat Lux', A" [1664] — 681, 682
Packer, J. I. (b.1926) — 686, 687
——, *Evangelism and the Sovereignty of God*, Inter-varsity Press, Chicago: 1961 — 688
Palau, Luis (b.1934). By permission. — 689, 690, 691, 692, 693
Parkhurst, Charles Henry (1842-1933) — 694
Pascal, Blaise (1623-1662), *Pensées* [1660] — 695, 696, 697, 698, 699, 700, 701, 702, 703, 704, 705
Patmore, Coventry (Kersey Dighton) (1823-1896) — 706, 707, 708, 709
Paton, David M. (MacDonald) (b.1913), *Christian Missions and the Judgment of God*, SCM Press, London: 1953 — 710
Peabody, R. G. — 711
Perrin, Henri (1914-1954), *Priest-Workman in Germany*, translated by Rosemary Sheed, Sheed & Ward, London: 1947 — 712
Phelps, Arthur Stevens (1863-1948) — 713
Phelps, Elizabeth Stuart (1844-1911) — 714
Phelps, William Lyon (1865-1943) — 715
Phillips, J. B. (John Bertram) (1906-1982) — 716
——, *Appointment with God*, Epworth Press, London: 1956 — 731, 732
——, *Church Under the Cross, The*, Highway Press, London: 1956 — 733
——, *Is God at Home?*, Lutterworth Press: 1957 — 737
——, *Making Men Whole*, Highway Press, London: 1952 — 717, 718, 719, 720, 721, 722
——, *New Testament Christianity*, Hodder & Stoughton, London: 1956 — 734, 735, 736
——, *Plain Christianity*, Macmillan, London: 1954 — 728, 729
——, *When God Was Man*, Lutterworth Press: 1954 — 730
——, *Your God is Too Small*, Macmillan, New York: 1953 — 723, 724, 725, 726, 727
Phillips, Wendell (1811-1884), *Christianity a battle, not a dream, a discourse.* [1869] — 738
Pierce, Bob, founder and president, World Vision, by permission. — 739, 740, 741, 742
Pike, Kenneth L. (1912-2001) — 743
——, *With Heart and Mind*, Eerdmans, Grand Rapids: 1962 — 744, 745, 746
Pink, A. W. (Arthur Walkington) (1886-1952) — 747, 748
——, *Sovereignty of God, The* [1918] — 749
Pinnock, Clark H. (b.1937), *Reason Enough*, Paternoster, Exeter: 1980 — 750, 751
Porter, Kenneth W. (Wiggins) (1905-1981) — 752
Powell, Lyman Pierson (1866-1946) — 753
Pusey, Edward B. (Bouverie) (1800-1882) — 754
Quarles, Francis (1592-1644) — 755
Raleigh, Sir Walter (1552?-1618) — 756
Ramsay, Sir William Mitchell (1851-1939), *Letters to the Seven Churches, The*, Hodder & Stoughton, London: 1904 — 757

——, *Pictures of the Apostolic Church: its life and teaching* [1910] — 758

Rashdall, James Hastings (1858-1924), *Principles and Precepts*, B. Blackwell, Oxford: 1927 — 759, 760, 761

Rauschenbusch, Walter (1861-1918) — 762

Reardon, Patrick Henry, *Christ in the Psalms*, Ben Lomond, California, Conciliar Press: 2000 — 763

Redwood, Hugh (b.1883), *Live Coals*, Fleming H. Revell, New York: 1935 — 764

Rees, Thomas (1869-1926), *Holy Spirit in Thought and Experience, The*, C. Scribner's Sons, New York: 1915 — 765, 766

Reeves, (Richard) Ambrose (1899-1980), Bishop of Johannesburg — 767

——, *Calvary Now*, SCM Press, London: 1965 — 768

Reich, Max I. (Isaac) (1867-1945) — 769

Reid, Gavin (b.1950), *Gagging of God, The*, Hodder & Stoughton, London: 1969 — 770, 771

Reindorp, G. E., Bp. — 772

Rhymes, Douglas (1914-1996) — 773, 774

Richard of Chichester, Bp. (1197-1253) — 775

Rieu, E. V. (Emil Victor) (1887-1972), *Four Gospels, The*, Penguin Books, London: 1952 — 776

Robertson, Frederick W. (1816-1853) — 777

Robinson, John (1576?-1625) — 778

Rolle, Richard (1290?-1349) — 779

——, *Commandments, The* — 780, 781

——, *Concerning the Love of God* — 782

Van Rooy, Cammie — 783

Rossetti, Christina G. (Georgina) (1830-1894) — 784, 785

Rufinus, T. (345?-410) — 786

Rupp, (Ernest) Gordon (1910-1986), *Six Makers of English Religion, 1500-1700*, London : Hodder and Stoughton, 1957 — 787

Ruskin, John (1819-1900) — 788

Rust, E. C. (Eric Charles), *Nature and Man in Biblical Thought*, Lutterworth Press, London: 1953 — 789

Rutherford, Samuel (1600-1664) — 790, 791, 792, 793

Ruysbroeck, Jan van (1293-1381), *Adornment of the Spiritual Marriage* — 794

Ryle, J. C. (John Charles), Bp. (1816-1900) — 795

Ryrie, Charles C. (b.1925), *The Ryrie Study Bible*, Chicago: Moody Press, c1976 — 796

Sadiq, John W. (1910-1980) — 797

Saphir, Adolph (1831-1891) — 798

——, *Hidden Life, The*, Gospel Publishing House, New York: 1877 — 799

——, *Christ and Israel*, Morgan and Scott, London: 1911 — 800, 801, 802, 803, 804, 805, 806

Saucy, Robert L., *Church in God's Program, The*, Moody Press, Chicago: 1972 — 807

Sayers, Dorothy Leigh (1893-1957) — 808, 809, 810

Schaeffer, Francis (1912-1984) — 811

——, *Death in the City*, Inter-Varsity Press, London: 1969 — 812

——, *God Who is There, The*, Hodder & Stoughton, London: 1968 — 813

Schaff, Philip (1819-1893) — 814

Scofield, C. I. (1843-1921), *Addresses on Prophecy* [1914] — 815

——, *Rightly Dividing the Word of Truth* [1930] — 816

Selden, John (1584-1654) — 817

Sergeant, Lewis (d.1902) — 818

Shedd, Charlie W. (b.1915) — 819

Sheppard, H. R. L. (Hugh Richard Lawrie) (1880-1937), *Two Days Before*, Macmillan Co., New York: 1924 — 820

Sherrill, Lewis J. (Joseph) (1892-1957), *Lift Up Your Eyes*, John Knox Press, Richmond: 1949 — 821

Shoemaker, Samuel M. (1893-1963) — 822

——, *Experiment of Faith, The*, Harper, New York: 1957 — 823

Short, Robert L. (Lester) (b.1932), *Parables of Peanuts, The*, Harper & Row: 1968 — 824, 825

Simeon, Charles (1759-1836) — 826, 827, 828

Singh, Sadhu Sundar (1889-1929) — 829, 830, 831, 832

Smart, Christopher (1722-1771), *Jubilate Agno*, Greenwood Press, New York: 1969 — 833, 834

Smith, Franc (ps. of S. F. X. Dean), *Harry Vernon at Prep*, Houghton Mifflin Co., Boston: 1959 — 836

Smith, Carl R., "Experiment in Suburbia," with Robert W. Lynn, in *Spiritual Renewal through Personal Groups*, Association Press, NY: 1957 — 835

Smith, Miles (d. 1624), *King James Bible*, Preface to the [1611] — 837

Smith, Sydney (1771-1845) — 838

Soper, Donald O. (1903-1998), *Popular Fallacies*, Hodder and Stoughton, London: 1938 — 839

Spurgeon, Charles Haddon (1834-1892) — 840, 841, 842

——, *Gleanings among the Sheaves* [1869] — 843

Stace, W. T. (Walter Terence) (b.1886), *Religion and the Modern Mind*, Macmillan, London: 1953 — 844

Stark, Rodney — 845

Stearns, Richard, President, World Vision United States — 846

Steen, Thomas M., "Renewal in the Church," in *Spiritual Renewal through Personal Groups*, Association Press, NY: 1957 — 847

Steuart, R. H. J. (Robert Henry Joseph) (1874-1948) — 848

Stevenson, Robert Louis (1850-1894) — 849

Stott, John R. W. (b.1921) — 850, 851

——, ed. *Obeying Christ in a Changing World*. v.1: The Lord Christ, editor John Stott – v.2: The people of God, editor Ian Cundy – v.3: The changing world, editor Bruce Kaye. Glasgow : William Collins & Co. Ltd, [c1977]. — 852

——, *Romans: Encountering the Gospel's Power*, Downers Grove, Ill.: InterVarsity Press, 1998 — 853

Streeter, B. H. — 854

Studd, C. T. (1860-1931) — 855, 856, 857, 858

Studdert Kennedy, Geoffrey Anketell (1883-1929) — 859

——, *Wicket Gate, The*, Hodder and Stoughton, London: 1923 — 860, 861, 862, 863

Summers, W. H. (William Henry), *Our Lollard Ancestors*, National Council of Evangelical Free Churches, London: 1904 — 864

Swete, Henry Barclay (1835-1917), *Holy Spirit in the New Testament, The* [1909] — 865

Synge, F. C. (Francis Charles) — 866

Tabb, John Banister (1845-1909) — 867

Tauler, Johannes (ca. 1300-1361) — 868

Warfield, Benjamin B. (1851-1921), *Inspiration and Authority of the Bible, The*, Presbyterian and Reformed Pub. Co., Philadelphia: 1948 — 960
Watson, David — 961
Watts, Isaac (1674-1748), *Hymns and Spiritual Songs* [1707] — 962, 963, 964, 965
——, *Psalms of David Imitated* [1719] — 966
——, *Psalms, Hymns, and Spiritual Songs* — 967
Webster, Douglas (b.1920), *Local Church and World Mission*, Seabury, New York: 1964 — 968
Wedel, Theodore O. (1892-1970) — 969
Weil, Simone (1909-1943) — 970
Wesley, Charles (1707-1788) — 971, 972, 973
Wesley, John (1703-1791) — 974, 975, 976
——, *Journal* — 977
Westcott, Brooke Foss (1825-1901), *Gospel According to St. John, The*, John Murray, London: 1882 — 978
Wetzel, Todd H. (b.1946), *Steadfast Faith*, Latimer Press, Dallas, Texas: 1997 — 979
Whale, John Seldon (1896-1997), *Christian Doctrine*, Cambridge University Press, Cambridge: 1966 — 980, 981
Whately, Richard (1787-1863) — 982
Whitefield, George (1714-1770) — 983, 984, 985
Whitehead, Alfred North (1861-1947) — 986
Whitemell, C. T., Mrs., "Christ in Flanders" — 987
Whittier, John Greenleaf (1807-1892) — 988
Wilberforce, William (1759-1833), *Practical View, A*, SCM Press: 1958 — 989, 990
Wilde, Oscar (Fingal O'Flahertie Wills) (1854-1900), *The Ballad of Reading Gaol* [1898] — 991
Willard, Dallas (b.1935), *Hearing God*, InterVarsity Press, Downers Grove, Ill.: 1999 — 992
Williams, Charles (1886-1945) — 993
Williams, Daniel Day (1910-1973), *Interpreting Theology, 1918-1952*, SCM Press, London: 1953 — 994
Williams, Roger (1603?-1683) — 995, 996
Wilson, Thomas, Bp. (1698-1755) — 997
Winter, Gibson (b.1916), *Suburban Captivity of the Churches*, Garden City, N.Y., Doubleday: 1961 — 998
Woods, C. Stacey, the first General Secretary of InterVarsity in the United States (b.1909) — 999, 1000
Wycliffe, John (1320?-1384), *Wicket, The* — 1001
Zinzendorf, Count Nicolaus Ludwig von (1700-1760) — 1002

SCRIPTURE INDEX*

* refers to the quotation number, not to the page number

The Authentic **Book of Christian Quotations**

40:12 —— 515
41:4 —— 321
42 —— 699
42:1-2 —— 240, 863
42:1-4 —— 514
43:3 —— 713
44:20-21 —— 690
46 —— 966
46:1 —— 287
46:10 —— 749
47 —— 81
48:1 —— 855
51:1-5 —— 86
51:17 —— 306, 490,
    826, 991
53:4 —— 132
63:1-2 —— 493
63:5-7 —— 357
63:11 —— 833
66:1-4 —— 81
66:7 —— 689
66:8-9 —— 115
66:18 —— 477
69:5 —— 515
69:32-33 —— 712
70:5 —— 670
71:1-3 —— 868
72:13-14 —— 672
76:7 —— 176
84:1-4 —— 878
84:11 —— 140
85:8 —— 291, 298, 352,
    473, 659, 777
85:9-13 —— 103
85:10 —— 230, 839
86:10 —— 699
86:11 —— 362
86:15 —— 830
89:30-32 —— 844
91:1-2 —— 287, 877
92:5 —— 42
96 —— 83, 262
97 —— 262
101:1-2 —— 636
103:1-4 —— 878
103:2-5 —— 739
103:8 —— 176
103:8-10 —— 830
103:10 —— 183
106:13-15 —— 719
107:8 —— 212
107:21-30 —— 548
108:5 —— 922
109:9-20 —— 763
110:1 —— 723
117:1-2 —— 642
118:22 —— 867
118:22-23 —— 698
119:11 —— 155, 421,
    675

119:11-12 —— 876
119:25-40 —— 876
119:64-68 —— 876
119:75 —— 341, 900
119:89-91 —— 411
119:142 —— 369
121:1-2 —— 154, 431
122:1 —— 878, 989
126 —— 967
126:5-6 —— 841
127:1 —— 629
130:1-4 —— 678
130:1-5 —— 323
130:1-6 —— 442
133:1 —— 88
136 —— 336
139:1-4 —— 7
139:7-8 —— 276
139:7-10 —— 592
139:13-14 —— 445
139:17-18 —— 421
141:1-2 —— 877
145:9 —— 212
145:11 —— 94
145:15-16 —— 671
147:4-5 —— 45
147:6 —— 638
148:13 —— 107

Proverbs 1:7 —— 30, 575
2:3-5 —— 835, 920
3:5 —— 585, 684
8:10 —— 591
10:2 —— 50
11:9 —— 320
13:10 —— 508
14:12 —— 624, 684
14:16 —— 132
15:8 —— 477
16:6 —— 673
16:18 —— 509
18:19 —— 595
24:17-20 —— 183
28:5 —— 38
28:14 —— 926

Ecclesiastes 3:14-15
    —— 986
10:3 —— 65
11:1 —— 503
11:10 —— 506
12:6 —— 153
12:12-13 —— 430

Isaiah 1:13-14 —— 93
5:11-12 —— 491
5:21 —— 624
6:1-8 —— 929
6:3 —— 179
6:5 —— 515
8:14 —— 12
8:21-22 —— 821

9:2 —— 653
9:6-7 —— 106
9:18 —— 455
25:8 —— 660
28:16 —— 20
29:13-14 —— 345
30:1 —— 325
32:4 —— 504
35 —— 544
35:1-2 —— 646
35:3-4 —— 702
35:8 —— 392
35:10 —— 506
40:1-5 —— 202
40:11 —— 645, 649
40:31 —— 133, 238,
    403, 557
41:10 —— 382
41:28-29 —— 210
42:6-7 —— 914
43:5-11 —— 15
43:7 —— 83
48:22 —— 301
52:7 —— 740
52:13-15 —— 437
53 —— 800, 914
53:2-11 —— 35, 223,
    737
53:3-4 —— 598
53:12 —— 385
54:13 —— 540
55:8-9 —— 62
56:7 —— 211
57:15 —— 638, 991
57:20-21 —— 455, 702
59:1 —— 382
61:1-2 —— 797
61:1-3 —— 783
61:6 —— 693
63:9 —— 854
64:6 —— 207, 624
66:2 —— 638

Jeremiah 7:23 —— 290
9:3 —— 325, 734
9:25-26 —— 125
10:12 —— 158
18:12 —— 821
22:1-4 —— 601
29:13 —— 203
31:31-34 —— 628
31:33 —— 294, 415
32:17 —— 882
33:10-11 —— 152
36:7 —— 335

Lamentations 3:17-18
    —— 942
3:19-23 —— 791

Ezekiel 20:37 —— 644
34:25 —— 119

36:26 —— 486

Dan. 3 —— 367
  6:10 —— 658
  7:13-14 —— 285
  9:3 —— 670
  10:21 —— 643

Hos. 6:6 —— 30, 103, 512
  13:6 —— 486
  14:6 —— 27

Amos 4:6-11 —— 215
  5:7-8 —— 601
  5:10 —— 816
  5:12 —— 455
  5:14-15 —— 122, 299
  5:21-24 —— 96, 527
  8:11-12 —— 699, 860

Jonah 1:14-17 —— 900

Micah 3:1 —— 769
  5:2 —— 769
  6:8 —— 290, 601
  7:7 —— 671

Nahum 1:3 —— 839
  1:6 —— 369

Habakkuk 2:3 —— 671
  2:4 —— 304, 305

Haggai 2:7 —— 721
  2:8 —— 450

Zechariah 3:8 —— 380
  7:5-6 —— 595
  7:12-13 —— 477

Malachi 3:6 —— 411
  4:2 —— 128, 987

Matthew 1:18-25 —— 584
  1:23 —— 8
  2:1-11 —— 962
  3:13-17 —— 980
  4:1 —— 912
  4:1-11 —— 564
  4:4 —— 556, 606
  4:10 —— 994
  4:12-17 —— 912
  4:19 —— 22, 857
  4:24 —— 46
  5 —— 730
  5:3 —— 484, 697
  5:4 —— 441
  5:5 —— 1001
  5:6 —— 508, 514, 863,
    930
  5:7 —— 37, 497
  5:8 —— 510, 991
  5:9 —— 334
  5:10-12 —— 816
  5:11-12 —— 245
  5:13 —— 224, 829

5:14-15 —— 608
5:16 —— 134, 198, 795,
  946
5:17 —— 104
5:19 —— 522
5:20 —— 430, 624
5:22 —— 151
5:23-24 —— 724
5:23-26 —— 334
5:25-26 —— 170
5:29-30 —— 496
5:40-42 —— 399
5:43-48 —— 895
5:44 —— 171
5:46 —— 706
5:48 —— 344, 482
6 —— 730
6:1-4 —— 181, 288, 542
6:1-18 —— 642
6:5-6 —— 894
6:6 —— 462
6:8 —— 947
6:9 —— 214
6:9-13 —— 716
6:10 —— 319, 476
6:12 —— 391, 512, 563
6:14 —— 171
6:14-15 —— 378, 391,
  512, 563
6:16-18 —— 315
6:19-21 —— 450
6:24 —— 869, 928, 932
6:25-34 —— 154
6:26-34 —— 550
6:28 —— 40, 834
6:33 —— 102, 911
6:34 —— 641
7:1-2 —— 873
7:3-5 —— 961
7:7-8 —— 42, 50
7:7-11 —— 383
7:9-10 —— 930
7:11 —— 57, 906
7:12 —— 104
7:13-14 —— 205, 339
7:15 —— 190
7:15-21 —— 657
7:21 —— 406, 711
7:22-23 —— 247
7:24-27 —— 180
7:28-29 —— 388
8:20 —— 815
8:21-27 —— 888
8:23-27 —— 620
8:24-27 —— 360
8:28 —— 273
9:10 —— 384
9:10-13 —— 615
9:11-12 —— 441, 458,
  703

9:11-13 —— 628
9:13 —— 72, 801
9:14-15 —— 95
9:20-22 —— 285
9:37-38 —— 116, 992
10:7-8 —— 358
10:16 —— 517
10:19 —— 958
10:19-20 —— 536, 934
10:22 —— 162
10:26 —— 571
10:26-28 —— 736
10:28 —— 673, 816,
  901
10:29 —— 40
10:29-31 —— 159, 916
10:32-33 —— 414
10:34-36 —— 309
10:37 —— 762
10:38 —— 832, 843
10:39 —— 286, 651
11:2-3 —— 405
11:4-5 —— 456
11:15 —— 152, 258,
  338, 415, 449,
  634, 696
11:15-17 —— 524
11:21 —— 677
11:25-26 —— 60
11:27 —— 412, 972
11:28-29 —— 61
11:29-30 —— 267, 558
12:1-13 —— 574
12:2-6 —— 113
12:3-4 —— 410
12:7 —— 43
12:10-13 —— 113
12:18-21 —— 13, 259
12:25 —— 725
12:25-28 —— 130
12:31-32 —— 562
12:33-35 —— 679
12:35-37 —— 475
12:36-37 —— 95, 298
12:38-41 —— 186
12:49-50 —— 291
12:50 —— 295, 932
13:20-21 —— 231
13:22 —— 313
13:33 —— 959
13:34 —— 836
13:34-35 —— 876
13:35 —— 31
13:44 —— 15
13:45-46 —— 633
13:51-52 —— 876
13:54-58 —— 773
14:19 —— 216
14:23 —— 217
15:2-20 —— 190

11:1 —— 217
11:1-4 —— 716
11:4 —— 391, 512, 565
11:9-13 —— 383
11:28 —— 289
11:35-36 —— 128
11:37-54 —— 37
11:39-41 —— 137
11:39-52 —— 224, 509
11:41 —— 697
12:2 —— 571
12:4-5 —— 673
12:6-7 —— 904
12:10 —— 562
12:11-12 —— 335, 718
12:15 —— 902
12:16-21 —— 58, 132
12:22 —— 451
12:24-28 —— 789
12:27-34 —— 89
12:33-34 —— 181
12:42-44 —— 300
13:1-5 —— 264
13:24 —— 427
13:26 —— 732
13:30 —— 529
13:34 —— 39
14:12-14 —— 610, 697
14:26-30 —— 903
14:28-30 —— 731
15:6 —— 553
15:10 —— 77
15:22-25 —— 553
16:13 —— 236, 278, 661
16:14-15 —— 247, 624
16:19-31 —— 64
16:29-31 —— 104
16:31 —— 160
17:3 —— 171
17:3-4 —— 512, 563
17:7-10 —— 72
17:12-19 —— 350, 542
17:20-21 —— 274
17:21 —— 946
18:1-7 —— 670
18:8 —— 304
18:9-14 —— 59, 207
18:10-14 —— 264, 713
18:18-27 —— 339
19:2-10 —— 338
19:10 —— 46
19:37-40 —— 872
19:38 —— 965
19:40 —— 965
19:47 —— 561
20:9-16 —— 830
20:17 —— 867
20:20-26 —— 36
20:38 —— 794

21:7 —— 304
21:8 —— 845
21:19 —— 549
21:34 —— 451
22:19-20 —— 99, 732
22:20 —— 393
22:25-27 —— 519
22:26-27 —— 29
22:31-32 —— 162
22:41-44 —— 492
22:44 —— 490
23:21-24 —— 451
23:43 —— 92
23:45 —— 939
23:46 —— 623
24 —— 420
24:1-12 —— 228
24:32 —— 233
24:45-47 —— 591
24:46-47 —— 262
24:46-48 —— 1002
24:46-51 —— 758
24:47-48 —— 83
24:50-51 —— 1

John 1:1 —— 753
1:1-5 —— 537, 570, 723
1:1-14 —— 546
1:4-5 —— 128, 653, 658
1:4-9 —— 987
1:7-9 —— 422
1:9 —— 425
1:9-10 —— 128
1:9-14 —— 607
1:11 —— 806
1:14 —— 408
1:17 —— 242
1:18 —— 412
1:23-36 —— 637
2:14-17 —— 604
3 —— 538
3:5-6 —— 436
3:9-10 —— 540
3:13 —— 584
3:16 —— 105, 846
3:16-17 —— 9, 15, 257, 259, 356, 916
3:18-19 —— 71
3:19-20 —— 455
3:19-21 —— 653
4:6-26 —— 216
4:7-14 —— 831
4:23-24 —— 936
4:31-34 —— 852
4:41 —— 10
5:19-20 —— 554
5:21 —— 330
5:25 —— 981
5:26-30 —— 750
5:30 —— 554
5:39 —— 701

6:9 —— 302
6:27 —— 256
6:32-35 —— 260
6:38-58 —— 584
6:39-40 —— 587
6:44-45 —— 463, 978
6:45 —— 540, 561
6:53-56 —— 393
6:63 —— 524
7:5 —— 748
7:6-8 —— 816
7:16-17 —— 136, 335
7:16-18 —— 38
7:24 —— 601
7:46 —— 330
8:12 —— 511, 607, 782
8:28 —— 349, 940
8:31-32 —— 890
8:31-36 —— 135
8:58 —— 35
9:4 —— 199
9:39-41 —— 247, 695
10:1-5 —— 52
10:9 —— 619
10:10 —— 723, 917
10:14-16 —— 239
10:27-28 —— 681
10:28 —— 203
10:29 —— 721
12:25 —— 997
12:35-36 —— 291
12:42-43 —— 655
12:49-50 —— 69
13:1-4 —— 732
13:4-5 —— 216
13:13-15 —— 117
13:14-15 —— 523
13:34 —— 910, 969
13:34-35 —— 488
14:1-4 —— 798
14:2-3 —— 54, 92, 616
14:6 —— 56, 551, 652
14:7-9 —— 312
14:9 —— 340, 704
14:12 —— 131
14:15 —— 95, 667, 668
14:16-17 —— 403
14:21 —— 780, 950
14:23 —— 457, 464, 465, 929
14:23-27 —— 886
14:26 —— 656
14:27 —— 659
15:1-8 —— 435
15:9-12 —— 780
15:10 —— 281
15:11 —— 63
15:13 —— 709
15:13-15 —— 459
15:16 —— 923

8:2 —— 386, 766
8:2-3 —— 363, 853
8:4-13 —— 538
8:5-6 —— 901
8:6 —— 766
8:9-10 —— 188
8:10 —— 396
8:11 —— 433, 632, 853
8:14 —— 53, 334, 765, 963
8:15 —— 135
8:15-16 —— 766
8:16 —— 963
8:17 —— 632, 853
8:18 —— 66, 145
8:22 —— 547
8:22-23 —— 493
8:22-25 —— 182
8:23 —— 766, 853
8:23-25 —— 632
8:25 —— 549
8:26 —— 120, 442, 865
8:26-27 —— 287, 374, 656, 828
8:28 —— 40, 97, 468, 548, 614
8:29-30 —— 53
8:31 —— 215
8:32 —— 742, 802
8:34 —— 777
8:35-39 —— 255, 885
8:36 —— 997
8:36-37 —— 974
9:15-16 —— 688
9:22-24 —— 342
9:31-32 —— 528
10:3 —— 624
10:8-11 —— 578
10:13 —— 707
10:14-17 —— 157
10:16-18 —— 123
10:17 —— 144
11:2 —— 174
11:5-6 —— 174
11:15-21 —— 626
11:17-21 —— 225
11:22-24 —— 628
11:33 —— 920
11:36 —— 460
12:1 —— 306, 368, 850
12:1-2 —— 138, 612, 729, 742
12:1-3 —— 856
12:2 —— 735
12:3 —— 258, 316, 638
12:4 —— 717
12:5 —— 465, 627
12:5-8 —— 256
12:9 —— 897
12:10-14 —— 295

12:12 —— 222
12:15 —— 627
12:16 —— 590
12:20 —— 849
12:21 —— 443, 497, 969
13:1-7 —— 172, 864
13:11-12 —— 851
13:12 —— 619
14 —— 466
14:4 —— 226
14:5 —— 426, 466, 603
14:5-8 —— 933
14:7-8 —— 261
14:13 —— 109, 969
14:14-15 —— 292
14:17 —— 274, 410, 766, 835
14:19 —— 629
14:19-21 —— 326
14:21 —— 292
15:1 —— 70, 110
15:2-3 —— 317
15:3 —— 889
15:4 —— 419, 474, 647, 686
15:5 —— 725
15:5-7 —— 334, 465, 590, 682, 910
15:7 —— 626
15:13 —— 766, 925
15:17-18 —— 638
15:18-19 —— 766
15:21 —— 733, 821, 842
15:30 —— 766
16:17 —— 640
16:19 —— 883

1 Corinthians 1:2 —— 254, 453
1:9 —— 798
1:9-10 —— 375
1:10-13 —— 640, 725
1:13 —— 146, 334
1:17-18 —— 275, 862
1:17-22 —— 934
1:19-21 —— 715
1:19-27 —— 409
1:20-21 —— 305
1:21 —— 674
1:22-23 —— 748
1:23-28 —— 196
1:23-29 —— 141, 428
1:28-29 —— 371
1:30 —— 173
1:30-31 —— 219
2:4 —— 766
2:4-5 —— 34, 934
2:7-10 —— 766, 896
2:9-16 —— 944

2:10 —— 418
2:12-14 —— 534, 753
2:16 —— 277
3:1 —— 765
3:1-7 —— 640
3:3 —— 765
3:4-6 —— 811
3:5 —— 282
3:5-7 —— 638
3:8-11 —— 1000
3:9-17 —— 983
3:11 —— 463
3:11-14 —— 176
3:13-15 —— 688
3:16 —— 525, 765
3:16-17 —— 460, 755, 766
3:18 —— 509
3:23 —— 434
4:10-13 —— 541
4:19-20 —— 34
5:6-7 —— 343
5:8 —— 351
6:1-8 —— 170
6:19 —— 766
6:19-20 —— 877, 916
6:20 —— 996
7:5 —— 95
7:12-17 —— 602
7:29-31 —— 331
8:6 —— 173
8:7-13 —— 165, 292
8:13 —— 12
9:12 —— 24, 178
9:22 —— 977, 1002
10:14 —— 21
10:16 —— 393
10:16-17 —— 732, 964
10:17 —— 150
10:19-22 —— 21
10:21-22 —— 732
10:27 —— 598
10:31 —— 996
10:32 —— 254
11:16-19 —— 640
11:20-34 —— 732
11:22 —— 254
11:27-30 —— 398
11:32 —— 644
12:3 —— 18, 765, 1002
12:4 —— 766
12:7-12 —— 424
12:8 —— 766
12:11 —— 137
12:12-13 —— 633
12:12-18 —— 995
12:13 —— 765, 766
12:22-23 —— 109
12:24-27 —— 650
12:28 —— 766

12:1 —— 549
12:1-2 —— 63, 193, 307
12:1-3 —— 637, 664
12:2 —— 221
12:3 —— 907
12:3-8 —— 341
12:6-7 —— 296, 644, 841
12:10-11 —— 501
12:16-17 —— 909
12:27-29 —— 71, 192
13:6 —— 849
13:9 —— 541
13:15-16 —— 352
13:20-21 —— 342

James 1:3-4 —— 549
1:4 —— 497
1:5 —— 766
1:5-7 —— 303
1:6-7 —— 477
1:8 —— 435
1:12 —— 443
1:14-15 —— 413
1:17 —— 102, 156, 411
1:19 —— 320
1:19-20 —— 268
1:21-23 —— 184
1:22 —— 194
1:22-25 —— 281
1:22-27 —— 435
1:25 —— 166
1:26 —— 320
2:5 —— 697
2:6-7 —— 902
2:10 —— 79, 149, 528
2:13 —— 898
2:14 —— 817
2:14-17 —— 662, 756
2:14-18 —— 796
2:24 —— 796
3:15 —— 766
3:17 —— 766
4:3 —— 477
4:4-5 —— 2
4:7-8 —— 935
4:8 —— 435
4:8-10 —— 909
4:11 —— 884
5:1-5 —— 840
5:10-11 —— 317, 389
5:16 —— 86, 318, 321
5:16-20 —— 364
5:19-20 —— 475

1 Peter 1:2 —— 175
1:5 —— 121
1:6-7 —— 162, 405
1:14-16 —— 283
1:15-16 —— 392
1:15-23 —— 666

1:18-19 —— 253
2:1-3 —— 875
2:5 —— 94, 539
2:7-8 —— 308
2:9 —— 630, 767
2:10 —— 626, 628
2:11-12 —— 139, 365
2:21 —— 372, 472, 844
2:21-25 —— 568
3:4 —— 258, 795, 887
3:8 —— 379
3:8-9 —— 590
3:15 —— 867
3:15-16 —— 248
3:18-19 —— 92
3:19 —— 858
4:4 —— 928
4:10-11 —— 195
4:13-14 —— 559, 892, 979
5:1 —— 155
5:1-4 —— 26, 366
5:5 —— 258, 316, 638
5:6-7 —— 532
5:10 —— 841, 892

2 Peter 1:4 —— 342
1:10-11 —— 162
1:16 —— 51, 206, 208, 452, 815
1:19-20 —— 686
1:21 —— 540
2:1 —— 329
2:1-2 —— 808
2:1-3 —— 345
3:15-16 —— 241, 778

1 John 1:3 —— 119
1:7 —— 633
1:8 —— 107
1:8-10 —— 86, 321
1:9 —— 119
1:9-10 —— 692
1:10 —— 435
2:1-2 —— 327, 676
2:16 —— 952
2:20 —— 766
2:27 —— 766
3:1 —— 950
3:1-2 —— 863
3:2 —— 600
3:14 —— 6
3:16 —— 598
3:17 —— 50, 902
3:17-18 —— 484, 846
3:18-20 —— 690
4:1 —— 597
4:3 —— 908
4:4 —— 443
4:4-5 —— 154
4:8 —— 674, 854, 906

4:8-10 —— 530, 758, 950
4:12 —— 191, 951
4:13 —— 992
4:16-21 —— 191
4:19 —— 460
5:1-3 —— 97
5:1-4 —— 903
5:4 —— 139, 773
5:5-7 —— 395
5:6-7 —— 314
5:16-17 —— 325
5:18-19 —— 219
5:19 —— 208, 580

2 John 1:7-10 —— 190

Jude 1:3 —— 74, 161, 234, 578
1:4-5 —— 320
1:14-16 —— 320
1:20-21 —— 30
1:21 —— 951
1:22-23 —— 361, 842, 858

Revelation 1:5 —— 678
1:5-6 —— 352
1:6 —— 359, 539
1:8 —— 705
1:9 —— 328
1:10-11 —— 409
2:4-5 —— 998
2:5 —— 909
2:7 —— 540, 561
2:11 —— 901
2:15-16 —— 757
3:14-16 —— 303
3:17-18 —— 247
3:19 —— 490
3:20 —— 931, 991
4:11 —— 73, 721
5:12 —— 233, 833, 867
5:12-14 —— 73
7:17 —— 646
14:6-7 —— 83
14:7 —— 73
14:13 —— 261
19:10 —— 540
21:4 —— 458
21:6 —— 705
21:10-27 —— 787
22:1-5 —— 513
22:14 —— 932

SUBJECT INDEX*

* refers to the quotation number, not to the page number

The Authentic **Book of Christian Quotations**

The Authentic **Book of Christian Quotations**